Hip Figures

Post 45 Florence Dore and Michael Szalay, Editors
Post•45 Group, Editorial Committee

Hip Figures

A Literary History of the Democratic Party

Michael Szalay

Stanford University Press

Stanford, California

Stanford University Press
Stanford, California

This book has been published with the generous assistance of UC Irvine.

Printed in the United States of America on acid-free, archival-quality paper

Library of Congress Cataloging-in-Publication Data

Szalay, Michael, 1967- author.
  Hip figures : a literary history of the Democratic Party / Michael Szalay.
     pages cm. -- (Post 45)
  Includes bibliographical references and index.
  ISBN 978-0-8047-7634-9 (cloth : alk. paper) -- ISBN 978-0-8047-7635-6 (pbk. : alk. paper)
  1. American fiction--20th century--History and criticism. 2. Politics and literature--United States--History--20th century. 3. Democratic Party (U.S.)--History--20th century. 4. African Americans in literature. 5. Popular culture in literature. 6. Liberalism in literature. 7. Race in literature. I. Title. II. Series: Post 45.
  PS374.P6S93 2012
  810.9'358--dc23
                          2012009458

Designed by Bruce Lundquist
Typeset at Stanford University Press in 10/15 Minion

Table of Contents

Acknowledgments

This project would have been impossible without the generous help of my peers. I owe a special debt to all my friends and colleagues in Post•45, many of whom I no doubt will fail to name here, but all of whom have contributed, in one way or another, to making our meetings as consistently rewarding as they are. I'd also like to thank all of those at Stanford University Press who decided to bet on Post•45 and who have helped it grow. I'm particularly grateful for the help of Emily-Jane Cohen, Mary Katherine Maco, Jan McInroy, and Emily Smith. I'd like to thank Amanda Anderson, Jami Bartlett, Marshall Brown, Ellen Burt, Abigail Cheever, Michelle Chihara, Jeff Clapp, Amanda Claybaugh, J. D. Connor, Miles Corwin, Mary Esteve, Paul Gilmore, Mark Goble, Lauren Goodlad, Brandon Gordon, Eric Hayot, Andy Hoberek, Amy Hungerford, Oren Izenberg, Cathy Jurca, Arlene Keizer, Lee Konstantinou, Julian Koslow, Richard Kroll, Rodrigo Lazo, Jayne Lewis, Alan Liu, Catherine Liu, Dennis Lopez, Steve Mailloux, Rolland Murray, Debbie Nelson, Sianne Ngai, Lauren Pey, John Plotz, Ken Reinhard, Bruce Robbins, Stephen Schryer, Stephen Shapiro, Victoria Silver, Eric Sundquist, Elisa Tamarkin, Harvey Teres, Alan Wald, Andrzej Warminski, John Williams, and Alex Woloch. I am particularly grateful to those kind souls who, in one capacity or another, read all of this manuscript: Dale Bauer, Jerry Christensen, Florence Dore, Barbara Foley, Eric Lott, Deak Nabers, Jack Matthews, Sean McCann, and Mark McGurl. The debts grow still larger here, toward the very bottom: Richard Godden read multiple versions of these chapters, and shaped each one of them in decisive ways. Thank you, Richard. Lastly, and most importantly, *Hip Figures* would not have been possible without the keen eye, critical acumen, and steady, loving hand of Andrea Henderson. I dedicate this book to her, and to my daughter, Clara.

Very early versions of this project appeared in the *Yale Journal of Criticism* and *Modern Language Quarterly*. Chapter 4 appeared in *American Literary History*.

Hip Figures

Introduction

Days after the inauguration of Barack Obama, the Republican National Committee elected Michael Steele, an African American, to become its chairman. In the following weeks, Steele embraced what National Public Radio described as a "hipper—some may say a hip-hop—vernacular to breathe vigor into the demoralized GOP." The *Washington Times* reported the chairman's desire for "an 'off the hook' public relations blitz targeting young Latinos and African-Americans in 'hip-hop settings.'" This was the Republicans' answer to the widespread perception that they were out of touch, too white and too set against the future to understand those beyond their traditional core. To be sure, Steele's search for a hipper vernacular didn't register a significant change in the GOP, and this was not simply because his chairmanship was contested from the start, and ultimately short-lived. Republicans remained attached at their grass roots to the modern conservative movement crystallized by Barry Goldwater, committed to consolidating white supremacy, concentrating wealth, and privatizing the New Deal welfare state. Steele simply announced the party's willingness to market new messages to new segments of the voting public as the situation demanded. The language might change, but the message would not: as Steele put it, Obama's "big government" stimulus package was "just a wish list from a lot of people who have been on the sidelines for years . . . to get a little bling, bling."[1]

Steele's gambit was of course pointedly counterintuitive: if one of the two parties had an obvious affinity with hip black culture, it was the Democratic Party. A tide of rappers had turned out during the 2008 race for Obama. Ludacris had led the charge: as his "Obama Song" put it, "You can't stop what's 'bout to happen, we 'bout to make history / The first black president is destined and it's meant to be." Breathless, *American Prospect* declared, "Whether or not he is aware of it, Barack Obama is the first hip-hop presidential candidate." The moment seemed to abound in historical firsts. The *New Republic* described

Obama's presidency, one year later, as the first "cool presidency," and *Politico* described the president as "the nation's first hip president." "Watch him walk," *Politico* urged. "Listen to him talk. See the body language, the expressions, the clothes. He's got attitude, rhythm, a sense of humor, contemporary tastes."[2]

These announcements bespoke the fervent hope that Obama's election represented a definitive departure from the nation's long and ugly history of racism. The American public had elected a man with dark skin to its highest office. Who could refrain from wondering what opportunities this would create for entire classes of people? In his epochal "race speech," Obama had sought to "remind" Americans that "many of the disparities that exist in the African-American community today can be directly traced to inequalities passed on from an earlier generation that suffered under the brutal legacy of slavery and Jim Crow." The candidate seemed poised to redress these disparities, and it was tempting to see his hip in this light. "Where did this man's cool come from?" asked Michelle Cottle of the *New Republic.* A white writer, Cottle cited African American journalist Donna Britt on the distinction between "cool" and "*brother* cool," and reminded her readers that maintaining a calm and collected outward appearance had often been, for black men, a matter of life and death. But in Cottle's hands, the defense mechanism became a potent weapon: possessed of a brother cool, Obama wielded a "controlled fire" that gave him "the upper hand" in virtually all his political dealings.[3]

Hip Figures seeks to understand the origin not of Obama's cool but of fantasies such as Cottle's. Its central contention is that, over the last fifty or so years, a range of predominantly white fantasies about hip have animated the secret imagination of postwar liberalism and, more concretely, organized the Democratic Party's efforts to redress "the brutal legacy of slavery and Jim Crow." Seen in this context, Obama's presidency, like that of Bill Clinton before him, realized trends first manifest during the presidency of John F. Kennedy, whose very person seemed to capture the newfound importance of style to American liberalism. At the start of the sixties, mainstream political thought turned with frequency to what the sociologist David Riesman called "the process by which people become related to politics, and the consequent stylizing of political emotions." As Riesman saw it, "If politics is a ballet on a stage set by history," then "style tells us . . . in what manner [the dancers] play their parts and how the audience responds."[4] An important insight, to which we must add: a given style tells us only what the dramatic conventions governing its performance allow us to hear. I am interested in a particular stage, one not only set by history but furnished by novelists, and I mean to insist that it matters a great deal, to our sense of both literary and political history, that the fantasies of hip that have mattered most to liberalism first emerged in novels.

Norman Mailer thought Kennedy's style recognizably black, and on the eve of the 1960 presidential election, he dubbed the senator from Massachusetts "the Hipster as Presidential Candidate."[5] We cannot understand the works of novelists like Robert Penn Warren, Ralph Ellison, Norman Mailer, William Styron, John Updike, E. L. Doctorow, and Joan Didion without understanding how they too invoked hip on behalf of the Democratic Party of their time. Principally, these novelists invoked hip, as Mailer did, to consolidate the voting constituencies of postwar liberalism. To be sure, the novelists to whom I turn worked within a larger "coalition culture"; their novels joined a range of expressive forms—jazz, rhythm and blues, and rock and roll prominent among them—that militated on behalf of new unions between black and white voters and, more broadly, the ends associated with the Civil Rights Movement and the larger project of integration. But *Hip Figures* argues that novelists played a far more significant role in that coalition culture than we might at first imagine. They were, in a very real sense, the most important political strategists of their time.

Though they were responsive in individual ways to the massive voter realignments then changing American electoral politics, these novelists were primarily male and primarily interested in other men. Electoral politics was for them—as in many ways it still is today—an insularly fraternal affair. We can be more specific and postulate that these self-consciously hip novels were written for white male professionals and managers in the Northeast who were then rising to prominence within the Democratic Party. Few of these white-collar workers were what the sociological literature of the moment would have considered authentically hip; most experienced hip as a distant echo. But they no doubt glimpsed, even if only vaguely, its ultimate importance to their class, whose political power would depend upon sponsoring the aims of the Civil Rights Movement. Styron had this class in mind when he complained, during the sixties, that liberalism in the North demanded little more than that you "smoke pot and dig the right kind of jazz" in order to demonstrate "that you really love Negroes."[6] Seen this way, literary hip provided yet one more cost-free means of expressing goodwill toward African Americans, one more way of embracing, in Greg Tate's words, "everything but the burden."[7] But the function of literary hip is more complicated, precisely because the "hip figures" that I describe exist on the page, not on the street or in jazz clubs or dance halls.

Those pages transform exploitative relations between people, in Marx's famous formulation, into "the fantastic form of a relation between things."[8] The literary hip with which I am concerned is a fetish, just as nineteenth-century blackface was. For Susan Willis, "blackface is a metaphor for the commodity. It is the sign of what people paid to see. It is the image consumed, and it is the site of the actor's estrangement from self into role." That site looks different, however, when the blackface in question, now removed from sight, appears in figurative language, as a metaphor for a metaphor for the commodity. Literary hip is a doubly deracinated sign, one that abstracts embodied, coercive relations and subjects them to particularly complex forms of profit-bearing exchange. Like the minstrel show from which it is descended, literary hip presides over a series of alienations that remove individuals from the conditions of their labor, from the social relations implicit in those conditions, and, finally, from themselves. Willis reminds us that "in mass culture many of the social contradictions of capitalism appear to us as if those very contradictions have been resolved. The mass cultural object articulates the contradiction and its imaginary solution."[9] The same is true of the literary objects that follow, each of which mobilizes hip to unite otherwise multicolored bodies possessed of different economic interests. But these novels indicate how members of the professional-managerial class might, *as readers of novels*, view themselves as simultaneously inside and cast out from the center of political power, as possessed of both white and black skin. In these works, which transport whites into the imagined bodies of African Americans, the burnt cork of blackface returns, dematerialized, as a figurative "second skin" meant to hold together the straining coalitions of a Democratic Party undergoing decisive change.

The Marxist critic William Haug describes commodities as promissory "second skins"—iridescent phantasms that drift "unencumbered like a multicolored spirit . . . into every household." The second skins with which I am concerned drift into households inside of novels, as hip figures. These skins—figures of skins and skins produced through figures—bear the imprint, or brand, that would define postwar liberalism, and render it subject to exchange. When Mailer dubbed Kennedy hip, he reasoned that the candidate had just enough "patina of that other life, the second American life, the long electric night with the fires of neon leading down the highway to the murmur of jazz"

(*PP* 31). Mailer conjured this shimmering patina to brand Kennedy voters, no less than Kennedy himself. It's a marketing cliché that brands create consumers. A recent study announces in familiar fashion that while "emerging" consumers are "a demographic fact and a sociological reality—in many ways they are a metaphor," a metaphor made fact by branding.[10] As with consumers, so with voters: metaphors call both into being. In the early seventies, Doctorow announced that "unlike the politicians we [novelists] take office first and then create our constituencies"; the novels discussed in *Hip Figures* go further, branding those constituencies on behalf of the Democrats.[11]

Reading hip figures against the grain, as efforts to elide contradictions in the interests that motivate liberal coalitions, I describe novelists struggling—with mixed motives and results—to create that brand. Whether or not these novelists did so successfully is a question for which there is no simple answer—a question, moreover, that opens out on at least four decades of debate within the humanities over the significance of symbolic forms to more ostensibly "real" political formations. In practical terms, voting constituencies are less forgiving than reading ones: no national politician could have championed the inflammatory interracial sexual unions dramatized by Updike and Mailer, for example. But in the decades following the Second World War, during the heyday of the American novel's prestige, when it was unclear to the Democrats how they should understand the base of their power or the nature of their interests, it seemed plausible to these novelists that they might change the party in significant ways.

The postwar Democratic Party began to take shape after the Dixiecrat revolt of 1948, and after Harry Truman marginalized Henry Wallace and other pro-Soviet voices within Franklin Roosevelt's coalition. Embarrassed by their commitment to big government, complicit in Cold War red baiting, traditionally dependent on the institutionalized power of labor unions but increasingly responsive to well-educated elites, postwar Democrats began to distance themselves from the New Deal's hostility to concentrated economic power. Most significantly, the rising clout of professional and managerial elites within the Democratic Party came at the expense of old guard southerners still committed to white supremacy and segregation, and took place alongside the increasing electoral importance of African Americans, who had turned en masse to the Democrats during the New Deal. In 1932, when Roosevelt ran against Herbert Hoover, the Republicans won more than two-thirds of the black vote.

Four years later, with another presidential contest under way, *Time* announced, "In no national election since 1860 have politicians been so Negro minded."[12] In a reversal that would change the face of twentieth-century American politics, Roosevelt won almost three-quarters of the African American vote. After this election, the steady movement of African Americans into the Democratic Party, and the party's subsequent if uneven embrace of the civil rights struggle, fundamentally changed the nature of its liberalism, in obvious and less than obvious ways.

Between 1936 and 1964 (when women first began to vote Democratic more than Republican) blacks represented the single largest new voting bloc to enter the party.[13] In electoral terms, black votes were crucial to the outcomes of numerous elections. In legislative terms, because of the unity that African Americans were able to exert within their rank and file, they steadily replaced southern racists as the minority interest group most capable of casting a decisive veto within the party—even if particular African Americans weren't allowed significant positions of party leadership until well after the formation of the Congressional Black Caucus in 1969. But just as importantly, "blackness" took on a symbolic importance in the party beyond the practical influence that black politicians were able to wield.[14] For in the eyes of many white liberals, African America represented more than actual individuals in need of state aid; in a very basic fashion, liberalism organized itself, to recall Michael Rogin writing about blackface, "around the surplus symbolic value of blacks, the power to make African Americans represent something besides themselves."[15] The "Negro," Ralph Ellison noted, was "a key figure in a magic rite by which the white American seeks to resolve the dilemma arising between . . . his acceptance of the sacred democratic belief that all men are created equal and his treatment of every tenth man as though he were not." In some versions of this rite, African Americans were cast as beatific ideals of public virtue, possessed of a deep moral warrant. In others, they were anarchic and rebellious, angry guardians of democracy because of their unwillingness to surrender or submit. Either way, black bodies demarcated what Ellison called "that area of the national life where political power is institutionalized and translated into democratic ritual and national style."[16]

I focus on a reinflection of this process, in which novelists institutionalized and translated the style of hip subcultures into the political power of the Democratic Party. For these writers, subcultural style does not, as it does for cultural critic Dick Hebdige, articulate a "refusal" of power or a "breakdown of consensus."[17] Rather, it struggles to reconcile differences between groups to produce a vision of naturalized, easy authority capable of consolidating a rapidly changing Democratic Party. As Henry Louis Gates Jr. puts it, for Ellison, "America, roughly speaking, means 'black.'"[18] The fact that blacks could be made to seem quintessentially American, in many ways more so than whites, explains why militating on their behalf might have provided the Democratic Party with a way to transcend what many took to be its atomizing pursuit of local interests. Committing to racial justice involved something more than committing to one group among many. It meant, rather, discovering the grounds for a deeper unity. In this respect, Johnson's dedication to civil rights exemplified the centrifugal tendency of what historian David Reynolds calls "interest group liberalism" even as it promised to mitigate its effects.[19]

As Mailer saw it, Kennedy committed the Democrats to hip and to civil rights together, in the same moment, but it was already clear, before 1960, how hip might identify the greater vision of American pluralism with the Democratic Party itself. Since the end of the forties, novelists had been treating the hipster as the paradigmatic liberal subject, as a vigorous example of how even the most intense expressions of difference and disaffection might contain within them the grounds for producing ever-more-encompassing groups and collectivities. Kennedy concretized and lent institutional warrant to this literary program. "I see little of more importance to the future of our country and our civilization," the president announced at a memorial service for Robert Frost, who had spoken at his inauguration, "than full recognition of the place of the artist." Never before had novelists in particular been so fully recognized, so enthusiastically invited into the corridors of power. They streamed in and out of the White House, and engaged the president in conversation. Thus Gore Vidal would later declare, while speaking of those admitted to Camelot, that 1960 marked the moment at which "politics and literature officially joined forces."[20]

Jazz Fictions

As John Leland puts it, hip is not "a marginal fillip but a central current in American culture," and today that current encompasses a wide range of phenomena. Remarkably elastic, contemporary hip polices the boundaries of countless cultural forms, fashions, and lifestyles—calibrating distinctions between the authentic and the ersatz and calculating degrees of proximity to the fountainheads of significant change.[21] The particular hip I take up, however, is a complex variant of the peculiarly American tradition of blackface minstrelsy. In Eric Lott's formulation, minstrelsy was a "theatrical practice, principally of the urban North, in which white men caricatured blacks for sport and profit." A "clumsy courtship" animated by complex motives, minstrelsy allowed white men to negotiate the "panic, anxiety, terror, and pleasure" attendant upon their identification with black men. To Lott, that courtship persists: "Every time you hear an expansive white man drop into his version of black English, you are in the presence of blackface's unconscious return"; the legacy of blackface "is so much a part of most American white men's equipment for living that they remain entirely unaware of their participation in it."[22] The white and self-conscious version of hip at work in the chapters that follow constitutes a particular moment in the afterlife of minstrelsy, a moment precipitated by the emergence of bebop on the one hand and R & B on the other, when anxious white men sought and found in black subcultures a means of negotiating the conflicted ideological and organizational imperatives of postwar liberalism.

I take it as axiomatic that hip on the page is no more or less authentic than hip on the street—in all its forms, hip remains quixotic, an imitative fantasy for which there is, finally, no definitive locus or referent. To be sure, novelists like Jack Kerouac, John Holmes, and Chandler Brossard (among many others) treated bebop as the fountainhead of hip, and understood themselves as constituting the tertiary stage of a phenomenon that began in the early forties in Harlem jazz clubs. Reading these novelists, we confront literary figures that reproduce with a difference the white hipster's imitations of the nonchalant authority and sartorial styles associated with black bop musicians (the sneakers, wide-lapeled suits, berets, "smoked-window" glasses, and goatees).[23] Still, this is not a study of bebop, which, in the apt words of Cornel West, "expressed the heightened tensions, frustrated aspirations, and repressed emotions of an aggressive yet apprehensive Afro-America."[24] Rather, it is a study in the political afterlives of the white fantasy that coalesced around that edgy and cerebral music—as well as the more demotic idioms that followed, from boogie-woogie and the jump blues to R & B and rock and roll.

There were undeniable differences between the conspicuously elite avant-gardism of bebop and the more incipiently commercial tendencies of the dance-oriented rhythms that animated youth in the fifties and sixties. But the second skin of hip that I depict is nothing if not elastic, and accommodates a range of tastes and styles that would, in any event, converge over time in the popular imagination. As Andrew Ross has it, "hip is the site of a chain reaction of taste, generating minute distinctions which negate and transcend each other at an intuitive rate of fission that is virtually impossible to record."[25] But we must attend to moments of fusion as surely as those of fission. Despite its sometimes studied antipathy to any but the most discerning audience, bebop was quickly assimilated into mainstream culture. In 1952, the editors of *Down Beat* handed Charlie Parker and Dizzy Gillespie awards before a national television audience; after Parker's untimely death in 1955, as "Bird Lives" began to appear scrawled on walls throughout the recently named East Village, his legend grew apace, galvanizing not simply an increasingly visible underground but a generation of suburban whites hungry for something beyond the confines of a Cold War America that seemed to have sprung from the insipid imaginations of Walt Disney and Dwight D. Eisenhower. Whether they listened to Parker live, or to Elvis Presley and Chuck Berry on radios and jukeboxes, or watched Lenny Bruce and Lord Buckley in nightclubs, or Maynard G. Krebs on television, these whites participated in an encompassing coalition culture. When in John Updike's *Rabbit, Run* (1960) the white Negro Harry "Rabbit" Angstrom—embraced as a namesake decades later by the "wigga" Eminem—flees his wife and child and drives south, he listens to a radio station that plays Sidney Bechet and Cannonball Adderley as well as Chuck Berry, the Impalas, and Dave Cortez. Updike's goal is less to produce distinctions between these artists than to suggest how, taken together, they provide Rabbit a solution to the problem expressed by one of his lovers: "You're too white."[26]

Popular music like the kind on display in *Rabbit, Run* was incipiently political—albeit in complex and contradictory fashion—long before the counterculture of the sixties declared it so. While the social democratic liberalism expressed by that counterculture had its origins in the Civil Rights Movement, for example, the impact on a generation of white liberals of jazz, broadly construed, had by that time already paved the way for the popular reception of that movement. Yale law professor Charles Black, a member of the legal team that won *Brown v. Board of Education* (1954), liked to describe the moment he ceased being a white racist: it was while watching Louis Armstrong play at a Texas dance. The same might have been said by the countless teens that danced to swing, boogie-woogie, R & B, early rock, or any other of the forms that grew, as Armstrong's did, from the cross-fertilizations that first created jazz. Indeed, jazz was hailed widely as the nation's first truly integrated art. In 1963, LeRoi Jones, soon to become Amiri Baraka, detailed how jazz was born in the first decades of the twentieth century from the fusion of European musical techniques popular among the black middle classes with an expressive folk tradition of the blues, popular among the black working classes. The merging of these idioms produced music representative of all classes of black society and, at the same time, allowed for whites to engage it in what seemed to be a non-exploitative fashion. To Jones, jazz "made it possible for the first time for something of the legitimate feeling of Afro-American music to be imitated successfully." It "enabled separate and *valid* emotional expressions to be made that were based on traditions of Afro-American music that were clearly not part of it." In short, jazz was the nation's first and most significant vehicle for cultural integration. "It was a music," Jones argues, "capable of reflecting not only the Negro and a black America but a white America as well."[27]

What was true of the music was true of the literature it inspired. Eager to counter the accurate perception that the United States trumpeted freedom abroad while denying it to black Americans at home, the State Department sent musicians like Dizzy Gillespie oversees to sell the promise of American democracy. But, in the words of *Down Beat* in 1959, "the question of how hip the State Department really is" remained "an open one."[28] Less committed to jazz per se than to its value as propaganda, the tours provide one example of James Baldwin's claim that white fantasies of black America facilitated "the sanctification of power."[29] I'm interested in the related fact that a striking number of postwar political novels mobilized hip not only to sanctify but to symbolize and thereby negotiate transformations in the Democratic Party's power.

In Edwin O'Connor's *The Last Hurrah* (1956), an old-school ward boss in Boston confronts the reality that the New Deal's national consolidation of the party and the subsequent importance of television in elections have, together, rendered machine politics obsolete. As if to drive home this point, O'Connor's novel describes a black bebop musician who wanders in and out of scenes whispering scat, an unwelcome agent of the forces then changing what it meant to be a Democrat. In Billy Lee Brammer's *The Gay Place* (1961), a Texas governor modeled on Lyndon Johnson surrounds himself with liberal "hipster-pols," hard-partying, jazz-loving hacks who clean up after the governor and struggle to reconcile the Democrats' racist conservative wing with the tastes and mores of its surging youth vote. In Saul Bellow's *Mr. Sammler's Planet* (1970), a black pickpocket exposes himself to the aging protagonist, who compares the man's penis to Lyndon Johnson's, before calling it "a symbol of superlegitimacy or sovereignty." That sovereignty belongs to the Democrats, but Sammler cannot understand the nature of its authority because, as a friend tells him, he is not hip. In Updike's *Rabbit Redux* (1971), Rabbit is similarly estranged from the Democrats, to whom he has been loyal all his life. A black man asks him, "What is lib-er-alism?" and he is unsure. But ultimately the answer comes in the form of Rabbit's apprenticeship to that man, who teaches Rabbit "to groove."[30]

Generalizing about the differences between white and black fiction risks obscuring the degree to which, as Eric Sundquist reminds us, European American and African American literary traditions are part of one tradition.[31] Certainly Ralph Ellison confounds any simple distinction between black and white literary traditions, and I use his essays and never-completed second novel, along with Norman Mailer's essays, as something like the code key for much of the analysis that follows. This said, it's worth noting that black novelists of the postwar period tend to insist upon the exploitative dynamics of liberal hip more than white novelists, who tend to mystify those dynamics. For John A. Williams and Ishmael Reed, for example, Democrats either betray the spirit of bebop or appropriate it for dubious ends. The protagonist of Williams's *The Man Who Cried I Am* (1967) "wanted to do with the novel what Charlie Parker was doing to music—tearing it up and remaking it; basing it on nasty, nasty blues and overlaying it with the deep overriding tragedy not of Dostoevsky, but an American who knew of consequences to come: Herman Melville, a super Confidence Man, a Benito Cereno saddened beyond death." Instead, a racist publishing industry keeps him dependent on the income he earns writing for a newspaper called the *Democrat.* In due course, the novelist finds himself writing civil rights speeches for John Kennedy, which only hastens his disillusionment with the party. He finds himself "bored with New Deals and Square Deals and New Frontiers and Great Societies." In Reed's *The Free-Lance Pallbearers* (1967), mainstream liberalism literally feeds on hip. "Why, they're real swingers," someone says of Harry Sam, a despot modeled after Lyndon Johnson. "Those kats" live in "a groovy nowhere." But Sam shrouds himself in hip to disguise the fact that he has been abducting and eating black children from the impoverished black neighborhoods that surround the capitol. When the novel's protagonist discovers Sam's secret, a white performance artist complicit with Sam tries to teach him "HOW TO BE A HIP KITTY AND A COOL COOL DADDY O."

The artist's name, Cipher X, captures liberalism's commitment to obscuring its atrocities with a mystifying cultural style; when Cipher discovers that the protagonist is steadfast in his desire to expose Sam, he says in disappointment, "I thought that you were hip."[32] Reed lampoons with single-minded focus what most of the novelists whose work is examined in this volume struggle to efface; though their efforts to do so are riddled with illuminating tensions, these preponderantly white writers seek to consolidate and bind together the interests that Reed would disarticulate. Where Reed's *Pallbearers* exposes the sanctification of liberalism, these novels enact it.

None did so more influentially than Robert Penn Warren's *All the King's Men* (1946), which established the template for how postwar novelists would register—if only to elide—uncomfortable realities facing white professionals and managers. My first chapter reads the novel in light of the South's transition from tenant farming to large-scale agriculture, as an account of why affluent southern liberals, who were pledged to the Democratic Party but still implicated in the former production regime, would ultimately fail to form a workable coalition with working-class blacks. Governor Willie Stark winks at Jack Burden and suggests that all southern whites have dirty hands, implicated as they are in the coercive extortion of value from black labor. More particularly, Stark insinuates that Burden's hands are dirty whether he understands himself as a liberal professional or as a descendant of a slave-owning family, and Stark's wink would haunt a subsequent generation of novelists whose literary office depended on sugarcoating an otherwise stark reality: that the professional and managerial class (PMC) in the North would be required to control a black working class previously controlled by southern bourbons. Following Warren north after the Second World War, and reading his most famous novel as a rumination on his own professional development, I describe the New Critics' commitment to poetic autonomy as a commitment to obscuring the PMC's role in laundering black labor power. In sublimating constitutive economic relationships into mystified accounts of aesthetic power, the New Criticism eased the transition of reactionary Southern Agrarians into a nationally oriented PMC, even as it suggested to political novelists how they might do the same by means of hip figures.

Most white members of the PMC came to their sense of hip by way of bebop, a musical style that was itself the product of contested labor relations. In the early thirties, its innovators gathered after hours in small Harlem clubs to evade representatives from the local musicians' union, which had forbidden public jam sessions on the theory that they constituted unremunerated perfor-mances.[33] Ralph Ellison faulted the music because it struck him, along these lines, as the product of upwardly mobile blacks who wished to put distance between themselves and not simply the rank and file of the musicians' union, but the vernacular musical traditions of the black working classes. Whether or not we agree with this ultimately uncharitable account of the music, we must acknowledge that many of the white professionals and managers who expe-rienced bebop—difficult to perform and yet seemingly committed to the ap-pearance of ease—took from it an aesthetic vision ultimately valuable for its capacity to sublimate demanding physical labor, and the social relations that organized that labor, into something more easily exchangeable.

Proceeding from this assumption, my second, third, and fourth chapters read Chandler Brossard's *Who Walk in Darkness* (1952), Ralph Ellison's *Three Days Before the Shooting . . .* (2010), Richard Condon's *The Manchurian Candi-date* (1959), and John Updike's *Rabbit, Run* (1960) as efforts to demonstrate hip's importance to the sale of commodities and, ultimately, the Democratic Party itself. I read these novels, more specifically, in light of cultural and economic changes in the North that led to the election of John F. Kennedy; each partici-pates in the shaping of Kennedy's interracial coalition by reproducing the pro-cedures of an advertising industry increasingly important to the fortunes of the Democrats. For politicians and admen, as well as for these novelists, hip made a fetish of racial difference even as it provided a conglomerating image designed to pass over and go beyond difference; it transported whites from their own bodies and into the images of other bodies, in the process dematerializing race and turning it—and, by extension, the project of integration—into an after-effect of consumption. Then as now, selling hip to white consumers involved selling them the fantasy that consumption could turn them black—but only for as long as they wished to be.

Some saw this blackening as potentially permanent, and the cause of the decade's crisis of masculinity. "All Americans," Mailer wrote, "suffer an un-conscious slavery to advertising."[34] He wanted white men, in particular, to embrace the interracial fraternity that he thought followed from this shared condition. But Mailer's hip, no less than Madison Avenue's, elided the labor relations toward which it seemed to gesture. In fact, much of sixties-era fiction would suggest, against all evidence to the contrary, that middle-class white men were like African Americans in their shared subservience, not simply to commodities but to owners and capitalists. Typically, when professionals and managers, those men were paid to oversee, discipline, or otherwise manage labor on behalf of capital; nevertheless, middle-class white men persistently worried about their downward mobility and cast their affinity with the working classes in racial terms. Nowhere is this dynamic more evident than in the decade's countless dramas of middle-class self-liberation. Chapters 5 and 6 examine novels that urged white-collared white men to free themselves from themselves, as black slaves would free themselves from white owners. This exhortation often invoked familiar clichés about black male sexuality, pitched as it tended to be to emasculated white men in need of vicarious invigoration. It also sat uneasily with the Great Society liberalism in whose name it was often advanced. Novels like Styron's *The Confessions of Nat Turner* (1967), Updike's *Rabbit Redux* (1971), Mailer's *Why Are We in Vietnam?* (1967), Bellow's *Mr. Sammler's Planet* (1970), and Doctorow's *The Book of Daniel* (1971) seem to militate on behalf of an interracial alliance between white and black workers; but, ultimately, these novels reassure their readers that white professionals and managers have it in their power to become owners and capitalists, in ways that black workers do not.

Attending to the emergence of rock and roll in Chapter 6, I read *Vietnam* and *Daniel* in particular as efforts to integrate raced voices, as opposed to raced bodies. Rendering racial difference ever more fungible, these novels embrace in vocal registers the racial hybridity then central to rock and roll. But they also, as a consequence, refine the operations of a white-collar economy oriented toward the processing of deracinated information. And in their preoccupation with integrated voices, as opposed to integrated public spaces, they establish the terms with which subsequent novelists (and politicians) would later reject Great Society racial politics. My last chapter, on Joan Didion's *Democracy* (1984), examines Didion's backlash against the legacy of John F. Kennedy and the vocal integration with which she associates it. Looking back on a "New Liberalism" that she takes to be too closely affiliated with the Civil Rights Movement and the counterculture, she conflates purging the Democrats of African American taint with doing the same to her own literary voice. She performs this racial cleansing even as she defends the interests of what she calls "the American business class." In so doing, Didion anticipates the neoliberal project of the Democratic Leadership Council (DLC) (formed one year after the novel's publication) and the presidency of Bill Clinton.

Metaphor and the Life of the Party

These brief summaries raise two related questions: what is a political party and what does it mean to consolidate one in a literary fashion? In the 1920s and 1930s, these questions arose most visibly in relation to the Communist Party, which exerted considerable sway over U.S. literary production. That party influenced American literature through a centralized organizational apparatus that channeled funds to publications like *New Masses*, which provided income for journalists during the Depression, and to organizations like the John Reed Club, which ran workshops across the country for aspiring novelists and poets. These forms of support underwrote a body of still underappreciated proletarian fiction. Of course, as that fiction often attests, those writers elaborated party ideology in idiosyncratic fashion. There remains considerable debate over how and to what extent the Communist Party sought to control writers, but whatever the outcome of that debate, it's worth noting that even as "the party" functioned in the minds of novelists and poets as an organizational apparatus, it became, by virtue of its incorporation into literature, more than that apparatus alone. Georg Lukács had offered a version of this claim when he announced, "The form taken by the class consciousness of the proletariat is the *Party*." Lukács thought that joining the party served as an "entry ticket" to "History" because the party was more than "merely a form of organization"— it was, rather, the theoretical vehicle through which the postulates of Marxism achieved a "dialectical unity" with revolutionary practice.[35] Though critics often disparage Lukács for his willingness to take directives from Moscow, his work is animated by the possibility that novels were themselves potentially revolutionary, and therefore potentially constitutive of a party that was, necessarily, something more than an organizational structure.[36]

In what follows, I assume that U.S. novelists understood the Democratic Party as something other than an organizational structure—as more than the actual machinery that coordinated the actions of politicians and those who supported them. Looking beyond the organizational components of party life is, of course, relatively easy to do in the context of American political parties, which have never wielded the centralized authority of the Communist Party in the Soviet Union. Thus, for example, in 1963, James MacGregor Burns regretted that the Democrats and Republicans were in effect each divided in two, with a "Presidential Party" and a "Congressional Party"; as he saw it, the organizational morass of the latter impinged upon the visionary possibilities of the former. Burns is apropos here because his terms lend themselves to an account of why writers might matter to parties. He thought that presidential parties in particular were effective to the degree that they addressed themselves in high-minded fashion to national audiences; in so doing, they rose above the machinery that conducted the business of the party on a local and day-to-day level. It's no surprise then that, for Burns, the incipiently literary presidential party drew into its orbit intellectuals and Eastern elites, while the congressional party spoke in the less cosmopolitan and more managerial voice of Middle America.[37] Committed to the notion that the political party existed in high and low incarnations, and to the corresponding notion that these incarnations mapped onto analogous distinctions between high and low culture, Burns suggested the larger significance of mandarin taste and literary distinction in the configuration of political parties.

It's relatively easy, and often fun, to find less-than-exalted examples of a given party's reliance on metaphor. In his introduction to *The Fabulous Democrats* (1956), an extended puff piece on the party issued to coincide with the elections of that year, House majority leader Sam Rayburn expounded on the essential nature of the Democrats: "As every man is the sum total of his inheritance, environment, and experience, so are political parties." The truth about the "inner nature" of the Democratic Party, Rayburn adds, is that it has "a good heart." To Rayburn, the properties of this figurative heart matter more than programs. For how, he asks, "does a party interpret a program? It does it in the only way it can do it. By its inner light, its instinctive feelings, its habits of thinking acquired through many decades." Voters should trust the party the way they would trust a person with whom they had been familiar for many years.[38]

We might, however, capture the properly figurative registers of party identity in a more immediately relevant way. In 2003, cognitive linguist George Lakoff consulted extensively with the likes of Hillary Clinton and Tom Daschle, in an effort to make the Democratic Party more attentive to its use of metaphor. Lakoff drew on what he called "conceptual metaphor theory" to argue that parties won ostensibly ideological debates before they started, when they linguistically "framed" themselves and those debates such that they appealed to voters on a visceral level. He thought that Republicans tended to frame themselves as "strict fathers," while Democrats framed themselves as "nurturing parents." Lakoff thought the GOP more successful in its efforts, and we might well attribute that success to its long history of producing "rhetorical winks," as Jerry Himelstein calls them, designed to communicate indirectly messages that might formally be disavowed. Richard Nixon appealed to racist resentment with phrases like "law and order"—code for the need to crack down on urban blacks. Other Republicans used terms like "inner city" and "at risk" to describe the putatively unredeemable black ghetto. These metaphorical condensations reached their apotheosis, reasons Thomas Edsall, when conservatives used the word "black" alone to describe "crime, poverty, welfare and drugs."[39]

The Democratic Party's use of racial framing and rhetorical winking has been more complex, in part because its central alliances have often been strikingly tenuous. One is tempted to venture that the Democrats have often traded in mixed racial messages in ways that the GOP has not. For example, historians like Alexander Saxton and Michael Rogin read antebellum minstrelsy as the expression of Democratic Party interests in Jacksonian America. Saxton contends that the "stylized form" of minstrelsy "propagandized metaphorically the alliance of urban working people with the planter interest in the South."[40] That stylized form was complex and contradictory, in all of the ways that Eric Lott has made plain, especially insofar as it allowed whites to mobilize profoundly ambivalent feelings toward African Americans. I argue that, more than a hundred years later, white literary performances of hip "propagandized metaphorically," in an equally agonized and contradictory fashion, on behalf of a very different Democratic Party.

We see this fraught process at work in Norman Mailer's infamous essay, "The White Negro: Superficial Reflections on the Hipster" (1957). This account of hip was one among many, but, its warped assumptions and histrionic posturing notwithstanding, it focused and brought to the forefront debate that had until then existed on the margins of political and cultural life. *The Cambridge History of American Literature* very rightly declares, "Among the literary figures who gained fame before the fifties ended," Mailer was "the most prophetic [and] most attuned to the cultural eruptions soon to come." It adds that if the literature of that moment "can be said to have crystallized in a single work, it would be Mailer's feverish essay 'The White Negro.'"[41] *Hip Figures* reads the political history of Mailer's moment through this agonized essay.

Throughout, I'm less interested in psychological ambivalence than in semantic and social contradiction. Paul Ricoeur offers a useful account, in this context, of how all metaphors are in some sense contradictory. He reminds us, first of all, that metaphor applies not simply to individual words but to sentences and, potentially, to larger semantic units as well: to the whole scaled range of linguistic phenomena that the novel comprises, for example. As he puts it, "A word receives metaphorical meaning within specific contexts, within which it is opposed to other words taken literally." This is true of an extended conceit in a novel no less than a phrase—an essay, like Mailer's, no less than its title, "The White Negro." Ricoeur treats the local phrase and the extended conceit as related forms of metaphor because, to him, metaphors produce "semantic clash" between lexical and figurative meanings—between the already or commonly agreed upon and what deviates from that agreement—no matter how elaborately articulated the meaning at hand might be. This clash takes place simultaneously with what Ricoeur calls a metaphor's "semantic innovation": its creation of an "emergent," context-specific meaning.[42] The key point for Ricoeur, however, is that semantic innovation retains in its structure a fundamental tension. "In order that metaphor obtains," he writes, "one must continue to identify the previous incompatibility *through* the new compatibility." Metaphor produces "new kinds of assimilation," he writes, not "*above* the differences, as in the concept, but in spite of and through the differences." Thus he will liken metaphor to storytelling, insofar as it implicitly announces, "it is and it is not." Though evocative of earlier accounts of metaphor, Aristotle's most notably, this formulation usefully describes how Mailer's metaphor simultaneously conceals and reveals constitutive tensions.[43]

The phrase "white Negro" is a catachresis or solecism; it strains credulity and produces a semantic clash. From Ricoeur's perspective, this clash leads to a semantic innovation that allows us to understand what it might mean to be both black and white at the same time. Ricoeur would call this "predicative assimilation": "white Negro" places two antithetical categories in relationship so as to rewrite the differences between them and thereby predicate a new category. At first glance, "white" modifies what seems to be a more basic category of identity: throughout the essay, Mailer speaks of "the Negro" but never speaks of "whites." From this perspective, the phrase "white Negro" suggests the contingent and subordinate relevance of the word "white": his adjective will not function as a noun. Indeed, while Mailer's hipsters look white, they are in the process of becoming something other than a group of "whites." But, crucially, in becoming "Negro," they change that identity such that it describes neither external markers nor inherited traits, but instead a set of performable dispositions. In making these dispositions available to those who didn't look like Negroes were understood to look, Mailer's phrase reinvents the category of "Negro."

Ricoeur's metaphor is a "performative" form of speech, "in which to *say* something is to *do* something." For him, metaphor does not describe an existing state of affairs; it is an action whose "semantic innovation" produces effects in the world. Of course, as J. L. Austin reminds us, speech acts upon the world most effectively when it has institutional backing: performative speech produces what he calls "happy" or "felicitous" results when it derives legitimacy from structures of authority antecedent to itself. Putting the doing in saying requires "*an accepted conventional procedure having a certain conventional effect, the procedure to include the uttering of certain words by certain persons in certain circumstances.*" Pierre Bourdieu faults Austin for failing to articulate more fully what he calls "the institutional conditions" of the "accepted conventional procedure." "One only preaches to the converted," Bourdieu writes. "And the miracle of symbolic efficacy disappears if one sees that the magic of words merely releases the 'springs'—the dispositions—which are wound up beforehand." This elaborates what is already implicit in Austin, but Bourdieu does importantly add that performative speech can be at once "classified and classifying, ranked and ranking"—that which winds as well as releases the springs of institutional legitimacy.[44]

Mailer's metaphor wound and released the institutional legitimacy of the Democratic Party. The term "white Negro" had an immediately political resonance; Theodore H. White's *The Making of the President, 1960,* for example, speaks of the "white-Negro relations" important to Kennedy's victory.[45] Ricoeur's account is apropos to those figurative relations because it insists that we never lose sight of the clash that gives rise to semantic innovation: in any metaphor, we remain fixed on the incompatibility of the old terms; metaphor is built, he tells us, on the still visible "ruins of the literal." In the case of the phrase "white Negro," we witness the strained union of two groups; it performs uneven integration on behalf of a party still committed, in 1957, to the aftereffects of Jim Crow. "White" joins not with "black," but with "Negro," the latter term an inheritance of the Spanish and Portuguese involvement in the slave trade and a designation, Ken Warren reminds us, that derives from the world of separate but equal even as it expresses the hope that "the cultural and spiritual resources" of the black underclass might "offset the demoralization and desacralizing of life under the advent of late capitalism."[46]

Simultaneously ideological and utopian, Mailer's figure expresses divisive interests as it struggles to articulate the grounds for a community that might transcend those interests. His white hipster endeavors with psychopathic fury to mimic urban black men, to absorb their "existential synapses" and thus move closer to the "apocalyptic orgasm" that Mailer, in his often repellent racism, believes black men enjoy (*A* 341, 347). At the same time, in what we might call the hip version of Calvinist salvation, the white Negro thinks that he feels as he does, and wants what he wants, because he is, in a sense, already black. Trapped between the democratic and the totalitarian, black men face "the simplest of alternatives: live a life of constant humility or ever-threatening danger" (*A* 341). Mailer's whites think they too feel the force of these alternatives; they fear the arbitrary violence of their state and as a result believe that they share with blacks an analogous relation to injustice. Uneasily conjoining bodies craving transcendence through physical release and bodies under threat, Mailer's hip is a rationale for self-gratification and, at the same time, a goad toward collective affiliation. Thus he describes the hipster as "an extreme embodiment of the contradictions of the society which formed his character" (*A* 347).

In reading such contradictions, I'm guided by Ricoeur's belief that the greater the semantic clash in a figure, the greater the strain and, as a consequence, the greater the figure's need to legitimate its authority. Mailer's claims about the influence of his sentences grow more aggrandizing to the degree that they describe progressively counterfactual states of affairs. The phrase "white Negro" encapsulates his sense that he can change political reality by writing about it in a particular way. But the persistence of semantic clash in that writing embodies the anxious self-positing that Eric Santner attributes to many performative visions of authority, be they Walter Benjamin's, whose "*law reaffirms itself*," or Austin's, whose speech actor officiates at weddings instead of reporting on them.[47] Hip communicates authority through its display of ease. But as I describe it, hip is inherently unstable and characteristically gnomic, and anxious in its ease, because it expresses social contradictions and because, most immediately, it performs the natural in a situation that is demonstrably "unnatural," not because it is at odds with biology or any "real" or "authentic" version of lived life (for Ricoeur, the "literal" is simply the most immediately available or commonly understood meaning) but because it is at odds with what seems initially definitive of the terms at hand: whites do not look like Negroes. Hip performances teeter on the edge of theater, if not melodrama, to the extent that they seek to efface their constitutive tensions. Hip must struggle to conceal its struggles. It endeavors to erase evidence of its labor—to insist that it is not insisting. Like the bebop musicians on which it once modeled itself, it is studied but nonchalant, passionate but detached; it works hard not to work. But work it does.

A New Class of Hipsters

Bernard Wolfe noted something like Ricoeur's hypothetical double structure at work in black jazz musicians who played for white audiences. In essays later important to Frantz Fanon, Wolfe described how these musicians performed expected stereotypical roles—which we might call "literal" roles, not because they represented what was intrinsic to the performers but because they represented the racist meanings that white listeners ascribed to black performers. Wolfe's larger point was that these musicians produced tensions within this horizon of expectation; they simultaneously fulfilled and satirized the roles they were expected to perform, and this gave their performances what Wolfe calls their "*as if*" character. Like Ricoeur's metaphors, these musicians held expectation and its subversion in tension, and thereby produced new kinds of assimilation through difference.[48]

The author of innovative essays on hip, Philip Ford identifies a different but analogous version of this productive tension in the musical structure of postwar jazz. "The hip gesture" that he finds in solos by the likes of Charlie Parker, Thelonious Monk, and Miles Davis is "still in some ways a recognizable version of the original thing. This is a deformation of gesture: its expressive effect is dependent upon a shared understanding of a normative gesture and of its distance from the altered version." In "So What," for example, Davis takes "the shortest possible trip"—"one semitone"—in his "travel between modes," and thereby creates a "lyric binary form [that] pares away all but the most minimally differentiating musical information." Even as they appeared supremely "nonchalant," musicians used a range of deformations like these to push continuity to the breaking point: "The increasingly complex improvised lines and chordal substitutions of bebop placed new strain on listeners' power to detect traces of the standard on which a performance might be based," and thus explored "the conceptual dissonance between mental horizon and the moment."[49]

We might extrapolate from this account of conceptual dissonance, the better to understand how the contradictory structures described by Wolfe and Ford speak not simply to the novels below, but to the material conditions governing their production and reception. What larger social relations, in other words, are coded into the deformations of gesture, or the hip figures, that these novels perform? Richard Godden suggests the beginnings of an answer when he explains why Ricoeur proves useful in reading reification, a process that "yields a fetish, or, an entity standing in the place of another," and thus describes a "quasi-metaphorical relation." Ricoeur's account of the "semantic clash" always visible in metaphorical relations suggests to Godden "that in fetish as in metaphor, a semantic excess, resulting from an impertinent conjunction of terms, leaves a generative remainder beyond the reconstituted possibilities of meaning (or the meaning of the metaphor). Put tersely: the tension and its residues do not go away." Rather, "the metaphor, divided by its own tensions, yields a 'split referent,' requiring in its reception a 'split addressee,' or one for whom 'meaning is depicted . . . under the features of ellipsis.'" Beneath any such ellipsis we view productive forces, to recall Marx, that take "the social characteristics of men's own labor as objective characteristics of the products of labor themselves."[50] Labor relations disappear, by figurative magic, into the products produced by those relations. But their residue remains and, in the case of the commodity form that I am calling literary hip, those residues point toward the disciplinary labors of the professional-managerial class.

I read literary hip as a fraught and self-divided fetish produced by a class of workers eager to forget the social relations that govern their labor, and that their labor governs. These workers were members of what, following Barbara Ehrenreich, I have been calling "the professional-managerial class," or what Alvin Gouldner calls the "New Class"—a predominantly white group whose votes and supervisory labor would prove vital to the fortunes of the postwar Democrats. Ehrenreich elaborates upon the social control performed by that group, and I rely on this account throughout. Gouldner describes the group as comprising "symbol specialists" inclined "to disrupt established social solidarities and cultural values" and to believe "that 'What Is' may be mistaken or inadequate and . . . therefore open to alternatives." Such a class has obvious affinities with Ricoeur's figurative disposition, in which readers experience a tension between figurative and lexical ways of describing "What Is."[51] At the same time, this class needed false consciousness more than "the ruins of the literal." It needed, most basically, to conceal from its members the nature of its most central function—that it existed in large part to extract surplus value from classes with less control over the conditions of their labor. The aura of ease so important to hip facilitated the production of that false consciousness.

As John Leland has it, bebop and its related styles suited members of "the new managerial class who made their living with their brains, not their bodies, [because] the music was more cerebral than visceral." Scott Saul adds, "The hipster's appeal was tied to new kinds of working conditions, namely the expansion of the clerical and service professions in America's postindustrial economy." Alan Liu elaborates when he describes how members of the PMC turned to "outsiders"—"cool," racially marked others—in order to concretize forms of dispossession that they did not themselves experience, and were in fact, according to Ehrenreich, themselves responsible for producing among the working classes. "White-collars," Liu argues, "displaced the very experience of alienation onto outsiders who could do the heavy lifting of being alienated for them"; they engaged in "regular indulgences in outlaw scenes. *I work here* [amid all these machines, protocols, procedures, codes], *but I'm cool.*"[52] Needless to say, these outlaw scenes neither imagined nor required any actual "heavy lifting." Quite the contrary, in the PMC's many hands, hip treated outsiders as exemplars of effortless exertion.

Hip conjured only to stylize the social relations that obtained between the PMC and the working class whose labor it was employed to oversee. No surprise, then, that white professionals and managers invariably misapprehended the black underground with which they identified. Whatever their individual financial fortunes, and however much some adopted revolutionary or anti-capitalist stances, the bebop musicians so important to figures like Norman Mailer, for example, were typically, in the words of Scott DeVeaux, "*professionals*: ambitious and opportunistic, eager to exchange their specialized skills for monetary advantage in the service of their careers." Overlooking this fact was crucial to Mailer's larger project, insofar as it allowed him to confuse what was, in essence, the slow absorption of an elite group of blacks into a predominantly white PMC with an alliance between that PMC and the African American working classes, from whence derived the preponderance of the Democrats' black votes. Thus Mailer's *An American Dream* (1965) centers on Stephen Rojack, a former Democratic Party congressman, evocative of John F. Kennedy, who must physically best a hyper-masculine jazz musician, Shago Martin, who grew up struggling on the mean streets of Harlem. Mailer modeled Martin on Miles Davis—this despite the fact that Davis was the son of a well-to-do dentist. Martin is a far cry indeed from the cerebral musician, who recalled that he and Freddie Webster used to listen diligently to Dizzy Gillespie and Charlie Parker "like scientists of sound."[53]

Mailer rewrites Davis and bebop, but revealingly so. Rojack doesn't want to emulate Martin. He wants to control him. Earlier forms of blackface offer a limited model for understanding the many postwar versions of this desire, and not only because bebop constituted a genuine "revolution in culture," as Ralph Ellison put it, while the minstrel show was a hall of mirrors in which working-class whites burlesqued slaves who were themselves often parodying the codes of southern gentility. The blackface on display in early Hollywood film, for example, offers as limited a model as the minstrel show. "Blackening up and then wiping off burnt cork" functioned for Jews in the film industry, argues Michael Rogin, as "a rite of passage from immigrant to American"—one in which the performance of blackness cleansed Jews of their ethnicity and humble class origins and left them able to pass as white.[54] However compelling with respect to Hollywood, accounts like these remain insensitive to the requirements of postwar capital and the formations organized to serve it, in large part because they dramatically underestimate the utility of multivalent and sustained, as opposed to symbolically discarded, interracial identifications—not only to Jewish Americans but to all members of the PMC.

At the start of the sixties, the popularity of the Catholic, Irish American Kennedy signaled a new relation between minorities and the administrative apparatus of industry and state. Jews in particular were to prove densely emblematic to a new elite eager to stress its difference from WASP America, not least because Jews, neither black nor white, seemed crucial to mediating symbolically between black and white on behalf of industry and the state. This mediation displaced in complex fashion what is, for Ehrenreich, the PMC's mediation between capital and labor. In the period's cultural imagination, relations between capital and labor disappear into relations between black and white. Poised between white and black on the one hand and capital and labor on the other, Jews were understood to facilitate this disappearance, possessed as they ostensibly were of a labile embodiment and a tenuous relation to still-entrenched forms of privilege.[55]

Mailer's *Armies of the Night* (1968) is an account of how Jews such as himself might perform this function. He characterizes the 1967 March on the Pentagon as a protest against "the technicians, bureaucrats, and labor leaders who ran the governmental military-industrial complex of super-technology land." The irony of the event, he thinks, comes from the fact that many of those participating in it are, like him, "good professionals."[56] But he's not just a professional;

he's a self-consciously Jewish one, and he shows why this matters. "A clown of an arriviste baron" (41), a "nice Jewish boy from Brooklyn" (134), Mailer sees himself in competition with the patrician Robert Lowell, whose "languid grandeurs" have been refined by generations "going through the best troughs in the best eating clubs at Harvard" (44). Jealous though he is, Mailer has something that Lowell doesn't: he can when speaking to the crowds do the police in many voices and speak to the audience in all its variety. Reaffirming his faith in "the democratic principle" and "the common man" (47), he displays what he elsewhere calls "Jewish genius" (170) by performing a series of roles. First, "showing hints of Cassius Clay," he decides to act as a representative of "*impromptu* Black Power" (38); later, he pretends to be "Lyndon Johnson's little old *dwarf* alter ego," while showing "shades of Cassius Clay again" (49). Mailer's desire is not, *pace* Rogin, to perform blackness and thereby discard his Jewishness in favor of a more purely white identity; it is, rather, to insist upon the value of his ability, as a Jew, to mediate between power blocs by channeling black style.

We glimpse the properly administrative nature of this claim later when, arraigned for his part in the march, Mailer witnesses the contest between his lawyer and a sitting commissioner. It was, he writes, "a battle," a "face-off between a tough Jew and a well-made son of Virginia gentry" (209). The Jewish lawyer wins the contest, and the commissioner gives him a wry smile, as if to communicate that "there was no lawyer like a good Jewish lawyer" (211). This is the case, Mailer suggests, because the good Jewish lawyer possesses exceptional agility before a legal code in which he has no overriding moral investment: "he did not believe many of the pious sentiments he was obliged to express—what he did believe, what stood out about him, was his love of the law as an intricate deceptive smashing driving tricky game somewhere between wrestling, football, and philosophy" (207). As with subject positions, so with legal positions: Jewish lawyers master the system because, not entrenched within it, they see it as a game requiring versatility. It is characteristic of Mailer, and the PMC whose interests he typically represents in ambivalent fashion, to describe that versatility as important, in one instance, to radicalism, and, in another, to the state apparatus.

Mailer and Doctorow are the only Jewish novelists treated in this volume. But Ellison, Styron, and Updike each identified or were identified with Jews in some way over the course of their careers, and a study longer than this one might demonstrate, in ways that I do not, the extent to which literary hip emerges under the sign of a deracinated Jewishness, less because particular Jews stood to profit from these mobilizations (no doubt some did), than because Jewishness seemed even to WASP novelists to represent the fungibility of ethnic and racial identity per se. To Mailer, "the Jews were a spirit of emancipation"—"emancipated at long last from being Jews," modern Jews had "become the very principle of emancipation."[57] I argue here, instead, though in a related vein, that African Americans sponsored fantasies of racial lability on behalf of the Democratic Party when, all objective evidence to the contrary, they were taken to represent "the very principle of emancipation," as opposed to any actual emancipation that might have threatened established relations of production.

Not even that principle was extended to women, who are treated like second-class citizens in the strikingly misogynist novels that follow, as little more than vehicles for triangulating desire between white and black men. Moreover, women are often cast as embodiments of all that these white men would leave behind. Barbara Ehrenreich describes a Beat sensibility in which "women and their demands for responsibility were, at worst, irritating and more often just uninteresting compared to the ecstatic possibilities of male adventure." Susan Fraiman rightly adds that in the larger "structure of feeling" associated with "cool," women are more than irritating and distracting: "the feminine is maternalized and hopelessly linked to stasis, tedium, constraint, even domination. Typed as 'mothers,' women become inextricable from a rigid domesticity that bad boys are pledged to resist and overcome."[58]

Robin Morgan rejected hip's structure of feeling in her feminist anthem "Goodbye to All That" (1970). Unwilling any longer to be part of what she called "the counterfeit, male-dominated Left," Morgan bid farewell "to Hip Culture and the Sexual Revolution, which has functioned toward women's freedom as did the Reconstruction toward former slaves—reinstituted oppression by another name."[59] Morgan misconstrued the goals and effects of Reconstruction, but her larger point was unassailable: much hip culture enshrined the power of white men. Armed with this insight, second-wave feminism unsettled many of the white novelists discussed here, Mailer most famously, because it threatened not only "patriarchy" but the fraternal relations between white and black men that these novelists wanted to serve as the symbol of the Democratic Party.

By 1972, the ongoing entrance of women into the Democratic Party had placed feminist issues at the top of the party's agenda. At the convention of that year, 40 percent of the delegates were women, and George McGovern committed to ratifying the Equal Rights Amendment, eliminating discrimination against women in employment, education, housing, credit, and social security, extending the Equal Pay Act, and amending the U.S. Tax Code to permit working families to deduct child care and housekeeping as expenses.[60] Unfortunately, a rapidly changing political context seemed to give warrant to the perception that these commitments came at the expense of the party's dedication to integration: feminism became important to the Democrats even as the party scrambled to adjust to the 1966 backlash against Lyndon Johnson's civil rights legislation.[61] There was of course no necessary trade-off between the rights of women and blacks, and it's by no means clear that the Democrats turned to one at the expense of the other. Still, the entrance into the party of large numbers of professional women in particular made it easy for a generation of male writers, needing little excuse to vent their misogyny, to imagine that the party did. Reporting from the 1972 convention, Mailer writes,

> Every injustice against a black man poisoned the root of America's existence. Whereas every injustice against a lady in Women's Liberation gave every promise of poisoning her husband's existence. But just this was the intolerable disproportion of Women's Liberation—they pretended to a suffering as profound as the Blacks, when their anguish came out of nothing more intolerable than the intolerable pointlessness of middle-class life.[62]

It's telling that Mailer not only sets the claims of blacks and women at odds, but that he sets the claims of presumably working-class black men at odds with the claims of white women from his own class. For years he had made a fetish of the black working class in order to escape the middle class; to him, the rise to prominence of women in the Democratic Party threatened that project.

Feminists epitomized all that Mailer wished to disavow in the PMC. Thus *The Prisoner of Sex* (1971) calls Kate Millett one among many feminist "literary lawyers" (109), a "mouthpiece for a corporate body of ideas" (112), a "lab assistant" (115), and a "technologist" (123). But the real anxiety that organizes that volume arises from Mailer's sense that "the sexes already were growing similar" (128), and that, no stranger to the PMC, he is potentially as much a mouthpiece for corporate ideas as Millett, who, much to his dismay, possesses what he calls "a totally masculine mind" (119). In fact, and despite the abuse he heaps on Millett, Mailer is forced grudgingly to admit that feminism had made possible, for the first time in literary history, he thinks, a prose style among women that was as hardened by hip as his own; "the language of the blacks was in that style" (39), he grants. Mailer no doubt feared that, penetrated by black language, women no longer needed his version of that language (just as he feared that, buttressed by technological means of artificial reproduction, women would no longer need men to make children).

In *The Prisoner of Sex*, Mailer senses not simply that his radicalism might be a vanguard form of a more conventional liberalism (he worries throughout about whether he is a "revolutionary" or a "conservative"), but also that his commitment to existential action (to choosing as opposed to simply accepting one's identity) sits rather well with "the technicians, bureaucrats, and labor leaders who ran the governmental military-industrial complex of super-technology land." Mailer was in fact at the forefront of a generation of novelists who helped a new technical elite—freed from constraining identifications with racial groups, traditional communities, and nations—facilitate the transition of state-sponsored capitalism into a more properly neoliberal dispensation. These novelists wrote on behalf of the many triumphs of postwar liberalism—among which the Voting and Civil Rights acts must figure prominently. But they also exemplified how hip would become what Thomas Frank calls "the public philosophy of the age of flexible accumulation."[63]

Novel Politics

If during the thirties political parties and the state seemed agents of liberation, by the end of the sixties they seemed to embody all that individuals needed liberation from. Advocating on behalf of a Freudian sexual politics, Norman O. Brown announced "the superannuation of the political categories which informed liberal thought in the 1930s."[64]

In the countercultural imagination, the foremost problem with liberal thought in the 1930s was its corrosive emphasis on "social security." Mailer denounced all that was "smug, security-ridden and mindless" in American life, and thought that "security is boredom, and therefore sickness" (*A* 284, 339). James Baldwin mocked "the vast, gray sleep which was called security." Hunter Thompson's early essay "Security" railed against the dulling condition named in its title. For Joan Didion, the New Deal culture of social security simply no longer applied: her story "Some Dreamers of the Golden Dream" (1966) describes a Depression-era style insurance scam—less the product of cagey grifters than of hapless losers. Hers is an all-American dreamscape gone wrong, one "in which a belief in the literal interpretation of Genesis has slipped imperceptibly into a belief in the literal interpretation of *Double Indemnity*."[65]

Liberal thought of the thirties also seemed unable to encompass sexual experience. In Sylvia Plath's *The Bell Jar* (1962), Esther Greenwood declares, "Instead of the world being divided up into Catholics and Protestants or Republicans and Democrats or white men and black men or even men and women, I saw the world divided into people who had slept with somebody and people who hadn't, and this seemed the only really significant difference between one person and another."[66] Greenwood's terms anticipated a larger shift, captured by all of the novelists below, as well as Kate Millett's *Sexual Politics* (1972), which eschews "that relatively narrow and exclusive world of meetings, chairmen, and parties" for "the relationship between the sexes."[67]

The intellectual origins of this opposition between institutional and sexual politics lay in the immediate postwar period, when stodgy white men argued earnestly about the fate of politics. "The progressive," reasoned Dwight Macdonald in 1946, "thinks in collective terms (the interests of Society or the Working Class); the radical stresses the individual conscience and sensibility."[68] Eager to save the center, Cold Warriors like Lionel Trilling and Arthur Schlesinger Jr. refused that distinction and lionized literature for its ability to mobilize conscience and sensibility on behalf of an appropriately vigorous liberalism. C. Wright Mills thought literature inadequate to this task. He averred that "serious literature has in many ways become a minor art," largely because "men of sensibility" no longer find in it the "suitable ways of feeling" and "styles of emotion" that they need to cope with "the historical reality and political facts of our time." Put in the unself-consciously masculine terms offered by Lukács, a man of letters whom Mills admired, literature was failing to personalize "the vital, but not immediately obvious forces at work in objective reality."[69]

According to Lukács, the "major realist" aims to "penetrate the laws governing objective reality, and uncover the deeper, hidden, mediated, not immediately perceptible network of relationships that go to make up society." This piercing requires revealing "man in the whole range of his relations to the real world, above all those which outlast mere fashion."[70] But when were "suitable ways of feeling" and "styles of emotion" more than "mere fashion"? And when did they express "vital . . . forces" as a function of embodiment? To Lukács, a realist novel should "discern and give shape" to "underground trends"; but a preoccupation with manners and sensibility did not to him represent appropriate instances of this discernment. Mailer, on the other hand, thought fashion, hip in particular, the most significant trend of his moment, and his work should be understood as an effort to provide an appropriately masculine living connection, as retrograde as it might have been, between Millett's political parties and sexual relations, as well as between both of these and Lukács's generative forces. "The next collapse in America may come not from the center of the economy," he declared, "but within the superstructure of manners, morals, tastes, fashions and vogue which shape the search for love of each of us" (A 215). This suggested to him the revolutionary significance of hip manners, morals, tastes, and fashions as well as the world-historical importance of the novel—which he wanted to "give shape" to future events.

Because hip captured how style and sexuality might transform the most intractable social facts even without seeming particularly eager to do so, because it seemed simultaneously local and systemic, at once the stuff of private experience and totalized social relations, it stood to reason that metaphors of hip embodiment—literary figures of street-corner figures—might provide the novel with an apt vehicle for reflecting upon how it impacted "man in the whole range of his relations to the real world." The range in question was undeniably limited, especially insofar as it was limited to men. But it's worth adding that in the eyes of its invariably male practitioners, this clubby affair was helped more than hindered by the fact that white novelists mimed white hipsters who were themselves miming black musicians. Hip was an art of copying that compelled further and increasingly self-conscious arts of copying; it was, in short, ideally suited to a generation of late modernists interested in what Clement Greenberg, describing the avant-garde's commitment to medium specificity, called "the imitation of imitating."[71] Speaking of "the avant-garde's specialization of itself," Greenberg described efforts to focus in on and thereby refine the core attributes of particular media.[72] As many have observed, bebop was similarly modernist in its desire to strip away everything extrinsic to jazz—all associations with dance music, popular song, or entertainment—until it became "*art music.*" Thus Scott DeVeaux describes the popular belief that "it is only with bebop that the essential nature of jazz is unmistakably revealed."[73] It makes sense, from this perspective, that bebop provided the novel with a means of becoming self-conscious about its capacity to elaborate connections between embodied experience and social relations—and that Mailer declared himself interested in "the more formal aspects of hip" (A 423).

We see these aspects at work when Mailer proclaims hip capable of "comprehending every circuit and process of society from ukase to kiss as the communication of human energy," and therefore the first step toward a "neo-Marxian calculus capable of translating the economic relations of man into his psychological relations and then back again" (*A* 357). In many ways, this describes an assumption intrinsic to all cultural politics: energy flows fluidly between the symbolic and the institutional, just as it does between the personal and the political. But hip was to Mailer visible evidence of these transfers, just as his own hip style was a means of achieving them. We track his figurative "communications" phonetically, as they affect our bodies: we hear the aspirated /k/ sound of "comprehending" turn into the sibilant /s/ sound at the start of "circuit," which is picked up by the repeated /s/ sound in both "process" and "society." The equation is then compressed and doubled, as both "ukase" and "kiss" move internally from /k/ to /s/ sounds; and then it is completed with the double /k/ sound in "communication." To hear the circulation of these sounds is to experience physically what Mailer's metaphor means to assert: we hear in the circulation of sound a circulation of energy. The experience of hearing the repeated sounds of /k/ and /s/ within "kiss" and "ukase" further specifies this circulation. "Ukase" is a Russian word derived from *ukazlivat,* which means to show, announce, or prescribe. The most common meaning of the word comes from Tsarist Russia, where a ukase was an edict or decree that had the force of law. Moving from "ukase" to "kiss," we move between two forms of assertion, one public and the other private. Knowing as we do that Mailer's is a "neo-Marxian" calculus, we surmise that he wants the authority of the former overthrown by the latter: just as the masses replaced the tsars, so too might kisses replace a Stalinist or capitalist commitment to what his essay calls "the super state." After all, we move *from* "ukase" to "kiss," and not in the reverse direction. But we don't just know this—we feel it. As "ukase" sounds like "you kiss," so an old guard edict turns toward a new sexual politics, organized by hip. Mailer attaches that sexual politics to the authority of his sentence and its ability to register physically the translation of energy that it describes. His language doesn't simply assert the newfound relevance of a neo-Marxian sexual politics; it performs that relevance by demonstrating its capacity to produce new kinds of political meaning and embodied experience.

What did such performances look like within the novel? Toward the end of the fifties, when Mailer wrote these words, politics and the novel were finding each other at important moments in their respective histories. Just as new modes of political thought were beginning to explore the relation between ukases and kisses, new forms of literary analysis were beginning to anatomize the novel's constitutive properties. In 1955, Joseph Blotner published *The Political Novel*. The year 1957 saw the release of Ian Watts's *The Rise of the Novel*, Richard Chase's *The American Novel and Its Tradition*, C. P. Snow's *The English Realist Novel*, Northrop Frye's *The Anatomy of Criticism*, and Granville Hicks's *The Living Novel*. But most importantly, it saw the publication of Irving Howe's *Politics and the Novel*.

A socialist, Howe wrote from the front lines of the intellectual revolution fought over how the American left should understand "the political." For the most part he was hostile to the privatizing of this concept begun after the Second World War and realized climactically in the new social movements of the sixties. In his opus on politics and the novel, he condemned those who rejected traditional venues for pursuing social change. "One of the most striking facts about American life," he argues, "is the frequency with which political issues seem to arise in non-political forms. Instead of confronting us as formidable systems of thought, or as parties locked in bitter combat, politics in America has often appeared in the guise of religious, cultural and sexual issues." Howe notes a similar phenomenon in the American novel, which tends to ignore the properly political. Howe appreciates European novels "in which political ideas play a dominant role or in which the political milieu is the dominant setting."[74] Exactly what constitutes a political idea Howe does not directly say, but he hazards, in modernist fashion, that a "political milieu" offers "an autonomous field of action" and "a distinctive mode of social existence, with values and manners of its own." Novelists like Nathaniel Hawthorne, Henry Adams, and Henry James gesture to but never fully grasp that autonomy. Unable to "focus on politics long and steadily enough to allow it to develop according to its inner rhythms," they fail to register the conventions that animate and remain integral to political institutions. Intent on "personalizing everything," they fail to "do justice to the life of politics in its own right" (*PN* 162–163).

Howe's defense of "the life of politics in its own right" anticipated his venomous assessments of those on the New Left who seemed eager "to adopt a stance which seems to be political, sometimes even ideological," but was nothing more than an expression of "personal style."[75] He thought Tom Hayden an authoritarian demagogue, and pronounced his "participatory democracy" a "confusion of realms."[76] Howe believed that "a judgment of one area of experience in terms of another [was] . . . almost always a dangerous kind of judgment to make" (*PN* 189–190). All in its proper place: he thought Millett "the ideal high-brow popularizer for the politics and culture of the New Left," because *Sexual Politics* was "a simplistic leap from one order of experience (psychological) to another (social policy)."[77] His criticisms no doubt reminded Hayden and Millett of why a more capacious account of the political was necessary, for Howe appeared in these instances a patriarchal gatekeeper, bent on stemming the tide of those seeking entrance to a once rarefied preserve. Unwilling to grant legitimacy to new voices on the left, he was hostile to any expression of radicalism that had not internalized his version of the lessons of the past. He seemed more committed to "the political" as such than to whatever particular interests might be expressed in its name. How else to understand his claim that the New Left offered an "apolitical politics" that raised "the question of whether politics in the traditional senses remain a viable human activity in the Western world"?[78]

As Todd Gitlin recalls, he and the leaders of Students for a Democratic Society (SDS) rejected Howe and the editors of the socialist journal *Dissent* because they studied what they should have expressed in their very persons: "They *had* politics; we *were* politics." To SDS, politics was something you embodied, not something you wrote about. Versions of this claim appear throughout postwar literature, and emerge most cogently within second-wave feminism, not just to assert the importance of putting one's body on the line in the service of one cause or another, but to insist that one's body was, finally, the ultimate site of contest. Tony Kushner's *Angels in America* (1991) glosses this history when Roy Cohn exclaims: "This is gastric juices churning, this is enzymes and acids, this is intestinal is what this is, bowel movement and blood-red meat—this stinks, *this is politics*, Joe, the game of being alive."[79] But in truth, this kind of game was never foreign to Howe; he never "had" politics in any simple way. Having founded *Dissent*, he remained unsure of its ideology: as he recalls, "What *Dissent* should be we were not quite sure." According to its editors, the journal understood socialism as an "ethos," and later as an "act of pain"; according to C. Wright Mills, the journal understood it as a "mood."[80]

Howe's literary criticism is thus important not because it reflects his contempt for those who fail to understand political autonomy, but because it anticipated a question that still haunts the assimilation of New Left thinking within literature departments: how to understand embodied experience in the novel as constituting and describing a "politics" that is linked to—even in its indifference toward or disavowal of—more traditional understandings of that word. *Politics and the Novel* extensively explores this question, especially when it negotiates the "inescapable" conflict between "experience in its immediacy" (20) and unmediated ideology, which "reflects a hardening of commitment, the freezing of opinion into system," and "represents an effort to employ abstract ideas as a means of overcoming the abstractness of social life" (160).[81] Howe thinks the political novel can counteract such ideology, especially when it "transforms . . . ideas astonishingly" (22), into a different order of knowledge. Forced into commerce with embodied experience, "ideas *in the novel* are transformed into something other than the ideas of a political program" (21). Thus Howe praises Malraux for being "concerned with revolution not as an algebra of ideology but as an arithmetic of emotion, not primarily as a political act but as the incarnation of human desire" (211).

For all their differences, Howe's "arithmetic of emotion" echoes Mailer's "neo-Marxian calculus." Like Mailer, he assumes that, in the novel, "telling relationships can be discovered between a style of social behavior and a code of moral judgment"—no less than between physical experience and what Lukács called "the vital, but not immediately obvious forces at work in objective reality."[82] Indeed, Howe attributes to good political novels a quality that Mailer attributes to hipsters: "*felt thought*" (254). These novels treat physical experience as both an instance of ideology and a means of transcending it. "This seems to me," Howe therefore writes, "as good a prescription for the political novel, if there must be a prescription, as we are likely to get: amidst the clamor of ideology—the indispensable, inescapable clamor—listen to your nerves" (234).

Versions of this inward-looking imperative to become audience to the performance of one's own body appear throughout postwar literature. Émile Zola described his naturalistic characters in *Thérèse Raquin* (1867) as "completely dominated by their nerves and blood, without free will." Subsequent literary movements turned Zola's social realist critique into a prized tenet: what was once an expression of determinism would become, instead, a fantasy of how art might transform bodily experience into new forms of cognition. Thus Arthur Symons described symbolism as "an art of the nerves," and T. S. Eliot, preoccupied with a "dissociation of sensibility," complained that Philip Massinger "dealt not with emotions so much as with the social abstractions of emotions. . . . He was not guided by direct communications through the nerves." Even as the novelists in this study shared Zola's desire "to discover and follow the thread of connection which leads mathematically from one man to another," they were each in their way guided by Eliot's imperative to communicate with the nerves and produce "a direct sensuous apprehension of thought, or a recreation of thought into feeling." "I try to immerse myself in the motive and *feel* toward meanings rather than plan a structure," Robert Penn Warren declared. You must trust, he explained, "in your viscera and nervous system."[83]

Novelists followed versions of that advice even when dissatisfied with their own nervous systems. Tellingly, Howe's imperative, "listen to your nerves," echoes Mailer's claim, in "The White Negro," that hipsters, and by implication hip novelists, wanted to construct for themselves a "new nervous system" (*A* 345), to which they would remain loyal, henceforth, above all else. The echo was not coincidental: Mailer published "The White Negro" in *Dissent*, edited by Howe, who would that same year publish *Politics and the Novel*. In significant ways, their visions were compatible—as were, in a very basic way, those of all the novelists examined in the chapters that follow. At once nervous and nervy, anxious and assertive, these writers fulfill the spirit of Howe's imperative even at those moments when their interest in hip takes them far from any recognizable "political milieu," and even when their versions of "*felt thought*" seem to embrace feeling at the expense of thought. Mailer rejected the notion that "hip shouldn't belong to writers" because it was a kind of "anti-expressionism." Hip was "involved with more expression, with getting into the nuances of things" (*A* 379). And so Mailer would demonstrate, with all of those who follow, that in the game of hip, even "small actions," like the construction of a metaphor, become "not necessarily more large, but more meaningful" (*A* 349).

Burden in Blackface

A political party is a very complicated menagerie.

Robert Penn Warren, *The Legacy of the Civil War*

"Reconstructed but Unregenerate," John Crowe Ransom's introduction to the Southern Agrarian manifesto *I'll Take My Stand* (1930), wonders whether it any longer makes sense for southerners to remain Democrats. "No Southerner ever dreams of heaven, or pictures his Utopia on earth, without providing room for the Democratic Party," he writes. But in the face of "many betrayals," he doubts whether it is possible for the party to be "held to a principle that . . . can now be defined as agrarian, conservative, anti-industrial."[1] He calls upon the South "to reenter the American political field with a determination and an address quite beyond anything it has exhibited during her half-hearted life of the last half a century." The South, he thinks, should unite communities across the nation opposed to "the insidious industrial system" and "thoroughly tired of progressivism and its spurious benefits." It should in particular rally to its cause "those who have recently acquired, or through the generations miraculously preserved, a European point of view—sociologists, educators, artists, religionists, and ancient New England townships. The combination of these elements with the Western farmers and the old-fashioned South would make a formidable bloc" (25).

In the years to come, the professional classes to which Ransom wished to appeal did not in fact align themselves with southern interests. Considered as a whole, "sociologists, educators, [and] artists" would commit to liberal causes and affiliate with the Democratic Party. Likewise, "the European point of view" so prized by Ransom would after the Second World War tend to encompass forms of state socialism that were anathema to the Agrarians. But increasingly, southerners would abandon their long-standing loyalty to the Democrats. Ransom anticipated an epochal change in party alignment, in which southerners sympathetic to corporate interests as well as newly reactionary forms of western populism began to vote Republican. Racism figured crucially in the shift; in 1968, for example, Richard Nixon embraced a "Southern Strategy" that courted southern whites who were hostile to integration and the Civil Rights Movement. The makings of this strategy were already under way when Ransom wrote. In 1928, Henry J. Allen, the publicity chief for Herbert Hoover's presidential campaign, signed on to "a new Republican line in the South." As Allen saw it, "the better class of white people vote for the Democratic ticket" in the South because "big *black* Republicans control the offices" and dictate "who shall go to the National Convention as Delegates." Allen advised Hoover and his party to "give the white folks down there a chance." As part of this effort, Republican leadership stymied efforts to incorporate into the platform of that year any advocacy of the Fourteenth, Fifteenth, and Eighteenth Amendments. They also eviscerated the ranks of black officials in the South under the guise of a crusade against corruption. The strategy worked: Hoover won Tennessee, North Carolina, Florida, Virginia, and Texas in the national elections, more than any Republican presidential candidate since the Civil War.[2]

The New Deal placed the Democratic Party on still more tenuous footing in the South. While landowners benefited from the farm policies of the Agricultural Adjustment Administration (AAA), Roosevelt's social welfare programs and gestures on behalf of civil rights alienated regional elites. In 1948, the New Deal and its legacy drove away significant numbers of southern Democrats. Already inflamed at the formation of Harry Truman's President's Committee on Civil Rights, thirty-five southern delegates walked out of the Democratic National Convention when Hubert Humphrey succeeded in getting the party to adopt a civil rights plank. They formed the States' Rights Democratic Party and were commonly referred to as "Dixiecrats." Faced with a threat from his party's left, in the form of Henry Wallace's Progressive Party, Truman now faced a threat from his party's right. The Dixiecrats nominated the openly racist Strom Thurmond as their presidential candidate. Truman won the election with a narrow margin, but Thurmond carried South Carolina, Alabama, Mississippi, and Louisiana.[3] It would take some twenty years for the Republican Party to consolidate these gains and transform the South into its most reliable constituency, but in 1948 the future course of national party politics was already visible.

Published one year after the so-called "Dixiecrat Revolt," V. O. Key's *Southern Politics in State and Nation* anatomized interest-group behavior and voting patterns throughout the ostensibly "Solid South." The Dixiecrats, he argued, were not able to speak for all the Democrats in their region; support for economic and social conservatism was not uniform. Because the Democratic Party enjoyed a monopoly in the South, substantive issues were absent from most campaigns, which tended to turn on personal loyalties, cliques, and demagoguery. This lent the party a surprisingly varied nature—local machines were often strikingly different state by state. Nevertheless, these machines were united in their antipathy to one symbolic figure: "Whatever phase of the southern political process one seeks to understand, sooner or later the trail of inquiry leads to the Negro." The South was solid for the simple reason that the prospect of African American independence united otherwise diverse interests and constituencies. The agricultural policies of the New Deal and the rapid emergence of a war economy had unsettled long-established social relations. To be sure, working-class whites and blacks, increasingly freed from the debt peonage structures of tenant farming, possessed new affinities. And Key believed that "the South ought, by all the rules of political behavior, to be radical." Poor and agrarian, "pressed down" by local oligarchs and "the colonial policies of the financial and industrial North and Northeast," the region offered "fertile ground for political agitation," in large part because working-class blacks and whites shared economic interests in ways they hadn't before.[4] Key thought that, ultimately, the Democratic Party would profit from this fact. Sooner or later, liberal whites would join with working-class whites and blacks and capture the party from the forces of reaction. But this never happened in a systematic manner, and Key anticipates why: local machines and landowners generated and sustained virulent racism in working-class whites, especially those living in the black belts once central to the region's plantation economy.

Huey Long was a striking exception. Championing a host of welfare services as governor of Louisiana, he declared "Every Man a King." Targeting "thieving" oil companies, "lying" newspapers, and "crooked" politicians, he garnered massive support from his state's working-class whites. More audaciously, he courted African Americans. Some argue he did so only when convenient, and ended up offering little to this constituency once he was elected. But one historian makes room for Long by making a "distinction . . . between the [typical southern] politician who framed his public appeal around racism, who deliberately stirred up white racial hatred in a vicious and calculating manner, and the one who merely resorted to 'nigger-baiting' as an occasional political device"; Long, he grants, was unusual for being "a politician of the second type." Another praises Long for being willing "largely to leave aside" racial prejudice; still another describes his outreach to African Americans as "large, almost revolutionary, far more than any other southern politician was willing to give."[5]

To students of American literature, Long is most famous as the model for Willie Stark in Robert Penn Warren's *All the King's Men*, published eleven years after the governor's assassination and two years before the Dixiecrat revolt. Like Long, Stark is assassinated before he is able to realize his political vision. Warren's novel attributes responsibility for this assassination and analyzes its larger significance, especially in light of Long's interracial coalition; seen in this light, the novel is an account of why the as-yet-unnamed Southern Strategy was destined for success. As Warren has it, Stark's program falls victim not only to the moneyed interests that it would reform but also to the state's liberals, who prove unable to grasp their imbrication in the South's racially exploitative system of wealth production. Liberals would never be a political force in the South, Warren suggests, because they refused to confront the more uncomfortable ramifications of their own economic interests.

Warren's novel became one of the twentieth century's most adopted and adapted templates for fictionalizing the relation of African Americans to white liberals in the Democratic Party. Billy Lee Brammer worked as a staffer for Lyndon Johnson during the late fifties; in 1961, he published *The Gay Place*, three novellas organized around a liberal southern governor named Arthur Fenstemaker whose character and fate echo Willie Stark's as much as if not more than Johnson's. This confusion of roles makes sense, insofar as Huey Long was something of a model for southern liberals, like Johnson, who risked alienating white voters by appealing to and in some instances militating on behalf of African Americans. Johnson reportedly identified with Long as much as he did with Franklin Roosevelt.[6] Norman Mailer connected Johnson to Long through Willie Stark. In *Armies of the Night* (1967), he pretends to be Johnson's "dwarf alter ego." Warren provided the impetus for this impersonation: "Ever since seeing *All the King's Men* years ago he had wanted to come on in public as a Southern demagogue." Shadowing the president provides Mailer with a way to reconcile public and personal experience: inhabiting the president's body by way of Warren, Mailer feels "two very different rivers, one external, one subjective . . . come together."[7] But this confluence is also racial in nature. Mailer's language is a direct reference to remarks Johnson had made two years previously when signing the Voting Rights Act. "Today the Negro story and the American story fuse and blend," he declared.

"The stories of our Nation and of the American Negro are like two great rivers." Long kept separate, the rivers were at last merging: "In our time, the two currents will finally mingle and rush as one great stream across the uncertain and the marvelous years of the America that is yet to come." Thus the "American Negro [claims] his freedom to enter the mainstream of American life."[8]

Twenty-five years later, these figurative rivers mingled in the person of Bill Clinton, whose body explained to Ishmael Reed and Toni Morrison how topes of blackness mattered to liberalism and the Democratic Party. The most notorious fictionalization of that body, Joe Klein's *Primary Colors* (1996), was also a point-by-point retelling of *King's Men*. That Klein's novel so faithfully retells Warren's even as it sticks closely to the actual events and personages of the 1992 primaries is surely testimony not simply to the abiding relevance of Huey Long, but to how cannily Warren's novel anticipates in coded form problems that would prove increasingly central to the Democratic Party. Crucial in this regard is Jack Burden, Warren's narrator; a southern liberal born to a wealthy and privileged community, he nevertheless supports Long's reforms. Burden's attraction to Stark has much to do with racial guilt, but Warren never links the two explicitly. Klein does. He merges Burden and George Stephanopoulos into a black narrator, Henry Burton, who agonizes over the nature of his homoerotic attachment to Jack Stanton, a philandering southern governor running for president who surrounds himself with African Americans and who may or may not have fathered a child by an underage black teen. Burton frets over his attraction to and need for Stanton, just as Burden does with Stark. Burton tells us that his father was black and his mother white. This leads him to believe that his propensity toward "servility" was "a slavery atavism." But upon further reflection, he realizes that his father was in fact "proud and angry," while his mother was patient and accepting. He laughs: "I was a genius at servitude because I was half white."[9] This makes sense as a reading of *King's Men*: Burden serves Stark, we're led to believe, because he wishes to atone for the racial crimes of his class—because he is white and because Stark, "proud and angry" as he is, is symbolically black.

Huey Long's readiness to transgress racial boundaries impressed the father of future Black Panther activist Huey Newton; raised in Louisiana during Long's reign, Walter Newton named his son Huey because he wanted his son to follow in the governor's footsteps.[10] The black power that Newton would later channel roils beneath the surface of Warren's novel. Stark is accompanied everywhere he goes, for example, by one "Sugar-Boy," who "couldn't talk"; "he wouldn't win any debating contests in high school," Burden reports, "but then nobody would ever want to debate with Sugar-Boy. Not anybody who knew him and had seen him do tricks with the .38 Special which rode under his left armpit like a tumor." The next two sentences give away the novel's game: "No doubt you thought Sugar-Boy was a Negro, from his name. But he wasn't." Burden's narration intimates the threat of black violence throughout, never so suggestively as when Stark is on the scene; the joke here is that in some basic sense Sugar-Boy is black, insofar as he is Stark's muscle and insofar as Stark's political might derives in large part from the specter of an interracial folk composed of whites and blacks who are, as Sugar-Boy is, "from the wrong side of the tracks."

The notion that black muscle backed up the machinations of white liberals became a cliché in the years that followed; Mailer returned to this idea consistently, as we will see. The cliché thrived during Clinton's presidency. Having distanced himself from the disquieting anger of rap during his 1992 campaign, Bill Clinton invoked the specter of black violence during his impeachment, at least according to Joe Eszterhas, who felt that the beleaguered president consciously surrounded himself with impassioned crowds of African Americans. This constituted to Eszterhas a "subliminal White House message that no one would ever articulate": "These are my beloved and loving constituents, Bill Clinton was telling America. They will go to the wall for me. They will be extremely unhappy if I am removed from office. Do you *really* want them to be extremely unhappy? Do you want that to happen *now*, when the economy is booming and you don't have a whole lot of worries in your life?"[11] Whether or not Clinton sent this message, Warren's Stark does, though he does so to ambiguous effect: ultimately, he reminds the gentry of his state that they depend on black bodies not as a coercive cudgel but as a form of wealth production. Warren lays Stark's downfall at the feet of liberals like Burden because, he thinks, they refuse to reconcile their reliance on black political muscle with their reliance on black labor power: they would wield the former without recognizing their dependence on the latter.

"The effluvium of brotherly bodies"

In an assessment of Warren's *Brother to Dragons* (1953), Cleanth Brooks offers by-now-familiar New Critical bromides about the relation between literature and politics: the poet is not "telling us *about* the experience; he is *giving* us the experience." The poem's truth "does not reside in a formula. It cannot be got at by mere logic." The antipathy between poetry and logic corresponds to one between literature and politics. Dismissing the notion that literature should "argue[ ] for the passage of a particular bill or for the election of a specific political party," Brooks insists that it should instead pursue "something deeper and more resonant."[12] Along these lines, Warren maintained that the subject of *King's Men* was not politics per se; the novel, he reasoned, "was never intended to be a book about politics. Politics merely provided the framework story in which the deeper concerns . . . might work themselves out."[13] Critics have tended to agree. An early review declares, "Warren is no more discussing American politics than *Hamlet* is discussing Danish politics."[14]

If disavowals like these seem implausible when made on behalf of poetry generally, they seem wildly so when made of a novel as wholly absorbed with political life as *King's Men*. Stark's reforms occupy a central place in the novel, and turn coherently on a conflict between legal and social rights. Stark mobilizes the down-and-out masses of his state in the name of a new vision of social democratic citizenship and, ultimately, to contest the idea that the judiciary is the best guardian of a citizen's rights. He battles a conservative judiciary, protective of constitutional rights, and strong-arms his legislature, in order to expand the rights of citizenship. Warren was preoccupied throughout his career with this struggle, with what he called the "opposing absolutes" of "'higher law' and 'legalism,'" "government by law" on the one hand and "government by sociology" on the other.[15]

Before Stark, power was in the hands of a "plug-hatted, church-going, Horace-quoting" (202) aristocracy that governed during its "little time off from duck hunting and corporation law" (46). Flouting such genteel paternalism—which serves to disguise the actions of an elite lining its pockets with graft from special interests—Stark builds roads, schools, and a large free hospital. These initiatives lead one judge to complain that Stark "is giving this state away. Free this and free that and free other. Every wool-hat jackass thinking the world is free. Who's going to pay?" "Government," a second judge reluctantly concedes. It "is committed these days to give services we never heard of when we were growing up" (124). Stark urges his constituency to understand these services not as charity but as a condition of their participation in a political democracy: "as a right" (261). He bellows to a cheering crowd, "It is your right that every child shall have a complete education. That no person aged or infirm shall want or beg for bread. That the man who produces something shall be able to carry it to market without miring to the hub, without toll. That no poor man's house or land shall be taxed. That the rich man and the great companies that draw wealth from this state shall pay this state a fair share" (261). Rejecting the hidebound institutional authority of the state judiciary as well as the primacy of natural rights, Stark constructs a populist, majoritarian, executive authority.

From this vantage, Jack Burden's equivocation over Stark's power grab looks like a New Deal liberalism taking a second look at the statism unleashed during the Second World War. Martin Horwitz explains how, paralyzed by a "lingering doubt . . . about whether they had won an illegitimate constitutional victory during the New Deal," reform-minded progressives turned after the war toward "consistency, uniformity, and neutral principles," embracing along the way the importance of the "institutional competence" and "procedures" championed, for example, by Henry Hart and Albert M. Sacks in *The Legal Process* (1958).[16] We might say, in this vein, that Warren's novel represents the turning back from the New Deal by a conflicted postwar liberal orthodoxy, weary of reform and eager to reassert the institutional competence and significance of the judiciary over and against an absolutist legislature and executive. Judge Montague Irwin captures this retrenchment when he says of Stark, "I was . . . for him at one time. He was breaking the window panes out and letting in a little fresh air. But . . . I began to worry about him knocking down the house too" (343). Irwin grants the justice behind Stark's reforms, but questions the extremes to which they are put. When Burden moves into the dead Irwin's house at the novel's close, he embraces just this ostensibly moderate vision; he retreats, like the political order generally, from state-orchestrated action to the rhetoric of individual responsibility.

These broad parameters constitute the explicitly political frame of Warren's novel. But *King's Men* would remain influential for decades to come because it casts Stark's political project in sexual and ultimately racial terms. "Kingship is fornication," Norman O. Brown learned from Sigmund Freud; it is "the identity of politics and sex."[17] Warren seemed to agree. One of the most rewritten political novels in American history, *King's Men* would offer countless writers a guide for representing what Irving Howe's *Politics and the Novel* (1957) calls "the problem that would dominate the 20th century novel . . . the meeting between politics and sex" (*PN* 166). Parties and platforms; campaigns and elections; policy debates and the tug-of-war between the judiciary, the legislature, and the statehouse: all of these preoccupy *All the King's Men*. But so do a raft of sexual concerns that the novel ties to its political milieu. Stark's wife, Lucy, fears that her husband's job impacts even her son's sexual indiscretions:

> "Oh, God," she breathed again, and rose abruptly from the chair, and pressed her clenched hands together in front of her bosom. "Oh, God, politics," she whispered, and took a distracted step or two away from me, and said again, "Politics." Then she swung toward me, and said, out loud now, "Oh, God, in this too."
>
> "Yes," I nodded, "like most things." (335)

The breathless melodrama suggests the calamitous conjunction of politics and sex. But more typically, Warren's characters simply assume that sex is political and that politics is sexual, in strikingly homosocial fashion. Burden tells us, "The story of Willie Stark and the story of Jack Burden are, in one sense, one story" (157); "many's the time," he reports, "we've settled affairs of state through a bathroom door, the boss on the inside and me on the outside" (28). Likewise, Burden acts as "Secretary of the Bedchamber" (39), managing Stark's sexual secrets and exposing those of his competition. In *King's Men*, political life is an erotic contest between men. "The struggle for power," Warren writes, is as "likely to occur in smoke filled rooms than at the polls" (*LCW* 45). These are the rooms in which the king's men—Burden calls them "behind guys" (137)— exchange favors while basking in "the effluvium of brotherly bodies" (13). An homage to Warren's novel like *All the President's Men* (1973) is awash in this effluvium: wracked with guilt over their rebellious presumption even as they know Richard Nixon to be corrupt, Carl Bernstein and Bob Woodward bring down the president by exchanging informational intimacies in a parking garage with a man named "Deep Throat."

But *King's Men* does more than cast traditionally political problems in sexual terms. Its sexual politics codes a racial politics. As Warren sees it, Stark weds "government by sociology" to an indulgent vision of natural rights, in a way that recalls the Bible-toting abolitionists. "With every man his own majority as well as his own law," he wrote in *The Legacy of the Civil War* (1961), "there is, in the logical end, only anarchy, and anarchy of a peculiarly tedious and bloodthirsty sort" (*LCW* 33). For Warren, a commitment to natural rights elevated contingent feelings over established precedents. He gives voice to this view in *King's Men* when a character muses, "The strength of the desire seems to give the sanction of justice and righteousness" (170). But the problem is not simply that Stark's reformism describes the indulgence of need and desire. The problem is that Stark's desire to help the poor codes the dangerous desire that Warren thought abolitionists had for African Americans.

In 1957, the year that Mailer published "The White Negro," Warren confessed to Ralph Ellison that segueing back and forth between what he called "the race problem" and "the sex problem" might in fact suggest "a poor parallel." Nonetheless, contemporary crusaders in both arenas, he argued, did just this: "You know the kind of person who puts on a certain expression and then talks about 'solving' the race problem. Well it's the same kind of person and the same kind of expression you meet when you hear the phrase 'solve the sex problem.'"[18] Warren traced this confusion to the abolitionists, whom he described with scorn as early as *John Brown: The Making of a Martyr* (1929). In *Legacy*, he describes these figures as Nazis *avant la lettre*: gripped by bloodlust, they were bent on what he calls a "total solution" (*LCW* 22) to the race problem. They were also, strikingly, proto-hipsters. Mailer's hipster searches not just for an "ineffable frisson" but for "an orgasm more apocalyptic than the one which preceded it" (*A* 342, 347). Though gripped by different motivations, Warren's abolitionists put their antisocial absolutism to similar use. He sees them acting in the name of black America not primarily from moral conviction, but in order "to achieve [what he calls] the apocalyptic *frisson*" (*LCW* 29).[19] Warren worries that interracial identifications made in the name of the "Negro Cause" produce precisely the sexually anarchic, antisocial passion that Mailer celebrates and locates within black sexuality.

In *Band of Angels* (1955), Warren's abolitionists confuse race and sex in an incipiently hip fashion. The novel tells the story of Amantha Starr, the daughter of a plantation owner who, just after her father dies in bed with a married woman, discovers that her mother was a slave. Starr later takes an Emersonian abolitionist for a husband. But before she marries him, she commissions a mutual friend to tell the groom what she calls "her secret." Years later, she discovers that the friend did not communicate to her now husband that her mother was a slave. "Then what in God's name was there to tell him—what?" she asks of the mutual friend. "I told him about your father," he replies, "that he was of libidinous nature, that there was a taint of immoral blood."[20] Presumably, only an abolitionist like her husband would believe that an adulterous father tainted the blood more than a black mother. But then *Band of Angels* is as much about the 1950s as the 1860s; it figures abolitionists as proto-hipsters, gripped by overzealous identifications with blacks and their culture. *Band of Angels* ends with northern liberals talking about a new product, a "curler that puts kinks in white folks' hair" (374). The curler, we must imagine, commodifies the abolitionist's sympathetic identification with blacks; it is Warren's wink to the reader, his suggestion that such identifications were finding a marketable form in the hip subcultures of the 1950s.

"You can't be a Southerner and not have the whole race question on your mind in one way or another," Warren said in 1967.[21] But some ways were better than others, and the protocols of hip seemed to him a step in the wrong direction. In *Who Speaks for the Negro?* (1965), Warren asks Robert Moses about "young white persons" who "try to enter romantically into Negro taste in music, Negro taste in this, that and the other—who want to enter, to join, to become more Negro than Negroes." Surely African Americans have no patience for the "the white man who tries to go Negro."[22] Warren has none. "Some young white people," he complains to Ellison, try to get "outside the flatness of their middle-class American spiritual ghetto" by trying "to absorb arbitrarily the Negro culture, Negro speech, Negro musical terms, Negro musical tastes—move in and grab, as it were, the other man's soul" (*WS* 338). As he puts it, "the Negro" is often conceived of as "the secret sharer in [our] darkness" (*WS* 438). He does not approve. Warren is especially concerned to debunk the notion, advanced by Mailer, that hipsters constituted a new kind of political vanguard. Warren writes, "We should forget that whole business [of the hipster] and accept the straight political view which holds that a vote is a vote no matter what motive prompts the casting" (*WS* 443). Refusing to vote was nothing more or less than refusing to engage in politics: he cites David Riesman, who claims that the "apathy" of the young "has its positive side as a safeguard against the over-politicalization of the country: the apathetic ones, often not so much fearful or faithless as bored, may be as immunized against political appeals, good or bad, as against commercial advertising" (50).

But, ultimately, Warren's engagements with the politics of hip could only be equivocal, and Mailer explained why. Mailer thought hip drew energy from and increased in importance in light of racial integration in the South. "The White Negro," he tells us, emerged from a letter he wrote to William Faulkner concerning the sexual panic that integration caused southern white men. "Can't we have some honesty about what's going on now in the South?" he asked. As Mailer saw it, "the white unconsciously feels that the balance has been kept, that the old arrangement was fair. The Negro had his sexual supremacy and the white had his white supremacy" (*A* 332). To Mailer, the South's racial problems were inextricable from its sexual problems; committed to pushing boundaries that found their most rigid expression in the South, hipsters made the inter-relation of these problems unavoidable to any subsequent political calculus. An argument like this was bound to elicit mixed feelings from Warren, whose concerns often mirror Mailer's, albeit without the trappings of hip. Indeed we might say that Warren's novel is a negative image of the fantasy of influence lodged at the heart of Mailer's essay. Despite Warren's protestations to the contrary, in *King's Men*, Jack Burden's sex problems are inextricable from his race problems and, despite Warren's commitment to "the straight political view," this confusion appears to precipitate significant political outcomes.

King's Men turns on Burden's abiding desire for childhood sweetheart Ann Stanton. That desire conforms to the dictates of his class. Ann is from old money, and Burden, born to the gentry as he is, disavows desire for any but the right kind of women. Accused of being a "nigger-lover" like Stark, Burden replies, "No sale . . . I like mine vanilla" (69). But Burden persistently casts Ann as a racial other. He claims that her charms have on him the same hold that Queequeg's harpoon has after it sinks "through four feet of blubber to the very quick" (278). A pierced whale, Burden struggles to penetrate Ann in turn, but comes closest to doing so when thinking of her as a black child. Alone with her in his mother's house, he arranges her hair so she will "look just like a picka-ninny" (292). Moments later: "I felt the new blood coursing through me as though somebody had opened a sluice gate" (293). Yet Burden cannot complete this fantasy, in which he takes possession of his younger and blackened part-ner. He hesitates and thinks, "I couldn't any more have touched her then than if she had been my little sister" (296). He's crippled by this sudden incapacity, born from a confusion of incest and miscegenation, and loses both Ann and his self-confidence as a result. Ultimately, he will need Stark to break through the incest prohibition that keeps Ann from him: Burden reunites with her only after he has been vitalized by the governor's incipient blackness and after she in turn has slept with Stark.

Having triangulated their desires through Stark, Jack and Ann need him removed: Burden's reunion with Ann requires Stark's death. In fact, as Burden sees it, his failure to consummate his relations with Ann as a teen leads directly to that death. Enraged with jealousy that his sister has been sleeping with Stark,

Ann's brother, Adam, assassinates the governor. Warren's novel works relent-
lessly toward the unstated conclusion that this is a racial crime, that killing
Stark amounts to killing (and at the same time appropriating) the black sexuality that Burden needs in order to consummate his relations with Ann, but that
cannot be openly acknowledged or allowed. Consequently, when Adam discovers that his sister has been with Stark, and then shoots him dead on the steps
of the state capitol, we see the ghost of Henry Sutpen from *Absalom, Absalom!*
(1936) shooting down Charles Bon at the gates of Sutpen's Hundred. Warren
bifurcates Sutpen into two characters, Adam and Jack. Stark is an appalling
figure to Adam because he presents a racial threat to his incestuously endogamous kinship group; at the same time, Stark is an attractive figure to Burden
because he represents the sexual potency that will allow Burden to break the
incest prohibition that keeps him from Ann: even as Henry Sutpen symbolically penetrates his sister, Judith, through Charles Bon, so Jack symbolically
penetrates Ann through Stark.

From this vantage, Stark's hostility to the state's moneyed interests, as
well as his emphasis on an unchecked and heedless state authority over and
against the judiciary's moderate, cautious resistance to change, codes the sexually charged threat of integration, which the South knew was coming but was
not, in either the 1930s or the 1940s, willing to accept. But it's not initially clear
how to read this code. Is the problem that Stark threatens to transgress tribal
taboos? That he threatens the financial interests of Adam's class? That he and
his henchmen threaten that class physically? What this novel calls "the curse of
Jack Burden" (159) derives in part from its narrator's inability to answer these
questions. Burden doesn't understand why he's drawn to Stark, and so cannot understand his relation to Stark's crusade. As a consequence, he doesn't
understand his role in Stark's downfall. But he suspects. Over and beyond his
sense that his sexual prudery contributed to Stark's eventual assassination, he
thinks he has participated in "a more monstrous conspiracy whose meaning I
could not fathom. It was as though the scene through which I had just lived had
been a monstrous and comic miming for ends I could not conceive and for an
audience I could not see but which I knew was leering from the shadow" (417).
The larger contours of this guilt emerge in two ultimately related trips into
the past, each of which centers on how Burden's supposed forbears made their
money: one at Stark's behest to unearth incriminating evidence about Judge
Irwin (Burden eventually discovers that Irwin is his biological father) and the

other to somehow lay to rest the story of Cass Mastern, a nineteenth-century plantation owner who comes of age in the years leading to the Civil War and to whom Burden initially thinks himself related.

"A diamond ain't a thing"

Working on Cass Mastern's journal for his PhD in American history, Burden finds the following: "I understand that Mrs. Turner flogged her Negroes for the same reason that the wife of my friend sold Phebe down the river: she could not bear their eyes upon her. I understand, as I can no longer bear their eyes upon me" (184). Eventually, Burden lays the journal aside "because he was afraid to understand for what might be understood there was a reproach to him" (189). The reproach seems clear enough: Burden remains willfully blind, unlike the eyes upon him, to the coercive and exploitative relation between his class and the African Americans upon whose labor that class depends. Later, when confronting the "black faces" of his mother's maid and cook, he slams a door on "those all-seeing, all-knowing eyes" (349). But here, too, sexual melodrama clouds the picture. Mastern's journal describes the consequences of an affair with his friend's wife, Annabelle Trice. The friend discovers the affair and kills himself. The guilt-stricken Annabelle then discovers that one of her slaves, Phebe, has learnt of the affair, and thus of her culpability for her husband's death. Annabelle sells Phebe into sure prostitution, and Mastern, now doubly stricken, sets out to find her. He fails, but channels his guilt over his dead friend into a fervent concern for the well-being of his slaves, whom he frees; his subsequent abolitionism, Warren suggests, expresses guilt displaced from his adulterous liaison.

That interests Burden. Having refused sex with Ann when she was a teen, he imagines himself responsible for Stark's death, because he believes that his prudery drove Ann from him and into Stark's bed, thus precipitating Adam's murderous jealousy. He concludes from this that his sexual repression, born of a misguided sense of "nobility," had had "in my world almost as dire a consequence as Cass Mastern's sin had had in his. Which may tell something about the two worlds" (297). If in the 1850s a licentious sexual indulgence eventuates in white southern guilt, then in the 1930s the failure to indulge sexually points to a similar guilt. Burden's world requires sexual enlightenment, and from this vantage, Mastern's story allows Burden to confess, on behalf of his class, to an overly strict and repressive fear of sexuality. What business did he have, he wonders, thinking back on his fateful failure with Ann, to refuse her in the name of lofty sentiment? Wasn't this sentiment, this desire to act "rightly and wisely" (297) in matters of sex, the real problem? These questions point, unavoidably, to the accusation with which Mailer prefaces "The White Negro": black men threatened southern white men because those whites believed themselves unequal by comparison to female desire.

But Burden's desire to atone for a repressive morality tells us relatively little about the relation between his sex and race problems. Mastern's story offers more than melodrama. He initially describes the slave who becomes the object of his guilt as "a comely yellow wench" (174). Presumably, Phebe is yellow because she is the product of sexual coercion between white male masters and black female slaves. But the moment that Annabelle Trice discovers that Phebe is aware of her (Annabelle's) infidelity, she realizes that Phebe's color is richer than yellow. Presumably in despair over Annabelle's infidelity, her husband removes his wedding ring just before taking his life. When Annabelle first discovers the ring it is in Phebe's hand. She thinks to herself, "It is gold, and it is lying in a gold hand. For Phebe's hand was gold—I had never noticed how her hand is the color of pure gold. Then I looked up and she was still staring at me, and her eyes were gold, too, and bright and hard like gold. And I knew that she knew" (175). The change in Phebe's color registers the broken trust figured in the gold wedding ring: she is more autonomous and consequently less trustworthy now that she knows that Annabelle has been untrustworthy.

At the same time, Phebe's newfound color highlights the extent to which Annabelle and Cass's infidelity threatens a larger compact, in which gold and human bodies are indistinguishable. Phebe is worth a particular amount of gold because she provides productive labor. But she threatens a loss greater than her own value; her dangerous knowledge destabilizes the hierarchy necessary to a southern system of wealth production dependent on human capital. Phebe isn't simply worth a particular amount of gold: less abstractly, her laboring body is itself the standard of value upon which labor lords like Mastern depend. Indeed, she is herself a kind of gold ring: slave women were ritually raped by their masters, for pleasure, but also as a means of producing more human capital, in the form of offspring, that the master could then use or sell. Consequently, Phebe's acquisition of threatening information (in the form of the broken promise of a wedding between a white master and his wife) destabilizes an entire production regime. It's appropriate, then, that Mastern, wracked with remorse, frees his slaves and attempts to run his plantation "on a wage basis" (182), and that having thus undermined the economy of his community, he fears "ostracism, or worse" (183).

Burden spends some time dwelling on Mastern's subsequent descent into poverty and unhappiness. Burden already thinks himself the son of an ineffectual and delusional man committed to Christian principle. He identifies Mastern as a forbear because he sees in this figure a similarly enfeebling commitment to moral rectitude. At the same time, Warren suggests that Burden learns the wrong lessons from the past—that, in fact, his particular way of thinking about fathers prevents him from thinking clearly about the relationship between sexuality and subjectivity on the one hand and between sexuality and wealth production on the other. The novel's first paragraph enacts the limits of his interpretive paradigm, and describes it as the product of misdirected attention. Speeding down a highway in Stark's car, Burden records the following:

> To get there you follow Highway 58, going northeast out of the city, and it is a good highway and new. You look up the highway and it is straight for miles, coming at you, with the black line down the center coming at you and at you, and the heat dazzles up from the white slab so that only the black line is clear, coming at you with the whine of the tires, and if you don't quit staring at that line and take a few deep breaths and slap yourself hard on the back of the neck you'll hypnotize yourself and you'll come to at just the moment when the right front wheel hooks over into the black dirt shoulder of the slab and you'll try to jerk her back on but you can't because the slab is high like a curb. And maybe you'll try to reach to turn off the ignition just as she starts the dive. But you won't make it, of course.

Just before the inevitable crash, "a nigger chopping cotton a mile away" registers the scene with his black workmates. "Lawd God," he cries out. "And [then] the hoe will lift," Warren writes, "and the blade will flash in the sun like a heliograph" (1). For Forrest G. Robinson, the worker's hoe communicates "a message in code, sent clearly enough, but not received"; this passage summarizes what Burden "knows and refuses to know about 'the race problem.'" Robinson sees Warren in similar terms, "divided between largely concealed feelings of guilt about Southern racism and slavery and the proud refusal to acknowledge those feelings—especially in the face of what he took to be Yankee Phariseeism." Warren is "pulled both ways in matters of race," and *King's Men* "reflects his competing impulse to address and to submerge painful questions on this topic."[23]

This may well be an accurate account of Warren's psychology. But Robinson misses the strategic manner with which Burden invokes self-consciously Freudian paradigms to effect his evasions. Burden trumpets clichés like "the truth always kills the father" (354). "Men have laid low their fathers," he muses, "only because they were fathers" (458). Preoccupied with paternity, Burden holds that "each of us is the son of a million fathers" (436). Hard not to commit an Oedipal crime in this crowded room, and indeed, Burden describes his narrative as "a visceral, Freudian nightmare" (271) because he thinks he kills at least two of his million. He fronts his "monstrous conspiracy" with Oedipal fixations: "afraid to understand" his relation to slavery, "for what might be understood there was a reproach to him," Burden takes Freud in hand and dramatizes his paternal attachments in programmatic terms. We understand Warren's novel more completely to the degree that we keep distance from these terms. After all, the scene above, in which Burden drives too quickly, is one of *self*-hypnosis, ours as well as Burden's. Breathless and hypnotic, the passage conflates the colors speeding toward the driver with those confronting a reader: entranced by a white background with black lines, we are tempted to let go, and see only what we wish to see.

What should we see? For starters, a particular labor regime: sharecropping. Not fully capitalist, sharecropping modifies the "total relations" between landowner and worker that legal historian Mark Tushnet attributes to slavery—relations in which, according to economic historian Jay Mandel, African Americans are "not slave, not free."[24] Sharecropping was an agricultural system in which allegedly free black labor worked land that it did not own, for a percentage of the total crop sufficiently small that the worker's economic debt to the landowner effectively replaced the legal bonds that once tied slave to master. Extracting maximum labor and offering little in return, this system appealed to a southern landowning class that, just before the Civil War, had up to 60 percent of its capital invested in slaves. But during the thirties, when Warren sets his novel, sharecropping was on its way out. Behind Willie Stark's welfare state reforms loom not simply Long, but Roosevelt and the New Deal. As Eric Foner has it, the New Deal was the South's "Second Civil War."[25] In 1933, faced with a worldwide glut of cotton, the AAA began paying southern farmers to cease production of their crops, to "plough it under." Additionally, the New Deal reorganized farming by making use of rationalized principles and economies of scale that, most were quick to see, threatened both sharecropping and what Southern Agrarian George O'Donnell, writing in *Who Owns America?* (1938), called "the good, healthy, Anglo-Saxon" practice of yeomanry.[26] The result was a massive reorganization of the South's economy: it now made more sense to pay wages for intermittent labor than it did to allocate portions of unused land to tenant farmers. Wages: like those Mastern tried to pay workers before the Civil War; like those that newly minted but still itinerant PhDs like Warren were receiving from English departments in the early thirties; and like those that Huey Long, committed to the tenets of Keynesian economics, was paying in work programs across his state. Thus while Stark's dynamic self-indulgence models the racial currents subtending the South's agonized debates over miscegenation, rights, and constitutionality, it distracts from and provides cover for the more impersonal aspects of the South's economic modernization, its structural transition toward an economy of salaried piecework.

It's useful to read *King's Men* in light of the far-reaching anxiety precipitated by that transition. To Richard Godden, William Faulkner's thirties-era fiction is organized by the disavowals of southern elites who, faced with their dependence on departing African American labor, sense that they are "little more than an extension" of the "collective body" of their laborers.[27] Bound to their workers in a Hegelian dialectic, Faulkner's masters are haunted by their identity with them. In Warren, Phebe turns into gold the moment that Annabelle Trice discovers the depth of her personal dependence on her; suddenly possessed of a threatening autonomy in her newfound knowledge, Phebe is transformed, as if touched by Midas, into an icon of the plantation's economy. The slave turns gold in the master's eyes when the master realizes his or her dependence on her. But as Godden has it, this same realization turns the master a different color altogether. For Godden, the master's melancholia comes from refusing to grant the constitutive role that slave labor plays not simply in the economy but in the personhood of the master himself. Fully allowing the significance of this role into consciousness threatens a kind of death—precisely the kind, we might hazard, witnessed at the start of Warren's novel by black field hands. Burden imagines himself dying before the testifying eyes of a black workforce in the process of chopping cotton. The conjuring of this hypothetical death is part of a broader effort to forestall an unwanted recognition of what lies beyond the margins of the highway upon which Burden keeps his eyes so maniacally fixed. Fearful that these fields and their workers will expose something about him, Burden keeps his eyes turned away from the newly mobile black labor upon which his class depends. He thus displays what Godden finds in much of Faulkner: "the denial of a social trauma associated with the recognition that the South's singular, coercive, and premodern regime of labor forced black into white, and so made each white black." Averting his gaze from the generative physical labor that makes him who he is, Burden avoids recognizing that he is what Godden calls, suggestively, "a black in whiteface."[28]

Stark offers a tentative solution to this melancholic whiteface; coded black, he shows Burden what it means to be in possession of one's body. Time and again, Burden marvels at Stark's robust physicality. The governor's impetuous self-indulgence—his impulsive gratification of both private and public need—differs sharply from Burden's strangled ambivalence. Stark is a man of the flesh, what Burden calls "a man of fact" (436). And his physical efficacy is indistinguishable from his political efficacy: if the "fact" of which Burden speaks gestures to the implicit color of Stark's flesh, it also gestures to the political realities subtending Stark's populism, tied as they are to the labor conditions of his state. The opening passage cited above is crucial because, in essence, the highway that it describes is in blackface. The road on which Burden speeds has been poured with concrete, which is why it is white. Tar-and-petroleum-based highways—which result in a black surface that is then painted with white lines—were common during the thirties, but were just then beginning to be replaced by cement, which produces a white surface that is then painted with black lines. As Burden tells us, the highway is "new"—no doubt Stark built it, as the governor's public works projects modernize old roads. Stark's workforce transforms a black surface covered with a superimposed white (a black road in whiteface) to a white surface covered with a superimposed black (a white road in blackface).

We must consider this workforce and how it is paid. Stark begins his political career in a small town by opposing a corrupt public works project that employs an all-white crew; he favors instead an integrated crew. Presumably, then, once elected governor, he builds his highways with an integrated workforce. This workforce introduces the prospect of an interracial folk, a proletarian alliance between black and white, precisely the kind invoked by Warren in his essay "The Briar Patch," collected in *I'll Take My Stand.* Warren's essay is the only one in that collection to wed an antipathy to industrialism to a working-class politics. He encourages the "realization that the fates of the 'poor white' and the negro are linked in a single tether. The well-being and adjustment of one depends on that of the other" (259). Warren's essential worry is that an increasingly industrialized South would exploit black labor at the expense of white labor, thereby exacerbating racial tensions in the region. "The factory may have come to be near its requisite raw materials," he writes, "but it has also come to profit from the cheap labor, black and white, which is to be had there. The negro labor is unorganized and unable to bargain effectively with its employer, and the white labor is in little better shape" (256). All the same, he thought that white workers would suffer at the hands of this system, insofar as factories, for example, would tend to favor black labor, knowing they could pay less and grant fewer concessions to their workers by doing so. Those opposed to industrialism, he insists, must look closely at "the relation of white and black labor to each other and to the capital which makes that development possible. If this industrialism is to bequeath anything except the profit of the few, the conscious or unconscious exploitation of racial differences, and a disastrous rancor, an enlightened selfishness on the part of the Southern white man must prompt him to encourage the well-being and possibly the organization of negro, as well as white, labor" (258). Published some three decades after the Agrarian manifesto, Warren's *Who Speaks for the Negro?* reminds us that Huey Long was ahead of his time in his commitment to just this perspective. He quotes Long: "I'm for the poor man—all poor men. Black and white, they all gotta have a chance. They gotta have a home, a job and a decent education for their children. That means every man" (*WS* 14).

Stark threatens to unleash the black labor power upon which Burden's class depends. Compelled by the governor, Burden considers breaking with his class and modeling himself on Stark: less a black in whiteface (a self-denying member of an exploiting class, one whose psychic and sexual repression echoes a foundational economic exploitation) than a white in blackface (a working-class white who finds emotional and sexual release in flaunting his allegiance with the racially and economically subaltern). But Burden doesn't break with his class. "The pocketbook is where it hurts," says our sullen narrator, full of self-loathing, at the start of the novel, when he thinks he has no real inheritance. "A man may forget the death of the father, but never the loss of the patrimony." This is an honest confession, given his later claim that "nobody down here," in the old-money enclave where he grows up and where Irwin lives, "ever wants to be rich-rich" (434). After Irwin kills himself and after Burden discovers that he is Irwin's son and heir, Burden decides to keep the judge's sizable holdings, thank you very much. He'll manage to convince himself that moving into Irwin's house is the upstanding thing to do. Burden begins his story believing "that nobody had any responsibility for anything" (435) and ends convinced that he himself has no end of responsibility. Apparently, this assumption of total responsibility, which recalls the system of total relations then coming to an end, requires Burden to keep for himself a family fortune derived from running a cotton plantation.

The fortune also comes from graft; Irwin tendered favors for a utilities company while serving as attorney general of his state. The judge kills himself after Stark exposes the fact that he is, as Stark repeatedly puts it, "dirty." But Irwin and his money are dirty in interesting ways. Most obviously, dirt names political corruption. Burden uses it in this sense when he tells Stark that he'll never find compromising information on the judge. Stark's response is richer in meaning:

> "Dirt's a funny thing," the Boss said. "Come to think of it, there ain't a thing but dirt on this green God's globe except what's under water, and that's dirt too. It's dirt makes the grass grow. A diamond ain't a thing in the world but a piece of dirt that got awful hot. And God-a-Mighty picked up a handful of dirt and blew on it and made you and me and George Washington and mankind blessed in faculty and apprehension. It all depends on what you do with the dirt. That right?" (55)

Dirt makes the grass grow just as it makes the cotton grow. In this sense, dirt makes diamonds in two ways: it is the substance from which diamonds form, as well as the substance from which the South's cash crop grows. And of course Stark claims that dirt makes humans as well, which completes the buried movements of his conceit: we are all, he tells Burden, black, because we are all made from dirt and from the laboring of bodies in dirt. More pointedly, he suggests, the white bodies of Irwin and those in his class make their diamonds from black bodies laboring in dirt—which renders their bodies black as well as white, as dirty as those of their workers.

A different version of this claim would have been familiar to followers of the minstrel show, the nineteenth-century entertainment that haunts Stark's account of dirt and *King's Men* generally. As a popular magazine announced at the turn of the century, "When a blackface comedian makes up with burnt cork, he is smearing diamond dust on his face. Can there be anything more wonderful than this? The diamond, the hardest substance known, and the soft, black soot in your chimney are exactly the same thing!"[29] This provides a useful way of understanding the relation of minstrelsy to wealth production. As Eric Lott has it, the minstrel show drew force from its acknowledgment of complicity in the extraction of surplus value from black bodies. Detractors of the practice, he shows, held that "white men have blackened their faces to represent [Negroes], [and] made their fortune by the speculation." This protest derived from the sense that "black 'owners' are not equal buyers and sellers on the market but are 'represented,' bought and sold by brokers." But the problem, as Lott sees it, is that these critiques assume that "whites would like to have imagined the expropriations of minstrelsy as nonanalogous to slavery," as "a denial or forgetting of the unremunerated labor of slavery." In fact, he insists, minstrelsy generated desire and enthusiasm by confessing its extraction of surplus value from black bodies. He takes as exemplary a passage from Herman Melville's *Confidence-Man* (1857), in which a blackface street performer works passersby for coins. "The consciousness of black commodification which the writing forces on us works all the more to make blackness into a marketable object of white interest," Lott writes. "Commodification," he argues of the performer, is "what seems blackest about him." As Lott sees it, the minstrel show "helped to produce the cultural commodity 'blackness.'"[30] We might, then, read the prosthetic skin applied literally in blackface and metaphorically in all subsequent performances of blackness as glittering not simply with diamond dust, but with the patina of capital itself.[31]

Stark's campy homily seeks to elicit an acknowledgment. With an insinuating wink, he would have Burden see. Warren's work consistently dramatizes the violence with which southern whites disavow what they should otherwise see: in *Brothers to Dragons*, for example, black bodies lie beneath the very foundations of the South's political economy; the poem describes two nephews of Thomas Jefferson who butcher a slave for breaking a teacup, and then bury him—beneath the dirt floor of their barn and, we presume, beneath Jefferson's legacy; the poem also describes the agonized reluctance with which its speaker comes to accept this information. Analogously, Stark confronts Burden with the prospect that Irwin is "a black in whiteface" and that, as a consequence, Irwin's corruption is the corruption of his class and his region: the judge is dirty less because of his corporate collusion than because he is constituted from the start by black labor that he would disavow. Stark's "blackmail" works to suggest, finally, that Irwin is a "black male." There's nothing repugnant to Stark about this. Pragmatic to the core, he solicits recognition that the whiteness tacitly claimed by Irwin and his class is theatrical, the product of a performed disavowal that requires the consent of an audience. A version of his message would have been familiar to followers of Huey Long, who is reported to have claimed that "all of the 'pure' white people in New Orleans could be fed on a half a cup of beans and a half a cup of rice, and there'd be some left over."[32] Of course Burden can no more see this than can Irwin. The few African Americans in his narrative have "all-seeing, all-knowing eyes" and he—poor Oedipus—does not. In fact, for Warren, as surely as for Hegel in the master-slave dialectic, recognition and death are synonymous. Recall that "black dirt" separates Stark's new highway from the black farmers laboring just beyond it. In the shocking process of crossing this dirt, and being forced to look too closely into the fields from which the South derives its wealth, Burden's imaginary driver plunges to his death.

"If they don't know, you can't tell 'em"

Annabelle Trice decides to renounce some of her dirty money. She sells Phebe and gives the proceeds to a blind black musician "picking on a guitar and singing 'Old Dan Tucker'" (176). First published in 1843, the song was an early staple of the minstrel shows. This is ground zero of the incipient hip in *King's Men*, in which damning money disappears into the patronage of blackface culture. Burden is not himself hip. He goes out of his way to suggest that he is something of an outmode. Walking on the beach, he meets "an indifferent stare" from the "brown, water-slick faces" of presumably African American children. Conflating skin color, generation, and style, and nodding to T. S. Eliot's Prufrock, Burden thinks himself a member of "that dull and purblind race which wears shoes and trousers" (338). Still, Burden's hard-boiled, detached demeanor aspires to a streetwise enlightenment. Struggling with early drafts of *King's Men*, Warren recalled, "turned on the question of getting a lingo for this narrator" (*RPW* 223). Burden's lingo is jaded in the extreme, and his noir and deadpan voice points us toward the hip dispositions that were taking shape in U.S. cities, like New Orleans, as Warren wrote.

Of course, New Orleans wasn't just another city; it occupied a central place in the history of jazz and in the subcultural styles that sprang from the music. Though historians debate whether jazz has a precise origin, there's widespread agreement that the music took its most popularly recognizable form in New Orleans during the first decades of the twentieth century, with the birth of "hot jazz" (a music sometimes referred to as "Dixieland" and thus regrettably linked to the Confederacy). The city is exemplary to Amiri Baraka because its racial and class stratifications delineate the influences that combined to form jazz. Soon after the inauguration of southern Jim Crow laws, light-skinned Creoles working in the city were forced from their places of employment in the city's downtown (Homer Plessy, the plaintiff in *Plessy v. Ferguson*, was one such New Orleans Creole). As Baraka has it, Creoles trained in western musical styles, especially those fluent with brass instruments and marching-band music, began playing with poorer African Americans uptown, who were versed in the expressive oral tradition of the blues. To Baraka and many others, these collaborations usefully describe the origins of jazz across the South. By the thirties, however, when the events in *King's Men* take place, swing had displaced hot jazz in popularity, and many black musicians were driven into the swelling ranks of the unemployed. While river steamers still tended to hire African American Dixieland bands, those running the "big bands" necessary for swing tended to hire white musicians—this despite the fact that swing was discernibly the product of African American musical traditions. It wasn't just former sharecroppers who headed north during the thirties; by the decade's end, the most important jazz was being made in the North and Midwest by black musicians who in leaving New Orleans followed in the footsteps of those, like Louis Armstrong, who had already left.[33]

The advent of swing has always seemed a particularly galling moment in the history of jazz, one of the more flagrant reminders that, as was the case in the tradition of minstrelsy, white performers stood waiting in the wings ready to cash in on black culture. There have been many such reminders. One of the most notorious involves Freddie Keppard, an African American New Orleans cornet player who passed up the chance to record the first jazz record. The oft-repeated story has Keppard and his band refusing the offer because they didn't want others to "steal their stuff." In what seemed an appropriately revealing turn of events, the Original Dixieland Jazz Band, an all-white group, recorded the first such record shortly thereafter. What followed placed white bands at the heart of jazz. As Baraka has it, during the thirties, "most white men believed that 'The biggest contribution to American music the Negro had made by this time was to swing.' And the 'King-of-Swing' was a white man, Benny Goodman, whose only real connection to Afro-American musical tradition was the fact that he hired a Negro arranger and later a few Negro musicians" (*BP* 170). Goodman got the glory and the gold, and black musicians were left on the financial margins of a musical form they continued to push into new territories.

But those in the know knew what those in the mainstream did not: hip was born, in part, as a strategy for asserting, in coded form, a wise relation to information that others cannot or will not handle. When asked about those who read *King's Men* as an apologia for Huey Long, Robert Penn Warren replied, "As Louis Armstrong is reported to have said, there's some folks that if they don't know, you can't tell 'em."[34] This kind of insider knowledge echoes Long's and Stark's relation to the politics of interracial labor that I have delineated above: they gesture to but will not directly invoke their willingness to mobilize black votes, and outrage, on behalf of their reforms. As I understand it, hip designates more than a particular set of styles (those associated with bebop, for example); more neutrally, it also designates a coded disposition toward otherwise unallowable information. From this vantage, Warren's gesture to Armstrong encapsulates his own narrative style. The point here is not that the speakeasy-frequenting, large-living Warren thought Armstrong hip (no doubt he did) and that he therefore modeled his style on Armstrong's jazz (no doubt he did not). The point, rather, is that we hear jazz in Warren's voice to the extent that we hear it gesturing to what it will not directly name.

More specifically, Warren's incipiently hip lingo secretes away the racial origins of money. Money, or knowledge of money, or knowledge worth money, appears and disappears throughout *King's Men*. An inveterate reporter, Burden writes his observations in little black books that he then places in safety-deposit boxes. The information they contain is "worth their weight in gold to some parties" (30), and so he keeps them locked away—in just the manner that Phebe, pure gold, must be sent away and rendered inaccessible. We never read the dirt that these black books presumably contain. All the same, similarly reflexive, protected knowledge abounds: Cass's brother, Gilbert, comes upon his brother reading. "You might make something out of that" (163), he says, tapping the book with his riding crop. How frustrating, Burden muses, that the book remains invisible: "We see the flick of the leather loop on the open page, a brisk flick, not quite contemptuous, but we cannot make out the page" (164). Moving downward now, from high to low, from books to oral knowledge, we return to the opening passage of the novel, in which Warren describes black field hands witnessing the crash of Burden's car. As if to relay news of this event, one of their hoes flashes in the sun, like a heliograph. For Forrest Robinson, the worker's hoe communicates "a message in code, sent clearly enough, but not received." This is encrypted information, potentially blinding, unavailable to those beyond an inner circle. This is also the heart of the novel's primal scene, the moment at which black labor—only reluctantly viewed as "gold"—becomes something more properly sublime and blinding: looking at African American workers is for Burden akin to looking into the sun.

Warren's studied excisions anticipated by-now-familiar accounts of modernism, whose formal experiments often depended on the self-conscious elision of crucial information. As Hugh Kenner tells us, modernists were fascinated by what appeared only as traces within the work of art. For example, he describes symbolism—the late-nineteenth-century French movement that greatly influenced Pound, Eliot, and Stevens—as an effort to capture stylistically the vestiges of what had "dropped out" from otherwise familiar language.[35] We see in the symbolist poem only fragments of a lost history, evidence of meanings once whole and now only partial. Ernest Hemingway elaborated a related version of this aesthetic when he declared, "If a writer of prose knows enough about what he is writing about he may omit things that he knows and the reader, if the writer is writing truly enough, will have a feeling of those things as strongly as though the writer had stated them. The dignity of movement of an ice-berg is due to only one-eighth of it being above water."[36] That the iceberg works like Freud's unconscious is hardly incidental: Hemingway's omissions—felt more than understood—take on talismanic power by virtue of their partial invisibility. The New Critical interest in "sensibility" represents another version of this dynamic. Sensibility was for the New Critics what it was for Matthew Arnold: an affective, embodied structure of feeling meant to stand in for more explicitly programmatic ideational systems. As John Guillory argues, for the New Critics, "*sensibility* takes the place of religious *belief*." He finds a Christian sensibility in the New Criticism's commitment to "paradox," which "names the very condition by which the poem does not *name* the truth to which it nevertheless gestures." As Guillory sees it, the New Critics learned from Eliot that literature "should be *unconsciously*, rather than deliberately and defiantly, Christian."[37]

Guillory considers the unconscious truth that the New Critical poem does not name religious in nature; but this is the New Critics' own mystified account of how particular poems should capture an unconscious. We must attribute to the New Criticism a different kind of unconscious, one grounded in the South's "singular, coercive, and premodern regime of labor." Mark Jancovich describes the origins of the Southern Agrarians: "It was the arguments which surrounded the Scopes Trial of 1925," he says, "which seem to have forced Ransom, Tate, and Warren to clarify and develop their positions." In their eyes, the trial was a drama in which self-righteous northerners came to gawk and impose their cold science on time-honored traditions mistaken for backwardness. Jancovich distills the resentment over this intrusion and comes to the anodyne conclusion that Agrarians placed themselves "in opposition to modern society."[38] To be sure, Ransom's terms were similarly broad; in "Reconstructed but Unregenerate," he singles out industrialism as the great evil facing the South. Industrialism is hostile to "that leisure which conditions the life of intelligence and the arts" (21). Wanting anti-instrumental values, Ransom defends traditional southern society and opposes himself to the teaching of Darwin in southern schools. But the so-called "Monkey Trial" was rife with racial undertones. William Jennings Bryan, Tennessee's prosecutor, had already opposed a resolution condemning the KKK during the 1924 Democratic convention. More pointedly, the Darwinian theory that Scopes was being prosecuted for teaching led to unavoidable conclusions: the *Chicago Defender* held that Tennessee legislators were suppressing evolution because of the Darwinian implication "that the entire human race is supposed to have started from a common origin." "Admit that premise," it continued, "and they will have to admit that there is no real difference between themselves and the race they pretend to despise."[39]

The Southern Agrarian iceberg remained mostly underwater. With the exception of Robert Penn Warren, none of the contributors to *I'll Take My Stand* treat southern race relations in a direct or sustained manner. The racial preoccupations are, instead, implicit. The collection, Richard Gray remarks, assembles often strikingly incompatible economic positions: for example, its contributors alternately invoke a populist vision of small-farm yeomanry and an Anglophilic vision of leisured aristocracy. All the same, "however much the individual essayists may be at odds at times, there is something holding them together, some force other than sheer blind conviction that draws them into the same orbit, the same field of discourse." "There is something there," he continues, "exerting a gravitational pull on each contributor to the volume": "Like any code, the one the Agrarians employed is as notable for what it does not say as for what it does, for the absences by which it is haunted; and *their* code seems intent on not bringing into speech, and therefore into the orbit of its attention, one figure in particular—the black, especially in his role as slave."[40] This is a compelling analysis. Nostalgic for a lost southern way, *I'll Take My Stand* calls attention to the one subject it appears to evade: race. Still, we might ask why these authors bothered to evade the one topic their commitments surely would have raised.

Fredric Jameson suggests that modernism was less "a way of avoiding social content" than a way "of managing and containing it, secluding it out of sight in the very form itself."[41] For Gray, the Agrarians did just this in their handling of race. But their goal was not simply to avoid socially explosive material. It was also to proselytize on behalf of the quasi-political agency lurking in form—or shared culture. For the Agrarians, keeping African Americans out of sight was a way, however paradoxical, of endowing southern culture with an organizing energy. The South's "established order of human existence" was cultural precisely to the degree that it converted African American labor into a more ineffable, charismatic principle of communal cohesion. Contributors to *I'll Take My Stand* did not try to conceal what readers might have considered racist. Frank Owsley, for example, describes the South after the Civil War as "turned over to the three millions of former slaves, some of whom could still remember the taste of human flesh and the bulk of them hardly three generations removed from cannibalism. These half-savage blacks were armed" (62). It is, rather, when discussing traditional southern culture that the volume becomes silent about the South's African Americans. Donald Davidson brags, "Southern people have long cultivated a historical consciousness that permeates manners, localities, institutions, the very words and cadences of social intercourse." In this way, they established a democratic culture "not at war with its own economic foundations" (53). For Davidson, as for the other contributors to the volume, these manners and speech cadences have an ambiguous relation to the African Americans who laid the foundations of the southern economy. Contributors like Davidson and Owsley gesture to virtues derived from the gentlemanly cultivation of the land. As Owsley has it, southerners were like "the Romans of the early republic, before land speculators and corn laws had driven men from the soil to the city slums." These Romans, he couldn't resist adding, were "open and without guile" (70). Had he been equally so, he might have compared the South to Imperial Rome, when slaves worked the land. In Owsley's sense of the past, African Americans are salient only when armed with northern rifles. In matters of culture they are invisible, precisely because they underwrite the vision of grace and leisure that animates Owsley's nostalgia for the organic community.

In *I'll Take My Stand*, African Americans are the ghosts in the machine, the spirit animating a whole that is deemed more than the sum of its parts. "The models of belief and behavior, and habits of language" that the Agrarians saw the South losing take shape only in negative form, when placed in relief against barely visible African Americans, who—Ransom in particular wanted his readers to know—were during the days of slavery so very much more than mere economic instruments. By the 1920s, the Great Migration was well under way; African Americans were leaving the South in vast numbers. But to the Southern Agrarians, they had already left and disappeared into melancholic recollections of what the South once was, when organized around the total relations of slavery. As traditional southern culture seemed to lose its cohesion before the onslaught of industrialization, these barely visible African Americans haunted the anti-bureaucratic imagination of the Southern Agrarians.

Cleanth Brooks admitted to reading *I'll Take My Stand* "over and over." His earliest research, published five years after the manifesto, meant to prove that "the Negro has made no innovations" in the southern dialect because he spoke an English traceable to the provincial dialects of southwest England. The premise is paradoxical, insofar as Brooks turns his attention to African Americans in order to establish that they have failed to exert any significant impact. He studies the dialect of the Uncle Remus stories and concludes that this speech was, after all, an import. African Americans hadn't hybridized the English language. But they also hadn't bastardized it; rather, due in large part to their reliance on oral tradition and their connection to agricultural labor, they had remained remarkably faithful to its historical spoken forms. In fact, Uncle Remus's speech was the language of Renaissance England. "That's an honorable lineage, isn't it?" he later asked Warren. Brooks insists that local dialect is, simultaneously, African American and British. Brooks understood T. S. Eliot's dissociation of sensibility as a "segregation of impulses"; in this context, identifying the intimacy of Negro dialect with Elizabethan English amounted to an integration that saved contemporary spoken English from the rationalizing tendencies of institutions. Denouncing "foolishly incorrect theories of what constitutes good English," Brooks makes clear that the "propagation of bureaucratese, sociologese, and psychologese, which American business, politics, and academics seem to exude as a matter of course," is far more dire a phenomenon than Remus-speak, like "the occasional use of *ain't*."[42] For Brooks, the grammatically incorrect locution humanizes English, insofar as it saves it from the organizational imperatives of officialdom. His African Americans thus signify an unassimilated institutional difference. Decades later, during the postwar information economy, a similar logic would find in hip argot a means of preserving the lost autonomy of knowledge workers alienated from corporate bureaucracies.

Paul Bové argues that the Agrarians declared themselves part of a unified movement at precisely the moment that the New Deal's agricultural policy in the South came into its own. "Two different types of intellectuals—one traditional: clerical, humanistic, petit bourgeois; the other technical: bureaucratic, scientific, professional—belonging to two different social formations compete[d] for leadership." This isn't entirely right: the Agrarians belonged to the first type but were often from wealthy families, whose money came not from office work but from the South's traditional crop economy. Thomas Wolfe described the Agrarians as "refined young gentlemen of the New Confederacy." A childhood friend remembered Warren's family as "real aristocrats." But Bové is right to see that the Agrarians had to lose in this competition, illconceived from the start as it was; even as they continued to champion the rhetoric of bureaucracy and charisma, they committed to literary expertise and based their cultural authority on professionalizing codes of specialization. Thus Bové deems them "unknowingly aligned with the practices and ideology of the Farm Bureau."[43] Ransom was the first to grasp the larger implications of this affinity. In the late thirties, he renounced his defense of southern traditionalism and headed north. In the following years, the most prominent Southern Agrarians would follow and reinvent themselves as New Critics in northern universities.

Interpretations of this migration into the university vary widely. Jancovich sees it as a strategic extension of the Agrarians' early commitments: John Crow Ransom, Allen Tate, and Warren's entrance into the university was "a politically motivated intervention which sought to establish a basis for their particular criticism of culture and society." Conversely, Gerald Graff sees the Agrarians' move north as part of an about-face and, moreover, as "a condition of becoming institutionalized." The New Criticism had to "sever its ties with the social and cultural criticism of which first generation New Critics were a part," mainly because the largely liberal universities for which they eventually worked demanded it. Other critics cast matters in a more personal light: Agrarians became New Critics not to further their program, or because they were required to renounce that program, but in order to evade the embarrassment of it.[44]

These critics differ in how they imagine individual New Critics' either renouncing or continuing to embrace their Agrarian beliefs. But none of them consider that Agrarian social and cultural criticism might have offered northern universities something that those institutions imagined they needed. Alan Liu offers us such an account. He claims that Brooks "and his generation preceded us along the path of modernization, new media, and the desire for a new Bildung."[45] Liu sometimes names that Bildung an "ethos of the unknown," but most typically names it "cool." This designation, he reasons, functions as a latter-day equivalent of New Critical irony and ambiguity—habituated or somatic forms of anti-scientific knowledge that resist translation into purely instrumental information. As Liu sees it, "When the New Critics so passionately argued that understanding poetry is different from understanding rational prose—nowhere more influentially than in Brooks and Robert Penn Warren's textbook *Understanding Poetry* (first edition, 1938)—they were protesting the colonization of sensibility by what we today call the information age."[46] For Liu, the New Critics did not just protest: their commitment to untranslatable poetic knowledge demonstrated to subsequent white-collar workers how "*information designed to resist information*" alters and humanizes the corporate contexts in which it is deployed.[47] In his account, "cool" functions as a self-preserving aesthetic that reconciles knowledge workers to their institutional arrangements: I work here, but I'm cool, his white-collar subjects declare in their pursuit of a plausible individuality. For Liu, cool takes two forms: on the one hand, it adapts workers to an ever-greater demand for efficiency, conditioning them in leisure pursuits that make them more productive at work; on the other, it preserves for them some critical distance between their humanity and the machines for which they labor (and often symbolizes that distance by invoking fantasies of racial groups more wholly alienated than the worker himself from the scene of white-collar wealth production). The not-fully-understood and the untranslatable—like the primal sexual drives of ostensibly primitive populations—matter crucially in this second capacity, insofar as they baffle the instrumental and technocratic rationality of the workplace.

Capaciously learned and incisive, Liu's comprehensive study changes how we understand the white-collar workplace. But the New Critics are appropriate analogs to Liu's present-day knowledge workers for a reason he does not fully elaborate: their shared meta-discursive commitment to providing theories of information designed to resist information itself scrambled the racially marked data that loom large in the evolution of postwar cool. As a theory of poetic knowledge, the New Criticism condemned "the heresy of paraphrase";

as Brooks explained, poems could not be converted into information other than themselves because they captured an inviolate totality, a wholeness of experience irreducible to any other form. But as an institutionally located practice that evolved out of nostalgia for the total relations of slavery and sharecropping, the New Criticism performed resistance to a much more specific informational payload: it obscured its foundational commitments with formal analysis designed to qualify away the biographical and historical origins of authorship.

The Agrarians romanced a vision of southern culture organized around theatrically hidden black labor; the New Critics adumbrated a formal program that guaranteed that such labor could never be read out of a poem, could never be grasped as anything other than a poetic effect. From this vantage, Liu's ethos of the unknown is Southern Agrarian false consciousness. Universities needed that false consciousness. Reincarnated as New Critics, Agrarians suggested in their personal histories as well as in their criticism, to recall Jameson, less "a way of avoiding social content" than a way of "managing and containing it, secluding it out of sight in the very form itself."

When New Critics did understand their work in political terms, they did so in a manner that sat well with the mystifying imperatives of their time. In *Democracy and Poetry* (1975), for example, Warren approvingly cites the *Port Huron Statement*'s commitment to safeguarding "consciousness" from "the brutalities of the twentieth century." These were the kinds of terms that appealed to administrators and intellectuals in the years following the Second World War, when once revolutionary critiques of industrialism and capitalism were assuming the broadly Weberian language earlier mobilized by the Agrarians. These were manifestly safe terms, never so much as when issued from the mouths of former Southern Agrarians: they seemed to constitute a rejection of a racist southern orthodoxy, in the absence of that rejection's ever really having taken place.

With this dynamic in mind, we might read *King's Men* as an allegory for the ambitions of a previously southern group of agrarian intellectuals who, having taken their place by the mid-forties in northern organizations, needed a story about the national relevance of otherwise parochial southern values and commitments. Such a story might explain the otherwise perplexing fact that Warren shifts the dates in the novel, whose events take place during the years when Huey Long was a U.S. senator and not a governor of Louisiana. Changing the dates, Warren suggests that Willie Stark represents his state to a larger national forum—that his charisma captures the particular energy that the New Criticism finds in poetry and teaches—as emblematic of the South itself—to an otherwise technocratic northern civilization. "It may be that poetry is the proper residence of charisma," wrote Kermit Lansner in the *Kenyon Review* in 1951. Similar claims appear across the works of the New Critics. In *The Hidden God* (1963), for example, Cleanth Brooks celebrates the "something deeper and more resonant" in literature that militates against a "spirit of industrialism" that, he claims by way of Paul Tillich, renders man "an object among objects, a thing among things." That something deeper derives from the fact that poetry constitutes, in Brooks's estimation, a "full" and "total" experience more than a reproducible meaning: "The poet is not telling us *about* the experience; he is *giving* us the experience." Reporting on an experience means rendering it a "formula": akin to "charts and timetables" and one more industrial object. Actually having the experience militates against the instrumental "logic" inherent in these mechanistic forms.[48]

Given these terms, Stark is a figure for the New Critical poem itself, his populism an expression of the mass-educational program championed by the ascendant school of which Warren was then a prominent member. In effect, Stark's charismatic energy turns out to be the same kind that, according to Warren, bursts from deep inside works of literature. In the 1962 essay, "Why Do We Read Fiction?" Warren defines fiction in terms of its ability to offer an escape from the "drab." Citing Freud, he notes that everyday life offers "meager satisfactions" that leave one "starving." A form of collective wish fulfillment— much like Stark himself—fiction is a "publicly available daydream." Readers embrace it as an instance of what Warren, citing Francis Bacon, calls "a greater grandeur." A "life more abundantly lived," he declares, "is what we seek."[49] We read fiction, then, for much the same reason that Jack Burden follows Stark: because it excites, and it saves us from our authenticity-deprived, mechanical lives.[50] Along similar lines, Warren's *Democracy and Poetry* claims that "the 'made thing,'" by which he means the poem, "nods mysteriously at us, at the deepest personal inward self." The made thing, Warren tellingly adds, "wakes us up to our own life" (*DP* 69, 71). These words recall Stark's relation to Burden. Stark wakes Burden up to his life; he revives him from years of alienation and lethargy that Burden refers to as "The Great Sleep." In fact, Warren's numinous literary object nods mysteriously at its reader in exactly the same way that, upon first meeting, Stark winks mysteriously at his pupil-to-be. Burden will return to this wink more than once, perplexed by its capacity to sound him and change his life.

The problem with this reading is that if we make Stark a New Critical poem, then we must make Burden a New Critic, the agent who assumes responsibility for representing poetic charisma to the world. This we cannot do, because Warren's novel implicitly faults Burden for failing to know and say more than he does. The reading makes sense only retroactively, I want to suggest, because Warren would grow more as opposed to less committed to the mystifying rhetoric of charisma after he left the South, this despite—or perhaps because of—the fact that his positions on racial tolerance and integration grew more recognizably liberal. Warren would come increasingly to believe in the efficacy of poetry's "greater grandeur," its ability to recast the prosaic social details that animate *King's Men*, a novel that very carefully traces "the curse of Jack Burden" to Burden's failure to see the relationships in which he is implicated. Burden's problem, the narrative everywhere suggests, is not that he suffers "meager satisfactions." Rather, it's that he feels he needs to be protected from the troubling information before him. This need to look away constitutes Burden's denial, to recall Godden, "of a social trauma associated with the recognition that the South's singular, coercive, and premodern regime of labor forced black into white, and so made each white black."

In the sixties, however, when he penned "Why Do We Read Fiction?" Warren would use a term like "charisma" to establish a point of comparison between political leaders and literary texts—and in so doing reproduce Burden's denial. This is most clearly the case in *Who Speaks for the Negro?*, where Warren describes the "publicly available daydream" that is Martin Luther King Jr. To Warren, King is less the leader of a political movement making demands on the government than he is a source of compelling aesthetic energy. When Warren first meets him in the early 1960s, he notices the "mystical hold" of King's authority and the "inner force" of his voice (*WS* 220). "It is easy," Warren observes, "to recognize the charisma. But, the charisma is not the product of publicity. It is real" (*WS* 206). The effort to explain what this means preoccupies the pages that follow. Most striking, he thinks, is King's capacity to focus his vision "inward" after being asked a question:

> Even if it is a question that you know he has heard a hundred times before, there is
> a withdrawing inward, a slight veiling of the face as it were. There is the impression

that for an answer for even that old stale question he must look inward to find a real answer, not just the answer he gave yesterday, which today may no longer be meaningful to him. It is a remarkable trait—if my reading is correct: the need to go inward to test the truth that has already been tested, perhaps over and over again, in the world outside.

Does the charisma inhere in this? (*WS* 210)

Beyond answering in the affirmative, Warren describes King's charisma in terms that echo his own critical project. Warren notes King's capacity to embrace "tension" and his "way of living with intense polarity" (*WS* 213). He notes his "balanced rhythm," his tendency to produce one "movement balanced by another." He praises King's ability "to include antitheses, to affirm and absorb the polarities of life" (*WS* 221). Looking inward, he generates an autotelic, centripetal force: gravity. These are precisely the qualities that Brooks and Warren celebrate in *Understanding Poetry* and *Understanding Fiction*, classroom aids meant to teach students how discrete literary objects mobilize irony, tension, and polarity. Removed from the world (he retreats behind a veil), King is an object that "is its own meaning." In short, he is a New Critical poem.

But though possessed of gravity, Warren's King feels empty, without content. Warren appreciates how King handles familiar questions; he's impressed by the profundity of the minister's commitment to discovering and testing "the truth." But this truth stays offstage. It's as if the pretext for eliciting King's charisma—an "old stale question"—must remain irrelevant and denuded of any specificity, as indeed it does: we hear neither the question nor the answer. Like his charisma, King's answer is "real" to the extent that it suffers no direct translation. Coming as it does at the heart of a book on black leadership in the Civil Rights Movement—*Who Speaks for the Negro?*—this suggests, at the very least, that Warren's analogy elides what makes King's project political in the first place. Warren registers the minister's power as a function not of ideology but of poetic power that models psychological power. If King is a poem, then this gives him an ability to access in any one of his followers their "deepest personal inward self." Possessed of a distinctly literary charisma, he nods mysteriously, or winks, at his listener. Consequently, though standing at the head of a very big organization—intent on political, economic, and legal reform—this curiously inward figure seems mostly to tap pre-political needs; Warren thinks King's followers find in him less a program than "the father-that-might-have-been" (*WS* 372).

"The noiseless, secret vote"

We work here, but we're cool. In *All the King's Men,* Jack Burden works for Willie Stark's administration, but stays cool. No slave to "the boss," he remains autonomous and critical of Stark. "No, I'm not in politics," Burden declares. "I've just got a job." He elaborates, "I'm an office boy" (123). The same might be said of the New Critics—of Cleanth Brooks and Robert Penn Warren in particular, who were the state's office boys. In the early 1930s, they taught at Louisiana State University, a campus swimming in newfound cash, courtesy of Huey Long. There they helped found the *Southern Review* and enjoyed the same freedom while running it that Burden enjoys while working for Stark. Writing in the *New York Times,* John Chamberlain noted of the nascent journal, "Huey may dictate to the Louisiana Legislature, but he permits free controversy in the new quarterly published by 'his' university." Warren agreed; he thought Long "too adept in the art of power to care what an assistant professor might have to say" (*RPW* 151). And yet, as the years went by, Washington, DC, seemed by all outward appearances to care a great deal what Brooks and Warren had to say. In fact, postwar liberalism's most concerted commitment to federally funding the arts took shape around recognizably New Critical claims.

In *I'll Take My Stand,* Donald Davidson denounces "the phantom of a theory in the air" that there should be "some formidable managerial body" like "a United States Chamber of Art or a National Arts Council, with a distinguished board of directors and local committees in every state" (28). Warren and Brooks benefited from a version of this theory. Warren was the third Consultant in Poetry to the Library of Congress, and the first Poet Laureate of the United States. President Johnson named Cleanth Brooks the cultural attaché to the American embassy in London in 1964, one year after the poet made his distinction between policies and elections on the one hand and something deeper and more resonant on the other.[51] Brooks's appointment was part of Johnson's sustained effort to make funding of the arts and humanities an ongoing project integral to the national interest—so was the founding that year of the National Council on the Arts, a body that resembled the "American Academy of Letters" that Ransom envisioned in a 1936 letter to Allen Tate. These efforts culminated in the National Endowment for the Arts (NEA) and the National Endowment for the Humanities (NEH).

Brooks's view that black dialect humanized an otherwise bureaucratic language turns out to be surprisingly relevant to Johnson's rationale for federally funding the arts and humanities. The president pushed through the NEA and the NEH in a rapidly changing political landscape. One year before funding the two endowments, he secured passage of the Civil Rights Act, landmark legislation that outlawed segregation in U.S. schools and public places. A year later he secured passage of the National Voting Rights Act, which lent federal support to unimpeded voter registration across the South. Such acts argued for the primacy of purely political action. As Johnson put it after the House's passage of the Voting Rights Act, "We have been awakened to justice by the sound of songs and sermons, speeches and peaceful demonstrations. But the noiseless, secret vote will thunder forth a hundred times more loudly."[52] And yet Johnson would suggest time and again that songs and other art provided a template for voting and political action. "Right now," he declared, "the affairs of men are struggling to catch up to the insights of great art" (1965:406). As he put it when signing the Arts and Humanities Act, on September 29, 1965, "It is in our works of art that we reveal to ourselves, and to others, the inner vision, which guides us as a nation" (1965:1022). If art helped spur political legislation in particular, it was also the case that political legislation opened the way for the kind of full democratic citizenship that the arts uniquely captured. "It is only the free man who can strike away the bonds of convention and the claims of ideology in order to express the world as he sees it," Johnson declared. "Only when men and women are free can they shape the intensely personal vision which is the heart of the artistic enterprise" (1965:218).

Johnson reinvented the Democratic Party with the aid of his civil rights legislation on the one hand and his arts legislation on the other; support for African Americans and art each earned its pride of place within the party almost simultaneously, and often with a mutually reinforcing logic. There was the superficial fact that Johnson often linked African Americans and their culture with the arts legislation: he singled out Harlem congressman Adam Clayton Powell Jr. for special thanks when announcing the establishment of the NEA and the NEH and, at the 1965 White House Festival of the Arts, when plugging the programs, Johnson declared, "From jazz and folk song to the most complex abstractions of word and image, few parts of the world are free from the spreading influence of American culture" (1965:659). But more meaningfully, Johnson's tacit plea to the attending artists was that they see his commitment to the arts as part of his commitment to black political freedom. Confessing the "true meaning of this occasion," Johnson noted that he was using the presidency "to help move toward justice for all of our people, not simply because I believe it, but because American freedom depends on it" (1965:660). "By your presence," he told the assembled group, "you help in the struggle to liberate all the talent and energy which this nation has in such abundance" (1965:600). As Johnson saw it, nationally funded art helped liberate African Americans not simply by paving the way for valuable legislation—directed at securing political freedoms—but by representing in turn a freedom that obtained beyond the pale of federal action. African Americans received the largesse of the federal government, in Johnson's words, only "so far as the writ of federal law will run."[53] Something more was needed, something that might supplement federal action and, at the same time, transcend its terms altogether.

Art worked there, but it was cool: it would declare itself able to move citizens beyond the state's agency at the moment it (and they) became most dependent on that agency. In this respect, Johnson reproduced the New Critical truism that art became most political when transcending politics. "Your art is not a political weapon," he told his audience at the Arts Festival, "yet much of what you do is profoundly political" (1965:660). Artists and intellectuals supported by the state were "profoundly political" less in their support of particular bills or parties than in their commitment to an existential vision of how to resist the killing abstractions of the state. As Johnson saw it, artists and intellectuals "seek out . . . the terrors and cruelties of man's day on this planet" (1965:660). Presumably, these terrors and cruelties were "profound" when they spoke to a human condition that no federal law could ever alter; acknowledging them captured all that was most resistant to what William Sumner had once called "stateways."

Warren shared with Johnson the sense that these terrors and cruelties played out on internal terrain: they were existential in large part because they transposed social arrangements organizing "man's day on this planet" into putatively timeless psychic realities. Important to Johnson's civil rights legislation was his sense that "laws and governments are, at best, coarse instruments for remolding social institutions or illuminating the dark places of the human heart."[54] Warren embraced the same language and agreed that art should look inward, the better to confront and make peace with mental atavisms well beyond the reach of legislation. From this perspective, the struggle for integration took place in "dark places" of the human heart more than in public facilities and institutions. *Who Speaks for the Negro?* describes a civil rights activist for whom "the integration of the Negro into American society would be . . . a correlative of the integration of the personality" (*WS* 171); Warren consistently used this correlative. As he puts it in the subtitle to *Segregation* (1956), a social conflict is, unavoidably, an "*Inner Conflict.*" Having interviewed southerners about their views on Supreme Court–ordered integration, Warren prominently cites a girl from Mississippi who declares, "I feel it's all happening inside of me, every bit of it." That is the point: Warren's interviews, he reveals on the final page, are all part of "an interview with myself." Committed to "the reality of self-division," Warren's text declares that "division between man and man is not as important in the long run as the division within the individual man."[55] These divisions could not be legislated away any more than the terrors and cruelties of man's day on this planet could be. Warren's larger aim is to insist on the importance of making peace with one's inner darkness, but crucial here is his sense that "darkness" is both that which resists integration and that which needs to be integrated. Making peace with his inner darkness (his prejudice, for example), the white man makes peace with the dark-skinned individual he would deny. The metaphoric elasticity of Warren's internal darkness therefore might be said to encompass and unite two otherwise antithetical coalitions beyond the mind: those who would resist integration (southern whites) and those who need to be integrated (southern blacks).

An account of how and why art should matter to the state, Warren's *Democracy and Poetry* pursues this line of thought in light of what it calls a "dark inner landscape" (*DP* 78). The book began as the third Jefferson Lecture in the Humanities, a series inaugurated by the NEH in 1972 as "the highest honor the federal government confers for distinguished intellectual achievement in the humanities."[56] Lionel Trilling delivered the first lecture in the series, and the proximity of his to Warren's was appropriate, for Warren cites Trilling and develops claims long associated with his *The Liberal Imagination* (1950), which stresses the congenial mutuality uniting liberalism and what it calls "the deep places of the imagination."[57] Reactionary forces thrived in those deep places; as Trilling sees it, art matters because it cultivates and allows for social inclinations otherwise unacceptable to a technocratic liberalism. Poetry is invaluable to democracy, Warren similarly reasons, because it complements the "apparent inevitability of the scientific project" with "other kinds of knowledge" (*DP* 47). Warren's lecture sets out to fuse a recalcitrant and oppositional southern sensibility with a commitment to the greater grandeur of poetic knowledge—less to deny the liberal mandate for racial justice than to transpose that mandate into more ambiguous psychic registers. Poetry helps the state, he reasons, when it forces us to confront and accept "the deep, dark inwardness of [man's] nature and his fate" (*DP* 31).

Like many Southern Agrarians, Warren began his career compelled by I. A. Richards's separation of poetic and scientific knowledge into two discrete domains, one emotive and one referential. In the early 1930s, Richards's account of the differences between these domains confirmed the incommensurability of organic southern culture and the aggrandizing industrialism and bureaucracy of northern liberalism; Southern Agrarians like Warren feared that science was erasing poetry from the world in the same manner that the North was erasing southern traditional culture, built as it was upon the backs of black workers. More than forty years later—the triumph of science, industry, and bureaucracy seemingly complete—Warren initially appears intent on justifying that fear. Echoing *The Manchurian Candidate*, he describes "selves" as "gadgets of electrochemical circuitry operated by a push-button system of remote control" (*DP* 59). This vision reaches its apotheosis, he claims, in what Carl Jung calls "the idea of the State as the principle of political reality."

In Warren's view, "the moral responsibility of the individual, a mark of his selfhood, is 'inevitably replaced by the policy of the State,' and the 'moral and mental differentiations of the individual' replaced by 'public welfare and the raising of the living standard'" (*DP* 65). Such antipathy to the welfare state confirms the widely held view, expressed by Marcus Klein, that New Critics like Warren wanted poetry "grounded in a felt antiquity of manners and belief"—and not in anything resembling modern governance.[58] And yet Warren had received a very large stipend to speak at the behest of the state. And so despite his ominous tones, he reaches a conclusion more in line with Trilling's establishment liberalism than with the Southern Agrarians' traditionalist piety. Warren bows to "the proudest monument of our society: the overarching, interlocking, and mutually supportive structures of science, technology, and big organization." Indispensable, this monument feeds "the present population of the planet" (*DP* 43). Given this fact, democracy, like the research universities at which Warren taught, needed poetic knowledge "not in place of, but in addition to, scientific knowledge" (*DP* 47).

Freed from its fealty to antiquity and ancient wisdom—and, ostensibly, supported by some big organization—poetry could take on its properly Blakean form: as a demonic life force that balances an overweening Reason. In *The Marriage of Heaven and Hell*, one of William Blake's persuasive devils insists, "Energy is Eternal Delight"; though "calld Evil," energy is in fact "the only life."[59] For Warren also: Klein reads the New Critics as resisting "antinomian fervor" (101), but Warren's lecture declares that poetry—"really art in general" (*DP* xi)—best supplements democracy when expressing an "untamable energy." For Blake, being a "true Poet" meant understanding yourself to be, like Milton "of the Devil's party" (56). But that party constituted a loyal opposition: Warren's was an ultimately functionalist vision of bureaucracy and liberalism, in which otherwise anarchic energies captured in literature make peace with and become useful to the organizations that those energies seem initially to oppose. By these lights, literature served democracy by expressing what seemed most untamable.

Trilling suggested the properly racial implications of this project in his Jefferson lecture, when he spoke against "the posture toward colleges and universities which of recent years has been taken by the Department of Health, Education, and Welfare." He decried the governmental mandate "that institutions of higher education which receive government funds shall move at once toward bringing about a statistically adequate representation on their faculties of ethnic minority groups." He thinks this effort will erode "the belief that no considerations extraneous to those of professional excellence should bear upon the selection of [academic] personnel."[60] The surprising fact is not that the temperamentally conservative Trilling held such an opinion, but that he viewed the NEH as an appropriate sponsor of it. What better forum to denounce affirmative action, he appears to suggest, than an NEH lecture, itself an extension of the Great Society welfare liberalism he ostensibly means to call into question? Seen from one vantage, his lecture appears hostile to the inclusion of blacks in the university workplace; but seen from another, it clarifies what function blacks must serve. They serve white-collar work (and liberalism more broadly) not by taking a "statistically adequate" place within it but by representing a charismatic darkness beyond its lethally scientific commitment to statistics.

As Trilling saw it, a claim such as this was less an assault upon liberalism than a constitution of it—an example of how culture was uniquely capable of offering an otherwise bureaucratic liberalism the internal tension it so badly needed. Culture offered this tension most successfully, he reasoned, not when it denounced liberalism outright, but when it captured "dark" knowledge that liberalism otherwise sought to deny. Trilling's position was not, finally, that different from Johnson's, which associated African Americans with the NEA by way of suggesting that man's inner "darkness" could not be legislated away, that it should be given creative expression and appreciated as a force countervailing otherwise arrogant state agencies. Warren extended this dubious logic in suggesting that liberalism might profit from the very forms of racism that it sought to eradicate. The Great Society could do only so much; the drive to engineer racial equality in particular produced a reifying quantification of social life that needed charismatic offset. Providing this offset required moving back and forth between liberalism and existentialism; between a commitment to dark faces and dark psychic places; between finding the roots of racial injustice, if not of all injustice, in economic relations on the one hand and human venality, broadly conceived, on the other. Poetic culture offered liberalism the internal tension it so badly needed, Warren suggested, not by endorsing the drive toward racial equality (which Warren did, in his journalism), but by resisting it (which he also did, as a poet). His vision of why poetry mattered to a racially torn United States required understanding the ways in which the state-orchestrated project of integration called forth (and even called for) a deep, dark resistance. That *Democracy and Poetry*'s vision of this dark resistance is denuded of any explicit reference to race suggests how fully that text completes the New Critical laundering of black labor power, the transformation of constitutive economic relationships into mystified accounts of cultural power.

Copycats

Chandler Brossard's novel *Who Walk in Darkness* (1952) was one of the first to chronicle Greenwich Village's hipster scene. It's set toward the end of 1948. "That was the time when we gave parties which changed people's lives," Norman Mailer recalls. "The Forties was a decade when the speed with which one's own events occurred seemed as rapid as the history of the battlefields."[1] Brossard offers a more pessimistic account of the relation between private and public events. His characters drift aimlessly between integrated bars, African American and Puerto Rican dance halls, and parties at which "dead-faced hipsters" mingle with bebop musicians.[2] All endeavor to be "really very hip" (80). This requires attention to the minutiae of personal style; even "the way you walk says a lot about you. Like your handwriting" (146). Bernard Wolfe recalls that time and place in similar terms:

> The first thing the Village insisted on was that nobody be defined in terms of where he came from, or of what he did. . . . All the same, you did get to be known as this rather than that. You took on an identity from the stride you showed as you walked down the main drags, the laxness with which you occupied a space on a Washington Square bench, the angle at which you tipped your beer mug, the frankness or sneakiness with which you eyed passing girls. You were . . . what you added up to in your day-to-day stances and gestures, your style at a bar, your bearings on the streetcorner, the sum total, in short, of your impacts on eyes and ears.[3]

Like commodities in shop windows, Wolfe's hipsters anxiously distinguish themselves from each other, and present themselves as alluring objects with no past.

In a similar fashion, the efforts of Brossard's characters to be "this rather than that" result less in self-expression than variations on a generic ideal. Being yourself, the Villagers announce, makes you an "underground man," a representative "spiritual desperado" (81). This "New Man," they speculate, "acts any way he feels like acting. Nothing is either good or bad, dignified or undignified. There's no experience he's not capable of having. He is completely mobile" (46). Curiously, though, this mobility doesn't produce a variety of experience; quite the contrary, it leads to, and in some sense springs from, a blank indifference. Though ostensibly differentiated in their personal styles, these New Men care little about anything—let alone the difference between Republicans and Democrats. When somebody asks the first-person narrator Blake Williams what he believes in, he responds, "Not an awful lot." He does "believe in eating and sleeping" (136) and would like to believe in love, but doesn't. "And what about politics," he's asked. "Don't you think one party is better than another?" Blake responds flatly, "I don't care about politics" (137).

Published one year before Brossard's novel, David Riesman's *The Lonely Crowd* emerged from similar conversations. Just before Riesman wrote his famous study, he was conducting research designed "to grasp the sort of communication that went on in a political survey." What did it mean, he wondered, for a respondent to answer "don't know" when asked to supply a political opinion? It's tempting to read *The Lonely Crowd* as a condemnation of this kind of answer, if not of the rudderless apathy on display in Brossard's novel. Riesman lauds the Romantics for having understood the nature of the process by which, as Jean-Paul Sartre later puts it, individuals "choose themselves." But he decries the betrayal of this process by "other-directed" personality types who are overly oriented toward reading and being read by those around them and are thus unable to identify their guiding convictions. The rise of this personality type had changed political life in deleterious ways; describing a bygone "inner-directed era," he recalls how once "leaders went into politics to do a job . . . rather than to seek a responsive audience." The hungry pursuit of that audience had left the political scene with a "general lack of imaginative alternatives."[4]

But Riesman confesses that he himself is no more interested in imagining these alternatives than he is "directly concerned with the political as defined from the point of view of the state or from the point of view of the groups, parties, and classes into which the state is divided for purposes of formal political analysis." Nor, for that matter, is he interested in political opinions themselves. He is "concerned instead with the process by which people become related to politics, and the consequent stylizing of political emotions" (164). Politics is to Riesman a process in which individuals affiliate with those who feel as they do—not with those who feel a certain way about certain things, but rather with those whose affective propensities seem familiar. At the heart of this work, then, we find both an analysis, and an exemplification, of a profound shift in the conception of "the political." As Richard Pells put it,

> The intellectuals of the 1950s had transferred their attention from the substance of politics to styles of behavior, from the sharecropper to the suburbanite, from labor to leisure, from "conditions" to consciousness, from revolution to resistance.
>
> Behind this new rhetoric and outlook lay a new set of values. The planned, orderly, equitable nation envisioned by the Old Left gave way to an admiration for any signs of marginality, eccentricity, self-expression, and private indifference to public life. Alienation was no longer a problem to be surmounted, but a virtue to be nourished. The individual had to free himself, not from the chains of capitalism, but from the smothering embrace of "other people."

This last reference is to Riesman, of whom Pells writes, "The possession of power was for him largely a question of 'interpersonal expectations and attitudes,' emotions and self-images."[5] And indeed, Riesman's interest in "the political" amounts to an interest in political style, which he considers a powerful "sort of communication." Success or failure in political life, he thinks, depends on cultivating particular styles.

Riesman describes an "inner-directed" personality that he thinks characterized the principled and task-oriented ranks of the "old" Protestant middle classes, among whom were numbered small bankers and entrepreneurs, independent professionals, tradesmen, and technical engineers. He details a shift from this personality to the other-directed: workers in the service and media industries, the bureaucrats and the salaried employees swelling the office spaces of the nation's suburbs and corporate offices—all those whom C. Wright Mills had just called "white collar." When speaking of politics, Riesman exemplifies the other-directed character type in what he calls "the inside dopester." This figure gestures to what Brossard calls the "underground": for example, by equating opiates ("dope") and inside information. Ralph Ellison would later use "inside-dopester" (*CE* 248) to describe jazz aficionados, and throughout his famous study, Riesman portrays the inside dopester as a kind of hipster. In general terms, the figure's increasing prominence represents a shift from the centralized decision making of a previously dominant Protestant elite toward the dispersal of power between "marginally competing pressure groups"; these groups tend toward "tolerance" rather than the moralizing "indignation" (163) characteristic of the inner-directed. More specifically, the inside dopester possesses an "ability to hold his emotional fire" (181); he wants desperately to be "modern" and "up to date" (37, 49), in touch with the latest and most popular trends; he wants to "know the score" (181). At the same time, he aims "never to be taken in by any person, cause, or event" (182). Often "indifferent" to political issues, he is given to "varieties of fatalism" (185).

The inside dopester isn't hip in any conventional sense of the term; he moves within mainstream political venues and hardly considers himself part of an underground. But Riesman's language, like his emphasis on style, suggests an intimacy between the period's political elite and those disaffected from the corridors of traditional power. However square Washington suits appeared to Village denizens, and however irresponsible hipsters seemed to the officially elected and duly appointed, each would with increasing frequency make sense of itself through reference to the other. In this and the following two chapters, I argue that changes in the production and attribution of value to commodities mediated these constitutive engagements, and helped forge the interracial coalition that returned the Democrats to power in 1960. John F. Kennedy took advantage of important developments in advertising, like the dawn of the "creative revolution" and the rise of market segmentation, to generate political capital from the popular perception that he was hip. Put in Riesman's terms, Kennedy in this way exemplifies how political style had become an "important consumable" (185).

I anatomize the structure of that consumable in light of Wolfgang Haug's claim that commodities extend to prospective consumers the promise of an alluring "second skin" and, more broadly, I examine the ontology of the chimerical secondary body offered by advertising at the end of the fifties. Riesman thought advertising unimportant sociologically. "Isn't is possible," he asks, "that advertising as a whole is a fantastic fraud, presenting an image of America taken seriously by no one, least of all by the advertising men who create it?" (228). Oriented toward people and styles, the other-directed, he thinks, are "simply unable to be as materialistic as many inner-directed people were" (229). Riesman presumes that "other people" are categorically unlike commodities, just as he presumes that ads require the unadulterated credence of those whom they address: like Brossard's hipsters, the other-directed possess a "consumer sophistication" (229) that leaves them immune to the siren songs of ads. But in the novels below, consumer sophistication, no less than literary sophistication, requires understanding bodies as exchangeable goods and refusing to distinguish between the authentic and the fraudulent. Fraud functions as an integral component of commodity and literary aesthetics, less the betrayal of a promise than a constitutive element of an endlessly innovative capitalist reality. For these novelists, hip expresses that reality at its most dreamlike when, extending a transporting if transient fiction, it urges consumers *cum* voters to imagine themselves, and their elected representatives, possessed of chimerical bodies necessarily not their own.

"A new way of looking at literature"

When asked if he thinks one party better than another, Blake answers, "If you really want to know, I think most of the people who have all this so-called political consciousness are all kidding themselves. They do it because they can't do something else they really want to do" (137). It's hard to take Blake at his word, in part because he devours the news throughout the novel, in the *Times*, *Life*, *Time*, the *Nation*, the *Atlantic*, and the *Journal American*. But even if we grant his lack of interest in establishment politics, it's impossible to overlook his peer group's preoccupation with the racial dynamics of what Brossard calls "the scene before us" (55). Blake's love interest, an Italian American named Grace, bitterly complains, "Democracy. What a laugh. . . . You don't know how lucky you are being an Anglo-Saxon" (190). Comments like these suggest that Brossard's characters displace their interest in political parties onto a different kind of "political consciousness." "That lousy status business again," one character complains. "Nobody can forget it, even for a minute" (235). What nobody can forget, above all, is that status is distributed unevenly among different racial groups.

Three years after Brossard's novel, Richard Hofstadter explained the significance of this kind of perception. "We have, at all times," he writes, "two kinds of processes going on in inextricable connection with each other: *interest* politics, the clash of material aims and needs among various groups and blocs; and *status* politics, the clash of various projective rationalizations arising from status aspirations and other personal motives."[6] Hofstadter means to explain "the pseudo-conservative political style" (95)—what he would later call "the paranoid style"—in American politics. He thinks that ethnic groups rapidly

gaining and losing social status were remaking the American right. In particular, he thinks "Anglo-Saxons are most disposed toward pseudo conservatism
when they are losing caste" (86). Previously assured that their cultural values
and styles were central to the nation, Hofstadter's reactionary Anglo-Saxons
bitterly resent the waning of their status relative to other ethnic groups perceived to be rising at their expense.

Grace thinks Blake lucky to be Anglo-Saxon. But it's not clear that Blake is
lucky, because if being an Anglo-Saxon removes him from certain kinds of overt
prejudice beyond the confines of the Village, it also hinders his ability within
the Village to enter the underground, and subjects him to physical danger. Brossard's characters are based on his circle of that time: William Gaddis appears as
Harry Lees, Milton Klonsky as Max Glazer, and Anatole Broyard as Henry Porter. Lees is conspicuously affluent and, with Blake, the only Anglo-Saxon in their
circle of friends. He confesses to Blake, "I don't know when to take this underground business as a laugh or to take it as the real thing" (90). It turns out to be
the real thing: the Village is stalked by Italian gangs that target Lees because he
"had the style of the people who . . . ran the game in America" (22). At the end of
the novel, one of these gangs beats him close to death. Brossard's final lines find
Blake and Grace responding to this and the fact that the underground seems to
be closing in on them. "I'm scared," he confesses. "So am I," she replies (245).

The Italian gangs prey on African Americans as well. They're given to ter-
rorizing black men seen walking with white women, for example. But it's telling that in Brossard's topsy-turvy underground, Porter fears relatively little,
even though many think he's black. "People said Henry Porter was a 'passed'
Negro" (5), Blake reports in the novel's first sentence, suppressed in the original
publication because of legal threats from Broyard. When confronted by Lees on
this score, Porter reacts angrily, but without real concern. When Glazer walks
into the room and discovers the cause of his anger, he laughs and responds, "Is
that all?" (232). Blake, on the other hand, feels he must unearth Porter's "secret," even though he doesn't know what would follow from doing so. At one
point, he suggests that the rumor about Porter's Negro ancestry is "supposed
to explain the difference between the way he behaved and the way the rest of
us behaved" (5). But later, when discussing that ancestry with Lees, Blake confesses, "I don't know whether that is his trouble." Lees responds that his trouble
might be just the opposite, that he is "camouflaging" (214) that ancestry. This
exchange haunts *Darkness*, which can't decide what kind of difference being

black does or should make—or, analogously, whether to disdain or embrace the hip underground that it describes.

Seen in this light, *Darkness* is a transitional text, caught between two competing visions of status: a nativist ethos that defined the lost generation of the twenties and that stressed the importance of Anglo-Saxon racial purity, and an emulative, hip ethos that would during the fifties and sixties urge whites, and Anglo-Saxons especially, to embrace racial difference. Brossard's novel rewrites Ernest Hemingway's *The Sun Also Rises* (1926), the better to negotiate these competing visions. Porter is Brossard's Robert Cohn. Jake Barnes finds the Jewish Cohn distasteful because he lacks the stylized mannerisms of the Anglo-Saxon narrator; so too, Blake finds Porter uncouth. This similarity extends to the novel's romance plots. Emasculated in the war, Jake envies Cohn for having slept with Brett Ashley. Likewise, Blake covets Porter's girlfriend, appropriately named "Grace": he's galled that Porter should possess and take for granted what he does not deserve. But it's also useful to see Blake's relation to Porter in light of Barnes's relation to the second of the two racially marked men who sleep with Ashley. Barnes finds little to like in Cohn, but much to admire and emulate in Pedro Romero, a Spanish bullfighter who possesses an effortless and presumably innate sense of style. Possessing the right style is the goal of every character in *Darkness*, as it is in *The Sun Also Rises*. But in Brossard's novel, the minority you don't like and the minority you wish to resemble are one and the same: Brossard collapses Cohn into Romero, which is why, in addition to describing Porter as a student of the Jewish Max Glazer—the most conspicuously hip member of Blake's circle— he describes him, through Blake's eyes, as someone who appears "Latin" (5).

In a similar way, Brossard attributes Blake's fusion of passion and detachment to what would have been for Hemingway two incompatible sources: the stoic masculinity of the beleaguered Anglo-Saxon and the "Negro hipsters" (121) who people the novel. This overlay of source material captures what is to Scott Saul an emblematic feature of 1940s hip, which "effectively synthesized Anglo-American ideals of cool (exemplified in the existential loner—the detective, the gunslinger—who repressed emotion and resisted temptation 'in exchange for an unimpeachable reputation for straight talk') with West African ideals of cool as a form of 'relaxed intensity,' the ability to take part in community rituals with simultaneous passion and detachment."[7] But Brossard's novel doesn't present us with anything so smooth as an effective synthesis. Rather, the debate surrounding Porter's race directs our attention to a problem signaled by Brossard's title. How and to what extent does "darkness," or colors and their absence, signify racially?

On a double date with Blake, Porter holds forth on "primitive dancing" and describes the differences between Negroes and whites like himself. The dinner having concluded, Blake and his date take leave of Porter, who wants them to remain. Blake refuses and Porter says, sarcastically, "That is really white of you." Blake replies, "It isn't a question of color" (54). The retort is jarring, since it points in two potentially incompatible directions. Blake might mean to repudiate the suggestion that his failure to include Porter speaks in any way to Blake's own "whiteness"—that is to say, to those imagined qualities linked through the color white to his Anglo-Saxon heritage. From this vantage, the retort chastises Porter for his earlier racial discourse and suggests that acting well or badly has less to do with race than with a personal code of conduct. But the declaration "it isn't a question of color" seems also to locate those racial qualities that Porter imputes to Blake—and that he wishes to secure for himself in his search for a style—beyond appearance, such that they remain unavailable to Porter. Seen this way, Blake's retort puts Porter in his place: you may be able to pass for white, because you look white, but you will never actually be white.

The larger problem indicated by this confusion is that an individual's race has come to seem potentially subject to repeated abstraction and exchange, and thus something like a commodity. In *Darkness*, looking for a race is tantamount to looking for a style, and however much characters find their styles by rejecting the grasping world of consumerism, the passion with which they reject this world masks a deeper entanglement with it. Blake declares himself unwilling to participate in a commercial "rat race" (173); he collects unemployment checks from the government instead. At his last job, he proved unable to hide his sense "that the place was no good. I should have been smarter about it," he says, "but I was not interested in being smart that way" (8). He's particularly contemptuous of advertising, an industry that permeates this novel. Blake combs the newspapers, hoping to find "clean work" for which "you did not have to tell lies" (141). What he finds, instead, are countless ads for advertising copywriters (194). He won't consider such work. "Being an advertising-agency copywriter," he thinks, "that was the worst" (141).

At one point, an advertising executive sidles up to Blake and his friends in a bar, and showers them with free drinks. In exchange, he wants to learn the ways of hip—he's paid as much as he is, he explains, so he can conduct research in just such a manner. Is that a "jive expression"? he asks one of them. Blake can't tolerate such "buying in" (83). But the presence of the executive indicates the extent to which the novel's underground is already permeated with the logic of sales. Porter works in a publicity office (6); the local dealer doesn't buy and sell marijuana, he "promotes" (199) it. Blake himself appears to others as marked by advertising. Lees calls him "the Hamlet of the Underground" (47) because he can't decide if he should fully embrace the alternative world of his racially marked friends. Blake acknowledges that he's only "partly underground" (90) and therefore partly "traditional [and] middle-class" (169). Recognizing as much, Glazer dubs him "the Arrow Collar man of the underground" (85), a reference to the Jazz Age advertising campaign that popularized the sporting life of the vigorous Anglo-Saxon (and which Daisy Buchanan references in *The Great Gatsby*). Blake might be partly underground, but his collar is as white as the adman's.

Brossard described his novel as a "nightmare presented as flat documentary."[8] Much of this nightmare comes from Blake's sense not simply that advertising permeates his environment but that the perceptual inducements of commodities refashion his subjective life, even aspects of that life that promise to remove him from commodities. He spends his time reading and writing when not drinking with his friends. In constant need of money, he sells books he's already read. But he does so at a profit, because the value of those books has risen. The "paperback revolution" was just beginning, and many titles were still out of print.[9] "People missed books during the war," Anatole Broyard later recalled of the postwar Village. "Now there was time for everything, and buying books became a popular postwar thing to do."[10] Having missed the war for medical reasons, and amassed a library while others were fighting, Blake owns a valuable resource. At one point, he examines his shelf, trying to decide which books to sell. "It seemed funny to me," he thinks. "I had never thought of their paying off in just this way. What a laugh. I was glad now that I had put all that money in books when I had it. It was a new way of looking at literature. Not how good is the book going to be. How much can you get for it when you have read it. That is the point. You had to think of these things" (92). Almost despite himself, Blake is in business. But what kind of business is this?

Wolfgang Haug helps explain Blake's "new way of looking at literature" in the context of advertising. In *Critique of Commodity Aesthetics* (1986), he delineates the basic process through which objects become commodities. Two people come together, a buyer and a seller, in order to make an exchange. As he has it, "non-owning need on the one side must coincide with not-needing ownership on the other. If those who have what I need do not need what I have, then they will not be interested in an exchange" (13). These conditions met, buyer and seller attribute a money amount to the object being exchanged. Thus "an abstraction is accomplished," as the agreed-upon exchange value "has detached itself from any specific commodity-body" and "become independent of any specific need" (14). The resultant differentiation of use value and exchange value is, he reminds us, one of the basic contradictions upon which capitalism is based. But Haug's ultimate interest lies in an extension of this contradiction, in which exchange value is still further separated from use value. He thinks a "double reality is produced" as advertisers disarticulate use value and "the *appearance* of use-value" (16). Commodities sell further abstractions of themselves; they promise their capacity to make more promises. Over the course of the twentieth century, he argues, advertising increasingly induces consumers to value not the prospect of an object's use but its ability to generate erotically alluring images that precipitate fantasies of further exchange. As Haug sees it, these images detach themselves from the actual body of the commodity and become what he calls its "second skin." This second skin appeals to consumers with "amorous glances" that promise the consumer a new body. And when the consumer takes on the commodity's second skin in place of his own, his "sensuality" becomes "the vehicle of an economic function" (16). From this perspective, Blake's "new way of looking at literature" involves perceiving its second skin, which is to say perceiving less its use value than "the *appearance* of use-value" promised by the further exchange of that literature.

Brossard's *Darkness* anticipates Haug's account of the commodity on an almost point-by-point basis. Coming from their double date with Porter, Blake and his companion arrive at Times Square, which is "crowded with thousands of people. They were walking slowly up and down. They overflowed the sidewalks" (54). Surrounded by these crowds, Blake observes the following:

> The Pepsi-Cola sign took up the north sky. In front of us a mammoth Ingrid Bergman in a suit of armor was charging on a horse. On my left a Union Pacific train was racing through the Rocky Mountains. In the eastern sky a giant mouth was blowing Camel-cigarette smoke rings over the square, over the crowds of people below.
>
> The thousands of lights were so bright they seemed to make a noise in the sky. But that was it. They were not. I felt something was missing in the scene before us. Then I realized what it was. There was no noise. It was all quiet. (55)

Missing here is any vestige of the labor required to produce the commodities that the advertisements sell. But this absence is overshadowed, if not in some sense replicated, by the more immediately palpable absence of any sound of the crowds that move around Blake and his companion. It's as if the spectacular and sensuous images that float above his head have, in their ability to suggest sound, replaced the bodies not simply of those who labor to produce commodities, but of those prospective consumers to whom the ads address their erotic appeals (Bergman an avenging virgin, a train pushing through mountains, smoke leaving puckered lips). These sound-bearing images are both the agent and object of a negation: "They were not." This sentence contradicts and at the same time renders more emphatic the claim that the lighted images were bright enough to make a noise in the sky. But the "they" also points to the next sentence: "I felt something was missing in the scene before us." That something is the crowd of which the narrator is a part, no longer entirely present and thus incapable of generating sound. The crowd has disappeared into the ads: in consuming, it has been consumed, though only for a moment.

The commodity, Haug explains, suspends a contradiction: it "is and is not what it is" (36). Brossard's vision of consumption temporarily suspends consumers in that contradiction. Thus the two short sentences in the second paragraph— "But that was it. They were not"—form a faulty echo: they register a loss. With the first word in the first sentence, "But," Blake both indicates and takes exception to his initial perception that the lights "seemed to make a noise." The object of this indication and exception, "that," points toward a moment of synesthesia and suggests the movement of his mind's eye and ear into the perfect second skin of the assembled images. However, this moment can only be pointed toward; it cannot fully be nominated. And it must be transitory. Indeed, we might say that Blake inhabits that promissory second skin, and experiences the lights making a noise, in the fraction of time between the sound of his first sentence ("But that was it") and its faulty echo ("They were not"). We might say that, in this fleeting moment, "he" and the crowds around him are indistinguishable from a "they" that refers to lights, sounds, and crowds, all together for a moment.

The woman accompanying Blake is a professional model and the two are headed back to her apartment, where Blake will repeat in more literal fashion the substitutive dynamic just delineated: he will disappear into her capitalized and spectacular body in the same way that he and those around him have just disappeared into the advertising images in Times Square. She's "perfect looking" (48) and Blake realizes that he's seen images of her in magazines and newspapers. She confesses that she's not sure if she's good at her job, but tells him that she makes a lot of money. Blake thinks she must be "good" because he thinks money "a good enough measuring stick" (57). Talk of money functions as foreplay. "Don't blame me if people pay a lot of money for something I happen to have," she says. "I'm not blaming you for anything. I'd like to make half of what you do," he replies. Her answer: "Why don't you make me, instead?" (58). And make her he does: her body is made of money, and he proceeds to lose himself within it. After coitus, Blake records a confusion of her body and his. "I lay on my back," he writes, "feeling her smoothness on my skin." He feels her skin on his skin, which is to say he feels her skin, the promissory second skin of the commodity form, as having in some sense become his skin. He has been made, as well.

This moment mimes in physical form the passage of Blake's mind's eye and ear into the impossible space of Times Square. Given new existence by the model's second skin, he is reincarnated but hollow. "I felt lonely and sad and empty. I had died the little death and now I was alive again" (58–59). Blake takes on and in some sense dies into the second skin of an advertising image, and his dubious rebirth elaborates his earlier experience: beneath the lights in Times Square, he momentarily experiences the promise that light might be heard, or that sound might be seen; in the model's apartment, he experiences that promise again, when she puts on a jazz record before beginning her seduction. They first listen to a record by "Danny Blue," whom Blake hears "blowing on and on and up and up, blowing one variation after another variation on what he had been blowing, getting hotter and faster, more alone in what he was doing, until I thought he was going to come right off the record. He flipped his wig when he was finished and they took him to a sanitarium" (57). The crescendo of frenetic but isolating energy anticipates what is to come: as Blake and the model make love, Dizzy Gillespie plays in the background. Afterward, as Blake lies in bed, feeling increasingly empty and lonely, the record repeats and repeats on the phonograph, until he flees the apartment in a panic.

The musical shift is telling. Danny Blue references Buddy Bolden, the legendary cornet player often credited with inventing the style of play later taken up by Joe Oliver, Freddie Keppard, Bunk Johnson, Louis Armstrong, and the many who followed. Bolden left no recorded music behind, however, and spent the second half of his life in an asylum, where he died penniless and unknown (jazz journeyman "Danny" Barker, married to singer "Blue" Lu Barker, started but never finished a biography of Bolden). As if to enact the advent of Bolden's era-sure, the music of Brossard's Danny Blue (the name a concatenation of Bolden's would-be biographers) gives way to the recurring sounds of Gillespie, who functioned in the late forties as an easily recognized and endlessly copied tem-plate of hip. In Michael Ondaatje's rendition of Buddy Bolden, *Coming Through Slaughter* (1976), the musician exists in a turn-of-the-century New Orleans long since "obliterated by brand names"; by the time of Brossard's novel, Gillespie was himself one such brand name.[11] In 1946, *Down Beat* complained that

> musicians wear the ridiculous little hats that have been seen around lately be-cause Dizzy wears one; musicians have started to laugh in a loud, broken way because that's the way Dizzy laughs; musicians now stand with a figure "S" posture, copying Dizzy who appears too apathetic to stand erect—and so on down the list. Surely this *copycatism* accomplishes nothing for the Dizzy fan, but, just as surely, it does Dizzy much harm.[12]

Blake experiences this harm as his own. Brossard juxtaposes Blue's agonizing anonymity and madness—which seem here the mark of authenticity—with Gillespie's oft-replicated style. In fact, the music in the apartment changes, seemingly on its own, from Blue to Gillespie, at the precise moment that the two start discussing the model's salary. What follows amounts to something like the mass production of Gillespie's sound within the apartment itself: Blue's music builds such that Blake thinks the musician is "going to come right off the record"; Gillespie's repeats again and again, becoming not less but more like a record, a broken record, losing its singularity in a mechanistic reiteration and becoming in the process more recognizably a commodity.

Brossard's two musicians also possess different kinds of color. Though leg-ibly a reference to Bolden, a black musician, Blue seems to have slipped the coils of his race, by way of Brossard's literary mediation: his name conflates the color blue, the musical origins of his sound, the blues, and the condition of being blue that leads him to an asylum. Gillespie is more recognizably the kind of black that hipsters wanted to appropriate, and Brossard views that color as the color of the imaginary second skin that Gillespie provides his listeners. Brossard thus countermands the cliché, common in writing about jazz, that, in the words of Andrew Ross, "commercialized music = whitened music."[13] This formula dominated popular accounts of bebop that saw the music corrupted by its entrance into mainstream markets. For Brossard, however, bebop colors the skin black just as the commodity does. If Blake dies a figurative death while entering the model's body, he emerges from this process only half alive, mechanically animated, and blackened, by the music that he hears: Gillespie's sounds replace the evacuating silence of Times Square and give Blake a substitute and racially marked body, as if in fulfillment of the promise extended there.

Blake's body disappears, and is replaced, in a way that recalls Anatole Broyard's "A Portrait of the Hipster" (1948), which Brossard later republished in a collection of essays on life in Greenwich Village, *The Scene Before You* (1955). Broyard's hipster presides over a series of removals. Broyard likens bebop to a form of "synthetic cubism" in which "specific situations, or referents, had largely disappeared."[14] Most immediately, the hipster presides over the disappearance of language. In *The Sun Also Rises*, Jake Barnes finds himself imitating the English "upper classes," which have "fewer words than the Eskimo." The English "talk with inflected phrases," he thinks, and use "one phrase to mean everything."[15] This linguistic reduction signifies upper-class breeding and is thus different in kind from the total silence, imposed from above, of a "nigger drummer" whose scat Hemingway registers only as absence: ". . . . . ." (70). As Broyard saw it, the argot of hip fell somewhere in between Hemingway's aristocracy and drummer. It consisted in at most "a dozen verbs, adjectives and nouns." This was a common view, reiterated in the 1959 essay "Cool," by Robert Reisner, who claimed, "The entire vocabulary of hip consists of perhaps three hundred words and phrases, but one word can be used in many ways."[16]

Broyard's hipster also does away with bodily expression. He describes the hipster's frequent use of "metonymy and metonymous gestures," in which simplified acts refer to more complex ones no longer visible, like, for example, "brushing palms for handshaking [and] extending an index finger, without raising the arm, as a form of greeting" (114). Broyard believes that the hipster's art of reduction takes its cue from bebop, which taught the hipster how to be an "ironical" master of "second-removism." As he sees it, "That which you heard in bebop was always something else, not the thing you expected; it was always negatively derived, abstraction *from*, not *to*" (116). At the end of the day, however, Broyard thinks these forms of abstraction compensatory for an already existing condition of physical loss. He describes the hipster as one who feels acutely the absence of his body. "The hipster was really *nowhere*," he writes, and longed "to be *somewhere*," in just the way that "amputees often seem to localize their strongest sensations in the *missing* limb" (113). Writing six years after Broyard, Norman Mailer would declare, "The only Hip morality is to do what one feels whenever and wherever possible" (*A* 354). Mailer's was an uncomplicated account of feeling: hipsters wanted what they wanted, and acted accordingly, especially when it came to sex. Broyard, on the other hand, suggests the emasculation with which we associate Jake Barnes: the hipster feels what he cannot feel; he experiences his strongest sensations in the part of his body that is not there. In a similar way, Blake's capacity to feel is dispersed across the surface of his imaginary skin. Standing in Times Square, he experiences spectacular advertisements as if they were his own second skin, even as he experiences the loss of his literal body. This skin has nothing inside it. "I just feel empty all the time," he says (38). Analogously, Broyard's hipster experiences his body as if he were not inside it—as if he could feel the hollowness of the phantom skin into which he has been displaced.

It's not clear what's inside these skins. Brossard's Village, like Wolfe's, is uninterested in interior states. "You were," to recall Wolfe, "what you added up to in your day-to-day stances and gestures, your style at a bar." Blake asks Grace, "What do you see in Porter?" (189). She doesn't see a Negro, insofar as Porter doesn't look like one, and she's not interested in any account of his racial origins, or interiors. This might appear to confirm the enlightened politics of the scene. Blake accuses Lees of being "too color conscious" (188), perhaps, because he thinks that being part of the underground requires a refusal to see race, and a commitment to seeing people as they truly are. The Italian gangs, for example, are "so far underground they don't need eyes any more" (14). But to put matters this way is immediately to see a problem, and this not simply because the gangs are violently racist. Not having eyes means seeing color in metaphoric terms; it means being race conscious in the presence of language about bodies that are absent.

The Color of Silence

Speaking of her feelings for Romero, Jake Barnes tells Ashley, "You'll lose it if you talk about it" (249). Such claims resonate with writing about hip, especially insofar as they seem to oppose language to bodily experience: talking, Barnes suggests, comes at the cost of an inexpressible physical sensation. One of the first white hipsters to commit his adventures to the page, Mezz Mezzrow announced in 1946 that hip requires consciousness of "the fraud of language." Twelve years later, the argot of hip now fully entrenched in popular culture, an episode of *Peter Gunn* directed by Blake Edwards finds a musician named "Streetcar Jones" describing a dead bebopper who "could never dig the original sounds." Gunn asks him to speak a language he can understand. "Semantics," Streetcar replies. "Sometimes words are a drag." In fact, according to Herbert Gold in 1960, "I'm hip" meant "no need to talk. No more discussion." As he saw it, "the language of hipsterism is . . . a signal for silence."[17] But this was an equivocal signal, one that promised release from the body at the moment that it became preoccupied with that body. The zero-degree affect to which Barnes aspired, like the metonymic reductions that Broyard described, constituted a quieting of the body, a minimization and mitigation of its ostensible presence.

We might read these silencing pleas in light of what Theodor Adorno, following Georg Lukács, calls "reification." For Adorno, "all reification is forgetting: objects become purely thing-like the moment they are retained for us without the continued presence of their other aspects: when something of them has been forgotten."[18] Broyard's account of hip, for example, emerged in light of his strategic desire to forget something about his body. In his memoir of Greenwich Village at the end of the forties, Broyard stresses the role of "books" in a substitutive process that gives readers new bodies:

> It was as if we didn't know where we ended and where books began. Books were our weather, our environment, our clothing. We didn't simply read books, we became them. We took them into ourselves and made them into our histories. While it would be easy to say that we escaped into books, it might be truer to say that books escaped into us. Books were to us what drugs were to young men in the sixties.[19]

This rhapsodic nostalgia records more than the fact that Broyard used books to effect the personal reinvention that Wolfe thought endemic to the Village. He was escaping into books, and allowing them to escape into him, because he was selling them. Broyard would spend seven years working for the advertising agency of Ricotta & Kline before becoming a book critic, essayist, and editor for the *New York Times*, where he worked for almost twenty years. But before holding any of these jobs he ran a bookstore in the Village. Start-up funding for this bookstore came from money he made on the black market in Tokyo during the Second World War—which Brossard obliquely records when Blake reads of Senate hearings convened to investigate wartime profiteering. Having returned from the war, Broyard was to books what a later generation was to drugs: a dealer.

He used his Tokyo money to enter the book business as if it were "the black market of personality" (46). For Broyard, being a dealer in books meant being a dealer in the imaginary second skins (or racially marked personalities) that he thought they provided. This much we learn from the story he tells of how he first decided to open a bookstore. While serving as an officer in a stevedore battalion on the docks in Tokyo, he oversaw efforts to "scrape a solid crust of shit off a dock a quarter of a mile long" (27). Watching "boxes of condensed milk" swing down on pallets from ships onto surfaces being cleaned of their dark residuum, Broyard thinks not simply of opening a bookstore, but of how such a venture might enable him to "trade in my embarrassingly ordinary history for a choice of fictions. I could lead a hypothetical life. . . . Nobody in the Village had a family. We were all sprung from our own brows, spontaneously generated the way flies were once thought to have originated" (29). But not even Kafka's insects are spontaneously generated, and most typically, flies breed in shit, the dark substance that Broyard removes, as if an epidermis, from the dock in Tokyo, as he sees floating through the air crates of alluringly white milk. Indirectly, Broyard associates the removal of that epidermis with the transcendence of his own family, which, though he makes no mention of this in his memoir, self-identified as African American. Broyard distanced himself from that family after he returned from the war and opened his bookshop. Having figuratively scraped his skin clean of its darkness, he treated literature as a kind of milk, finding sustenance in its capacity to enable metaphoric rebirth. "I want to be transfigured" (51), he told his psychoanalyst soon after the war. And so he was. Nearly all of his friends, and all of his children, knew nothing of his family's past until almost the moment that he died.[20]

Blake's "new way of looking at literature" owes much to Broyard, for whom a given book's use value and appearance of use value had become confused. Broyard made a living selling books and then a career and a considerable fortune selling his opinions of them. "We didn't simply read books, we became them": this was powerfully the case for him, not simply because his romantic evocations of the literary inspire a confusion between "where we ended and where books began," but because the racial transfiguration that resulted from that confusion allowed him to rise to prominence in what was at the time a bastion of white privilege.[21] Blake's relation to use value and the appearance of use value is surprisingly similar. We might say that the use of a given novel, like *The Sun Also Rises*, lies in the reader's amusement and instruction. But the second skin promised by such novel is something more elusive. A master of literary marketing, Hemingway confused his own skin with that of his novels; the author's bullfighting, boxing, and big-game hunting all lent the appearance of authenticity to his stories about the renewing power of bodily experience. Irving Howe thought Hemingway "the most influential novelist of our time," one "for whom life consists in keeping an equilibrium with one's nerves." This equilibrium evokes the equivocal consciousness of fraud that I attributed to commodity aesthetics. As Howe saw it, Hemingway branded a unique "moral style," a bodily dispensation that pretends "as if there were— the drama consisting in the fact that there is not—a secure morality behind it." If this "drama" derives power from its willful blindness, it also derives power from an equally equivocal commitment to embodied feeling. For Howe, the "gestures" and "manners" of characters in a Hemingway novel everywhere bespeak "the hope that in direct physical sensation . . . there will be found an experience that can resist corruption."[22] But only the hope: it's more accurate to say that Hemingway's fiction proceeded "as if" it could impart "direct physical sensation" to readers eager to feel what Hemingway once felt, and thus to assume a second skin that was in spirit his.

Brossard sells a version of this skin, even as he acknowledges that doing so constitutes a kind of literary profiteering, and makes him, if not "an advertising-agency copywriter," then at least a writer given to copying. Put simply, Blake's confession of literary arbitrage is Brossard's confession that bringing *Darkness* to market involves buying and reselling *The Sun Also Rises*. Brossard knew he was using Hemingway to advertise a Village underground that had not yet received novelistic treatment, and Blake's unease with advertising suggests his creator's awareness that the logic of sales permeates the scene before each of them. A moment such as this suggests the same: upon entering Times Square, Blake notes, "The smell of it was like the used smell of the subway. Only this was not underground. Or maybe it was. Maybe it was at that" (54). If the implication is that while not literally underground, Times Square is part of "the" underground, then it's equally the case that the underground partakes of the illusory advertising dreamscape that dominates the skyline. Brossard imagines himself reselling Hemingway's novel in order to ascend to this dubious firmament.

More precisely, Brossard understands himself to be selling the promissory second skin of *The Sun Also Rises*. What is the color of this skin? Insofar as it encourages emulation of the "moral styles" that Hemingway attributes to his most famous protagonist, *The Sun Also Rises* asks its reader to identify with and adopt the white skin of Jake Barnes, and by extension Hemingway himself. And yet, Jake's skin doesn't work, and its dysfunction is either a sign or the source of his sexual incapacity. Thus Hemingway's novel might be said to describe Jake's search for a new, sexually functional skin. He finds that skin in Pedro Romero, the young bullfighter whose elegant cape work in the ring captures the novel's ideal of literary style.[23] For Hemingway, both bullfighter and writer strive to "hold him tight": the bullfighter's imperative to keep the bull close to his body modeled the writer's imperative to keep the reader absorbed in physical experience.[24]

Jake can do this to a point: he understands the bullfight because he possesses "afición," which, he tells his friends, "means passion" (136); at the same time, his ability to experience passion for bullfighting contrasts sharply with his inability to experience sexual passion. In many respects, the former stands in for the latter, in just the way that Romero will stand in for Jake when he becomes Brett Ashley's lover. When Robert Cohn discovers that Romero is sleeping with Brett, he knocks Jake down at a café. Jake sits on the floor, unable to rise to the occasion. "I tried to get up," he recounts, but "felt I did not have any legs." Romero has vital legs. When Cohn knocks him down, this time in Brett's bedroom, "he kept getting up" (205). Cohn accuses Jake of pimping Brett because he understands that Romero is acting at Jake's behest, as his prosthetic phallus. To understand this fact is also to understand the novel's preoccupation with taxidermy. One of Jake's companions becomes obsessed with buying the stuffed hides of dead animals. "Simple exchange of values," he says. "You give them money. They give you a stuffed dog" (78). Jake accomplishes something like this exchange of values: he gives Brett to Romero and, in return, gets Romero's sexually operational skin, with which he is preoccupied. "I noticed his skin," Jake says of the bullfighter. "It was clear and smooth and very brown" (189).[25]

Jake's not so "simple exchange of values," in which he gives Brett to Romero and in return receives Romero's skin—a figure, I would ultimately suggest, for Jake's capacity to tell his story—models Brossard's literary arbitrage, in which he sees in books the personae that they offer readers and thus, as Haug would have it, their promissory second skins. Blake's "new way of looking at literature," then, in which he sees in books the possibility of future gain, is Brossard's way of looking at Hemingway's novel as an advertiser who sees the value of Romero's very brown skin. Like Jake, and presumably like Hemingway's readers, Blake is an embattled Anglo-Saxon who, though possessed of a stoic and seemingly self-sufficient personal code, finds himself longing for connections that require the mediation of a dark double—that require, in effect, a metaphorically brown second skin.

No doubt it mattered to Hemingway that the brown skin promised by his novel was European as opposed to African or African American. But for Brossard, the bohemian, underground literary commodity had since the twenties become a different kind of dark. It had become increasingly black—this because of and not despite the fact that those most eager for its promissory skin were white. If Blake is, by virtue of being Anglo-Saxon, half out of the darkness in which his friends walk, he is also half in it, a fact registered in his name, which evokes the word "Black." For Brossard, black and white are locked in a mutually defining embrace. Porter might be a "passed Negro," but he avidly studies black culture. He's a hall of mirrors whose claims to darkness depend upon corresponding claims to lightness. Blake notices "a black hipster" at a party and thinks to himself, "He was a nice looking boy. He had a slightly East Indian face. I tried to imagine what he would look like if he were white" (121). Something like this transposition takes place moments later when Porter faces the hipster on the dance floor and assaults him. Blake leaves the party as Porter and the hipster fight, each entangled in the other's arms; there's something in the scene before him he cannot see. Porter wants to be a white Negro, not a black hipster, and his figuratively black body seems to require violence toward a visibly black one. Blake no doubt intuits that this spectacle echoes his own battle with Porter: Blake wants to reveal Porter's "secret," and so destroy him, the better to consume (and subject to further exchange) the blackness that it signifies.

Blake flees the fight between Porter and the hipster with a wealthy gangster, who takes Blake and the model discussed above to an expensive restaurant. Blake thinks about the price of his food and listens to the model discuss the numerous clothes she wears while working. When Blake takes leave of the gangster, he thinks to himself, "He was all right. He was not square. Not like Goodwin" (139), the advertising executive. But this Hamlet of the Underground protests too much the presence of an adman learning jive, in part because he puts on and takes off his own white, Arrow Collar skin as readily as the model does her clothes. As we have seen, Blake views consumption itself as a process in which he sheds his skin and adopts another, ultimately black one.

Brossard's novel is typical of much postwar fiction, which departed decisively from fiction of the previous decade in its handling of race, labor, and consumption. Popular Front and working-class fiction of the 1930s often dwelt on the pathos of the laboring white body. When John Steinbeck's *The Grapes of Wrath* (1939) describes Tom Joad's body, "wet with sweat," we have no doubt as to the color of its skin. "Farm labor in California," Steinbeck predicted, "will be white labor, it will be American labor." This putative whiteness saved "labor," considered as an abstraction, from degrading working conditions. "White labor," Steinbeck continued, "will insist on a standard of living much higher than that which was accorded the foreign 'cheap labor.'"[26] But the sweat of prewar labor would become the sweat of postwar desire, most interestingly, if equivocally, in popular fiction that dwells on the pathos of a laboring black body that is, also, a consuming body. The black figures conjured in some postwar fiction suggest to whites that to consume is to become black, simultaneously liberated from and enthralled to a capitalist economy at the moment of what looks like gratification. This doubling—in which blackness is at once a liberating escape from and a despairing confirmation of consumerism—is powerfully on display in novels about hip, like Brossard's, which derive their imaginary second skins from dark bodies ostensibly geared for physical pleasure, but possessed at the same time of a surprising affinity with death.

Alternately, a novel like Jack Kerouac's *On the Road* (1957) celebrates the laboring black body, and in so doing transforms it into an exchangeable product. Dean Moriarty hungers for "old-fashioned spade kicks," and asks, "What other kicks are there?" (252). He would sweat as black bodies sweat, kicking with pleasure. In one instance, while listening in a trance to a black jazz musician, Moriarty stands "oblivious to everything else in the world, with his head bowed, his hands socking in together, his whole body jumping on his heels and the sweat, always the sweat, pouring and splashing down his tormented collar to lie actually in a pool at his feet" (201). As Andrew Ross suggests, the sweat on the black musician's brow signifies in a potentially complex fashion: "It is the sweat of the vestigial minstrel clown (Satchmo's ever-ready handkerchief), but it is also the reminder of the sweat of slave labor. It is a comforting reminder to a white audience that labor exists, and is elsewhere, in a black body, but it is also a militant negation of the racist stereotype of the 'lazy' i.e. underemployed black male."[27] Kerouac's work holds this troubling complexity at bay, and understands Moriarty's imitative sweat as the expression of a will to pleasure. In fact, Sal Paradise experiences even the sweat of hard physical labor as an indulgence. Picking cotton for three cents a pound, Sal Paradise works alongside "an old Negro couple" who "picked cotton with the same God-blessed patience their grandfathers had practiced in ante-bellum Alabama" (96). At the end of the day, relishing his exhaustion, he sighs "like an old Negro cotton-picker" (96–97). But Paradise quickly quits this scene; he feels "the pull of my own life calling me back" (98). He wires his aunt for money and when it arrives he leaves picking behind. He wants to have had the experience of working as a black man: he works in the fields less to labor than to transform labor into a commodity he might buy.

Brossard endows his characters with the same freedom of movement that allows Paradise to quit picking cotton and move on to other pursuits. Those characters move in and out of the Village. "They tell me Africa is very nice," says Grace, in one of the novel's many gestures to Hemingway. "Wonderful," replies Blake. The two go on to dream of taking a cruise liner to South Africa, where they will "hire native boys" (177) to pick up diamonds that wash onto the beach. In *All the King's Men*, Willie Stark tells Jack Burden, "A diamond ain't a thing in the world but a piece of dirt that got awful hot." As we've seen, this reminds Burden that the white bodies of his landowning class make their diamonds from black bodies laboring in dirt—a fact which renders their white bodies black as well as white, as dirty as those of their workers. In *Darkness*, fantasies of affluence depend on black labor, but that labor seems no labor at all: rather than working mines, these native boys gather diamonds while strolling on the beach.

This whimsy elides concrete relations: considered as a group, the black men living in postwar Manhattan from whom Blake and company borrow their styles faced unemployment rates appreciably higher than those of white males, dim prospects for more than physical labor, and a wage gap that was 68 percent in 1960 and widening.[28] *Darkness* doesn't show us hungry black men looking for work, or black men engaging in poorly compensated physical labor while looking for better work. It shows us "black hipsters" listening to or playing jazz. Blake and his circle see no more than this, because they are part of an underground, not part of an underclass. Possessed of white-collar skills and white skin, their dispossession is figurative, and temporary. When considering the rise in crime around them, Blake and Grace wonder whether they shouldn't just move out of the Village altogether. Brossard, Broyard, Klonsky, and Gaddis eventually did.

Deadpanning Democracy

Looking back from the vantage of the sixties counterculture, it's easy to view Blake's hip as an intimation of the popular sentiment, proclaimed by Charles Reich in *The Greening of America* (1970), that "the political activists have had their day and have been given their chance"—and have "failed." In 1966, *Time* reported, "Students once aflame with political causes are drifting toward the introspective life of psychedelic life and the beat life." The magazine quotes Berkeley assistant chancellor John Searle, who described this drift as "a move from the political culture to the hipster world."[29] But this antithesis belies the way in which, during the fifties, many viewed "the hipster world" organized by jazz less as an example of the "great refusal" than as an example of what "political culture" might ideally be.

Paul Anderson notes that "in the New Deal era," jazz came to be seen as "a uniquely democratic, pluralistic, and tolerant cultural form." The music was also, to some, tacitly socialist: in 1939, the *New Republic* wrote that Benny Goodman's integrated quartet—which featured Goodman, Lionel Hampton, Gene Krupa, and Teddy Wilson—was "a collective thing, the most beautiful example of men working together to be seen in public today." Jazz offered an arena in which, as Sterling Brown put it in 1945, "Negro and white musicians meet as equals to improvise collectively."[30] By the mid-fifties, critics were rushing to declare jazz a uniquely American and democratic form of collective labor. As Marshall Stearns put it in 1954, jazz "offers a common ground on which the conflicting aims of the individual and the group may be resolved." Two years later, Congressman Frank Thompson Jr. extended this logic: "The way jazz works is exactly the way a democracy works. *In democracy, we have complete freedom with a previously and mutually agreed upon framework of laws; in jazz, there is complete freedom within a previously and mutually agreed upon framework of tempo, key, and harmonic progression.*" In 1959, Willis Conover declared that jazz was "structurally parallel to the American political system." In 1960, the editor of *Down Beat* argued, "Jazz is democracy, that is freedom of expression of self, sometimes angry, sometimes exclamatory, with a social (the group members) and judicial (limit imposed by 'musical laws') structure."[31]

Almost from the moment that bebop found mainstream audiences, critics began to debate the particular nature of its appeal and the kinds of community that it might produce. The music's spirit of improvisation lent it an aura of restless social democratic idealism. Here was a collective activity in which a group of individuals seemed to organize themselves spontaneously, without the heavy hand of a leader. Indeed, to many, bebop seemed nothing like swing; critics rushed to note that it was polyrhythmic and played with asymmetrical phrasings, whole-tone scales, and flattened fifths; the drummer tended to keep the beat and maintain the music's often blistering pace on the top cymbals instead of the bass drum; solos and accompaniments were improvised in conjunction with each other, through extended chromatic harmonies. Amid this astonishing range of technical innovation, the musicians coupled a "hot" virtuosic style with a "cool" and detached demeanor. Many black musicians described this synthesis as part of an effort to develop a music that couldn't be stolen or imitated by pretenders and non-initiates. As Gillespie put it, bebop was meant to "scare away the no-talent guys." Nevertheless, the typically poker-faced affect associated with bebop's difficulty marked the hip styles associated with it. Philip Ford argues that the music of Miles Davis, influenced as it was by first-generation bebop, was "an instant signifier of hip" because it produced an aura of "nonchalant authority." The apparent ease of that authority reconciled the technical difficulty of bop to what Ford calls "the utopian, demotic, communitarian, and antielitist modes of the 1960s and 1970s counterculture."[32]

"Nonchalant" aptly describes the ambition; but "deadpan" more usefully captures the unanticipated costs associated with hip's incipient political culture. Deadpan facial expressions proved easy to copy, and thus provided one of many opportunities for the otherwise unlike to become, triangulated through shared fantasies of jazz, contingently alike. At the same time, fifties-era narratives of hip, like *Who Walk in Darkness*, suggest something more equivocal. Brossard's novel describes bodies rendered deathly by moments of consumption that promise transcendence: having consumed his model, Blake Williams listens to Dizzy Gillespie, and feels himself dead. His deadpan affect, in this moment, is less the vehicle than the product of the figurative bodily transposition implicit in his experience of Gillespie. Any metaphor, argues Paul Ricoeur, retains within it "ruins of the literal": the phrase "white Negro" conjures a new identity; but it also retains the lingering incompatibility of its terms. Blake experiences his body as a version of that ruin, as the incompatible remainder that haunts him after he passes into Gillespie's music, and the capitalized body of the model.

George Panetta's *Viva Madison Avenue!* (1957) elaborates this logic by situating hip in more explicitly economic and political contexts. Panetta chronicles the madcap adventures of George Caputo and Joe Caruso, two boisterous Italian Americans who work in one of New York City's largest advertising firms. Though they bear no resemblance to the gangs that stalk Brossard's Village, Caruso and Caputo imagine themselves at war with their coworkers, whose upper-class airs bespeak assumed privilege. George, the narrator, puts it simply: "It was us against the Anglo-Saxons."[33] We sympathize with their struggle to slough off the yoke of their antagonists. "The Anglo-Saxons owe us something," George announces, ". . . . something big—America, maybe—and me and Joe, scared as we are, are determined to get it" (250). Of course the joke is that, in a basic way, they've already got "it," insofar as their deferential coworkers think them hip. Panetta's WASPs are eager to apologize for themselves. The hard-partying George and Joe invoke their heritage to secure advantageous treatment from their colleagues, who scramble to demonstrate their lack of prejudice. Some invert the one-drop rule to claim they have Italian ancestors; "that's all the Anglo-Saxons needed," George reports, "just a drop, to make them noble" (145). Anglo-Saxons want to claim Italian blood, we're told, because they "have very little blood" of their own (121).

The protagonists are hip, ultimately, because they are "scared," and because, embattled, they are proximate to death in ways their antagonists are not. Though hip typically opposed the black skin of African Americans to the white skin of Anglo-Saxons, it didn't require blackness. Whites might style themselves hip by embracing Italian American styles or, as we will see at the end of Chapter 3, ancient Chinese culture and religion. But some suggested that white existentialists might style themselves hip simply by virtue of their preoccupation with the transient nature of their flesh. Published the same year as Panetta's novel, Norman Mailer's "The White Negro" argued that hip required an existential outlook: whites become white Negroes by imagining themselves subject to a sudden and arbitrary death, and by living with a "profound despair" (342) that distinguishes them from those who plan endlessly for the future.

Gripped by despair, George and Joe distinguish themselves from their Anglo-Saxon coworkers by viewing their bodies—and those of the consumers to whom they would sell—as simultaneously hypersensitive and senseless, alive and dead. Commissioned to film an episode for "the Brewery Television Theater" (145), they dramatize a man dying from an incurable brain disease. The sponsors want a transcendent "symbol" (160) that will leave people happy and eager to consume beer. The symbol must be ecumenical—it must produce a coalition out of diversity. As an advertising executive puts it, "Our audience is made up of all kinds, Baptists, Episcopalians, Catholics, Moslems, Jews. We don't want to do a Baptist miracle and then find out we offended the Catholics" (160–161). The sponsors want the sick man to survive his illness, the better to dramatize "plain human courage, without religion or anything" (160). But Joe broadcasts the drama with its original ending: the hero sits on a park bench, "his voice full of courage . . . like poetry," contemplating "how beautiful it was to die" (173)—and then dies. Here, Joe thinks, is a universal symbol. The episode is titled *Death in the Sun*, and thus invokes *Death in the Afternoon*, in which Hemingway insists that, in fact, death was the only truly universal experience. "Death," he writes, is "the one thing any man may be sure of; the only security . . . it transcends all modern comforts."[34] But Joe repurposes death (as Panetta does Hemingway) in order to sell a modern comfort (beer) and, it turns out, a flagging Democratic Party.

"The day President Roosevelt died," the narrator reports, "we wore black ties, and we cried, real tears" (209). The two remain fiercely loyal to Roosevelt's party because they think "the Democrats are better for people like us" (243). But George and Joe witness the erosion of their party's competitive edge. The narrative opens with their elation over Harry Truman's victory in 1948. Four years later, Dwight Eisenhower defeats Stevenson and brings with him "bankers, businessmen, chairmen of the board—people who were our natural enemies" (211). These enemies include the protagonists' thin-blooded coworkers, all of whom like their Ike. There are subsequent glimmers of hope. After Eisenhower's heart attack, "the Anglo-Saxons began to worry a little because they had visions of the New Deal coming back, and some of them were already talking of moving to Maine, where things like the New Deal never really reach" (212). Nevertheless, Ike recovers and for a second time defeats Stevenson, whom Panetta singles out for blame. Hemingway proves valuable in part because his hard-boiled populism contrasts with Stevenson's gentility. George and Joe complain to the local Democratic Party headquarters that Stevenson "should talk our language" and "say what he feels" (233). They are regular guys—two of many "poor people who were used to the simple talk of Roosevelt" (234)—and they're baffled by the candidate's lofty literary rhetoric. The candidate doesn't get that the party is, like the potential consumer base of beer drinkers, "made up of all kinds." They want evidence of "plain human courage," not frippery. "We don't understand a word he says," they say of Stevenson. "He's too literary"

(237). Hemingway's hard-nosed existentialism, however, redeemed the literary for selling products on the one hand and Democrats on the other.

Mailer used Hemingway in an analogous fashion. As he saw it, Hemingway defined "the categorical imperative" at the heart of hip: what made the adventurer "feel good became therefore The Good" (*A* 340). To Mailer, "the only Hip morality . . . is to do what one feels whenever and wherever possible." This was a consumer-friendly creed sprung from the likes of Jake Barnes, Nick Adams, and Frederic Henry: there are for Mailer's hipster "no truths other than the isolated truths of what each . . . feels at each instant of his existence" (*A* 354). Advertising executives didn't need Hemingway to sell these isolated truths but, Mailer believed, politicians did. Writing in the *Village Voice* one year before Panetta's novel, Mailer offered an unusual candidate for the election of 1956: "Yes, it may seem a trifle fantastic at the first approach, but the man I think the Democrats ought to draft for their Presidential candidate in 1956 is Ernest Hemingway." His reasoning was simple: "There is no getting around it—the American people tend to vote for the candidate who gives off the impression of having experienced some pleasure in life" (*A* 311). Papa's commitment to pleasure made him "one of the germinal influences of the birth of the hipster" (*A* 310) and endowed him with an ability to combat "the hopeless conformity that plagues us" (*A* 311). Unlike the implicitly feminine Stevenson, Hemingway said what he felt and felt like a man. No doubt he often felt like drinking beer.

More importantly, Hemingway buttressed an existential vision of why death mattered to a political world that might be saved by consumerism. Beneath its strident declarations about pleasure, and its prurient fascination with black sexuality in particular, "The White Negro" announced a new manifesto of liberal citizenship. It defined a pervasive anxiety gripping white America, which it traced to the threat of annihilation by atomic explosions and death camps. It then declared this anxiety commensurate with the fear experienced by African Americans that they might at any moment be subject to death at the hands of white supremacists. Though they were less than equal before the law, or indeed any contemporary political institution, Mailer's blacks and whites were equal before death—and, by extension, equal because similarly subject to the disembodying procedures of capitalism, in which the laboring body disappears, in a figurative death, beneath the abstract exchanges required in the production and sale of commodities. To Mailer, the death camp that incinerated bodies but kept hair and teeth suggested capitalism's capacity to extract exchangeable value from laboring bodies. From this vantage, living with death is, for Mailer, a metaphor that both recalls and obscures lost labor: his hip bodies die as the empty husks of workers, and live as consumers who ingest social relations reified, transformed into relations between things.

Mailer figured his own body as similarly doubled when he reframed "The White Negro" with the "self advertisements" that structure *Advertisements for Myself.* "The way to save your work and reach more readers is to advertise yourself," he announced (*A* 21). Advertising yourself meant sacrificing yourself. "*The shits* are *killing us,*" he opined, referring to the "little institutional lies from the print of newspapers, the shock waves of television, and the sentimental cheats of the movie screen" (*A* 23). But, preoccupied as it consistently is with narration that issues from corpses, *Advertisements* suggests that Mailer was already dead. Immanent within this collection, we find the ghost of a slave mortified by a commercial world he could not escape. Imagining himself free of a once-constraining body, Mailer as hipster cannot but imagine the death of that body. Hence the alternating elation and dread that permeates his hip and, especially, its encounters with the commodity form. Even as it offered a transporting escape from once-constricting racial categories, his hip seemed, equally, a remanding into a more totalized prison.

In It to Win It

No liberal politician could run on Mailer's vision. But Mailer thought that John F. Kennedy came close to doing so, by way of Hemingway. Published the same year as "The White Negro" and Panetta's novel, the senator's *Profiles in Courage* begins like this: "*This is a book about the most admirable of human virtues—courage.* 'Grace under pressure,' Ernest Hemingway defined it." Kennedy continues, "A nation which has forgotten the quality of courage which in the past has been brought to public life is not as likely to insist upon or reward that quality in its chosen leaders today—and in fact we have forgotten." Kennedy would recall the nation to its lost courage, even or especially when doing so involved cultivating, as he thinks it did for John Quincy Adams, "an unbending will" before "death."[35]

By the time Adlai Stevenson received his second nomination, there were stirrings that intimated the eventual appeal of Kennedy's language. During the fifties, the party had urged its upwardly mobile voters to look past dollar signs and toward the sweetness and light that might be theirs. "It isn't just social *secu-*

rity we want," Stevenson declared in 1956. "We want a chance to be somebody." As he had it, "free society cannot be content with a goal of mere life without want. . . . Now that physical security has been so very largely achieved, we are reaching out for more spiritual values, for better quality in our living, for a higher purpose and a richer life."[36] To many, this seemed too ethereal by half, and out of step with young voters. In his introduction to *The Fabulous Democrats* (1956), House Majority Leader Sam Rayburn declares that it is as "essential for the prosperity of a political party to improve its 'product' as it is for a commercial corporation to improve what it sells." In the same breath, as if to reassure that packaging the Democratic Party would make it more rather than less current, he adds that none who cared to look would "find any old fogies among us. Nor will you find what is still worse—young fogies."[37] The party, Rayburn all but announced, was hip. But his language betrayed him, as did the party's candidate. *The Fabulous Democrats* failed to convince voters that the famously "egg-headed" Adlai Stevenson was not a fogey.

Kennedy was an easier sell, and in 1960, on the eve of the presidential contest between Kennedy and Richard Nixon, Mailer set out to convince the American public that the Democrats had in fact improved their product, in a widely read *Esquire* article titled, appropriately enough, "Superman Comes to the Supermarket." Arguing on behalf of Hemingway's candidacy, he had speculated four years earlier that the ideal presidential candidate for the Democrats "must of course be Hip, and yet not display himself unduly as a hipster" (*A* 310). As we've already seen, in his *Esquire* article, Mailer dubbed Kennedy "the Hipster as Presidential Candidate"; Mailer thought the candidate had just enough "patina of that other life, the second American life, the long electric night with the fires of neon leading down the highway to the murmur of jazz." Compelled by the evidence, he added, Kennedy "was In" (54).

In part, Mailer thought Kennedy "In," and able to compete in the supermarket of American public opinion, because he kept death before him at all times. For Hemingway, in *Death in the Afternoon*, violent death was "one of the simplest things of all and the most fundamental" (2). Embracing this reality promised unique benefits: "The matador," Mailer reasons, "living every day with death, becomes very detached, [and] the measure of his detachment is of course the measure of his imagination" (56). Kennedy was Mailer's matador. The candidate possessed the detachment of one who had confronted his own violent death. "Kennedy's most characteristic quality," Mailer writes, "is the remote and private air of a man who has traversed some lonely terrain of experience, of loss and gain, of nearness to death, which leaves him isolated from the mass of others" (48). He thinks the candidate "a man who has lived with death, who, crippled in the back, took on an operation which would kill him or restore him to power" (44).

The prospect of Kennedy's victory thrilled Mailer because it suggested that the nation was on the verge of embracing the renewing power of existential bravery over the tedium of what he called "housing projects of fact and issue" (27). In fact, he thought that Kennedy's isolating experience amplified "the murmur of jazz" that accompanied him: the "patina" of America's second life was, to Mailer, black by virtue of its proximity to death. Mailer later extended this association in *Miami and the Siege of Chicago* (1968), which views politicians as hipsters because of their exposure to the violence that he had long since associated with bullfighters and African Americans. Since Kennedy's assassination, "major politicians—no matter how colorless, they all had hints of charisma now that they were obviously more vulnerable to sudden death than bullfighters, and so they were surrounded with a suggestion of the awe peasants reserve for the visit of the bishop—some rushed to touch them, others looked ready to drop to their knees."[38] To Mailer, the hint of death transformed the otherwise "colorless" into the implicitly black. Kennedy shimmered with the patina of jazz because he was cloaked in a second skin, and Mailer wanted a victory for Kennedy because he thought that skin might cover the Democratic Party's ethnic coalition.

But what did it mean for Mailer to declare that Kennedy "was In"? In where, or what? Calling someone "in" leaves unspecified the social group or political entity with which the preposition establishes a relation, while at the same time suggesting that such a group or entity might coalesce or come into being around that individual. Riesman's *The Lonely Crowd* captures something of this equivocal reciprocity in its account of the shifting hall of mirrors between crowds and individuals, each of which forms around the other. Riesman's "inside dopester" is a cipher, a conduit for a range of emotions borrowed from those around him, which is to say borrowed from the crowd that those around him constitute. Missing the internal "gyroscope" that characterizes the inner-directed, he develops "radar" that registers the emotional states of those around him. The sum of these states, he personifies the social whole. The inside dopester thus turns his skin inside out; so good is his radar that his innermost emotions track those of the social totality that he anxiously scans, to the point that what is inner and what is outer lose distinction. The other-directed in general, Riesman writes, have internal crowds "implanted early" (21) in life. These implanted crowds, he avers, have been getting bigger:

> There has been a general tendency—facilitated by education, by mobility, by the mass media, toward an enlargement of the circles of empathy beyond one's clan, beyond even one's class, sometimes beyond one's country as well. That is, there is not only a great psychological awareness of one's peers but a willingness to admit to the status of peer a wider range of people, whether in one's own immediate circle or vicariously through the media. The problem for people in America today is other people. (xliii)

As an individual "admits" an increasingly wide range of people, he approaches the point at which his internal crowd is identical to the crowd that he and many like him together constitute. The crowd of Riesman's title is lonely because it cannot experience something other than itself; once all are in the crowd, there is nothing but that crowd. This collapse of what is in and what is out stems in complicated ways from Riesman's methodological assumptions. *The Lonely Crowd* studies "social character," a term that equates individual and group by way of Freud's application of individual to group psychology. Riesman borrows from psychoanalysis "the temerity to tackle whole cultures" (xxxvi) as if they functioned like isolated psyches. "Other direction" thus functions as both the premise and the logical conclusion of the decision to represent crowds and individuals as if they were each other's most natural and self-confirming vehicles. Committed at the start to the idea of social character, Riesman fortuitously "discovers" the near impossibility of distinguishing between individuals and the mass of "other people," both within and beyond themselves, to which they refer. From this vantage, the study is itself a symptom of the anxious adjustment between inner and outer reality that it describes.

More resigned to the loneliness in his title than Riesman is to the loneliness in his—and, ultimately, more apropos to Kennedy's election—Brossard describes hipsters in *Who Walks in Darkness* as taking their cues, and consequently their prosthetic skins, not from a crowd but from an increasingly spectacular world of promissory commodities. In Times Square, dazzling representations of those commodities absorb, transform, and render collective the many persons in the square—they constitute the new and shared body of the crowd. The circulation of these commodities changes what it means to be "in."

Looking out the window from their bebop party, Blake and Grace see a crowd of Italian hoodlums gathered on the street below. She asks Blake to guess what they are thinking. He responds, "That they are out and you are in" (125). Still, Blake's circle allows for forced entry. Max Glazer thinks Goodwin the advertising executive is "buying in" to their crowd with his money, but grants, "You get in however you can. In this case you buy in. One way is as good as another" (84).

Maybe so; but Mailer was convinced that Kennedy was in by way of Mailer's own writing. With one felicitous preposition, "In," Mailer conflated the assumption of presidential office and the attainment of the elusive social approbation captured by hip. Significant here is the fact that the word "in" finds its first use as a noun in the context of political office some two hundred years before it comes to function as an adjective, to describe the fashionable. The OED tells us that to be one of the "ins" meant, in the eighteenth century, to be associated with the party in power. It's not until 1960, the year Mailer writes his article, that being "in" comes to mean belonging to a select group defined by mercurial social codes rather than access to institutional power. Mailer's conflation of these registers turns on the particular properties of his preposition. To say someone is "of" the Democratic Party, for example, is to establish a metonymic relation between an individual and the group to which he belongs. "Of" points to what Broyard calls a "*somewhere*." But when used without an object, "in" creates a *somewhere* from a "*nowhere*." To say that someone is "in" is to leave unspecified the social group or political entity with which the preposition establishes a relation and, at the same time, to suggest that such a group or entity might coalesce or come into being around that individual. Broyard's hipster, for example, wants to be where others already are: he has "a desperate, unquenchable need to know the score" (114). At the same time, this figure's intense preoccupation with being "*in-there*" (119) expresses his thinly concealed desire "to conquer the world" and to "direct human traffic" (114). Even in the midst of his anxious group identifications, he longs to define "the score" that others must come to know.

This mutually constitutive emergence of individual and group identity returns us to the power of performative speech to act upon and change the world to which it is addressed. J. L. Austin refines his notion of the performative by distinguishing between "in" and "of." He defines an "illocutionary act" as the "performance of an act *in* saying something as opposed to [the] performance of an act *of* saying something."[39] Mailer viewed his work as possessing just this illocutionary relationship to politics, most powerfully when that work described the embodied social codes through which blacks and whites were then forging a new liberal coalition. Mailer found evidence of these codes in the "murmur of jazz" surrounding Kennedy. But he also thought that the power of hip to alter political life testified to the power of his own language about hip to do the same. "In such places as Greenwich Village," Mailer announces in "The White Negro," "a ménage-à-trois was completed—the bohemian and the juvenile delinquent came face-to-face with the Negro, and the hipster was a fact in American life. If marijuana was the wedding ring, the child was the language of Hip" (*A* 340). Symbolic unions of the otherwise unlike are the essence of hip. "I believe in mixed musical marriages," said Ray Charles, of the myriad borrowings between white and black musicians that resulted in "White America . . . getting hipper."[40] But Mailer doesn't just report on his marriage—he indulges in it, as Austin would say, as its officiant. And the sentence's passive construction ("a ménage-à-trois was completed"), its agential ellipses, suggests that just as the child gives birth to its parents, language about hip—such as Mailer's—gives birth to hipsters themselves. What Mailer calls "the special language" (*A* 348) of hip functions as both the product and the agent of the wedding here described.

Mailer wielded that special language for political ends. Thus we find him officiating a second, related wedding when, reporting from the convention that nominated Kennedy, he seeks to "dress" the Democrats "with a ribbon or two of metaphor." The Democrats are to Mailer "a crazy, half-rich family, loaded with poor cousins, traveling always in caravans with Cadillacs and Okie Fords, Lincolns and quarterhorse mules, putting up every night in tents." He trusts these motley hordes because "in tranquility one recollects them with affection, their instinct is good, crazy family good." At the heart of this large family, Mailer finds evidence of another "marriage": the Democratic Party is to him "the Snopes Family married to Henry James." Mailer uses this metaphor to join together two groups crucial to Kennedy's precarious coalition: (1) starting in the fifties, affluent whites in the South would begin leaving the Democratic Party almost twice as quickly as working-class whites—like the Snopeses—who were more interested in earning money than in old racial taboos; and (2) during this same period, Brahmins in the Northeast, guardians of the nation's cultural establishment, would expand their grip on the party, as it absorbed liberal but fiscally conservative whites who had once voted Republican.[41] First invoking Wordsworth, and then Faulkner and James, Mailer aims not simply to describe these constituencies, but to reconsolidate them with his language.

This project imagined a transfer of power from political to literary institutions, and then back again. One of the chief architects of Lyndon Johnson's Great Society, Richard Goodwin, a consummate insider, described his "rejection of politics as a vehicle for social change in America." After 1968, he came to believe that "Washington is the capital of illusion, a caricature of society, a fabricated city inhabited by strangers. It's impossible to change. The bureaucracies are too well entrenched. To change them is like asking a whale to fly."[42] But Mailer imagined his writing politically significant precisely because Washington was the capital of illusion—because it was constructed from the ground up by caricature and flights of fancy. In fact, Mailer had little difficulty in asking a whale to fly—especially when that whale was the Democratic Party. Reporting from the Democratic Convention in Chicago, chronicling the tumultuous showdown of the party's progressives and conservatives, he writes, "It was as if the war had finally begun." It was "as if the military spine of a great liberal party had finally separated itself from the skin, as if, no metaphor large enough to suffice, the Democratic Party had here been broken in two before the eyes of a nation like Melville's whale charging right out of the sea" (*MSC* 172). No metaphor phallic enough for Mailer—who had spent the fifties trying to finish a sprawling, 1,000-page novel about hip that he thought of as a "descendant of Moby Dick" (*A* 156)—the military spine of the party separates from its foreskin just as Melville's whale charges from the sea. But insofar as Moby Dick's spine remains attached to its white skin, and insofar as we know that it will return to the deep, Melville's resurgent animal heals an otherwise severed body, and in so doing reconstitutes under new auspices the party to which it is compared. The rebirth at hand is as literary as it is rooted in the hyper-masculine sexual politics that Mailer would promote throughout his life. Moby Dick represents a new incarnation of the Democrats even as the animal embodies the literary authority at stake in that figurative renewal.

3. Selling JFK in *The Manchurian Candidate* and *Rabbit, Run*

Postwar popular culture, argues David Riesman in *The Lonely Crowd*, "teaches the other-directed man to consume politics and to regard politics and political information and attitudes as consumer goods. They are products, games, entertainments, recreations; and he is the purchaser, player, spectator, or leisure-time observer."[1] Between 1952 and 1968, the advertising industry taught these lessons as well. During this period, the Democratic and Republican parties turned to Madison Avenue for help in selling presidential candidates. Later, the two parties would develop their own internal media strategists and consultants, but during the bulk of the fifties and sixties, private firms played central roles in national elections and in the dissemination of party ideology.[2]

Accepting the Democratic nomination in 1956, Adlai Stevenson denounced this trend: "The idea that you can merchandise candidates for high office like breakfast cereal—that you can gather votes like box tops—is, I think, the ultimate indignity in the democratic process." But the words rang hollow: he spoke from a platform designed by the advertising agency that had organized the convention at which he spoke.[3] Published in 1956, John Schneider's satirical novel *The Golden Kazoo* tells the story of an agency similarly involved in a national election. Adman Blade Reade, "the boy wonder of Madison Avenue," has been hired to run the 1960 Republican presidential campaign.[4] "Look," he explains to his team, "I don't want you to come back and tell me what our boy should do or say about farm policy, foreign affairs, tariffs, taxes or civil rights. Don't sell the welfare state, the free enterprise system or whatever screwball Utopia you've got figured out for the U.S.A." The candidate is "your product. He's a can of beer, a squeeze tube of deodorant, a can of dog food. Sell him" (22).

Reade believes that selling a president requires understanding "the Political Admind," which has become, he says, "a Dominant Force in our society, just as was the Liberal Mind of the early 'thirties." The Political Admind, he explains, caters to "the good old Lowest Common Denominator" (35). As Reade sees it, this approach is justified because "*There ain't any high brow in low-brows, but there's some low brow in everybody*" (34). Replace Reade's "low-brows" with "middlebrows" and his remark usefully schematizes Madison Avenue in the fifties. This was the heyday of "mass society," when images of white, middle-class suburbanites suffused advertising. With few exceptions, firms pitched their products to members of this demographic, exhorting them to move up a ladder of conventional status hierarchies by engaging in agreed-upon forms of conspicuous consumption: the right house in the right neighborhood, the right car, the right shirt, and so on. Advertising sold these hierarchies to a mass audience; it assumed that they applied to all possible consumers. If you weren't actually part of white, middle-class suburbia, the reasoning went, your acts of consumption probably reflected your desire to be. As Dwight Macdonald saw it, assumptions like this led to a homogenization of taste—to what he called the "midcult."[5]

But homogenization doesn't present a problem to Blade Reade, whose favorite piece of music is Beethoven's "Old Number Five." He loves the piece because it "became popular [and] therefore vulgar." "Look," he explains with brio, "you mention Beethoven's Fifth, you are a commuter who bought a hi-fi outfit and are playing with culture. You are a square." Reade thinks this makes Old Number Five "the most nearly perfect musical entity ever created" (180) because, all trends to the contrary, he loves the square; he thinks that it is still, in 1960, the secret of advertising success. This belief is the source of ironic humor throughout the novel. Reade instructs his team to come up with "big, 1960 ideas" (19), but they're stumped. Faced with a deadline, one of Reade's copywriters engages in "a secret vice. Lust to indulge this vice would come on him at the damndest times" (87). Satisfying this lust helps him generate ad copy, and while the narrator delays specifying what this entails, we're told that doing so involves trips to "broken-down sections of semi-slum areas such as the 1960 Village" (89). We follow the adman to the Village and as he climbs creaking stairs to reach a "Madame." She's drunk and encourages him to relax with a glass of cheap whisky. But this is no scene of transgression: she sits him at a piano and plays Brahms's *Lieder*; he jumps in with a hearty baritone. The implicit punch line replicates the reasoning with which Reade extols "Old Number Five": if you must visit Greenwich Village for help hawking product, avoid the underground. Square, Germanic culture still sells; it's what an Anglo-Saxon mass market wants.

Published one year later, George Panetta's *Viva Madison Avenue!* disagrees. Each of his chapters begins with humorous observations about Anglo-Saxons and advertising, in which the narrator enjoins the reader to participate in his mockery.

> Have you ever been on Madison Avenue? It's the street of the Anglo-Saxons, the great ad men, and sometime you should sit on the curb and watch them. They look like humans, but take a long look and you'll know they're different; they're something better. They walk with their heads in the sky, not looking at anybody, just up and ahead. . . . [and] think of headlines, of slogans, of money. (6)

Madison Avenue was at the time an Anglo-Saxon preserve, though as we will see, a predominantly Jewish-American firm was then creating a paradigm that would change the world of advertising. More immediately noteworthy, however, and indicative of the innovations then sweeping Madison Avenue, is the fact that this passage's implied reader is not Anglo-Saxon, and that, curiously, this doesn't make the reader part of a minority so much as part of a "human" race. This is not to say that the novel doesn't want Anglo-Saxon readers; it's rather to say that it extends to these readers the promise that they might, even if only for a moment, be something other than members of an oppressive white majority. If there is a mass market to which this novel directs itself, it's a market that wants to be something other than Anglo-Saxon.

Panetta's term of art can be specified, in light of changes then reshaping the Democratic Party. In 1957, when he published his novel, a sociologist named Andrew Hacker narrowed the category of "Anglo-Saxon" so that it might more accurately describe the group ridiculed by the likes of Panetta's protagonists. Though the term "WASP" found its first popular audience in 1964, with the publication of E. Digby Baltzell's *The Protestant Establishment: Aristocracy and Caste in America*, Hacker used it first in an essay called "Liberal Democracy and Social Control." His aim was to establish the centrality of old money, high-caste Anglo-Saxons, or WASPs, to the Democratic Party and the postwar liberal tradition. "Ed Flynn might boss the Bronx," Hacker argued, "but he would defer to Franklin D. Roosevelt (of Harvard); Carmine De Sapio rides behind Averill [*sic*] Harriman (of Yale); and Jake Arvey cleared the way for Adlai Stevenson (of Princeton). The seeming inconsonance of the fact that the party of the immigrant accepted old-stock patricians as its leaders is good evidence of the deference that was paid to the *ancien regime*."[6] Hacker likes this deference: he thinks only an aristocratic elite can stave off the value-eroding tendencies of capitalism. Conversely, Panetta articulates a growing impatience with Hacker's deference, embodied in *Viva* by the Democratic Party's commitment to Stevenson, which I discussed in Chapter 2. At bottom, the novel insists that the party would not continue to win national elections under the rubric that Hacker describes.

Hacker was committed to Riesman's "inner-directed" world, but as Daniel Bell would later explain, building on Riesman, new forms of labor and leisure were leading to the collapse of that world and the "abandonment of the Protestant ethic." Corporations urged individuals "to work hard, pursue a career, [and] accept delayed gratification"; but they also promoted "pleasure, instant joy, relaxing and letting go." Warren Susman described a similar tension between a work "culture that envisioned a world of scarcity" and embraced "hard work [and] self-denial" and a leisure culture that embraced "pleasure, self-fulfillment, and play."[7] As I've been insisting throughout, hip dramatized these tensions in racial terms, and in so doing suggested how systemic changes in work and leisure might adjust WASPs to the political realities of integration. Hip accommodated the enfranchising of ethnic and racial interest groups by enjoining WASPs who wished to remain white at the office—where they would jealously guard their Protestant work ethic—to become black at the shopping mall. Norman Mailer described white Protestants as a "Faustian, barbaric, draconian, progress-oriented, and root-destroying people."[8] As he had it, "they must vote, manipulate, control, and direct, these Protestants who are the center of power in our land, they must go for what they believe is reason, when it is only the Square logic of the past" (*A* 388). But he thought Protestants might free themselves from this self-imposed tyranny by committing to "the freedom of the body and the democracy of the flesh" (*A* 388). In flight from their predilection to "think of headlines, of slogans, of money," they might become white Negroes, in order to satisfy both their physical cravings and a new vision of democracy. In making this case, Mailer adopts a variant of Panetta's mode of address: even as he appeals to those disaffected from a WASP majority, he encourages the individuals who constitute that majority to imagine themselves as disempowered and on the racial margins of society.

One version of this claim is familiar enough. As Ralph Ellison put it, the increase in freedom experienced by black Americans "acted on the youth at least as a sort of sudden release for which they were unprepared. It was as though the word had gone out that the outsider, the unacceptable, was now acceptable, and young people translated it to mean that all of the repressed psychological drives, all of the discipline of the instincts, were now fair game. 'Let it all hang out,' they said. 'We have become black men and women'" (*CE* 784). But I am interested less in how individuals let it all hang out than in the figurative strategies with which novelists and advertising agencies transformed the white insider into a black outsider. To Anatole Broyard, who worked at an advertising agency, self-abstraction was one such strategy. The hipster, he thought, cultivated the art of "second-removism." An "ironical pedagogue," he spread the lessons of bebop, in which the musician, radiating "coolness . . . comes to a standstill in his observance of his position in the world." This stance is "his attempt to move from the performer to the omniscient and superior spectator—the spectator looking upon himself."[9] Richard Condon's *The Manchurian Candidate* (1959) and John Updike's *Rabbit, Run* (1960) replicate that stance: they describe hip figures who contemplate the white communities of which they are a part as if they are from the outside and possessed of a black second skin. If we understand cultural pluralism as a commitment to seeing the sameness of a larger community in and through the difference between the diverse groups that constitute it, then the hip pluralism figured in and aggressively promoted by these novels generates an encompassing communal sameness in and through the difference it generates between an individual and his or her own skin.

Ironic Advertising

Theodore White, in *The Making of the President, 1960*, stresses the importance of white Protestants in the election of Kennedy when, having catalogued the Democrat's outreach to minorities, he announces, "Even when the Catholic vote is added to the Negro vote, the Jewish vote and the suburban vote, one still has no true picture of what happened in the election of 1960 nor how its totals came about" (356). This is the case, White maintains, because "the greatest success of Kennedy planning" lay in reconciling a dominant mainstream demographic to the party's increased reliance on minorities: "John F. Kennedy cast his appeal, *above all*, to the overwhelmingly Protestant majority of the American people, and ran uphill to convince them that whatever differing pasts and heritages they brought to 1960, they shared a common future and common conviction for the years ahead" (357). In assuaging "the pride of the Anglo-American peoples" (358) of the nation, Kennedy reconciled them to the changing composition of their party. In "Superman Comes to the Supermarket,"

Mailer elaborates this logic. Kennedy didn't just reconcile Protestants to the minorities in his party; he made them want to be minorities. Mailer thought WASPs would be happy with a victory for Kennedy, which promised them the chance to be something other than members of an elite. "The fact that he was Catholic," he wrote, "would shiver a first existential vibration of consciousness into the mind of the white Protestant. For the first time in our history, the Protestant would have the pain and creative luxury of feeling himself in some tiny degree part of a minority, and that was an experience which might be incommensurable in its value to the best of them" (*PP* 49). Here, then, the same turn that is built into the narrative address of *Viva*: the ritualized castigation of a WASP majority, and the celebration of all beyond the pale of that majority, performed for the benefit of that majority, which is asked to identify with and assume the bodies of once caricatured subalterns.

George Panetta's protagonists enjoy the "creative luxury" of feeling themselves "part of a minority." George and Joe combine their hard-nosed existential cynicism with an antinomian opposition to WASP authority, thereby producing a stance that WASPs themselves want to claim as their own. As we saw in Chapter 2, Joe is asked while filming a television drama to discover a universal symbol that won't alienate any particular constituency. He does so by staging a death scene and, predictably enough, the sponsor is livid. But surprisingly, Joe's show turns into a hit, and he's celebrated at the office. Parallels present themselves: the more he mocks the Anglo-Saxons, the more they try to please him; the more his work offends their sense of propriety, the more successful it is.

With Joe's ad campaign, which appeals because of its commitment to offend, Panetta anticipates what has since been described as the advertising industry's "creative revolution." As Stephen Fox puts it, this creative revolution was, "first and most enduringly," also "an ethnic revolution": advertisers changed the way they sold their products both by diversifying their own ranks and by cultivating in their ads a diffuse and coded version of the antipathy toward WASP culture that we find in Panetta's novel.[10] At the core of Madison Avenue's twinned revolution was an ad campaign mounted by the predominantly Jewish firm of Doyle Dane Bernbach (DDB). The company faced a formidable challenge: how to sell to the American public a brand, Volkswagen, closely associated with Nazi Germany and, by extension, at least in the fecund imagination of Mailer, all that was most lethally technocratic in white Protestant culture. DDB faced this challenge by overturning many of the industry's most cherished tenets.

The dominant tone of its campaign was irony; the ads winked at their readers and allowed them critical distance on strategies typically used to compel their consent as consumers.

As Thomas Frank has it, "remarks about the fraudulence of consumerism and expressions of disgust with the system's masters run as a sort of guiding theme through virtually everything DDB did. Disgust with consumer society was both the agency's forte and its best product pitch, applicable to virtually anything: Buy this to escape consumerism." The Volkswagen campaign sent shock waves down Madison Avenue: "No longer would advertising construct an idealized but self-evidently false vision of consumer perfection."[11] To Frank, the hip style inaugurated by these ads proved central to exploding youth markets because it stoked leisure consumption as a form of protest against a mass society characterized by leisure consumerism. But consumers never understand ads as simply false: an ad's fraudulence and promissory appeal are mutually constitutive, and DDB's campaign assimilated this insight into mainstream advertising in ways previously unimaginable. According to Frank, DDB's ads gave birth to "a new species of hip consumerism, a cultural perpetual motion machine in which disgust with the falseness, shoddiness and everyday oppressions of consumer society could be enlisted to drive the ever-accelerating wheels of consumption."[12] This might just as easily be expressed the other way: the Volkswagen ads encouraged individuals to express their difference and disaffection from, and even disgust for, those who failed to acknowledge that "disgust with the falseness . . . of consumer society" was fake disgust.

Frank's terms offer tidy categories, and one way to express the difference between *The Golden Kazoo* and *Viva Madison Avenue!* is to say that the former dramatizes the already established, square, conservative tastes of the fifties and the latter anticipates the hip, liberal tastes of the decade to come. There's truth in this: voters did respond to different appeals in each decade. Eisenhower hired the staid and predominantly Anglo-Saxon firm of Batten Barton Durstine Osborne (BBDO) to assist in his 1952 presidential campaign; Kennedy hired DDB, the predominantly Jewish firm that revolutionized the industry with its Volkswagen campaign, to run his reelection campaign. Lyndon Johnson ended up using DDB instead in his 1964 landslide, en route to which the firm produced the most famous political advertisement in U.S. history—officially titled "Peace, Little Girl," but often referred to as "Daisy," after the flower from which a young flower child picks petals, as a clock ticks down to a nuclear apocalypse, precipitated, ostensibly, by the rash Barry Goldwater. The Democrats' choice of DDB, we might surmise, says it all: they were more closely attuned to the changes in taste that led to the creative revolution, as would become clear over the course of the sixties.

But these changes in taste also reflected structural changes in production regimes, and developments in advertising accommodated these changes in complex fashion. The United States was transitioning from a Fordist to a post-Fordist economy, in which newly flexible and contingent forms of assembly specialization, small-batch production, just-in-time inventory control, and decentralized management called for new ways of selling commodities to highly articulated consumption communities. Instead of mass-producing and amassing stockpiles of a standardized product designed for a mass market, companies began to tailor differentiated versions of that product to variegated demographics. These communities were not simply discovered. Advances in market research made it possible to produce the communities as surely as the products they were being sold. In 1956, the year that Schneider published *The Golden Kazoo*, Wendell Smith described the virtues of what he called "market segmentation." He insisted that products would "find their markets of maximum potential as a result of recognition of differences in the requirements of market segments."[13] Isolated versions of market segmentation had been in place since at least the 1920s. But in the late fifties and early sixties, the advertising industry adopted segmentation wholesale. The consequences were far-reaching. No longer would the industry assume that all consumers aspired to white middle-class culture. Instead, it would cater to—but also in many instances create—a range of finely grained consumption communities, even as it produced new forms of intergroup affiliation in order to capitalize on the spirit of desegregation. No sooner did Madison Avenue narrow its appeals to already recognizable demographic categories than it invented new categories and suggested new points of access to established ones.

Frank's hip consumerism relies on these developments in production and advertising in obvious ways. It's hard to register protest through acts of consumption if the commodities you're buying are the same as those your neighbor is buying. It's easier if you have an array of choices that promise membership in counter-hegemonic communities. It's easier still to register this protest if the process of group differentiation itself comes to take on an antinomian élan. Market segmentation turns group distinctions organized around class into distinctions organized around lifestyle, and tethers lifestyle distinctions to fantasies of contestation, in which groups struggle to assert their rights against others. In *Viva*, George and Joe distinguish themselves from their bosses almost solely in terms of perceived differences between Italians and Anglo-Saxons. Tensions between management and labor are secreted away, and in their place emerge tribal taxonomies that express conflicts of interests in terms of attitudes and styles allegedly expressive of the groups in question. But these tribal taxonomies were as flexible and contingent as the antinomian élan that Frank describes; there was nothing self-evidently true or false about them.

The rise of market segmentation led to the production and consolidation of an array of subcultural, gendered, racial, and ethnic group identities. This was a process that reached beyond any simple accounting of the true or false. According to John Kenneth Galbraith, advertising brings "into being wants that previously did not exist."[14] So too market segmentation brings into being collective groupings that previously did not exist, and encourages consumers to imagine themselves part of these groups based on how they spent, wished to spend, or could be convinced to spend, their disposable income. A flexible form of corporate hailing, segmentation interpellates individuals and groups together, at once, allowing each to constitute the other. The rise of the "youth market" attests to this powerfully. By the end of the sixties, appeals to this new segment were producing far-reaching political and economic changes. Advertising encouraged the young to see themselves as part of an interest group capable of changing history—albeit in ways amenable to the needs of the greater economy. But Madison Avenue didn't "discover" the youth market any more than it understood that market to include only the young; as Stanley Hollander demonstrates in his account of the so-called "Pepsi Generation," advertisers sold to young and old alike an ideal of "youthfulness or what might be labeled youngness—a nostalgic and fantasized state of looking and feeling young without having any of the cares and concerns that youth actually face."[15] The young weren't a segment; they were segmented: they became youthful as a function of having been hailed as such.

Madison Avenue's creation of a youth market is instructive in light of its relation to black consumers, who were early objects of segmentation. These consumers were consolidated with what were called "race records": jazz and blues recordings made by and marketed to African Americans. One of the earliest, Mamie Smith's *Crazy Blues* (1920) sold 150,000 copies in its first year of release, thus proving, in the words of Amiri Baraka, "the existence of a not-yet exploited market." To Baraka, "the Negro as *consumer* was a new and highly lucrative slant, an unexpected addition to the strange portrait of the Negro the white American carried around in his head." He points out that in addition to bringing this new figure to light, early jazz recordings provided the opportunity for what was perhaps the first marketing campaign to lionize black culture as something to which non-whites might aspire. Founded in Harlem in 1921, Black Swan was the first black-owned record company in the country; Baraka reports that it "advertised its products as 'The Only Genuine Record. Others Are Only Passing for Colored.' (A wild turnabout!)."[16] That appeal was decades premature and Black Swan quickly went bankrupt, in 1923, only to be bought by Paramount the next year.

The recording industry sold black products to black consumers well before other industries did. It wasn't until the fifties that large Madison Avenue advertising firms, like BBDO, established "special market units," staffed by blacks to sell to blacks. But by the end of the decade, most firms were targeting specific ads to African Americans.[17] The result was that, in place of ads for cosmetics with white models, for example, readers of *Ebony* began to find ads featuring black models wearing recognizably black hairstyles. As Elizabeth Cohen has it, these changes were crucial to "a civil rights movement that continued to mobilize blacks at the point of consumption—through sit-ins, selective buying campaigns, and boycotts." But she adds that market segmentation also "paralleled the larger evolution of civil rights from integration to black power," insofar as it instantiated separatism in place of universalism. And insofar as this separatism took shape under the aegis of corporate power, it led to the disenfranchising of small black businesses. Cohen reports that as market segmentation took hold, the proportion of black income that went to black-owned businesses dropped by half.[18] Market segmentation didn't simply appeal to consumer groups; it fashioned such groups into objects of corporate power, instead of into agents capable of wielding it.

Marketing to African Americans did, however, bring problems as well as rewards to large corporations. For advertisers, the challenge was determining how to sell products to increasingly variegated groups without differentiating those products so much that the cost of their production outweighed the revenue earned by winning over new consumers. This problem was particularly complicated with respect to the black community. In 1962, an industry trade journal described African Americans as "the least understood, most controversial, and yet most promising consumer group in the nation." Jason Chambers reads this line as an indication that "the question of the day was, in light of the rapid social changes ongoing among blacks, how to successfully reach them as a market segment without alienating white consumers in the process." In Ralph Ellison's second novel, Adam Sunraider articulates this alienation when he laments the use of Cadillacs by blacks. "We have reached a sad state of affairs," he says, "for this fine product of American skill and initiative has become so common in Harlem that much of its initial value has been sorely compromised."[19] Those selling the Democratic Party faced an analogous problem: how to balance the needs of the party's racist white constituencies without sacrificing an inclusive sense of mission that might bind these constituencies with emergent ones. Whether selling cars or Democrats, advertisers faced the same problem: how to appeal to blacks without alienating racist whites.

Hip offered a solution, in some obvious and not so obvious ways. It represented an effort to generate socially permissible codes of identification between white and black Americans; faced with the increasing momentum of the Civil Rights Movement, both the advertising industry and the Democratic Party realized at the start of the sixties that their fortunes depended on these codes. Both realized, also, that these codes were most effective when tolerant if not productive of racial fluidity. As an instrument of sales, hip dramatized the ever-shifting nature of the criteria that determined membership in any given group. Even as the most racially conscious forms of hip made a fetish of how blacks were presumed to live, they acknowledged with a wink the contingent nature of the identifications necessary to the pursuit of this or that imagined lifestyle: even when a vision of the authentically black, hip was, at the same time, an aslant recognition that racial authenticity is staged under klieg lights, and thus is subject to endless reinvention.

These terms provide one way to understand Milton Klonsky's claim that *"Hip is merely the local habitation and the name assumed by irony in our times."*[20] The irony at the heart of Frank's hip consumerism generates consumer desire by allowing for critical distance on that desire: we consume while expressing our difference from the act of consumption; it does not define us. The commodity, Wolfgang Haug explains, "is and is not what it is." To this we might add that the hip consumer, possessed of a doubled incarnation, is and is not what he is. The irony at the heart of this consumerism generates racial identification by allowing for critical distance on that identification. Appeals to hip render racial difference both authoritative and subject to exchange—they invoke racial characteristics as the basis for interpersonal affiliations even as they decouple race from its ostensibly literal moorings and suggest that it is, instead, something performed, a mantle to be assumed or discarded, a figurative rather than a literal means of seeing color. Thus hip bespoke more than the propensity toward other-direction and more than what sociologists call "allophilia": one social group's "liking or love of the other."[21] It also extended the promise, written through with something more than simple fraudulence, that members of one group might become members of another, and yet remain themselves.

As early as the start of the twentieth century, copywriters argued that the goal of advertising was "expressing the inexpressible, of suggesting not so much a motor car as speed, not so much a gown as style, not so much a compact as beauty."[22] An extension of this trend into heretofore restricted terrain, hip expressed not so much race but the idea of race. Anyone might come to own the idea. The music industry, to take a prominent example of hip marketing in action, would learn by the end of the fifties to negotiate the perception that much of popular music was, in a very basic and yet complicated way, indebted to African American traditions. That perception was important to young consumers for any number of reasons, but valuable to marketers only insofar as it didn't restrict consumption. Thus the industry gradually detached its musical categories from the imagined racial communities to which they were initially marketed: moving, for example, from "race music" to "rhythm and blues," and eventually to "rock and roll." In 1957 *Billboard* announced, "No abstract categories prevent the teenagers of today from buying records of Fats Domino, Elvis Presley, Bill Haley, Carl Perkins, or Little Richard at one and the same time. The trade, therefore, must revise and perhaps abandon some of its old boundary lines." As one columnist put it, R & B reached white and black consumers alike, and was "an interesting case of the integration of the tastes of the majority into the tastes of the minority."[23]

Advertising facilitated that integration. Randall Rothenberg reports that after the Volkswagen campaign, ad companies were "no longer punished but *rewarded* . . . for using ethnic locutions."[24] This new vogue expressed more than recognition that the nation's consumer base was diverse, or even that members of the majority liked "the tastes of the minority." Ethnic locutions in ads functioned much as Panetta's narrative address: they appealed to those in the majority eager to distance themselves from Anglo-Saxon life in their acts of consumption. Long before the sixties, white Americans used black Americans as screens upon which to project fantasies of anarchic and unrestrained desire; while these scenes had long dramatized, for example, threats to white womanhood, so too could they dramatize the amorous fits of antinomian consumption that hip consumerism performed. Rhythm and blues and early rock and roll were ideally suited to this task. The music was "an expression of *solidarity* with the social and political aspirations of black people," argues Andrew Ross, even as it was characterized by "its vigorous lyrical praise for the liberating promise of endless teenage consumption ('with no particular place to go'), and its cheerful swerve away from the middle-class ethic of deferred gratification ('a fool about my money / don't try to save')."[25] This is exactly right, but "*solidarity*" often encompassed more than shared aims. Throughout the fifties and sixties, advertisers asked white consumers to see themselves as potentially hip, and by extension as potentially black. This meant, in effect, asking them to confirm the fantastical power of consumption generally to remove them from their skin and provide them with another.[26]

How transcendent must consumption be if it had the power to propel consumers across a barrier so aggressively policed as that between black and white skins? Of course the period's borders were policed unevenly, and proved porous for whites in ways they did not for blacks. Over the course of the sixties, African Americans risked their lives by crossing physical barriers, at the front of buses, at lunch counters, in classrooms, and at voting stations, to name just a few. These barriers, once crossed, gave way to more immaterial ones. In *Viva*, the Italian Americans George and Joe refuse to assimilate to their Anglo-Saxon coworkers, who cross over, symbolically, to them. The office politics facing black advertising agents were less congenial. Writing in *Advertising Age* in 1968, Edgar Hopper, a former account executive at Foote, Cone, and Belding, asked that ad companies not compel newly hired African American copywriters to emulate whites. These companies were coercive with black employees in ways they were not with white ones: "We have to become black Anglo-Saxons to make it," he lamented. "If you let your hair grow out, you're Rap Brown. Speak out and you're coming on too strong." He recommended, instead, along lines suggested by Panetta, that "when you hire a black creative person, hire him for his lifestyle, not because you want him to imitate the white." The important point here, however, is that Hopper's proposal—white employees should emulate black employees, as opposed to the reverse—is more than a plea for workplace tolerance: he wants firms that hire black talent to craft appeals that change the consumer's sense of what it means to ascribe to "the white."

Hopper's term "black Anglo-Saxon" begins to explain how literary figures might craft similarly transformative appeals. Nathan Hare's 1965 study of the black middle class, *The Black Anglo-Saxons*, follows in the footsteps of E. Franklin Frazier's *The Black Bourgeoisie* (1957). Hare describes his subjects as middle-class "Negroes" who "disown their own history and mores in order to assume those of the biological descendants of the white Anglo-Saxons" and, as a result, become "more conservative and conformist than the whites."[27] Hare's subjects look black and are in this respect counterparts to "the whites." But they become through the force of his figurative conjunction something other than black as an identity category: more white than the whites, they become more Anglo-Saxon, itself a conjunction that captures a particular set of attributes and styles more fully than the simply descriptive "the whites." Indeed, part of what's noteworthy about this study is that it uses the word "black" pejoratively and the word "Negro" to describe members of the ostensibly more authentic working classes. Hare's "Negroes" give up this authenticity and become "black"—that is to say, merely dark-skinned—the moment that they aspire to becoming "Anglo-Saxon." As with Norman Mailer's use of "Negro" in the phrase "white Negro," the ability of the conjunction "Anglo-Saxon" to capture a set of performable properties requires that it function as a noun in relation to what initially seems an antithetical adjective; for Hare, "black" throws properties associated with "Anglo-Saxon" into relief, and makes those properties available for adoption, by suggesting the contingent nature of visual registers otherwise taken to define identity categories.[28] Adding his adjective, Hare changes what it means to refer to something as "Anglo-Saxon": if there can be black Anglo-Saxons, then being Anglo-Saxon must necessarily involve performing codes more than possessing a certain kind of ancestry.[29] The border-crossing novels that follow replicate this process on a wider scale: with an eye toward the mutable and fungible nature of group identities, they conjoin and transform the otherwise contradictory on the way to selling Kennedy.

The White Oriental

Translated into nineteen languages and used as the basis of two major motion pictures, Richard Condon's *The Manchurian Candidate* describes an American GI captured by the Chinese during the Korean War and returned to the States with his brains "not merely washed" but "dry-cleaned."[30] Unbeknownst to himself, Raymond Shaw becomes the triggerman in a communist conspiracy—organized in China and led in the United States by his mother, Eleanor—to catapult his stepfather, Johnny Iselin, into the Oval Office. The novel touched a nerve. Greil Marcus calls it "simultaneously a bestseller and a cult book, casual reading for a public and the subject of hushed conversations among sophisticates: could this really happen?"[31] Something at least superficially like it did happen. One year after the release of John Frankenheimer's film of the novel, Kennedy was killed by a marksman who, like Shaw, had spent time behind the iron curtain and had likely seen *The Manchurian Candidate* (playing two blocks from his apartment) just weeks before. Supposedly wracked with guilt, Frank Sinatra, who owned the rights to the film, pulled it from circulation.[32] Since then Condon's story has served as a template for countless retellings; its vision of sleeper agents infiltrating the state continues to organize the persecution anxiety expressed by what Richard Hofstadter named "the paranoid style" of American politics.[33]

A mindless vessel for agencies not his own, Raymond Shaw suffers from an unconscious slavery to advertising. For Condon, Chinese communism is an extrapolation of American capitalism, less its antithesis than its fulfillment. He insisted that *The Manchurian Candidate* was about an "all-American brainwashing" that had nothing to do with Red China. He argued that "words such as communism [and] fascism" were instead part of a schizophrenic fantasy that Americans invented to distract themselves from capitalist forms of dispossession and self-alienation. "I am suspicious," Condon announces, "of the term 'free will.'" In fact, he claims to have written *The Manchurian Candidate* as he "had been conditioned to do in successful merchandising."[34] When Condon tells us that the purpose of Yen Lo's conditioning is "to concentrate the purpose of all propaganda upon the mind of one man" (41), we should see that conditioning as an extension of Condon's experience as a Hollywood publicist and merchandiser. Americans had a "packaged soul," Vance Packard had just declared in *The Hidden Persuaders* (1957). Advances in advertising like "psycho-seduction" and "subliminal communication" made consumers into conditioned robots.[35] Raymond Shaw's soul has been packaged in just this manner.

But Shaw's conditioning rewards him with new kinds of physical experience; it provides him with what are, in essence, two incarnations, which embody the lethal contradictions at the heart of early sixties hip. At the novel's start, he is a parody of postwar whiteness; "his skin," Condon writes, "was immoderately white" (24). A quintessential square, he's sexually bottled and profoundly un-happy. An embodiment of repressed, flannel-suited Protestant alienation, Shaw leaves for Korea "a sexual neutral" (227). The brainwashing that he receives there liberates him from the effects of his heritage. Yen Lo, the Chinese scientist who conditions him, points out that "at the core of his defects is his concealed tendency to timidity, sexual and social, both of which are closely linked" (41). Buttoned down, he is helpless in the face of authority, so much so that he flees the love of his life, before even his first kiss, at his mother's command. Though Yen Lo makes Shaw a gun trained on authority figures, he also reaches into Shaw's unconscious to free him sexually. As a result, Shaw's "consciousness of guilt, that rough lip-print of original sin," is "wiped off" (88). He leaves for Asia uptight and abstinent, and returns as "a man who could get exactly what he wanted sensually" (5). Transformed, Shaw disparages the "square" after "ex-changing intense joy" (13, 12) in bed. The opposite sex now strikes him as "with it" (106). He remains supercilious and stiff. But he's suddenly able to participate in a growing sexual and racial liberalization. As one woman breathlessly insists, "Everything is changing right in front of our eyes" (106). Raymond experiences those changes firsthand, for example, during a tryst with a variety artist "of Hawaiian, Negro, and Irish extraction" (109).

Published one year before *The Manchurian Candidate*, and repeatedly cited in it, Jack Kerouac's *Dharma Bums* models for Condon one version of the coun-tercultural ferment behind these changes. The narrator, "Ray" Smith, initially declares himself "afraid to take my clothes off," unwilling to have sex "in front of more than one person."[36] But he is instructed in "Zen Free Love Lunacy" by Japhy Ryder, a thinly disguised Gary Snyder, who looks like one of "the old gig-gling sages of China" (11). Ryder teaches Smith and "the intellectual hepcats" with whom they associate that "the greatest Dharma bums of them all [were] the Zen lunatics of China" (11, 9). Smith embraces Ryder's Chinese "theories about women and lovemaking" (27). After learning from Ryder that "there was no question what to do about sex," Ray realizes that "this is what I always liked about the Oriental religion" (31). From this vantage, Yen Lo's psychological con-ditioning serves Condon as Zen Buddhism served the Beats: as a vehicle for renouncing the white Protestant's ratiocination and as a gateway to hip.

By the end of the decade it was well established that things "Oriental" pro-vided one avenue to hip. As Herbert Gold wrote in 1958, "In recent years some have taken to calling themselves Zen hipsters and Zen Buddhism has spread like the Asian flu so that now you can open your fortune cookie in one of the real cool Chinese restaurants of San Francisco and find a slip of paper with the straight poop: "'Dig that crazy Zen sukiyaki. Only a square eats Chinese food.'"[37] Gold aims less to distinguish Japanese from Chinese Zen (though figures like Snyder gave the matter serious thought), than to dramatize that Oriental hip was well enough established to accommodate and even encourage the narcissism of minor differences. Gold's dizzying distinctions—in which a cool Chinese restaurant disparages the impulse that leads consumers to its door—consolidate deeper divisions between the hip and the square. Similarly, in John Updike's *Rabbit, Run*, Rabbit double-dates with his ex-coach, whom Rabbit considers akin to "the Dalai Lama," and who procures Rabbit his date. The two couples eat at a Chinese restaurant and are served by a waiter whose speech and deferential mannerisms conform to a stereotype: "Tank you vewy much, sir. We tank you vewy much." But as Rabbit leaves, he listens as the same waiter, "in a perfectly inflected voice," finishes telling the cashier a story: "—and then this other cat say, 'But man, mine was helium!'"[38]

Kerouac's romance with Chinese culture did not conflict with the Beats' romance with black culture. In *On the Road*, his alter ego, Sal Paradise, wanders through "the Denver colored section, wishing I were a Negro, feeling that the best the white world had offered was not enough ecstasy for me, not enough life, joy, kicks, darkness, music, not enough night. . . . wishing I could exchange worlds with the happy, true-hearted, ecstatic Negroes of America" (180). To Paradise and Dean Moriarty, "kicks" are typically African American: as Moriarty puts it, he's looking for "old-fashioned spade kicks, what other kinds are there" (252). But Kerouac also records the remarkable flexibility of the hipster's efforts to leave himself behind. Walking the streets of Denver, Paradise adds, "I wished I were a Denver Mexican, or even a poor overworked Jap, anything but what I was so drearily, a 'white man' disillusioned" (180). In some basic sense, not being "a 'white man' disillusioned" mattered more than being any other particular thing, and being a "Jap" or an "old giggling sage of China" promised to remove the scare quotes that Kerouac places around the imprisoning form of Paradise's default identity.

Of course Raymond Shaw never ceases to be a white man disillusioned, never truly wakes up from his hypnosis. He remains a slave to his conditioning, tragically so, not despite but because of his newfound access to physical pleasure. Upon returning from China, he's able, as he was not before leaving for

Korea, to consummate his relationship with his adolescent love, Jocelyn Jordan. For the first time in his adult life, he experiences happiness. But, no James Bond, he cannot function as an assassin and a lover at the same time. Jocelyn is destroyed by his contradictions: he kills her while sleepwalking through a mission. Condon's novel is most interesting, however, when it struggles to bind Raymond's constitutive contradictions with the second skin of hip, on behalf of the Democratic Party.

That the novel might be mobilized for liberal ends was immediately obvious to John Frankenheimer and those associated with the production of the film *The Manchurian Candidate* (1962), which was from its inception closely associated with Kennedy and the Democratic Party. Frank Sinatra starred in and helped produce the film. He was intimate with Kennedy through British matinee idol Peter Lawford, Kennedy's brother-in-law, and had both recorded the anthem of Kennedy's campaign—"High Hopes"—and organized the president's inaugural gala. Sinatra's costars Janet Leigh, Angela Lansbury, and Laurence Harvey had all campaigned for Kennedy throughout 1960. United Artists made the film, and the president of UA at the time, Arthur Krim, was the national finance chairman of the Democratic Party. In fact, Kennedy's enthusiasm for the project convinced Krim that it was okay to proceed with the politically explosive material. The president had read and loved the novel. "Who's going to play the mother?" he reportedly asked Sinatra. Looking to insulate the candidate from his decision to hire a blacklisted writer for another project during the 1960 campaign, Sinatra told the press, "I do not ask the advice of Senator Kennedy on whom I should hire [and] Senator Kennedy does not ask me how he should vote in the Senate."[39] But *The Manchurian Candidate* testifies to a far greater alignment of interests than Sinatra would grant. Without Kennedy, the film would never have been made.

Condon's novel was ready-made for Kennedy. Tellingly, Shaw's conditioning begins in 1951 and continues until 1959. An "eight years' lapse" (228), his friend and one-time commanding officer Ben Marco calls it. Lest we miss the significance of this time span, Marco repeats it: "They are inside your mind. Deep. Now. For eight years" (231). These eight years correspond closely to those between Dwight D. Eisenhower's first presidential campaign and the 1960 presidential campaign, and in this respect, Shaw's conditioning signals a larger malaise, marked by Eisenhower's time in office. When in *Viva* it becomes clear to George and Joe that Adlai Stevenson will lose to Eisenhower and the forces of Anglo-Saxon reaction, one tells the other, "If we lose, we're all robots." As he sees it, "this is a new world we live in. They don't want people any more, not people like us anyway; they want machines, more machines" (246). Shaw is an Eisenhower machine.

But *The Manchurian Candidate* presents a more equivocal picture of life as a white machine; it seeks to reconcile military efficiency and erotic freedom. Describing the flurry of advertising that accompanies his fictional 1960 Republican Convention, Condon directs our attention toward "printed partisan displays, the backs of which carried the same message in the name of the other party, whose convention would follow in three weeks" (292). The notion that there was little difference between the nation's two political parties—that each appealed to an undifferentiated, "mass" audience—was familiar enough in the period. And in a fundamental way, Condon viewed the political process as nothing more than an exercise in mass marketing. And yet, his own marketing of the political process was considerably more sophisticated than these printed displays, and reflects the advances in market segmentation discussed above. To wit, Condon calls forth and unites what might otherwise seem antithetical constituencies crucial to John F. Kennedy's government coalition: Cold Warriors and the progressive young.

Addressing enslaved white Protestants of Northern European descent who are, at the same time, liberated, Sinophilic Americans, Condon appeals simultaneously to two key elements of Kennedy's coalition: Cold War hawks and the idealistic young. Running against Richard Nixon in 1960, Kennedy used a strategy that had worked in his 1952 Senate race: he embraced a hard-nosed realpolitik abroad even as he appealed to liberal cultural freedoms at home; as one historian puts it, Kennedy liked "going to his rival's right on foreign policy and to his left on domestic policy."[40] This strategy demanded negotiating the often conflicting demands of militarism and progressivism, and Condon's novel does just this. Dismissive of almost everything but the U.S. Army and an emergent counterculture, *The Manchurian Candidate* demonstrates why "the military mind [is] called a juvenile mind" (216). The claim throughout is that voters can be committed at the same time to the defense of the United States and to nascent forms of cultural and social liberalization associated with the young.

Condon makes this claim in light of what was then a fissure opening within the Republican Party between its liberal and reactionary wings, which Tom Jordan and Eleanor Shaw represent, respectively. A Republican senator, Jordan deplores Eleanor Shaw for having "very nearly destroy[ed] our party"

(265). He speaks too soon. She does destroy their party: she commands her son to assassinate Jordan and open the party to adherents of "Father Coughlin," "Gerald L. K. Smith," and "the clan" (258). Eleanor Shaw first rises to political prominence in the "Middle West" by realizing that "the outstanding Norse nature of her father's name and his heroic origins could be turned into blocs of votes" (74–75). She believes in white supremacy. She wants the country "purified back to original purity" (136). Her strategy for purification is torn from the pages of American modernism. She wants sex only with members of her biological family: her son, Raymond, and her father, who dies with a history of Scandinavia on his lap and whose "heroic origins" (70) consolidate the constituency that propels her into politics.

Condon turns the tables on this nativism, which he casts as the source of the republic's weakness. Outraged by his mother, Raymond thinks of her as "'a caricature of the valiant pioneer women of America who loaded the guns while their husbands fought off the encircling savages' in that he saw his mother and Johnny as the savages" (23). Condon also insists that flag-waving white Europeans are savages and Native Americans models for a new kind of American identity. But not only Native Americans: Chinese as well. Condon casually notes that some of Ben Marco's ancestors hailed from what would become Manchuria. Marco has what Condon calls "the aboriginal look" (26) because his forebears were Spanish and Native American; he's the product of centuries of intermarriage between colonizers and the colonized, and this means that he traces his lineage not just to Latin Europe but also to the steppes of Asia. Looking aboriginal is the same as looking part Chinese because so-called aboriginal Americans crossed the Bering Strait from Asia. Marco "looked like an Aztec crossed with an Eskimo, which was a fairly common western American type, because the Aztec troops had drifted down from Siberia quite a long time before the Spaniards of Pizarro and Cortes had drifted north out of the Andes and Vera Cruz" (26). Siberia is, to Condon, close enough to Manchuria: when Marco gives Shaw a recording of "We Three Kings of Orient Are" (231), he means the title to refer to himself, Shaw, and Yen Lo, and not solely because, with his own deck of cards in hand, Marco takes Yen Lo's place at the novel's end. Marco, whose name gestures to the inaugural convocation of East and West, is the novel's true Manchurian candidate.

Far from being the origin of communist infiltration, then, Manchuria is the homeland of the first Native Americans who crossed the strait so many years earlier, an iconic population whose descendants were viewed by Anglo settlers as Jean-Jacques Rousseau's natural children during the American Revolution, as icons of Anglo-Saxon cultural purity during the 1920s, and as sage victims of modernization during the 1950s.[41] As the Beats did time and again, Condon suggests that embracing Chinese culture amounts to claiming a legitimately Native American heritage. The novel's most arresting display of this logic comes when Marco first encounters his future partner, Eugénie Rose, on the commuter line from Washington. Marco immediately notices Rose's brooch, fashioned in the likeness of the Aztec god Quetzalcoatl. Moments later, and in response only to the observation that they are passing through Delaware, she declares herself "one of the original Chinese workmen who laid track" (159) for the rail on which they are riding. To Greil Marcus, this is one of many "absurd" moments in Frankenheimer's film. Rose "seems," he ventures, "to be conducting a random search for the spoken trigger that will replace Yen Lo's version of Marco's mind with her own."[42]

In a sense this is right: Rose's comments do evoke Yen Lo's conditioning and thus suggest a version of the Chinese influence we imagine at work on Marco. But Rose claims China not for its communism but for its ability to reorient the project of American nativism for countercultural ends. She expresses her antipathy to becoming "crypto-Republican" (203), a phrase with which she indicates the cultural and racial politics of the right. Rose is instead "crypto-Democratic": a personification of ethnic and racial diversity. Marco thinks her nose marvelously "Semitic"; she makes him think, also, of "Moslems" and the "*huanacauri* rock of Incan puberty" (157). She has, in addition, "Tuareg eyes . . . the eyes of a lady left over from an army of crusaders who had taken the wrong turning, moving left toward Jarabub in Africa, instead of right, toward London, after Walter the Penniless, to settle forever in the deep Sahara" (197). These figurative concatenations suggest her affinities with what the Beats called the "fellaheen": cosmopolitan nomads who were, as Neal Cassady put it, "world-citizens, world-pacifists, and world-reconcilers."[43]

Like Marco, however, Rose is no simple pacifist. She was engaged to an FBI agent before meeting Marco, and her choice of men moves her from one wing of law enforcement to another. And this is Condon's point: she and Marco conjoin an otherwise Beat racial politics with the power and authority of the United States military. Marco embraces the military because he finds in it a system of submission, "terraced ranks of fief and lord, where a major can always remain a peasant to a general and a lieutenant a peon to a major" (27). The language appeals less to those in command than to those who "remain" beneath them. But Condon weds this Establishment perspective to Marco's demonstrable hip. Sexually voracious, he is "excitatory" (26), libidinous, and insatiable. Like Mailer's white Negro, he inhabits "only the present," a state that "did not connect with the past nor had any possibility of the shape in the future" (107). An orphan who never knew his parents, he grooves to "the zeitgeist of zither music" (278). The world is his home. A "thirty-nine-year-old bachelor who has been batting around the world for most of his life," he "transshipped boxes of books . . . between San Francisco and wherever he was stationed at the time" (203, 23). Sinatra was appropriately cast in this role, since Marco is the organization man cum James Bond: globe-trotting, learned, lethal, and loving. An enlightened internationalist liberal with the weight of the army behind him, he possesses the worldly interests and countercultural affinities to which Kennedy (an avid Bond fan) would soon lend his name: he represents a militaristic cosmopolitanism as impatient with Congress as it was committed to the Cold War.

Marco is a hip figure able to contain his tensions, in ways that Raymond is not. He outflanks Republicans—he's good at "going to his rival's right on foreign policy and to his left on domestic policy"—in part because he's able to crack the codes of his own conditioning. "Marco treasured poetic, literary, informational, and cross-referenced allusions, military and non-military. He was a reader" (23). Adept with figures, he understands what it means to negotiate sameness through difference. As does Condon, who writes that Marco has "metallic (copper-colored) skin" (27). Marco holds together, and contains his tensions, because of the figurative strength of that metallic skin, marked by Condon as it is with hybrid racial vigor. Shaw's "immoderately white" skin does not possess this binding strength. Of course, as we have seen, skin is a metaphor, and Marco's metallic surface stands in for, and covers over, a vision of difference that, at least during the fifties, underwrote all difference. We discover, in the final moments of the novel, after Marco suffers a road accident that shears off "the right side of his face," that beneath his skin he is black, "as black as the far side of the moon" (304).

"Lose yourself"

In *The Golden Kazoo*, Blade Reade thinks that attending to the lowest common denominator in presidential elections promises to revise how parties conceive of their constituencies. "For more than a generation now," he declares, "neither party had known how to count. Both parties had wooed the AFL, had made passionate love to the farmer and courted the small businessman" (73). The problem is that these groups don't possess sufficient votes. More numerous, Reade thinks, are consumers, who have never been treated as a single voting bloc. Why not appeal to this group en masse? What voter wouldn't think herself part of an interest group committed to cheaper food? Reade traces his idea to the Democrats when "FDR was their mathematics teacher" (69):

> FDR counted the unemployed, distressed homeowners, rebellious farmers, impoverished old folks, hopeless young folks, workers who lacked weapons with which to fight economic royalists, even thrifty citizens who couldn't get their dough out of the banks. A superb salesman—if not an adman familiar with the concept of the LCD—Roosevelt worked up a different sales spiel for each of his several markets. Jobs. Loans to save homes and farms. Cheap electricity. Old-age pensions. Collective bargaining by government ukase. Money out of, as well as in, the banks. (77)

Roosevelt's genius, Reade suggests, lay in his ability to reach multiple interest groups with multiple appeals and, at the same time, unite these groups into one constituency. Reade imagines himself learning from Roosevelt insofar as he imagines all voters as consumers. But his strategy erases difference: he can conceive of uniting diverse constituencies only through the inclusive and explicitly square appeals of the mass market.

According to Theodore H. White in *The Making of the President, 1960*, Richard Nixon insisted on a similar approach while running against Kennedy. "He offered no vision of a greater future to any minority—Catholic or otherwise," White wrote. He appealed, almost exclusively, "to the great majority Protestant stock of the country" (357) as if they were not simply a majority, but the whole of the nation's population. He didn't do so out of naïveté: "No subject is more intensely discussed in the privacy of any campaign headquarters," White writes, "either state or national, than the ethnic origins of the American people and their voting-bloc habits" (222). Those running "a national ticket for the Presidency," he notes, "must concern themselves with all the delicate inheritances of the subordinate tribal communities of America and address themselves to the imposing task of convincing each little group that somewhere in the candidate's mind and affections they will find a reflection of their own concerns and aspirations" (223). Nixon's approach notwithstanding, one community loomed far larger than others in 1960. Since 1948, White points out, "as the Negro migration from the South has quickened in pace and size, the importance of the Negro vote has grown to be almost obsessive with Northern political leaders. . . . It represents power" (233). As White sees it, "Never in any election before 1960 had any group, under leadership of such talent, presented its specific community demands in such blunt and forceful terms" (234). In short, "even more than the election of 1948, the outcome of 1960 was to be dependent on Negro votes" (236).

As we've already seen, Democratic appeals to and on behalf of blacks became an important if last-minute part of Kennedy's campaign. As White has it, Nixon made substantial gains in the South because of these appeals, especially among social conservatives who had remained with the Democrats since the Civil War for largely institutional reasons: though never fully comfortable with the New Deal, they controlled the party machine in their region and endeavored to retain that control for as long as possible. But Republicans began effectively to straddle the Mason-Dixon Line by uniting these conservative southerners with Northeast business interests and members of the working class amenable to the party's rightward cultural lurch. This unification depended on the expulsion of the party's black voters, as Kevin Phillips would make plain when explaining Nixon's "Southern Strategy." The Republican Party wanted increasing numbers of African Americans to vote for Democrats. Granting that "from now on, the Republicans are never going to get more than 10 to 20 percent of the Negro vote," Phillips thought the party "would be shortsighted if they weakened enforcement of the Voting Rights Act. The more Negroes who register as Democrats in the South, the sooner the Negrophobe whites will quit the Democrats and become Republicans. That's where the votes are."[44]

Though Schneider's *Golden Kazoo* avoids any explicit engagement with race, it anticipates a version of that strategy when it announces that Blade Reade's proudly square Republican candidate is "Henry Adams Clay. A semantically fortunate name which neatly straddled the Mason & Dixon" (37). Henry Adams Clay is a candidate whose very name might appeal to old-world WASPs in the Northeast, like Henry Adams, and institutional pragmatists tolerant of racial injustice in the South, like Henry Clay.

Liberals were straddling the Mason and Dixon in a different fashion. The challenge facing the Democrats was retaining sufficient white votes in the South while gaining black votes there and the votes of white professionals and suburbanites in the Northeast: these efforts organized what White called the party's "white-Negro relations."

Eight years later, Abbie Hoffman offered a countercultural version of those relations. Riffing on Mailer's "white Negro," he described "white niggers"— middle-class adolescents from all over the country who identified with the powerlessness and anger presumed to characterize black life. For Hoffman, being a white nigger entails experiencing "police harassment previously reserved only for blacks." He likens the "servitude" of child to parent to a form of "bondage," describes "bounty hunters" who function like slave catchers, and details an "underground railway" that assists children in their flight. Making his analogy explicit, he announces, "A fifteen-year-old kid who takes off from middle-class American life is an escaped slave crossing the Mason-Dixon line." Hoffman's metaphor supersedes actual geography. The transition he tracks from literal to figurative identity (kid to slave) redresses an already accomplished transition from literal to figurative space: the kid leaves her home, and a "middle-class American life" analogous to slavery, because the South is no longer contained in the South, because her home, no matter where it's located, is already a part of what Hoffman calls the "United States of Mississippi."[45]

John Updike's *Rabbit, Run* begins by dramatizing literal and figurative crossings of the Mason-Dixon Line. Floundering in a world of commodities, Rabbit wants a black "second skin" that is somehow resistant to those commodities. He finds this skin, however, only as a function of his commitment to consumption. Before he flees his home and heads south across the Mason-Dixon, Rabbit sells the "MagiPeeler" kitchen utensil, a device that removes skins from fruits and vegetables—not to make the more desired food beneath available, but to enable the consumption of the skin alone, which contains fortifying vitamins. He would flee the drudgery of selling this gadget, as well as the domestic world of mindless consumption with which he associates it. But he cannot flee, and his efforts to exchange his white skin for black simply recapitulate the deracinating function of the MagiPeeler, and the abstractions of value upon which its sale, like the sale of any commodity, depends. Rabbit does not replace one ill-fitting skin with another to which he is more suited; rather, he makes a fetish of skin itself, of recycling and exchanging skins, and eventually, like the consumer of the MagiPeeler, discards everything but these surfaces.

The novel opens with Rabbit playing basketball, a sport that was by 1959, when the novel's events take place, already associated with African American athletic prowess. Between 1957 and 1959, John McClendon's African American Tennessee State teams won three consecutive National Association of Inter-

collegiate Athletics titles, only four years after the tournament had been integrated; by 1959, Bill Russell had established himself as the National Basketball
Association's most dominant and game-changing presence; by the early sixties,
it was already trite for white men wistfully to admire, as Norman Podhoretz
did in 1963, the "physical grace" of black basketball players.[46] The waning of
white dominance in basketball is an organizing metaphor in Updike's Rabbit
tetralogy, which ends, in *Rabbit at Rest* (1990), with Rabbit dying on a basketball court, after having played with African American children. *Rabbit, Run*
begins on the very same court, and while the children with whom he plays have
no discernible race, they remind Rabbit that his body is not what it should be,
and that he no longer enjoys the physical grace he once did.

Rabbit searches for a new body on the road. Updike reported that Jack Kerouac inspired the novel. He "found *On the Road* liberating," and thought his
own title offered its protagonist important "advice": run away from domestic
entanglements and the spiritual alienation of white middle-class consumerism.[47] Rabbit hears that advice soon after the basketball game that opens the
novel, while listening on his car radio to a "beautiful Negress" sing "Without a
Song." Listening to the voice of this allegedly beautiful but invisible body, the
surface of his own body becomes erotic: "his scalp contracts ecstatically." In
fact, he becomes nothing but skin, possessed as he is of "a cleaned out feeling
inside" (22). All at once, he is overcome by a desire to leave his Pennsylvania
suburb and "go south, down, down the map into orange groves and smoking
rivers and barefoot women" (23). Inspired by an African American work song,
he wants to find "sweet low cottonland" (29)—perhaps to sigh at the end of a
hard day's work, as Sal Paradise did, "like an old Negro cotton-picker."

But there is no outside to his world, which is composed only of outsides,
and fleeing south isn't easy. He can't find highway signs that point the way; the
roads send him east instead of south. When finally he drives across the Mason-
Dixon Line, he's accosted by a stream of commercials that punctuate the music
on the radio, many of which focus on beautiful or beautifying surfaces: "a commercial for Rayco Clear Plastic Seat Covers," "a commercial for Tame Cream
Rinse," "a commercial for New Formula Barbasol Presto-Lather, whose daily
cleansing action tends to prevent skin blemishes and emulsifies something," "a
commercial for Wool-Tex All-Wool Suits," and "a commercial for Speed-Shine
Wax and Lanolin Clay" (28–29). Organized as they are by the compulsion to
keep surfaces new and alluring, the promissory images extended by these ad-

vertisements speak in turn to the music they ensconce: mostly the bubblegum schlock rock that dominated the airways at the end of the fifties. Along with songs by innovative artists as different as Sidney Bichet, Cannonball Adderley, Chuck Berry, and Sam Cooke, the radio plays dross by the likes of Fabian, Frankie Avalon, Dodie Stevens, Connie Francis, Dwayne Eddy, the Diamonds, the Impalas, and the Admiral Tones.

It makes sense that Rabbit can't find the "real" South, or the authenticity that he craves, while listening to this hodgepodge, because, as Glenn Altschuler puts it, schlock rock "replaced distinctive regional sounds with homogenized voices, raucous riffs with lush orchestration, sexual themes with teenage yearning, rebellious white southern singers and rhythm-and-bluesy black ones with boys-next-door (and a few girls) whose looks were more important than their musical ability."[48] Embracing a Southern Agrarian fantasy, Rabbit wants the South conjured in a slave work song, a South ostensibly beyond the depredations of capitalism—not because he wants to own slaves, but because he longs for the simplicity that he thinks this labor regime provides. Before he drives south, he fondly recalls working with his body in a previous job, "his palms black" (13) with grime; after returning from his trip, he will quit his job selling the MagiPeeler, and work again as a physical laborer. But on his drive, he can't find the South with which he associates this labor. Instead, he hears songs that produce glossy abstractions of black southern musical traditions, reifications indistinguishable from commercials that urge him to beautify the surfaces of his world, the better to forget the toiling bodies that lie beneath.

It makes sense, then, that when Rabbit tries to cut straight toward the Gulf of Mexico, he's "drawn into Philadelphia" (23) instead. The clearinghouse of schlock rock, "American Bandstand," was based in Philadelphia, and had gone national the year before Rabbit makes his drive. Philadelphia "became the nation's opinion leader in popular music," writes Charlie Gillett, the model for consumer markets that knew no regional differentiation. "The rule of thumb became that what did well in Philly would probably do well elsewhere."[49] But Clark's show was also integrated, and it makes sense that, ultimately, the music to which Rabbit listens provides him with the imaginary skin that he needs, or at least deserves. In "Ace in the Hole" (1955), the short story that led to *Rabbit, Run*, Updike describes a high school basketball star blissfully dissolving into the pop music that he hears on the radio: "The music ate through his skin and mixed with nerves and small veins; he seemed to be great again."[50] The schlock rock to which Rabbit listens dissolves his body in similar fashion, the better to replace it with something more elastic and encompassing. To William Haug, the commodity that promises an alluring "second skin" both "is and is not" what it purports to be; the skin that beckons to Rabbit on his drive is, similarly, both black and not black, both white and not-white.

After he crosses the Mason-Dixon Line, Rabbit finds a map, but is forced to read it through a commercial haze: "He unfolds it standing by a Coke machine and reads it in the light coming through a window stained green by stacks of liquid wax." Standing proximate to a prominent brand, and reading a map bathed in the color of money, from light filtered through a product designed to polish surfaces, he senses that "the farther he drives the more he feels some great confused system . . . reaching for him" (29). He thinks, initially, that there is only one boundary that matters in this system: "There are so many red lines and blue lines, long names, little towns, squares and circles and stars. He moves his eyes north but the only line he recognizes is the straight dotted line of the Pennsylvania-Maryland border. The Mason Dixon Line" (33). But that boundary turns out not to matter, and just after looking at the map, Rabbit gazes at "a young but tall colored boy whose limber lazy body slumping inside his baggy Amoco coveralls Rabbit has a weird impulse to hug" (30). We're uncertain if he wishes to hug the boy because his "colored" skin promises an antidote to the product phantasmagoria through which Rabbit has been driving or because the boy is, like Rabbit thinks himself, trapped beneath a branded second surface. Ultimately, Updike suggests that these alternatives amount to much the same thing, insofar as the black skin that Rabbit imagines would save him from his own is itself a branded product: Rabbit's desire for blackness is a desire for a commodity that promises escape from commodities.

After Rabbit sees the boy, the music on the radio changes; first becoming "old standards and show tunes," the melodies later "turn to ice as real night music takes over, pianos and vibes erecting clusters in the high brittle octaves and a clarinet wandering across like a crack on a pond. Saxes doing the same figure eight over and over again." On the heels of this account of what we must assume is some version of bop, music so presumably anti-commercial that it must be described with a dense concatenation of figures as opposed to song names, Rabbit enters a diner and feels himself "unlike the other customers" (30). He then asks himself, "Is it just these people I'm outside or is it all America?" This is, in a nutshell, the experience for which he has been longing. Feeling that "the land refuses to change"—having discovered, in essence, that the South, or the African American South, is no longer confined to the South—Rabbit heads back, marveling at the ubiquity of "billboards for the same products you wondered anybody would ever want to buy" (31). He heads back, in other words, an ironic consumer, blackened by his trip, self-differentiated by a prosthetic skin that allows him to consume as a knowing outsider, nobody's fool.

All at once, signs point his way, and facilitate his decision to return to the normative world from which he sought release. So thoroughgoing is his interpellation that it need no longer operate on him explicitly. And just as suddenly, the music on the radio is "unadvertised" (34):

> Throughout the early morning, those little hours that are so black, the music keeps coming and the signs keep pointing. His brain feels like a frail but alert invalid with messengers bringing down long corridors all this music and geographical news. At the same time he feels abnormally sensitive on the surface, as if his skin is thinking. (35)

Presumably as "black" as "those little hours," the music seduces with erotic insistence. Again, Rabbit becomes all surface, as his skin assumes the functions of his brain. The commercials are gone, but their effects linger, in part because Rabbit is himself, now, written through with the logic of commodities. Blinking lights bring to mind young heiresses; he recalls the du Pont women, who had caused him on his trip south to muse, "You think of millions [of dollars] as being white" (24). Neither wealthy nor entirely white, he can, now, only wonder. All skin, and at one with his car, he is divested of agency, a vehicle for fantasies of money that seem to emerge from nowhere.

Upon his return, Rabbit becomes more than ever "a man of impulse and appetite." He defends a simple philosophy: "The world just can't touch you if you follow your instincts" (94). But there's a reason the world can't touch him: he will follow his instincts into a series of surrogate skins. It's soon after his return that he double-dates with his old coach, and a prostitute, Ruth, to whom the coach has introduced him. In a manner that anticipates Haug, "sensuality" becomes "the vehicle of an economic function." He agrees to spend the night with her, and contribute to her rent, in exchange for sex. As the two leave the restaurant, he looks where "the heart of the city shines" and sees a welter of phantasmagoric advertisements: "a shuffle of lights, a neon outline of a boot, of a peanut, of a top hat, of an enormous sunflower erected, the stem of neon six stories high, along the edge of one building to symbolize the Sunflower belt" (64). Updike closely reprises Blake Williams's movement, in *Who Walks in Darkness*, from Times Square into the body of a model: mesmerized by these alluring images, Rabbit will enter Ruth as if it were the body of the commodities he has just seen advertised; "I'm all skin," she beckons to him. "Come on. Get in" (72). To Rabbit, women are akin to blacks; "they're a different race" (81), he thinks to himself, as he makes love to Ruth. This conflation solves the problem implicit in Rabbit's trip south. As Ruth tells Rabbit, "You're too white" (150).

Made less white by occupying Ruth's skin, Rabbit strikes those around him as something of a hipster. "You just don't seem the institutional type" (204), he's told by one of his admirers. But in fact Rabbit is institutional in a densely emblematic way, for his trip south solves in symbolic fashion a problem then facing the Democratic Party. Rabbit doesn't simply run away; he runs from a wife who "has everyone on her side from Eisenhower down" (139), which is to say that he "runs" as a Democrat. Set in the spring of 1959, but published on November 12, in 1960, just four days after the presidential election of that year, the novel takes place in a state, Pennsylvania, that would vote for Kennedy by a narrow 2.4 percent margin. Support for Kennedy was even more equivocal in Berks County, on which Updike modeled his fictional Diamond County. Berks County would vote for Nixon despite the fact that the majority of its precincts were Democratic, and had turned out well for Stevenson four years earlier (the only reason the numbers seemed even close in Berks was because Reading, the model for Updike's fictional Brewer, turned out strongly for Kennedy). At bottom, the county went for Nixon because its heavily Lutheran population disapproved of Kennedy's Catholicism and, with the knowledge of hindsight, we might read the extended courtship between the Lutheran Rabbit and the progressive Episcopal reverend Eccles as a supplement to Rabbit's trip to the South:[51] Rabbit learns that his affinities lie with the young and open-minded "Jack" Eccles, whose catholic, all-embracing religiosity suggests a way beyond the sectarian tensions soon to be roused by Kennedy's candidacy. From this vantage, Rabbit's trip south creates the interracial coalition that would complement Kennedy's interdenominational coalition.

Updike didn't know for sure that Kennedy would run when he wrote, so it might be hard to see the novel's negotiations of religion in an immediately political light. But Updike must have known that the party of which he was a faithful member needed to produce a new coalition to win the presidential election of 1960, one that would unite white voters in suburbs like Rabbit's with African

American voters from states south of the Mason-Dixon Line. We might venture, then, that Updike sends Rabbit on his journey in order to bind these groups together, the better to unite them with a stylized, sensitized second skin—a skin doubly effective for seeming, as it does in *Rabbit, Run,* an alternative to the commodity form that it nevertheless reproduces. "All under him," Updike writes, "Harry feels these humans knit together." The metaphor is spatial: Harry feels himself looking down from a "cool height" (250). But these humans are also, in a sense, under his skin, which he understands as something like a fabric holding them together.

The properly institutional contours of Updike's project would become plain roughly ten years later, in *Rabbit Redux,* a novel explicitly interested in the changing makeup of the Democratic Party. "What is lib-er-alism?" (229), asks Skeeter, a fugitive Black Nationalist to whom Rabbit gives temporary shelter. This is an institutional question, not a theoretical one: what makes a liberal a liberal and a Democrat and Democrat are for Updike intimately related questions. Gore Vidal accused Updike of being "right wing" (*CU* 224). Updike responded that he wasn't right wing, because he always voted the Democratic ticket. He was a loyal party member, which proved his broadly liberal views (*CU* 246). You didn't vote Democratic because you were a liberal; you were a liberal because you voted Democratic. All the same, as *Rabbit Redux* makes clear, the election of 1968 had called this formula into question, so sharply did the contest between Hubert Humphrey and Eugene McCarthy divide the party into antithetical camps.

In *Rabbit Redux,* Rabbit reports having pulled the lever for Humphrey because, unlike McCarthy, the vice president supported the war in Vietnam. As far as domestic politics are concerned, Rabbit belongs to the "silent majority" (40); he seethes with racial resentments and disdains the counterculture. But as Updike knew, the future of the party was in the hands of the likes of McCarthy, which begins to explain why, despite his antipathies, Rabbit gives shelter to Skeeter and to a runaway flower child. Updike's novel recasts Rabbit's liberalism in order to reconcile him to a changing Democratic Party, such that he might embrace politically radical African Americans and the counterculture. And Rabbit does change, not simply by "trying to be Skeeter" but by committing to "being a nigger" (257). Skeeter encourages him: "As a white man, Chuck, you don't amount to much, but niggerwise you groove" (241). In 1971, holding together the straining coalitions of the Democratic Party required not "white-

Negro relations" but "white-nigger relations," and as we'll see in Chapter 5, that distinction indicated the increasing importance of black self-assertion to white fantasies of hip in the sixties. More pertinent here is the fact that, confronted with a solidly Republican South, there was no longer any reason for Democrats to travel south of the Mason-Dixon. The votes that would henceforth matter most were those in the North, where working-class whites like Rabbit were growing increasingly resentful about the newfound visibility and political clout of the African Americans in their midst. The North had become the new South; or, as Skeeter puts it, "the South is everywhere" (180). Hence the pressing need to gather the party's diverse and often hostile constituencies under one roof, Rabbit's roof—which in this context simply concretizes the encompassing function of its owner's flexible second skin.

Ralph Ellison's Unfinished Second Skin

The Ralph Ellison papers in the Library of Congress contain a short story dated 1983 and titled simply "Norman." The story's four pages describe a Jewish couple who take their pampered son "luddle Normundt" for a walk in New York. The couple imagine their son's golden future even as they ogle "long lean swartzas full of Super spade larceny." He will, they hazard, "Spikindt the language like a dook uv de realm. A cool thinker in a cool shade of greenbacks, tellin all the goys whose the boss."[1] The African Americans, one guesses, are the source of the cool that the child will someday exploit to his advantage. This gratuitously nasty piece—which concludes with "luddle Normundt" throwing a tantrum and shitting on the sidewalk—captures Ellison's abiding distaste for Norman Mailer. Indeed, so offended was Ellison by Mailer's pronunciations about black life that he was still, when he died in 1994, planning to include a send-up of Mailer's notorious essay "The White Negro" (1957) in his long-awaited second novel. Mailer's essay celebrated white "psychopaths" who emulate ostensibly hip black men to achieve an "apocalyptic orgasm." Mailer, Ellison wrote to Albert Murray, "thinks all hipsters are cocksmen possessed of great euphoric orgasms." This was, he pointed out, "the same old primitivism crap in a new package."[2] Ellison's second novel, released in 2010 as *Three Days Before the Shooting . . . ,* strips Mailer's primitivism of its new packaging, when an outraged but obviously titillated elderly southerner named "Norm A. Mauler" writes his senator to protest a sexual technique called "backwacking." The technique, which he describes in detail, leaves its black practitioners "as close to dying as any normal human being can possibly come and still not die."[3]

To Ellison, Mailer's Negroes were "dream creatures" and, as such, expressions of personal need.[4] But Mailer was part of a larger problem. Ellison viewed him as one of "those [white] professionals, who in order to enact a symbolic role basic to the underlying drama of American society assume a ritual mask"

(*CE* 103). A residue of nineteenth-century minstrelsy, that mask simulated black skin on behalf of a far-reaching pantomime. As Ellison had it, "The mask was an inseparable part of the national iconography" (*CE* 103); its persistence confirmed not simply the mystique of blackness but the abiding importance of white racial fantasy, we will see, to the American political imagination. Seen in this context, Ellison's animosity toward Mailer is evidence of a struggle central to the literary landscape in the decades following the Second World War, not simply over who controlled the national iconography, but over and how and on behalf of whose political interests fantasies of blackness were mobilized. Ellison was hardly the only African American writer to express alarm about Mailer's essay. James Baldwin despaired that "so antique a vision of the blacks should, at this late hour, and in so many borrowed heirlooms, be stepping off the A train." Lorraine Hansberry added her voice to Baldwin's and a swelling chorus of protest when she declared, "Who knew *where* to begin in the face of such monumental and crass assumptions."[5] But Ellison's response to Mailer was particularly freighted, and revealing, because, their considerable differences aside, the two were fascinated by the "symbolic role" played in the postwar Democratic Party by conspicuously hip "ritual masks."

On the eve of the 1960 presidential election, when Mailer dubbed John F. Kennedy "the Hipster as Presidential Candidate," he described Kennedy as having just enough "patina of that other life, the second American life, the long electric night with the fires of neon leading down the highway to the murmur of jazz."[6] By "jazz," Mailer means bebop, and Ellison thought bebop functioned for Kennedy exactly as Mailer thought it did. All the same, Ellison scorned both the music and the politician, and dramatized what Mailer elided: he viewed the creative destruction in bebop as an elision of the "jagged grain" of "brutal experience" (*CE* 129) at the heart of the blues—and thus appropriate to a Democratic Party eager to forget its roots in the interracial South.

Ellison felt that American democracy was, like American culture generally, "jazz-shaped" (*CE* 602) at its core, and his views on the democratic promise of jazz figure prominently, for example, in the writings of Albert Murray and Stanley Crouch, and in the contentious battles fought over the status of Jazz at Lincoln Center. Invariably, however, accounts of Ellison's influence run up against the fact that while he wrote on jazz with great nuance, he understood "democracy" very broadly. "American democracy is not only a political collectivity of individuals," he wrote, "but culturally a collectivity of styles, tastes, and traditions." He added,

"In order for democratic principles and ideals to remain vital, they must be communicated not only across the built-in divisions of class, race and religion, but across the divisions of aesthetic styles and tastes as well" (*CE* 602). This suggests the need for precision when communicating "democratic principles." But Ellison was far from precise. In addition to considering it "the ground-term of our concept of justice, the basis of our scheme of social rationality, [and] the rock upon which our society was built" (*CE* 31), he used the word "democracy" to capture "that condition of man's being at home in the world" (C 154) and the individual's experience of the nation's "complexity and diversity" (*CE* 768).

These latter definitions have confirmed for some a familiar account of postwar literary politics; Ken Warren claims, for example, that "the institution of the American novel" was, in the hands of writers like Ellison, "deeply implicated in redefining race in America away from the realm of political parties and movements into the intimacies of personal life."[7] I mean to insist, on the contrary, that Ellison's interest in jazz was intimately connected to his interest in political parties, which is why his implicit engagement with the Communist Party in *Invisible Man* (1952) becomes, in *Three Days*, an implicit if much more complex and equivocal engagement with the styles and tastes of the Democratic Party at the end of the fifties.

Ellison names the ostensibly white protagonist of *Three Days* after the zoot-suit-wearing hipster in his first: Adam "Bliss" Sunraider takes his name from "Bliss Rinehart," the hipster in *Invisible Man* who runs numbers, a prostitution racket, and a storefront church. Other echoes: the narrator of *Invisible Man* believes himself victimized by those who conspire "To Keep This Nigger-Boy Running"; the Senator in Ellison's second novel "runs" more successfully.[8] Invisible Man is an upwardly mobile African American who, even after moving to the North, remains indelibly marked by his education in the South; Bliss moves north with greater ease, and attains the political office for which he runs, because the color of his skin allows him to exploit a different kind of southern education.[9] After he flees the black community in which he had grown up, Bliss retains vestiges of the man who raised him, a streetwise trombone-player-turned-preacher named Alonzo Hickman, who concatenates the word of God and a vernacular, jazz-shaped culture. "You might *look* square, but you solid have *been* there!" (542), a stranger tells the minister. And indeed, Hickman thinks himself a servant of the Lord and, at the same time, a "*hep cat*" (858). Bliss learns at Hickman's feet, and the signs of this early education remain after he's left the minister's care: as one black character puts it, "Even if it appeared obvious that none of us had strayed into the boy's 'genes' pile there was no question but that we were hiding in his 'style' pile" (685).

Attending to Sunraider's style pile, we experience what Ellison experienced whenever he listened to Ellington: "the white American's inescapable Negroness" (*CE* 681). Seen in this light, Sunraider is a down-home variant of what Norman Mailer called "the white Negro": he is Negro by virtue of his southern black style, as opposed to his skin. The problem, however, beyond the obvious fact that Sunraider repudiates his blackness, is that he is as deracinated as Ellison took Mailer's "dream creatures" to be. Raised as a child minister, he rejects the church and the organic community around it in favor of an incipient capitalism. As a child, he wants payment for his ministerial services; he wants, as Hickman puts it, "to go into business with the Lord" (311). Ultimately, this is what he does, and in the process, his style becomes redolent of the wrong kind of jazz.

Ellison celebrated the blues and swing and lionized Louis Armstrong, Lester Young, Charlie Christian, and Duke Ellington for embracing the physicality of their music and defining themselves "against the ravages of time through artistic style" (*CE* 682). He viewed the ascendancy of bebop in a more negative light. "The lyrical ritual elements of folk jazz," he wrote, "have given way to the near-themeless technical virtuosity of bebop, a further triumph of technology over humanism." Though Ellison granted Charlie Parker's brilliance, he considered Parker a case in point. "As miserable, beat and lost as *he* sounded most of the time," the saxophonist contributed to "fucking up the blues." Many in his generation, Ellison complained, "don't even know the difference between a blues and a spiritual"; musicians "should know the source of their tradition."[10] Ellison wanted his jazz-shaped culture informed by knowledge of the blues, black folk traditions, the black church, and the dance hall: only then did it function as the true "soul" of the nation's "democracy." At the same time, he granted the power of bebop and its attendant styles—which is why Sunraider rises as high as he does. And Ellison's dilemma, if we can call it that, was that the novelist's power seemed also to increase to the degree that he too embraced the reification epitomized in bebop. One way or another, the black novelist depended upon black cultural styles: "If our black writers are going to become influential in the broader community," he reasoned, "they will do it in terms of style" (*CE* 368). But different styles promised different degrees of influence, and in *Three Days* Ellison dramatizes the disturbing fact that the wrong styles were winning the day.

Put another way, Bliss's journey—from an agrarian black community to commerce and national politics—articulates an impasse fundamental to Ellison's work between utopian and symptomatic accounts of black style. Ellison wanted to see black style as an agent of integration rather than a product of segregation, as an expression of a pre-capitalist wholeness rather than an example of reification. He wanted to endow style with a transformative promise, and view it as more than a reaction to racism, or the reflexive effect of exploitative structures. Ellison mapped these alternatives directly onto his conception of jazz, so that the blues and swing promise forms of creative agency and interracial community that are betrayed by bebop, which seems both a symptom of exploitation and a dangerously powerful vehicle for it.[11] Ellison mapped the same alternatives onto his engagements with the Democratic Party. *Three Days* envisions the utopian union of a New Deal liberalism and a blues-based black style only to discover that postwar liberalism was branding itself with more self-consciously hip styles derived from bop and the jazz that followed. This perception could only have increased in intensity as Ellison's writing, begun in the fifties, continued into the sixties and beyond: he wanted a therapeutic rapprochement between conservative southern whites and blacks still identified with the agrarian traditions of the South, but found in the Democrats a party increasingly dependent on stylized affiliations—organized by the likes of Charlie Parker—between northern white liberals and blacks torn from their southern roots.

These affiliations were unavoidably fraught. As Ellison saw it, Parker died from a failure to contain the tensions that his style embodied. He "stretched the limits of human contradiction beyond belief" (*CE* 263). His "vibratoless tone," which sounded "as though he could never quite make it," concealed the desire of "a do-it-yourself culture" (*CE* 264) to forget the past and the embodied relations that defined it. This was why Parker's "greatest significance" was for "educated white middle-class youth," represented most tellingly by "the so-called white hipster" who, after "casting off" the "education, language, dress, manners, and moral standards" of "American life" (*CE* 262), turned to black life for answers. As if to suggest the transfer to the hipster of Parker's contradictory blackness, Ellison claims the musician died "like a man dismembering himself with a dull razor on a spotlighted stage" (*CE* 261). The symbolic castration is simultaneously a symbolic razing off of Parker's reified skin. "The mask was the thing," Ellison writes of the burnt cork applied to nineteenth-century blackface performers, "the 'thing' in more ways than one" (*CE* 103). Figuratively detached,

Parker's black skin clothes the hipster, who has cast off his own. Ellison's second novel suggests that this same skin, stretched further still, holds together the otherwise disparate constituencies of the Democratic Party. This is a lot to place at the feet of a musician. But to see the problem in this light is to see that bebop expresses a larger problem. *Three Days* is contradictory to the core because, finally, it cannot imagine any self-consciously black style, least of all Ellison's own, capable of escaping reification. Ellison was preoccupied with the ontology of the surrogate skins offered by figures like Parker because those skins seemed to paper over so very much.

Coloring the News

The first chapters of *Three Days* recount the experiences of a white reporter, named Wellborn McIntyre, who witnesses and then investigates the shooting of Adam Sunraider. McIntyre is at the hospital where the mortally wounded Senator has been taken when he discovers that LeeWillie Minifees, a jazz musician who recently burned his Cadillac on the Senator's lawn, has been remanded to the building's psychiatric ward. He wonders if there's some connection between the shooting and the automotive immolation. Forbidden access to Minifees, he strikes up a conversation with a hipster named Charleston (ostensibly white in *Three Days*, but black in earlier versions of the novel) who works as an orderly, and who idolizes the detained musician. "LeeWillie is way out. He's gone" (209), he tells the reporter. "Everything LeeWillie *does* is interesting" (210). But Charleston won't allow McIntyre his visit until he demonstrates a sufficiently deep appreciation of "the language that goes with LeeWillie's music" (214). McIntyre is transfixed by the language—it "contained depths and traps which I had not suspected" (219), he thinks—and listens rapt as Charleston says of Sunraider's would-be assassin, "before he could catch the shuffle, that cat had leveled down—*bam! bam!*—and wasted him!" The hipster continues, "Oh, he garbaged him, man! *Ruined* him—*sieved* him!" (208). Excited, McIntyre asks, "Where did you read all that?" Charleston answers, "Oh, hell, man, are you kidding? I didn't read it that way, I'm just translating it into my own way of speaking so I can get the feel of what was put down. You know no newspaper writes like that." But they should: "You have to change that stuff so it will move, man. You see the headline said the man 'fired' at Sunraider and so on, but if it had said something like 'Mad Cat Blasts Sunraider, In God We Trust,' you'd know right away that he blasted him in the Senate standing on top of all that power" (208).

Charleston describes these revisions as "coloring the news" (209), and *Three Days* is an inquiry into the language most appropriate to the news of the early civil rights era. As Ellison saw it, imitative language like Charleston's had its place. In fact, his unfinished manuscript is awash in such performances; that language does not ask, as Ken Warren suggests it does, why "someone who didn't have to be a Negro [would] choose to become one 'one of us'" so much as it adjudicates between a wide range of instances in which whites chose to act Negro.[12] Ellison thought racial borrowing and emulation central to the nation's identity. "Americans seem to have sensed intuitively," he wrote, "that the possibility of enriching the individual self by . . . pragmatic and opportunistic appropriations has constituted one of the most precious of their freedoms" (*CE* 515). But these appropriations were appropriate only when they were born from a genuine appreciation of black traditions. At one point in the novel, Hickman listens as a white policeman adopts black mannerisms. "*What on earth does he think he's doing?* he thought. . . . the white man spoke in a voice that had become a thick-throated, inept imitation of Amos and Andy doing an imitation of a black, streetwise hipster." The routine is manifestly offensive; "Not only does he think he's become a Negro, Hickman thought, he thinks he's become a super Negro." More gallingly, the performance is "inept," "a tin-eared imitation of Negro speech." The detective thinks "that with no more than a clumsy change of accent and manner" he might "transform himself from white to black" (438–439). What most bothers Hickman is that the policeman hastily appropriates a property whose importance he makes no effort to understand.

Charleston is not the same as the white policeman. Born from love, his emulative language is adept and, as a result, possesses the kind of power that Ellison wanted for his own—the power to change the world that it would describe. Though white, Charleston considers himself black; "He's one of y'all" (213), he says to McIntyre, referring to a white man. This claim is less counterintuitive than Charleston's skin color might otherwise suggest: his speech actually alters his racial phenotype. Having provided McIntyre with a demonstration of what it means to speak of LeeWillie's music in an appropriately southern black patois, Charleston switches gears, and adopts the officious and self-consciously white lingo of a hospital employee. As this happens, McIntyre watches "his features becoming subtly more Anglo-Saxon, more refined, and when he spoke again his speech was precise, Northern, as though he were doing a mocking interpretation of a white man" (215). In the midst of this transformation, Charleston looks to McIntyre like two things at once: an Anglo-Saxon and what Sunraider, meaning to insult African Americans, calls the "black white Anglo-Saxon Protestant" (24).

Ellison here references *Really the Blues* (1946), the widely read memoir of jazz musician, weed pusher, and white Negro extraordinaire Mezz Mezzrow, who was known for his belief, transcribed by Bernard Wolfe, that "after his long years in and under Harlem" his "lips had developed fuller contours, his hair thickened and blurred, [and] his skin had darkened." These physical changes were metaphors for the transformative power of a metaphoric blackness. As Gayle Wald has it, Mezzrow's claims to bodily conversion expressed his desire to assert the primacy of a blackness performed by but not tethered to his body. Accentuating his allegedly changed lips, hair, and skin demonstrated the extent to which his true conversion was elsewhere. "Physically speaking," reads an article written with Mezzrow's assistance to promote his book, "Mezzrow couldn't pass for Negro by any stretch of the imagination; his skin is too white. His conversion to 'the race' has taken place largely within himself. In psychological makeup, he is completely a black man and proudly admits it." This was a claim opposed to the one found, for example, in John Howard Griffin's *Black Like Me* (1961). Griffin reports looking in a mirror after undergoing chemical treatments to darken his skin: "I had expected to see myself disguised, but this was something else. I was imprisoned in the flesh of an utter stranger, an unsympathetic one with whom I felt no kinship. All traces of the John Griffin I had been were wiped from existence." But after further contemplating his image, Griffin realizes "that there is no such thing as a disguised white man, when the black won't rub off. The black man is wholly a Negro, regardless of what he once may have been. I was a newly created Negro."[13] The black pigment disguising Griffin's skin does in fact rub off; nonetheless, for Griffin, adopting black skin means becoming black. Not having black skin means being white. Ellison was closer to Mezzrow than he was to Griffin. He sought to change the reality to which his language pointed by inducing a double vision: speaking a particular way about color, Charleston changes colors.

Such a metamorphosis is central not just to the plot of *Three Days* but to the structure of the novel, for Ellison is himself "doing a mocking interpretation of a white man." The reporter listens to a white man speaking as a black man; at the same time, we read Ellison, whose first-person renditions of McIntyre constitute a conspicuous act of whiteface. Ellison wanted Hickman's narrative framed by McIntyre's. The reader must "approach [Hickman and his] group from the outside," he wrote, the better to "prepare the reader for the mystery of experience." Hickman's contingent "must retain their strangeness" (974). This statement might seem to indicate who Ellison took his readers to be: identifying with McIntyre, they approach black characters as whites, "from the outside." But Ellison was interested in a "mystery of experience" more fluid than this. His commitment to writing as McIntyre dramatizes his investment in the linguistic constitution of race, the way in which talking and writing in one way as opposed to another makes listeners and readers perceive differently—or, to paraphrase Joseph Conrad, makes them, before all, see color differently. "There are many ways of being black," proclaims a Native American shaman in the novel. "There are the ways of the skin, and the ways of custom, and the way a man feels inside him." There are, in addition, many ways of "being black behind a white skin" (775). We're also told that, in the South, it's *a wide open secret that many Southern 'whites' were black and many 'blacks' white—at least visually*" (527); and we hear of "the whiteness hidden in blackness, or blackness concealed in whiteness" (587). Drinking in an integrated bar, a character with black skin is pleased to discover that he recognizes "not a single 'white' white face" (862) among those around him. One self-identified Negro describes the change she perceives in a child she has not seen in years, since raising him as her own. "Back then he was white-*looking*, yes; but he was one of us, a Negro; now he's white and one of *them*. Then he had *our* manners and *our* ways; now he has theirs—you know what I mean!" (741).

Ellison thought this kind of coloring, or re-coloring, a civic duty. "Just as there is implicit in the act of voting the responsibility of helping to govern," he wrote, "there is implicit in the act of writing a responsibility for the quality of American language" (*CE* 744). Above all, writing was like voting, and possessed of estimable quality, when it reorganized the reader's experience of individuals and groups whose figurative and literal colors were not the same. And yet, however energetically he pursued this project, he worried that there was no effective difference between the contemptuous policeman (who copies without knowledge) and Charleston (who copies from love)—and that he adumbrated what was, in effect, a phenomenology of the commodity. Ellison was one of many who asked how and in conjunction with what larger forces literary language changed the perception of color. In *The Fire Next Time* (1962), James Baldwin invoked a day when individuals would cease to see color altogether. He observed that "color is not a human or a personal reality; it is a political reality," just before insisting, "this is a distinction so extremely hard to make that the West has not been able to make it yet." Baldwin hoped his prose would help readers make that distinction. Responding one year later, Norman Podhoretz took issue with Baldwin's appeal for "the transcendence of color through love." As Podhoretz saw it, "color is indeed a political rather than a human or personal reality and if politics (which is to say power) has made it into a human and a personal reality, then only politics (which is to say power) can unmake it once again."[14] But power took many forms, and Ellison's work invariably acknowledges the confused interpenetration of political and economic reality.

In *Invisible Man*, for example, the narrator purchases a pair of sunglasses to conceal himself. The disguise works, and as he walks the streets of Harlem, strangers mistake him for Bliss Rinehart. The narrator marvels, "It was as though by dressing and walking in a certain way I had enlisted in a fraternity." He's not entirely sure how to understand his membership in this fraternity. "I was not a zootsuiter but a kind of politician," he reassures himself, before wondering, "Or was I?" (484, 485). The question is hard to answer, because the choice it presents elides the politics promulgated by the Brotherhood and the politics embodied in Rinehart, who expresses, among many things, the emancipatory promise of consumerism. *Invisible Man* ends by dramatizing the 1943 Harlem Riot, which contemporaries termed another "zoot-suit riot," after the pitched battles fought in Los Angeles earlier that year between Latino youths and white sailors and marines. The zoot suit was political, but it was so as a marker of conspicuous, unchecked consumption. Fueling the racism that caused the riots was the perception among whites that the large amount of fabric required to manufacture the clothes violated rationing guidelines set down by the War Production Board. As Andrew Ross explains, embracing the suits meant sloughing off restraint and embracing "the world of consumer capitalism." This was certainly the case in Harlem, where the suits expressed "the social aspirations of the ghetto teenager, newly introduced, like Malcolm X, to the attractive world of consumer credit."[15]

Writing of the "myths and symbols" surrounding the voluminous garments, Ellison speculated after the riots, "Perhaps the zoot-suit conceals profound political meaning."[16] But the zoot suit's political reality, no less than its economic reality, existed on the surface, as surface—in a way that recalls Wolfgang Haug's phenomenology of the commodity. As we've already seen, according to Haug, seductive images of advertised products offer consumers a "second skin." Assuming the commodity's second skin in place of his own, the consumer's "sensuality" becomes "the vehicle of an economic function." *Invisible Man* repeatedly describes the ever-renewing promise of prosthetic second skins that present themselves as vehicles of economic functions. Clothing and accessories figure this substitutive process with frequency, perhaps because the acutely fashion-conscious Ellison once worked in a men's store, dressing window dummies in bespoke suits.[17] The novel describes its narrator's compulsion toward men's clothing. He dreams of dressing in "a dapper suit of rich material, cut fashionably," and working as "one of the men you saw in magazine ads, the junior executive types in *Esquire*" (164). He discovers that this suit is cut from fraud, its promises, lies. But he is entranced by lies, and moves from one to the next. Committed against his own better judgment to a cycle of illusion and disillusionment, to entertaining renewed promises and sustaining further disappointments, he finds a different suit of clothes. Dressed in "a new blue suit" by the Brotherhood, about to begin his first speaking engagement, he feels reborn: "The new suit imparted a newness to me. It was the clothes and the new name and the circumstances. It was a newness too subtle to be put into thought, but there it was. I was becoming someone else" (335). Yet he discovers that these clothes are also cut from fraud, and is again stripped of the fantasy they embody, before turning hopefully to the zoot suit. Haug helps us understand the drive that animates this inexhaustible appetite for deceit: the perceptual inducements of advertising encourage individuals to see fraud and look beyond it. At every point, he explains, consumers see the commodity as something that "is and is not what it is."

That double vision is implicit in Susan Willis's observation that blackface was "a metaphor for the commodity," and thus a particularly complex deceit. Blackface amalgamated what is and is not, which is why Eric Lott characterizes the minstrel performer as a "seeming counterfeit." The formulation nicely captures how blackface performances held in abeyance the status of their authenticity. "As for the counterfeit," Lott writes, "it is clear enough from the evidence that consciousness of the copy did not foreclose on a variety of responses to its 'blackness.'"[18] Along these lines, Ellison declared that the "Negroes" one tended to find in American literature were "counterfeits," "projected aspects of an internal symbolic process through which, like a primitive tribesman dancing himself into the group frenzy necessary for battle, the white American prepares himself emotionally to perform a social role" (*CE* 84). But Ellison understood that counterfeits were no less effective for being seemingly unreal. Black Americans had important roles to play—as counterfeits. He believed, for example, that "the Negro," as imagined by whites, was the "keeper of the nation's sense of democratic achievement" (*CE* 782).

Preoccupied with vision in *Three Days*, Ellison sees the commodity, and the racial counterfeit, two ways: as something that is and is not what it is. Hickman is interested in what happens "in the blanks between seeing and not-seeing" (131). McIntyre thinks "the seen and the unseen" have been "stewed together" (136) by the nation's racial unrest. "We are held together by a delicate system of alliances and agreements as to the nature of reality" (77), he claims. Ellison is drawn to figures that violate that system and, in so doing, make manifest through a kind of double vision the abstractions required by capitalism. Thus he describes one Jessie Rockmore, an old man who, having been freed from slavery as a child, grows up entranced by the promise of democracy, but sinks into despair in his final hours. Rockmore spends his life "pulling dollars and pennies out of [his] black hide" (151), and amasses a fortune. But feeling betrayed by Congress, he ceases to believe in the larger value of the currency that he earns. Doubly alienated from the product of his labor, he hires a blond prostitute to dance for him, in a costume made from gold certificates. She materializes before him, "in the very flesh" (168), but covered in money. Moments later, a man we presume to be Sunraider bursts through the door. For no immediately explicable reason, Rockmore refers to him as a "yellow Negro" (169). Sunraider's "inescapable Negro-ness" appears as the color of gold: yellow. He's not unmasked as a racial hybrid (one meaning of "yellow") so much as he is covered by the dancer's second skin—a shimmering suit of gold that has been pulled from Rockmore's hide, a figure for the transformation of labor into an exchangeable and alluring property. Sunraider's particular brand of blackness, Ellison suggests, doesn't inhere in the traces of his lost connection to Hickman so much as it is a fetish produced through the symbolizing of black labor.

"Black and White unite and sweat and swing"

McIntyre considers himself "a liberal man" (132), but the nature of his liberalism has changed over the years. In the hospital, waiting for news of Sunraider's condition, he replays in his mind the end of a relationship he had with a black woman from Harlem, just before the entrance of the United States into the Second World War. His girlfriend, Laura, was pregnant and he visited her parents, flush with optimism, to declare his good intentions. The mother responded with fury, and drove him from the apartment, and by implication the relationship. Feeling guilty about the readiness with which he left, McIntyre stopped at a Harlem jazz club known for its jam sessions, the preferred late-night destination of musicians just off from their jobs downtown. The time and place suggests Minton's Playhouse, the Harlem club associated with the rise of bebop. Ellison wrote an essay on Minton's pivotal role in precipitating "changes which have reshaped the world, [and] a momentous modulation into a new kind of musical sensibility; in brief, a revolution in culture" (*CE* 239). McIntyre's experience begins to explain why this revolution was, to Ellison, something less than cause for celebration, and something with which it made sense to associate Senator Sunraider on the one hand and unchecked capitalism on the other.

McIntyre first met Laura at a swing ballroom. Gripped by the idealism of the thirties, the two became model progressives; he recalls that "in our circle it was agreed that Laura and I represented, if not the future, at least a good earnest of that time when the old conflicts left unresolved by the great war between the states (and we were nothing if not historical-minded) and the wounds, outrages, and inequalities which haunted contemporary society would be resolved by transcendent love" (101). McIntyre adopted as his "personal slogan" the phrase "democracy is love, love is democracy" (102). The end of the relationship dealt a crippling blow to McIntyre's liberalism, oriented as it was around fantasies of racial uplift. Walking the streets of Harlem after he's been thrown out of her parents' apartment, looking at the faces of destitute African Americans, he thought, "*I've suffered a defeat of hope. Our love had been meant to help them, and now it is broken*" (111). He does not recover. "The end of my relation with Laura," he sums up, was the end "to my efforts at social action" (126).

Dreamy as it was, McIntyre's idealism was doomed to failure, but Ellison takes seriously the promise embodied in swing and the New Deal. In drafts of the novel now published as part of *Three Days*, he describes how venues like the Savoy ballroom, where McIntyre dances with Laura, allowed "Black and White [to] unite and sweat and swing."[19] These unpublished drafts elaborate upon all that Ellison associates with that vision of collective and interracial exertion. At one point, a Harlem street-corner preacher admonishes her audience:

> Y'all don't believe in F.D.R. or Eleanore! You don't believe in Joe, in Sugar Ray, or in Mary McLeod Mawthume; Maw Rainey, Bessie Smith or in Louie Armstrong. . . . You don't believe what you read in the papers, except those ads; you don't believe

what you see on TeeVee—and I don't have to even *mention* the Bible. All you do is *pretend* like you do—And then you puts it all down as square. That's why you so dumb and ignurant! That's why you round here acting so hip when in fack you ain't paid no dues.

The self-consciously hip crowd, she insists, has lost sight of the importance of black history, and flounders in an artificial world of manufactured products: she will fulminate at length, for example, on their romance with rubber, a machine-made substance that keeps them at a distance from an otherwise bracing actuality. Her point is not that "hip" as such produces this distance, any more than it spelled the end of either the New Deal or the musical styles enumerated above. Rather, she imagines herself addressing those committed to the wrong vision of hip, which is why she wants to "hip y'all to the truth."[20] And as we will see, for Ellison, that mistaken vision is most insidious and, at the same time, most potentially evocative of Ellison's own project, in the credence it lends advertisements.

Three Days begins to elaborate the relationship between postwar hip and advertising when McIntyre drifts into the bebop club, and finds in its chaotic music an objective correlative for his newfound resignation. He hears a "dazzling burst of improvisational pyrotechnics," as "spurred by the big man with the saxophone, the music soon reached a hysterical pitch of surprise-producing unrestraint" (120). Tears flood his eyes as he watches a musician invoke and then shred a popular melody—as the musician "ridiculed its sentiments [and] mocked its pretension," the song is "transformed by a mood which belied the man's appearance, the people, the place, the very banality of the song itself" (121). As if in response to the music, forms lose their clarity: "faces suddenly flowed, liquid and loose with a sudden slackening of feature" (123). A woman with a tambourine seems to become, among other things, "a prancing horse, a fish on its tail, a circus bear" (122). McIntyre's deranging experience echoes his rumination on senators, and establishes one of many links between bebop and Sunraider. Senators, he thinks, are mercurial, shape-shifting creatures. "Shouldn't it be expected," he muses, "that, figuratively, lions, tigers, chimpanzees and jackals—chimeras even—should prowl the atmosphere around them" (76).

Ellison's novel likens jazz to a kind of backroom persuasion. "Jazzmen, jazzmen," he thinks. "What moneymen do with political influence and cash they do with horns, rhythm, and reeds . . ." (731). Indeed, *Three Days* provides a sustained account of how bebop in particular is not simply like money, but a version of commodity fetishism. The phantasmagoria surrounding senators and the musicians to whom McIntyre listens in Ellison's fictional Minton's displace a forgotten reality. The hallucinatory transmogrifications in the club, for example, take place by way of a violent exclusion, in which a street-corner preacher (the one who fulminates about advertisements) protests the music, precipitates a fight, and is then thrown out of the bar. "It makes for too much confusion, bringing religion into a jazz joint" (124), the proprietor says. As we've seen, Ellison characterized bebop by its rejection of the vernacular traditions of the blues and the black church; those at Minton's, he thought, were "screwed up musicians" (356) in part because they rejected the idioms that once sustained black music. Thus the music's apostasy invokes Rockmore's (who experiences "the loss of his lifelong religious convictions" [147] just before hiring his dancer) and, more centrally, Sunraider's (who served when young as a minister in Hickman's church, before renouncing God and entering politics).

Of course Sunraider loses more than his religion. "*Let Hickman wear black, I, Bliss, will wear a suit of sable*" (392): Hickman's "black" refers, by way of *Hamlet*, both to his mournful ministerial cloth and to his skin, just as Bliss's "suit of sable" refers to the way in which money will, as a function of conspicuous consumption, "prowl the atmosphere" around him, and thereby replace what was once his blackness. Bliss reinvents his skin, and when he cries, "*The past is in your skins*" (392), he means to insist upon the ability of the African Americans with whom he grew up to shed their skins, by forgetting their pasts, as he does his. The issue is not memory per se, however, but how a style either does or does not retain vestiges of its origins. "Imagine," one of Hickman's congregation says, "going up there to New England and using all that kind of old Southern stuff, our own stuff, which we never get a chance to use on a broad platform—and making it pay off" (1011). Sunraider personifies the commodity fetishism that haunts any black style that is torn from its roots, and made to pay off. A human commodity, he produces himself through self-alienation.

According to Marx, a commodity takes on a life of its own—and becomes, to take one famous example, a dancing table—by obscuring its origins in concrete social relations. This process of reification turns social relations into things, even as it accords things what seem to be human, social dimensions. Following Georg Lukács, Theodor Adorno claims that "all reification is forgetting: objects become purely thing-like the moment they are retained for us without the continued presence of their other aspects: when something of them has been forgotten."²¹ (Adorno considered jazz a particularly acute instance of this forgetting: in "Jazz—Perennial Fashion," an article that Ellison kept stored with the many drafts of his second novel, he describes the music's relationship to syncopation as inherently fetishistic, given as he thought it was to recycling technical effects that gestured in incomplete fashion to more sophisticated musical structures.) For Sunraider, making black stuff pay off requires actively obscuring domestic and agrarian labor. Rejecting his adoptive father and the community that raised him, Bliss sloughs off domestic entanglements and what Hickman calls "*the ties that bind us to this land*" (724).

That strategy allows Sunraider to thrive, but only for a time. Ultimately, his estranged son, "Severn," kills him. The name is appropriate, since Sunraider is by that point "severed" from his past. Of course, as this return of the repressed might suggest, Sunraider doesn't actually forget anything (which is why he can make his southern stuff pay off). The issue, however, is how and in what way he's legible to others, and here it's important to recall that the reification at work in commodity fetishism doesn't involve absolute erasure so much as a lingering if coded awareness of what seems to have been forgotten. To imagine a dancing table is to reify the labor that made it and, at one and the same time, to see that labor as having been transmuted into the table's dance. Thus, as we've already seen, Sunraider's personal style condenses the personal history and labor relations that he would disavow.

And yet, it's hard not to feel that the disavowal is Ellison's. Timothy Bewes reminds us that even as Adorno claimed "all reification is forgetting," he recognized that "all remembering is *necessarily* a forgetting, and vice versa."²² We might use this observation, and Bewes's larger contention that reification is inseparable from the consciousness of it, to register Ellison's equivocal relation to forgetting. For example, Ellison insists but hardly elaborates on the ties that bind Hickman to the land; there is little mention of the South's political economy during Jim Crow and virtually no depiction of physical labor anywhere in this gargantuan novel. Beyond uneasily indicating his own distance as a cosmopolitan intellectual from the kind of community that he nostalgically evokes, this ellipsis recalls Ellison's overly emphatic dismissal of Amiri Baraka's claim that the blues emerged from the isolating labor conditions of tenant farming. For Baraka, the blues were an expression of "the leisure that could be extracted from even the most desolate sharecropper's shack in Mississippi." Large slave plantations gave rise to collective work songs; "the small farms and sharecroppers' plots produced," he claims, "a form of song or shout that did not necessarily have to be concerned with, or inspired by, *labor*" (*BP* 61). To Baraka the blues are born from, even as they represent an effort to forget, specific social relations. Such a claim unsettled Ellison, committed as he was to the notion that his own style did more than reflect conditions of inequality, and no doubt suggested his uncomfortable affinity with the beboppers—upwardly mobile professionals infatuated with "technology" and eager to forget anything but the emancipatory powers of their art.

Put another way, we might say that Ellison, while committed to his ability to inhabit the consciousness of a white reporter, a black preacher, and a mountebank shape-shifter turned politician, suspects he is most like the shape-shifter, who, after leaving Hickman, wanders the country selling second skins in many forms. Bliss exploits the doubled vision with which African Americans "were [then] looking at themselves and yet *not* at themselves" (798). After performing in minstrel shows, but before producing movies, Bliss goes into the business of making skin bleach and hair straightener, and finally wigs, hairpieces, and straightening combs. He then moves into designing advertisements for the cosmetics trade (707). In one business venture after another, he generates illusory surfaces that appeal with amorous glances. The business of politics is no exception: one of the novel's characters might well be speaking of Sunraider when he says, "Today politicians . . . talk more flimflam than the admen" (960).

As Ellison has it, Sunraider and bull fiddle player LeeWillie Minifees talk this flimflam together, almost out of the same mouth. This point is made forcefully when Minifees burns his Cadillac on the lawn of Sunraider's estate, in response to the Senator's proclamation that, due to its popularity with African Americans, the Cadillac should be considered a black brand, and should be rejected by white consumers. Feeling personally assaulted by Sunraider's claim, Minifees sacrifices his own car, the better to preserve all that it represents. But in doing so, he echoes the Senator in a number of telling ways, and not simply because he does the Senator's bidding by symbolically divesting his Cadillac of its blackness. Minifees is "the black man in the white suit" and Sunraider "the white-capped Senator" (39), described moments earlier as "invulnerable" behind "a suit of blackmail" (34) (he is covered in figurative "black mail" by virtue of his willingness to cow white enemies whom he suspects have black ancestry). The deeper irony, of course, is that both are black men covered by protective white surface: Minifees has his suit, and Sunraider is "black behind a white

skin" (775). Their actions rhyme as well. McIntyre understands the Senator's
radio speech as "an act" or "a happening" (47); Minifees ups the ante, but his
happening parallels Sunraider's. When Minifees arrives at the estate, Sunraider
is "cooking in a large, chrome grill cart" (36). Minifees proceeds to set his car
alight, like "a huge fowl being flambéed" (39).

The eye-catching nature of the flambé leads local journalists to describe it
as "the new style of conspicuous consumption" (49). One of them jokes, "Thor-
stein Veblen, sir, today your theory has been demonstrated to the tenth power"
(50). Minifees's Cadillac is conspicuously "consumed" in flames; it becomes the
pretext for a public spectacle more than an object possessed of a particular use
value. And though Minifees will understand his action as an expression of his
freedom from the constraints of ownership, those in attendance see the action
as the apotheosis of consumerism. Ellison insists, in paradoxical fashion, that
the conflagration must be seen both ways because it expresses the logic of the
commodity. As Minifees begins his happening, McIntyre listens "for the horn
of a second car or station wagon which would bring the familiar load of pretty
models, harassed editors, nervous wardrobe mistresses, and elegant fashion
photographers who would convert the car, the clothes, and the Senator's elegant home into a photographic rite of spring." Even as Minifees covers the car
with gasoline, McIntyre thinks he witnesses the filming of a commercial: "For
so accustomed have we Americans become to the tricks, the shenanigans and
frauds of advertising, so adjusted to the contrived fantasies of commerce—
indeed, to pseudo-events of all kinds—that I thought that the car was being
drenched with a special liquid which would make it more alluring for a series
of commercial photographs" (37). Beneath the skin-like veneer of the gasoline,
we find the same intriguing conjunction discussed above from *Invisible Man*:
a heightened consciousness of fraud makes one more rather than less likely to
embrace illusion and fantasy. Ellison lends warrant to this embrace. The liquid
is not intended to make the car more alluring; it is gasoline, and Minifees ig-
nites the car. But McIntyre is right to compare the event to an advertising stunt.
Ignited, the car becomes dramatically perceptible and symbolically redolent.

Minifees conceives of his act while listening to Sunraider on his car radio.
As he takes in the diatribe, he undergoes a change akin to the one experienced
by Invisible Man after he puts on his sunglasses. "The *scales* dropped from
my eyes. I had been BLIND, but the Senator up there on that hill was making
me SEE" (43). Minifees brings this new sight to those witnessing his arson;

he accomplishes what McIntyre calls a fraud of advertising by replacing the use value of his car with a shimmering membrane that produces a spectacular image. The fraud and the skin are coextensive: the fire that results from the membrane destroys the car but saves the brand. As Charleston sees it, "every one of those dollars" that it takes to build a Cadillac "has a rainbow around its shoulders. Hell, yes, every one of those caddidollars has some glamour added" (210). Minifees repurposes this glamour in his own act of branding. Doing so involves the further abstraction of labor, in which the material form of the commodity is destroyed to produce a still-more-phantasmagoric second skin. Assuming this skin, figured as brand, no longer requires the purchase or experience of an actual object. The Cadillac expresses for Minifees "an aesthetic as well as a utilitarian value." Destroying the car, he destroys its utility. At the same time, destroying the car leaves him better positioned to consume the brand. Minifees explains that "for me that Caddy wasn't simply a car." Rather, "she was like a guaranteed freedom to move—*when* I wanted to and *where* I wanted to—you dig?" (228). Confined in his cell, Minifees is able more fully to enjoy the "glamour" promised by the idea of this freedom. "Now it's gone," he says, speaking of the body but not the spirit of his car, "and I'm free" (229). The irony is heavy: physically confined, Minifees experiences freedom not in a moving car that burns gasoline, but in gasoline that burns a car—in the imaginary skin of a brand lit by gasoline.

The *OED* tells us that the word "brand" referred to "destruction by fire" and "the burning rays of the sun" before it was used to describe the carefully managed image worlds that corporations built around their products. It's significant, then, that Minifees brands the Cadillac by destroying it in fire even as Sunraider, whose name evokes the burning rays of the sun, fulminates on the Cadillac brand while speaking of "the bedazzlement fostered by the brightness of our ideals" (243). Each brands the Cadillac so that it becomes, simultaneously, white and black. Before Minifees burns it, the car is pointedly white, and it burns, Minifees wants us to know, with the aid of "good white wood *alcohol* and good *white* gasoline" (44). But we might hazard that while burning, it begins to turn black. The Cadillac has two skins, which is one reason why it makes sense that, however different their motives, Minifees and Sunraider both brand the car with jazz and its attendant freedoms. Sunraider thinks the "crass and jazzy defiance of good taste" (243) at work in the black appropriation of the Cadillac suggestive, however improbably, of the nation's capacity for self-renewal.

To Minifees, the Cadillac epitomizes his music: it is "what good jazz is to noise" (229). Burning the car, he shifts this association to seemingly unrepeatable registers: he doesn't rebuke the Senator so much as challenge him with a presumably unrepeatable solo. As Dizzy Gillespie put it, bebop was meant to "scare away the no-talent guys"; so too with Minifees and his display of conspicuous consumption, which Ellison describes as a "duet" (45) with the fiery Cadillac.

Upon whom did Ellison model the players in this cutting contest, in which a race-baiting senator and a jazz musician seem, even as they denounce each other, to accomplish the same ends—united, as it were, underneath the figurative skin of the Cadillac? Minifees, it's safe to say, works in either bebop or a post-bop mode. Charlie "Bird" Parker offers one probable model, not simply because of the nature of Charleston's commitment to Minifees but because Ellison has McIntyre witness the burning of the Cadillac when returning from a "bird-watching" (35) expedition. Indeed, the fact that McIntyre views Sunraider through binoculars intended for this expedition suggests that bebop mediates the reporter's perception of the entire event. As well it should: Ellison described bebop in terms that echo Minifees's action—as a form of anti-commercial commercialism. Ellison admired jazz musicians of the thirties, among other reasons, because "their motivation wasn't primarily economic" (*LM* 261). This innocence meant that the dance experience central to swing, for example, was an unalienated, "total experience" (*LM* 274). Conversely, despite the fact that swing bands were far more revenue-dependent than bop bands, which first assembled at Minton's in flight from musician union representatives bent on preventing musicians from playing in public without remuneration, Ellison thought that the progenitors of bebop were seeking "a fresh form of entertainment which would allow them their fair share of the entertainment market, which had been dominated by whites during the swing era." He adds, "Today nothing succeeds like rebellion" (*CE* 283). When Charleston says, "You have to change that stuff so it will move, man," we hear Ellison's unease with bebop—that it was a vehicle for moving goods more than bodies on a dance floor. Certainly Minifees consolidates his own brand in his act of defiance. "I shook my head, closing my eyes to find flashes of flame streaked behind my lids," reports McIntyre, when thinking of the event; the very name of Minifees "struck fire in my mind" (133).

But even more than Parker, bull fiddle master Charles Mingus offers a likely model for this act of branding. The self-styled "Angry Man of Jazz," Mingus used to smash his bass onstage in what Scott Saul calls acts of "creative destruction." The term, borrowed from Joseph Schumpeter, evokes what we saw above: the creation of a brand through the destruction of an individual car. It also aptly describes Mingus's relation to the business of jazz. He protested the commercialization of the music by record companies, complaining in 1953, "'Jazz' has become a commodity to sell, like apples or, more accurately, corn." At the same time, he considered himself a "stone cold capitalist." Famously theatrical and given to spectacle when it came to collecting what he considered his pitifully small royalties (we might call them "mini fees"), he once donned a safari suit and helmet and, shotgun in hand, visited the accounting department at Columbia Records to demand payment. But Mingus is most compelling as a model for Minifees because of his famous satire of Orval Faubus, the Democratic governor of Arkansas who in 1957 blocked the court-ordered integration of schools in Little Rock. In 1959, Mingus recorded "Original Fables of Faubus" (1960), which savagely mocked the racist politician.[23] It's hard not to hear echoes of that recording when Minifees offers his send-up of Sunraider's views.

Skinning the President

Though we are never told what party he belongs to, Sunraider is cut from the same cloth as southern Democrats like Faubus. In many ways, *Three Days* is an agonized love letter to southern whites who rush to disavow the intimacy they shared with blacks as children and who, as adults, hatefully reject their imbrication in black culture. But Sunraider is a complex amalgam (he's analogized at one point to "a monster with two heads inhabiting a single body" [685]), and there are compelling reasons to read him as a fusion of Lyndon Johnson and John F. Kennedy. Ellison considered Johnson "the greatest American President for the poor and for Negroes" because he changed "the iconography of federal power" (*CE* 566). Northern artists and intellectuals could not understand, Ellison maintained, "meanings that went deeper than the issue of the government's role in the arts or the issue of Vietnam" (*CE* 559). These meanings were available even in Johnson's speech. As Ellison has it, "What one listens for in the utterance of any President is very similar to what one listens for in a novel: the degree to which it contains what Henry James termed 'felt life'" (*CE* 560). At bottom, Ellison hears in Johnson the "accent of speech" (*CE* 559), the "unreconstructed Texas accent" (*CE* 561), that he associates with the felt life of his youth. Thus he imagines that Johnson's "style and idiom form a connective linkage between his identity as representative of a particular group and region of people and his identity as President of *all* the people" (*CE* 560). When Hickman hears the styles and idioms of the black church in Sunraider's political oratory, he mourns the Senator's refusal to commit to the connective linkage already manifest in his voice. At one point Hickman recalls a "Texas white boy who was always hanging around till he was like one of us." The boy's black compatriots ask him, "*Tex, why you always out here hanging round with us all the time? You could be President, you know.*" Tex answers: "*Yeah, but what's the White House got that's better than what's right here?*" (480). Bliss was to be the answer to that question, a walking exemplification that a white southerner's commitment to "hanging around till he was like one of us" might under the right circumstances lead toward rather than away from the White House.

If Johnson is the president that Bliss fails to be, then Kennedy is the one that he most resembles in that failure. Many of Sunraider's commitments "seem forward looking" (24): he supports preserving national parks and shorelines, and nationalizing broadcast television (24, 165). Kennedy aggressively supported parks and shorelines, and used television for political ends in an unprecedented fashion. Sunraider appears to be on the Foreign Relations Committee and advocates aid to Third World nations, in order to silence their opposition to U.S. racism (1010); also on the Foreign Relations Committee, Kennedy did the same. Many of Sunraider's less than forward-looking commitments also resemble Kennedy's. When Hickman first visits Sunraider's Senate office, he finds a bust of pro-slavery vice president John Calhoun; in 1957, Kennedy chaired a Senate committee that named Calhoun one of the nation's five greatest senators. Sunraider is still more visibly like Kennedy when he listens to one "O'Brien," who tells him "to lay off the nigger issue because the niggers and the New York Jews are out to get us. This year they don't have to take it and they won't" (259–260). A draft in the Ellison collection makes clear how to understand this "us": "we're losing your state and my state and even New York seems doubtful," an advisor tells the Senator, "except for the niggers and the Jews in the city."[24] Only a Democrat could have spoken those lines. But not just any Democrat: Kennedy's early career was dogged by the perception that he was anti-Semitic as well as hostile to civil rights, and his campaign manager in 1952, 1958, and 1960, Larry O'Brien, was credited with mitigating that perception. There was much to mitigate: the year that Kennedy memorialized Calhoun, he was one of the few non-southern Democrats to join southern Democrats and conservative Republicans in undermining the Civil Rights Bill of 1957. This, combined with his proclivity to side with regional interests against his party's interests (which earned him the moniker "the Senator from New England"), finds echo in Ellison's remark that Sunraider, who represents an unnamed New England state, "flaunted his association with the Southern bloc to the embarrassment of his party." Sunraider embraces "collaborations across party and sectional lines" as necessary to "governing a diversified nation." Consequently, "certain party leaders" view him as a threat to "the very foundations of their power" (23). Adlai Stevenson, and the liberal core of the party that had supported him since 1952, viewed Kennedy in just this manner.[25]

Like Kennedy before him, Sunraider suggests a contradictory liberalism; raised in the South but representing a constituency in the North, both "forward looking" and reactionary, Sunraider is an embodiment of the incongruous imperatives then animating the Democratic Party. Courting or otherwise relying on African American voters was not at first prominent among those imperatives, and *Three Days* indicates as much. Ellison published the first part of his novel in March 1960, three months after Kennedy announced his candidacy for the presidency. The title and substance of the piece are suggestive: "Hickman Arrives" begins with Hickman, evocative of King, arriving in Washington, DC, with his congregation, to see Senator Sunraider. Bliss rejected them years ago, and has been antagonizing blacks ever since. But they are sure he needs their help. It's hard not to read this scenario as a comment on the readiness of black voters to throw in with a New England senator like Kennedy, who needed their assistance even if he refused to ask for it. A southerner in the novel puts this clearly, if in a more paranoid light: "We know for a fact that nigras are moving up North in keeping with a long-range plan to seize control of the American Government" (54). Beware, he adds, of those Negroes who "brag about the nigra vote electing the President of the United States" (60).

Yet Sunraider refuses Hickman's assistance, just as Kennedy refused to court black votes and sidestepped the issue of civil rights throughout the initial stages of his bid for the presidency. The candidate limited himself to a series of late gestures toward blacks. He hired University of Notre Dame's Harris Wolford to lead the campaign on civil rights; he ran advertisements featuring himself with Harry Belafonte, who introduced himself as an artist on the one hand and "as a Negro and as an American" on the other.[26] Most famously, on October 19, just before the election, he called Coretta Scott King to express his sympathy over the fact that Martin Luther King Jr. had been jailed in Atlanta. "Did a Phone

Call Elect Kennedy President?" asks an article in an issue of the *Negro Digest* saved with Ellison's drafts. "The Kennedy-King phone relay looms as the single headlined incident of the campaign. Previously there was little difference between the parties as Negroes appraised the records of the candidates and the promises."[27] Before entering politics, a friend of Bliss's declares that "*the colored don't need rights . . . they only need rites. You get it?*" (393). The strong support that Kennedy received from black voters in return for his symbolic gestures perhaps suggested as much. However, Kennedy's rites were coded. He won not simply because blacks voted for him, but because his shimmering patina appealed to suburban whites in the Northeast ready to embrace jazz in their living room more than black families on their blocks. In comparing Sunraider to Kennedy, and in claiming that Ellison's character shares something of the patina that Norman Mailer perceived around Kennedy, I've been suggesting that Sunraider glosses (gives luster to even as he obscures) an ellipsis integral to Kennedy's appeal—the way in which his style telegraphed commitments to racial justice that, during the election, he rarely avowed openly.

But it's perhaps more useful to say that Sunraider expresses the dialectical nature of Kennedy's liberalism—the necessary and mutually constitutive relation of what only seem to be its incompatible terms. Sunraider is no simple illusion, no mere fraud. Echoing Invisible Man, he calls himself "*a walking personification of the negative*" (408). He is, in fact, what Fredric Jameson, paraphrasing Adorno, calls "a movement of negation that can never reach a synthesis, a negativity that ceaselessly undermines all the available positivities until it has only its own destructive energy to promote." The Senator articulates what Jameson calls "the contagion of the dialectic" and defines as the "essential restlessness or negativity that fastens on our thinking at those moments in which we seem arrested and paralyzed by an antinomy." According to Jameson, that negativity allows us to see simple oppositions as constitutive of a larger whole; the "constructional function of the negative," he explains, inheres in its ability to describe the necessity inhering in a given set of relationships, of which it is itself a part. Even when it refuses synthesis, the negative delimits a boundary; it produces a formal system, at the same time suggesting what must become, at a second remove, a more encompassing dialectic between that system and what at first seems beyond and inassimilable to it. Sunraider's destructive energy delineates the relationships that define the Democratic Party at the end of the fifties, even as it suggests what lies beyond them.[28]

Put in more concrete terms, *Three Days* describes a dialectical relation between northern white professionals (like McIntyre) fascinated by what it means to be black, and southern blacks (like Hickman) fascinated by that fascination. McIntyre and Hickman meet each other, and offer their respective narratives, while they wait together for news of the dying Sunraider, who mediates their relationship even as he pushes beyond it: himself a white acting black and a black acting white, the Senator strains to the breaking point the politics of interracial identification. He does so intentionally, but—and this is Ellison's surprise gambit—he understands his bigotry toward blacks as inseparable from his desire to help them. The Senator ridicules "Negroes," he claims, in the hopes that they might give up their folk mannerisms and traditions; doing so will allow them to *"change the rules!"* and *"strike back in collaborative anger"* (392). He sets out to free African Americans by burlesquing their styles, tastes, and traditions—in effect, by destroying them, as Minifees does his Cadillac. He musters his hate, he believes, in the service of love. This perverse strategy—in which appreciative emulations and bitter rejections of black culture are bound together—suggests the necessary, reciprocal self-constitution not simply of northern liberals and blacks but, at another remove, of northern hipsters and southern bigots. "The different is not confronted by *any* other," Hegel insists, "but by *its* other." Jameson explains: "The slave is not the opposite of the master, but rather, along with him, an equally integral component of the larger system called slavery."[29] It fell to Ellison to point out that the hipster was not the opposite of the racist southerner, but rather, along with him, an equally integral component in the larger system called the Democratic Party.

Moving now beyond the Democratic Party, allowing our vision to encompass the larger system of relationships of which it is itself a constitutive part, we return to Ellison's favorite if often mystifying term, "democracy." From this more encompassing vantage, Sunraider personifies the interrelation of Republicans and Democrats. Indeed, it might be said that *Three Days* is an elaborate account of the dialectical relationship that obtained between Kennedy and Abraham Lincoln, a figure who possessed the virtues and sympathies that Ellison wanted Democrats to possess. Hickman sees Lincoln as symbolically black, and therefore capable of uniting black and white through properly Christian values. He sees what southern racists see, a black president, but hopes that love and compassion might lead to the integration of black and white. Looking upon the Lincoln Memorial, Hickman thinks that the president was *"one of us"*

in part because of the president's "*brooding facial expression.*" Hickman understands Lincoln's color in two ways, literally and figuratively: it isn't "*the darkness
of his flesh*" (575) that makes him appear black—it is his capacity to embody suffering. Appreciating that capacity begins to turn racial antagonists into brothers, he thinks. Hickman raises Bliss with this in mind; he hopes the boy, white
to the eye but culturally black, might unify the country as Lincoln did. "*And to
think,*" Hickman despairs while gazing at the memorial, "*we had hope to raise
ourselves that kind of man*" (421). But Hickman might have said, "We had hope
to raise ourselves a liberal Republican like Lincoln but, betrayed by the reversals
of history, find ourselves stuck with a conservative Democrat like Kennedy."

Cognizance of these reversals might seem to do no more than confirm the
essential sameness of the two parties. All his life, Ellison denounced the Hayes-
Tilden Compromise, the 1877 agreement between Democrats and Republicans
that ended Reconstruction. From that moment on, it seemed reasonable to
think, the nation's two political parties conspired to hold identical positions on
black civil rights. This seemed especially true in the years immediately following *Brown v. Board of Education*, when it was unclear which party represented
the interests of African Americans, who had been voting since 1936 with the
Democrats. Though seemingly indifferent to the nation's systemic racial inequality, Eisenhower had appointed Earl Warren to the Supreme Court, and
Stevenson, the champion of liberalism, had shown no enthusiasm for civil
rights. It was therefore possible, in 1957, for Samuel Lubell to write of the 1956
presidential contest, "One of the striking paradoxes of the whole election was
that the Negro and the white Southerner could cast a protest vote against one
another by voting for the same man, Dwight D. Eisenhower."[30] Thus Ellison remarks in the surrealistic "Tell It Like It Is, Baby," written between 1956 and 1965
as a teaser for the second novel, that the "Negro American novelist" who "tries
to write about desegregation" must remain aware, when describing North and
South, or white and black, of a "whirling nightmare of terms and attitudes" that
"change constantly into their opposite" (*CE* 31).

Undeniably, Ellison felt intense frustration that the two political parties
were at moments strikingly similar. Over the course of the fifties, he watched
in dismay as the Democrats sacrificed Franklin Roosevelt and Harry Truman's
tentative commitments to civil rights to placate reactionary southerners. Ellison had cut his teeth on the New Deal; as Lawrence Jackson puts it, he "saw
the WPA, with all of its shifting political ground, contested hallways, and cross-

purposes, as a model for interracial antagonistic democracy in cooperative action." But as Arnold Rampersad adds, Ellison subsequently struggled with his allegiance to the Democrats. He wrote of the 1956 presidential contest that though he was a registered Democrat, he couldn't support Stevenson. "I can't stand American politics for the moment because I can no longer swoller [*sic*] the southerners and Ike is still a hick," he added.[31] This said, Ellison is typically absorbed less with the absolute identity of the two parties than with the dialectical motion of their reversals, the calibrations with which each seemed to ghost the other: he knew the Civil Rights Movement was meeting furious political resistance during the fifties because the parties were changing in relation to each other. The Republicans had long had a liberal wing; indeed, as Rick Perlstein sees it, before about 1958 the GOP was on the whole more sympathetic to civil rights and blacks than was the Democratic Party.[32] But by the middle of the decade it was already possible to see the party extending its typically upper-class vision of white Protestantism to middle- and lower-class whites, and becoming in the process more committed to reactionary forms of populism and to what Richard Hofstadter, in 1955, called the "status politics" of WASP nativism. The Democrats, on the other hand, had been for some time more divided than the Republicans; they drew power from labor unions, urban ethnic machines in the Northeast, and racists in the South who were loyal to the party ever since the Civil War for the simple reason that Republicans had freed the slaves and instituted Reconstruction. But the party was slowly breaking free of the Old South—winning increasing numbers of black votes and making inroads among suburban professionals in the Northeast—and becoming in the process less connected to the populist traditions that once defined it.

Preoccupied by these reversals, and motivated by anger at the "Southern Congressmen's defiance of the Supreme Court" (*CE* 27), Ellison's "Tell It Like It Is, Baby" announces that "even the word 'democracy' . . . changes into its opposite, depending upon who is using it, upon his color, racial identity, the section of the country in which he happened to have been born, or where and with whom he happens to be at the moment of utterance" (*CE* 31–32). We might understand this as a comment on the similarity of the two parties. But it is, more revealingly, a comment on how the entire democratic system, defined as it is by two parties, seemed sometimes to turn into something other than itself. For Ellison, as we will see in one moment, telling it like it is about American racial politics requires describing how the capitalist underpinnings of democracy intimated the emergence of an imperial militarism antithetical to democracy. In this context, the imperative to "tell it like it is" promises a radical critique, in which the defiance of southern congressmen is implicated in the global politics of the sixties. But as is so often the case in Ellison, that imperative requires qualification, and recognition that truth telling is necessarily bound up with falsification. The dangling "Baby" attached to the title recognizes as much: the essay was prompted by a letter from a working-class friend, a companion from Ellison's days in Oklahoma, who mockingly goads the literary intellectual (so deracinated as to be working in Rome upon receipt of the letter) to remember whence he came and provide insight into the politics of desegregation. In this context, the "Baby" is a mask, a rhetorical affectation that allows Ellison to adopt for a moment a reified blackness. No less than when selling commodities, telling it like it is requires telling it like it is not.

In the "is-and-isn't world" (*CE* 42) of the essay, Ellison recounts a dream in which he witnesses "cracker senators" (*CE* 29) defiling Lincoln's corpse. When first he sees the slain president, Ellison marvels that he has "a complexion darker than I'd ever imagined" (*CE* 37). But in this remorseless and desacralizing dream, a mob, wanting souvenirs, appropriates Lincoln's blackness. In a reprise of his account of Charlie Parker, Ellison describes the president's "dismemberment": the mob uses razors to tear off Lincoln's "black coat" (*CE* 38). Ultimately, nothing remains but his undergarments. After further indignities—in which he is manipulated into "the cordwood postures of Dachau" (*CE* 41)—Lincoln's body swells and distends, in one last futile protest, until it resembles "the body of the figure in the Michelin trademark" (*CE* 43). Robbed of his blackness, Lincoln becomes a corporate logo—and an especially meaningful one at that. The Michelin Man is white because the pneumatic tires invented by the Michelin brothers at the end of the nineteenth century were white, but by the mid-1960s, that whiteness had come to bear a particular freight. During the 1920s and 1930s, Michelin ran vast rubber plantations in Indochina. Labor conditions were brutal, and historians credit an uprising at one of these plantations, Phú Riềng Đỏ, as a turning point in the history of the Vietnamese Communist Party, which was able for the first time effectively to organize workers' unrest.[33] By 1965, when Ellison published "Tell It Like It Is," Lyndon Johnson had substantially expanded the use of U.S. troops in Vietnam, to fight that very party, and in doing so had begun fatally to undermine the progress of his ambitious "Great Society"—if not the promise of democracy itself.

In "The Myth of the Flawed White Southerner" (1968), Ellison revisited the support he expressed in 1965 for Johnson's commitment to the war. He admits that, eager to defend Johnson from white intellectuals in the North who failed to appreciate the president's importance to black working classes in the South, he "underevaluated the issues which so concerned my fellow intellectuals" (*CE* 558). He surely regretted the fact that the first Democratic president decisively to champion civil rights—a president he credited with preserving the cultural styles of the South for liberal ends—was, in the moment of his triumph, the moment of his party's triumph, defending the residues of a colonial labor regime that bore uncomfortable similarities to the one Lincoln had endeavored to end, and in the process turning American democracy into something it should not be. "It's happening again" (*CE* 35), the dreamer thinks; everything seemed to be changing into its opposite. No wonder Edmund Wilson appears as part of the mob that defiles Lincoln: Wilson had just published *Patriotic Gore* (1962), which equates the North's war on the South during the Civil War with the long history of U.S. imperialism in Asia, and with the Cold War tendency to "clothe" (xxxi) otherwise naked national aggression in the language of moral virtue. Ellison wanted to believe in that virtue—in Lincoln's, especially. But he saw double: the Democratic Party's jazz-shaped culture, on the one hand, and a trademark beneath it, on the other.

5 White-Collar Liberation and *The Confessions of Nat Turner*

"Who ain't a slave?"

Herman Melville, *Moby Dick*

"What does it mean to be a slave? What does it mean to be free? And, even more, how does it *feel*?"[1] With these questions, B. A. Botkin introduces *Lay My Burden Down*, a 1945 volume of ex-slave narratives compiled during the late thirties by workers on the New Deal's Works Progress Administration (WPA). Botkin volunteers no answers. He would rather the narratives speak for themselves. They are, he avers, "the first attempt[s] of Negroes to write their own history." The narratives are "folk history—history from the bottom up, in which people become their own historians." A professional folklorist, Botkin believes that histories from the top down can too easily "be dismissed as a patronizing gesture, a nostalgic wish, an elegiac complaint, a sporadic and abortive revival—on the part of paternalistic aristocrats going slumming, dilettantish provincials going native, defeated sectionalists going back to the soil."[2] Whatever his own thoughts about the meaning and felt experience of slavery and freedom, he doesn't offer them.

At the same time, compiling the narratives did involve a certain amount of ventriloquism. Botkin valued the project because he believed that "history must study the inarticulate many as well as the articulate few" (xiii). In an important sense, the ex-slaves remained inarticulate, and spoken for. Botkin acknowledges in his introduction that the narratives are not actually written by ex-slaves, most of whom were well over seventy years old when interviewed. He further grants that the narratives often betray the "personal prejudices and sympathies" (xii) of the typically white writers who conducted the interviews on which they were based. Historians add that while a few of the interviews were conducted with an early version of the tape recorder, most were based on notes and only later transcribed into narrative form, at which point multiple officials at different New Deal agencies edited them. This was an unavoidably bureaucratic affair. A subdivision of the WPA, the Folklore Division of the Federal Writers' Project compiled the interviews. As head of the Folklore Division, Botkin reported to Henry Alsberg, director of the Writers' Project, who reported in turn to Harry Hopkins, director of the WPA, who reported in his turn to Franklin Roosevelt. Overseen by numerous offices and agencies, the editing of the narratives was inconsistent and the subject of sometimes heated debate. The WPA's national editor of Negro Affairs, Sterling Brown, adjudicated these debates with interoffice memos describing, for example, how to transcribe dialect and offering guidelines concerning whether to adhere more faithfully to pronunciation or idiom.[3]

The narratives remain an invaluable resource and offer unmatched insights into the lives of American slaves. Of the roughly 100,000 ex-slaves still alive when the project began, the WPA interviewed more than 2,000, a significant percentage by most sampling criteria. Even correcting for bias and inconsistent editing, the sheer number of the interviews makes them a definitive resource.[4] But at the risk of further dispossessing the subjects of the interviews, we might nevertheless ask what it would mean to understand the narratives as expressing something other than the experiences of ex-slaves themselves—that is, as a form of governmental speech. Harry Hopkins said the goal of the Writers' Project was to have the government "appear in the role of an author" in a way that "would have been considered fantastic a few years ago."[5] To him, anything written under the auspices of the Writers' Project was in some basic way an expression of the New Deal. From this perspective, the slave narratives constitute an act of blackface, an impersonation by a sitting Democratic administration of once enslaved African Americans.

What value did Roosevelt's administration derive from this minstrelsy?[6] Typically, the New Deal supported cultural programs so that they might call attention to and generate sympathy for those most in need of the state's ministrations. The documentary project on the Farm Security Administration, for example, paid Walker Evans to take the photographs that would later be collected in *Let Us Now Praise Famous Men* (1941), in order to capture the severity of the poverty that the New Deal intended to redress. The motivation behind the Writers' Project's production of the American Guide Series was slightly different. Each of the states participating in the project created a guidebook designed to recount the history of that state and thereby spur domestic tourism. More grandiosely, the series aimed to capture the national spirit. "The creative forces of the nation were being mustered," declares a Writers' Project employee in a novel written by a former project writer, "to produce The Story of America.

Not just the history, not merely the politics, the economics, the village folklore, the literature, but the whole thing. Think of it, to tell the story of AMERICA!"[7] Michael Sandel explains the significance of this undertaking when he reminds us that the New Deal's

> embrace of the nation was a decisive departure. From Jefferson to the populists, the party of democracy in American political debate had been, roughly speaking, the party of the provinces, of decentralized power, of small-town and small-scale America. And against them had stood the party of the nation—first Federalists, then Whigs, then the Republicans of Lincoln—a party that spoke for the consolidation of the union. It was thus the historic achievement of the New Deal to unite, in a single party and political program, what Samuel Beer has called "liberalism and the national idea." . . . In the twentieth century, liberalism made its peace with concentrated power.[8]

The guidebooks provided an outlet through which the Democratic Party might speak on behalf of consolidated national interests seemingly irreducible to party interests. In doing so, the party became more than a particular coalition of constituencies—it became, instead, the voice of the civic ideals that united all Americans.

The Democratic Party found in the ex-slave narrative project another vehicle for expressing its cultural nationalism. The decision to frame the narratives as the "bottom-up" self-expression of ex-slaves made sense given the fact that the WPA began the widespread collection of ex-slave narratives the same year that African Americans began to vote Democratic. The Roosevelt administration wished to speak on behalf of ex-slaves, and African Americans generally, but it wanted to avoid the impression that its doing so foreclosed the possibility of their self-expression.[9] This said, the narratives were a form of governmental speech addressed to whites as well as blacks. A Republican president had freed the slaves, but a Democratic one would, in bringing their stories to light, free them again and, in the process, claim for the Democrats not simply the votes of black Americans but the liberating powers of government itself. Abraham Lincoln's Emancipation Proclamation represented what was to the Democrats an unimpeachable exercise of federal power, and the New Deal was eager to recall that act on behalf of a wide-ranging expansion of federal authority. We therefore see in the decision to collect the narratives the implication, made explicit by radical historians during the sixties, that working-class whites suffering from the excesses of industrial capitalism were analogous to slaves in their need for a state-orchestrated emancipation.[10] Government had freed the slaves, the WPA seemed intent on suggesting, and it could free working-class whites as well.

This was and would remain dangerous terrain. Roosevelt described African American culture as quintessentially American; more pointedly, he viewed black music as especially evocative of the hardships then confronting all citizens. This was a period, after all, during which, in the words of one contemporary commentator, "the blues are on everyone's lip."[11] But did the blues on the lips of a white worker's face transform that face, and render it symbolically black, in a politically useful way? This question was as acute after the war as it was before it; associating working-class whites and blacks was, for Democrats, as fraught with peril during the sixties as it was during the thirties. White backlash decisively changed the party in 1966 when the Democrats lost, in the congressional elections of that year, the extraordinary majority they had won in 1964. The midterm elections of 1966 represented a watershed in the party's history, and while historians continue to argue about exactly what precipitated the reversal and who participated in it, these arguments typically begin from the assumption that working-class whites left the party in response to Lyndon Johnson's commitments to working-class blacks.[12]

Fueling racist resentments over the Democrats' commitment to African Americans were violent urban uprisings and the radicalization of the civil rights movement, both of which reflected a fundamental shift in black attitudes about slavery and political emancipation.[13] Bebop and hard bop also reflected that shift; these were the idioms, as opposed to the blues, that were on the lips of the decade's most politically assertive African Americans.

Over and beyond the strictly technical differences between bop and the blues, the two forms offered different answers to the questions with which this chapter begins: what does it mean to be slave or to be free? What does it feel like to be either? As Amiri Baraka points out in *Blues People*, the blues derived from the labor relations of the agrarian South. They drew from the collective work songs prevalent during slavery and evolved in idiosyncratic fashion during Reconstruction when African American laborers, now working in greater isolation from each other on smaller lots of land, developed more personally expressive voices and styles. According to Baraka, who discarded his "slave name," LeRoi Jones, in 1968, bebop broke with the agrarian labor metaphysic at the heart of the blues. "I am certain," he writes of Charlie Parker's *Ornithology*, "the Negroes who made the music would not, under any circumstances, be willing to pick cotton" (200). Claims like this suggested the broadly revolutionary attitude animating bebop and then hard bop. John Leland sees this music asking, "Could America accommodate black expression at its least accommodating? In short, could it embrace its own persecution?"[14] The stakes could not have been higher, at least to Baraka. As John Gennari puts it, "Having grown up with bebop and having derived from it a sense of the possibility of an assertive black male ego, Baraka very much wanted this music to be seen as a threshold in black-white relations, as a cultural fault line marking the distinction between slavery and freedom."[15]

The white novelists who follow here and in the next chapter negotiate the "black-white relations" of the late sixties by speaking in the name of "an assertive black male ego." But they do not justify the hope that the United States was ready to "accommodate black expression at its least accommodating." In William Styron's *The Confessions of Nat Turner* (1967) especially, often egregious acts of ventriloquism, offered on behalf of an angry black slave, express sixties-era cultural nationalism at its most self-contradictory. Elaborating these contradictions in light of the Democratic Party with which Styron was preoccupied, on the one hand, and the professional-managerial class (PMC) for which he wrote, on the other, will require understanding two related developments: the generalization of "slavery" such that it described an alarmingly wide and imprecise set of economic and ultimately cultural relationships, and the concomitant internalization of the struggle for emancipation that was deemed appropriate to these new understandings of slavery.

PMC Poetics

The PMC was invaluable to the Democrats during the Depression, when its allegiance to Roosevelt helped contain and absorb the radicalized working classes and buttress the ostensibly enlightened standards of expertise at the core of the New Deal.[16] During the moderate fifties, when little separated the parties on social issues, this group moved back to the center, and voted with others in their tax bracket. But starting at the end of that decade, as the Republicans moved out of the Northeast and abandoned their moderate voice, professionals and managers flooded back to the Democratic Party. By 1968, pundits like Arthur Schlesinger Jr. were noting that "the level of education had superseded the level of income as the dividing line in our public affairs," and that, as a consequence, "the rising professional, managerial, and technical classes" would figure centrally in any version of the Democrats' future.[17] By 1972, when George McGovern laid claim to the "constituency of conscience" first assembled by Eugene McCarthy, these classes had replaced labor unions decisively as the party's most powerful bloc.

Over the following decades, members of the managerial and technical classes remained receptive to and moved between both major political parties. Professionals, on the other hand, stayed loyal to the Democrats—this despite the fact that their economic interests often conflicted with the party's programs of wealth redistribution. This particular allegiance had a powerfully symbolic component, one that helps to explain the professional's imagined affinity with African Americans. In 1951, C. Wright Mills announced that "bureaucratic institutions invade all professions and many professionals now operate as part of the managerial demiurge." Once proudly autonomous, members of their own self-regulating guilds, professionals were being forced to "work in some department, under some kind of manager; while their salaries are often high, they are salaries, and the conditions of their work are laid down by rule."[18] Mills appealed to professionals made anxious by their transformation into a well-paid proletariat, as well as to a far larger group: all those members of the PMC who found themselves a small cog in a larger machine. Theodore White analyzed the 1960 census data and concluded that Americans "worked more and more for other men, in larger and larger enterprises. The giants of American employment . . . were baronies in themselves, self-governments, huge, almost unbelievable bureaucracies—as large as the government bureaucracies, with which they clashed and warred."[19] Reactions against this trend defined the period's intellectual life. These were years in which social critics decried the alienating effects of management and the saving graces of an unfettered creativity. Whether revisiting John Stuart Mill's elevation of Samuel Taylor Coleridge above Jeremy Bentham, reproducing Max Weber's romance with charisma and suspicion of institutions, or elaborating what James Burnham called a "bureaucratic collectivism" that applied equally to totalitarian societies and faceless corporations, intellectuals described the plight of the professional as emblematic of a larger social malaise—and, with surprising frequency, as evocative of the plight of African Americans.

Ostensibly, African Americans were natural allies of professionals—who often thought themselves at war with managerial and market forces. Talcott

Parsons reasoned that the professions provided a model of social organization antecedent to and able to check market forces. His thinking expressed the widespread belief, reiterated by critics and historians, that the professional embraced "self-consciously pre-capitalist 'quality of life' values over the competition for profits."[20] By this logic, professionals possessed a special affinity with blacks, who seemed, in the racist logic of the moment, to represent a wellspring of charismatic value beyond market utility and bureaucratic rationality. In "Ecstatic in Blackface" (1949), an essay that influenced Frantz Fanon, Bernard Wolfe offered an incisive account of this assumption: "Every community calls out a string of 'unnecessary' sounds and movements from its members. In these mass rituals of voice and body the whole subjective state of a people can be read, its fulfillments and its frustrations. These 'nonuseful' exercises must be doubly revealing in America—for here they have become overwhelmingly Negroid in both content and form." "The Negro image," he added, "pleases us in some 'nonfunctional' way."[21] Others claimed that the African culture of slaves was inimical to Max Weber's Protestant ethos. Much of the blues, Amiri Baraka insists in *Blues People*, came from "the circumstance of finding yourself in a culture of white humanist pseudo-Puritanical storekeepers." "The cruelest psychological and cultural imposition of all," he adds, while describing the American slave's jarring encounter with American life, "was the inculcation of this Puritan ethos on a people whose most elegant traditions were the complete antithesis of it" (10, 126).

Norman Mailer reproduced this logic when describing the hipster as the harbinger of a sexual politics in which charismatic heroism, violence, and the pursuit of pleasure broke through the stultifying ethos of the managerial demiurge. Hip was to him what literature was to Lionel Trilling: the embodiment of an atavistic romanticism that might counterbalance liberalism's managerial commitment to rationality. Mailer's hipster was thus what Fredric Jameson calls the "charismatic hero," a figure who embodies "a vision of the liberated self . . . a self integrated beyond the contingencies of the fallen world of the historical present, in a realm in which meaningful action is once more possible, in which means and ends are one and henceforth never to be disjoined."[22] This vision held in abeyance, among many things, a tension that would define postwar American professionalism. To Stephen Brint, "social trustee professionalism" would, over the second half of the twentieth century, give way to "expert professionalism": once committed to civic ideals and public causes, and to their independence of judgment in the face of financial reward, professionals came increasingly to view their services as "a resource sold to bidders in the market for skilled labor."[23] White hip reconciled these alternatives in a politically sanctioned fantasy, one that cast African Americans as suffering citizens in need of paternal ministrations and, at the same time, as streetwise rebels skilled in the art of self-promotion. Professionals committed to hip might draw on both these alternatives, and thus embrace the notion that they need not choose between civic ideals and market forces.

Whereas the early Civil Rights Movement dramatized altruism and moral elevation, Mailer's preeningly masculine hip offered a conspicuously self-serving calculus. The curious fact, however, is that his views were understood to accommodate professionals wanting involvement in the movement. According to August Meier, "hipster personality types" were widely prevalent on the 1961 Freedom Ride to Alabama and Mississippi, to take but one example. Many, he says,

> fitted quite neatly into Norman Mailer's concept of the "white Negro." Alienated from the middle-class conventions of their parents, they glorified the most alienated and outcast group in American society, lower-class Negroes. They accepted the stereotypes whites hold about lower-class Negroes—the stereotypes of personal sloppiness and uninhibited sexuality. Only, instead of considering these qualities bad, they regarded them as the warp and woof of a superior way of life. As one bearded Johns Hopkins graduate student gravely informed me: "Of course Negroes are more promiscuous and uninhibited sexually than whites. I envy them and wish I could be like them."[24]

Meier's graduate student affiliates with the movement precisely because he valorizes what he takes to be the self-interested nature of black sexuality. "There but for the grip of my superego go I," wrote Anatole Broyard in an early satire of the hipster.[25] Longing for the loss of his superego, Meier's professional-in-training understands his commitment to civil rights as a commitment to a version of himself freed from the oppressions of his mind and society. As Tom Wolfe described matters, in *Radical Chic and Mau-Mauing the Flak Catchers* (1971), the Black Panthers appealed to liberals in just this way. To Wolfe, "radical chic," which "is only radical in style," served the needs of "social-welfare professionals in the Kennedy Administration," who decided to fund those racial groups most willing to engage in belligerent self-aggrandizement. He describes a meeting between two blacks, with "the look of hip and super-cool and so fine," and welfare "bureaucrats" who, eager to appear sympathetic, "thickened up their voices and threw a few 'mans' and 'likes' and 'digs' into the conversation."[26] For the reactionary Wolfe, pushy black hipsters conspired with fawning state-employed professionals to produce the culture of liberalism. "Shock me, shock me," cry Wolfe's caricatured liberals, who are eager to learn how to stand up and emancipate themselves from their privilege.

Wolfe's account is extreme and mean-spirited, but it was the case, during the sixties, that numerous left-leaning liberals and radicals described white-collar workers as suffering something akin to slavery. Influenced by the struggle for civil rights in the South, but also responding to the growing pathos surrounding the routinization of knowledge work, students participating in the Free Speech Movement depicted Americans as "slaves of their own industrial creations." As Mario Savio explained, this bondage wasn't simply economic. He lamented the fact that "America is becoming ever more the utopia of sterilized, automated contentment." Expounding on this line of thought, Herbert Marcuse's *One-Dimensional Man* (1964) announced the apotheosis of a "technocratic rationality" that left white-collar workers "slaves of developed industrial civilization."[27] William Styron's *The Confessions of Nat Turner* begins from an analogous premise. He wrote the novel, he told James Jones, because he wanted to determine what kind of person "actually revolts from IBM or the big-corporation complex, which is a form of slavery." To Styron, white-collar work conditions suggested the legal ownership of persons, and the experience of historical slaves spoke to the alienated experience of "modern man" generally.[28]

Needless to say, these are figurative accounts of slavery: they do not describe the legal ownership of one class by another. But they do capture an important development in the postwar experience of middle-class self-estrangement. Mills called the white-collar worker "the hero as victim, the small creature who is acted upon but who does not act" (xii). Thus described, this new worker seemed to exemplify what Marx called "alienation." But Marx's terms didn't map easily onto white-collar workers. He characterized alienation as the estrangement of object from subject: "The object which labor produces—labor's product—confronts it as something alien, as a power independent of the producer. The product of labor is labor which has been embodied in an object."[29] But, as Mills pointed out, "as a proportion of the labor force, fewer individuals manipulate things, more handle people and symbols." This was especially the case with white-collars, who do not "live by making things; rather, they live off the social machineries that organize and coordinate the people who make things" (65). Historians of knowledge work point out that these social machineries tended more and more to process fungible and deracinated bits of information. For Alan Liu, the shift to a "*post*industrial" economy that began during the fifties and sixties, and that was attended by what he calls the rise of "informating," precipitated an awareness that "where once matter was the essence (in the industrial age a corporation not only processed matter but *was* its material factories, inventory, and people), now matter work [was] for the developing world." This new regime confined itself to "information processing or (since durables and consumables must still be produced) at least [to] matter that can be made to act like information processing—that is, plants, goods, and people, endowed with the quick-turnaround responsiveness, flexibility, and ultimate eraseability of bits."[30] The shift here from "matter" to "information" corresponds to the shift in Mills from "products" to "symbols": in both cases we track a "derealization."

At the same time, lest we make too much of the difference between manipulating matter and manipulating information, we should recall that, for Marx, "derealization" results from the structurally required forgetting of the relations that organize production. That forgetting didn't require members of the professional and managerial class to overlook their impending proletarianization. Recognition of this predicament suffuses most everything written by or on behalf of that class, which is why so much of that writing embraces solidarity with the working classes and African Americans in particular. Rather, the derealization crucial to the PMC required forgetting the ultimately coercive nature of its managerial function—the way in which that class saved itself from proletarianization by controlling classes beneath it on behalf of capital. As Barbara and John Ehrenreich put it, the PMC comprises "salaried mental workers who do not own the means of production and whose major function in the social division of labor may be described broadly as the reproduction of capitalist culture and capitalist class relations." Barbara Ehrenreich adds that the PMC has since the start of the twentieth century deployed its expertise as a form of "nonviolent social control" on behalf of capitalists who believed "that a cadre of professionals was cheaper than an army of Pinkertons" when it came to pacifying the working classes.[31] Absorbed with their transformation into a proletariat, members of the PMC—teachers, government workers, engineers, nurses, lower- and middle-level managers, journalists, advertising personnel, lawyers, and doctors—overlooked the disciplinary nature of their jobs, and instead dramatized themselves as slaves subject to the authority of another.

Psychic slavery in particular was for members of the PMC a figure through which to live and reconcile basic contradictions in their relations to production. This class worked on behalf of and aspired to join the capitalist class. But that aspiration could not be avowed explicitly; quite the contrary, effectively managing labor typically required the white-collar to disavow his role in extracting surplus value from those beneath him. We might hazard that the therapeutic exhortation so common to this period to free the mind from its self-incarceration emerged in part to mediate this contradiction. A legion of psychoanalysts supplied the raw material for these dramas, no doubt. But it also mattered that members of the PMC could hear what they needed to hear in the Civil Rights Movement. In a speech in Montgomery, Alabama, in 1954, for example, Martin Luther King Jr. described a

> type of slavery which is probably more prevalent and certainly more injurious than physical bondage, namely mental slavery. This is a slavery that the individual inflicts upon himself. History abounds with individuals who have enjoyed physical freedom and who have at the same time inflicted mental and spiritual [slavery] upon themselves. Deep down in their souls and minds they were slaves.[32]

Torn from their context, arguments like these suggested a solution to the PMC's class anxiety: though "salaried mental workers" enjoyed great physical freedoms, they were also perpetrators of what King called a "mental slavery," not against others but against themselves. Locating the slave inside trivializes the structural inequity confronting the working class—an inequity that the PMC is paid to sustain. But it also allows the professional or manager to imagine himself both a (white) capitalist-owner and a (black) worker-slave. And, as a consequence, it allows the professional or manager to transcend, in an act of self-liberation, the class conflict that he is paid to mediate.

The figure of psychic slavery mystified the PMC's contradictory class position even as it militated on behalf of the progressive coalitions into which that class was then entering. Critics have long noted the tendency of U.S. literature to assume, as Richard Poirier has it, that "freedom" is "a creation not of political institutions but of consciousness, that freedom is that reality which the consciousness creates for itself."[33] This is an accurate account of much postwar fiction, which often borrows its retrograde racial assumptions from psychoanalysis. Sándor Ferenczi wrote to Freud, for example, that "blacks represent the unconscious of the Americans. Thus the hate, the reaction formation against one's own vices."[34] Postwar fiction is rife with versions of this claim. As John Berryman put it in the concluding line of "The Imaginary Jew" (1945), "Every murderer strikes the mirror, the lash of the torturer falls on the mirror and cuts the real image, and the real and the imaginary blood flow down together."[35] If racial prejudice was a projection outward of internal strife, then liberating oneself from self-hatred and racial prejudice was the same, and making peace with one's prejudice against African Americans was tantamount to making peace with actual African Americans. The integrated personality was a model for, and a step on the way to, the integrated society.

Needless to say, this project was profoundly limited. The novels that follow here and in the next chapter are novels of desublimation, in which revolutionary black voices seeming to reside within white men militate against restraint. These voices function as goads toward personal liberation and suggest the extent to which personal and political freedoms might coincide under the aegis of the Democratic Party. But these novels, each in its own way, are instances of what Herbert Marcuse called "repressive desublimation"—they release contained sexual and aggressive energies, the better to channel those energies toward gratification in already extant capitalist markets and labor relations. Ralph Ellison provides a useful illustration. In *Three Days Before the Shooting . . .* , the white liberal Wellborn McIntyre slips into a dream. A lawn statue, a "hitching-post boy, a little iron groom" (180) shaped into the figure of an African American, speaks to him. The voice berates McIntyre with cagey insinuations and hip braggadocio—"Oh, I know you, baby" (188), he sneers. The implied intimacy is unsettling, as the voice addresses McIntyre as "McGowan," a racist southerner with whom he works. But McIntyre accepts the label, and thinks, "There's nothing to do but pick up McGowan's burden" (187). A good liberal, divided in his mind into a southern racist and an angry black voice no longer willing to accept an ornamental role, McIntyre appears ready to free himself. But his thoughts betray him. As he struggles with the weight of his implied sin, he thinks of turning the iron statue into capital that he can reinvest in a productive process. He thinks it a "natural resource," and imagines it "melted down, rolled into ingots, [and] made into the small screws and bolts of some vast anonymous machine" (190). The mental-worker-as-liberal dreams like a capitalist: discovering a black voice inside, he extracts voice from body in just the way that he dreams of extracting surplus value from the body of the iron groom. The novels that follow utilize black voice in an analogous fashion, expropriating it from its laboring base.

"Imperious moral duty"

The publication of William Styron's *The Confessions of Nat Turner* precipitated a tempest, easily the most significant literary controversy of the decade. White critics celebrated the novel. It shot to the top of best-seller lists, garnered a movie contract, and won the Pulitzer Prize. But numerous black critics and novelists—many of whom voiced their opinions in *William Styron's Nat Turner: Ten Black Writers Respond* (1968)—excoriated Styron, who recalled of the time following his novel's publication, "I would experience almost total alienation from black people, be stung by their rage, and, finally, be cast as an archenemy of the race, having unwittingly created one of the first politically incorrect texts of our time."[36]

Styron had set out to dramatize what the novel's "author's note" called "the only effective, sustained revolt in the annals of American Negro Slavery," an 1831 uprising in Virginia during which some fifty-five slaves led by Nat Turner killed a roughly equal number of whites, and after which some two hundred blacks were killed in random acts of retaliatory violence. Many objected to the assumption that Turner's was the only significant American slave rebellion. Others decried Styron's depiction of slaves defending their masters' plantations against Turner's followers, or faulted Styron for suggesting that Turner was sexually conflicted, alternately attracted to a young black man and a white woman. More broadly, many saw in Styron's novel yet one more example of a white establishment profiting from the black experience. *Nat Turner* represented a literary theft, not simply because it promulgated a controversial image of the historical Turner, but because it rendered "blackness" a fungible and deracinated sign at precisely the moment when black activists were struggling to exert a proprietary interest in black history and culture.

John Oliver Killens felt that Styron used Turner to impugn the emergence of a militant black vanguard: it seemed that this white southern author, descended from a slave-owning family, had turned a symbol of black male outrage and empowerment into a case study in contemporary pathology. Even favorable reviews saw the novel as less about the 1830s than the 1960s.[37] And Styron himself acknowledged that he "was never anything but intensely aware of the way in which the theme of slave rebellion was finding echoes in the gathering tensions of the Civil Rights movement" (439). But he hadn't fully appreciated the extent to which Nat Turner had become a figure worth fighting over. Speaking at the 1963 March on Washington, John Lewis, the chairman of the Student Nonviolent Coordinating Committee (SNCC), declared, "The revolution is at hand, and we must free ourselves of the chains of political and economic slavery."[38] He advocated peaceful emancipation. But by 1965, SNCC was questioning its advocacy of nonviolence. Stokely Carmichael replaced Lewis as the head of SNCC in 1966, as Styron was writing his novel, and soon thereafter orchestrated the expulsion of the organization's white members in the name of what he called "Black Power." Turner was a touchstone in this larger trend. In his 1965 autobiography, Malcolm X used Turner to malign the pacifism of Martin Luther King Jr.: "Nat Turner," he said, "wasn't going around preaching pie-in-the-sky and 'non-violent' freedom for the black man." In 1968, Addison Gayle agreed that Turner's uprising "negated the absurd and nonsensical philosophy" of King. "Cut deeply enough into the most docile Negro, and you will find a conscious murderer," concurred Larry Neal. "Behind the lyrics of the blues and the shuffling porter loom visions of white throats being cut and cities burning." Eldridge Cleaver added that "the embryonic spirit of kamikaze, real and alive, grows each day in the black man's heart, and there are dreams of Nat Turner's legacy."[39]

As Killens intuited, Styron strongly disapproved of that legacy; *Nat Turner* did express a liberal's horrified reaction to revolutionary black fervor. But Styron suggested in more anodyne terms that despite his misgivings with Turner's rebellion, he wanted to understand more than to rebuke. "It is impossible to live in America these days without giving the racial problem a great deal of thought," he said. "And I suspect that the efforts I made to recreate Nat Turner, to bring him back to life, represented at least partially the accomplishment of an imperious moral duty: to get to know the blacks" (*CWS* 81). Two years before the publication of his novel, Styron wrote, "The Negro may feel that it is too late to be known, and that the desire to know him reeks of outrageous condescension. But to break down the old law, to come to know the Negro, has become the moral imperative of every white Southerner" (*QD* 14). Styron would get to know the blacks whether they liked it or not.

Nat Turner is perhaps the most striking example of how this imperative shaped writing of the sixties, much of which describes or arises from instances of whites endeavoring with mixed motives and results to understand blacks better than they have. In Harper Lee's *To Kill a Mockingbird* (1960), Atticus Finch tells his children, "You never really understand a person until you consider things from his point of view . . . until you climb into his skin and walk around in it."[40] Fascinated by murderous white trash, the novel struggles unevenly to climb into the skin of its black characters. A work of nonfiction, John Howard Griffin's *Black Like Me* (1962) takes up Finch's admonition; it follows the author and future civil rights activist as he darkens his skin and then lives in working-class black communities in Louisiana and Mississippi. In Flannery O'Connor's "Everything That Rises Must Converge" (1965), a disingenuous liberal tries awkwardly and with little success to engage in conversation a black man on a recently integrated bus. In James Baldwin's *Another Country* (1963), a white hipster and aspiring novelist struggles to become intimate with a black jazz drummer and his sister. Terry Southern's "You're Too Hip, Baby" (1967) describes a white hipster much like Baldwin's sidling up to an African American couple. In *Rabbit Redux* (1971), John Updike's bigoted protagonist opens his home to an angry black fugitive, whose perspective he tries understand.

As these examples might suggest, Styron's "imperious moral duty" wasn't forcefully imposed. The duty lay at the core of sixties-era liberalism, and Styron was an earnest liberal Democrat, which is why the criticism of *Nat Turner* cut him. Nor was his duty born simply from a desire to be moral—it traded heavily in the sexual romance of racial difference. Years after the publication of his controversial novel, he described his early efforts to get to know the blacks. He was overcome, he reports, by "a near paralysis of affection" for black peers he could never fully know.[41] "I fell under the spell of *negritude*," he recalls of his childhood in the South, "fascinated by black people and their folkways." Transfixed by "a secret passion for blackness" he "wanted to confront and understand" it (436). But to Killens, Styron's prose revealed him as an interloper. Killens maintains that "Styron misses entirely the beauty of Afro-American idiom . . . the unique-to-our-blackness methods of expression." He concludes, "In attempting to write Afro-Americanese, [he] is like a man trying to sing the blues when he has not paid his dues."[42] Thus Styron appears as one more white man pretending to black cultural forms he cannot master. Compelled by negritude, he remains alien from it.

Accusations like these no doubt rankled because they suggested that Styron was, in his anxious efforts to perform "negritude," more like Norman

Mailer than he would have liked to be. Styron put distance between himself and Mailer's fantasy of hip; his second novel, *Set This House on Fire* (1960), describes the "hipster" as a form of "idiotic infantilism."[43] The novel's narrator announces that he is "white, Protestant, Anglo-Saxon [and] Virginia-bred" (4), and adds, "It is with neither pride nor distress that I confess that—in the idiom of our time—I am something of a square" (5). Another postwar Nick Carraway, the mild-mannered narrator chronicles the exploits of the sybaritic swinger Mason Flagg, a thinly veiled Mailer. This "solemn apostle of the groin" strikes the narrator as "three times as alive as any other mortal could hope to be" (195). A not entirely unfair caricature of Mailer, Flagg pontificates, "Sex is the last frontier." It is "the only area left where men can find full expression of their individuality, full freedom. Where men can cast off the constrictions and conventions of society and regain their identity as humans. And I don't mean any dreary, dry little middle-class grope and spasm, either. I mean the total exploration of sex, as Sade envisioned it" (151).

Styron sacrifices Flagg in the name of a more praiseworthy liberalism. The novel's narrator contrasts Flagg to his father, who he thinks is "the only true liberal" he has ever known. "To be one of this breed in New York is childishly simple; to be one in the South surpasses all ordinary guts" (13). Even so, Styron wasn't above negotiating his own liberalism by way of Mailer's favorite categories. When disgusted with supporters of Hubert Humphrey at the 1968 Democratic Convention, for example, he called them "square, seersuckered fraternity boys and country club jocks with butch haircuts" (*QD* 234). More generally, he defended the core premise of Mailer's project. Responding to his critics, Styron insisted, "I think it is a denial of humanity, of our mutual humanity, to assume that it is pretentious and arrogant and wrong for a white man to attempt to get into a black man's skin" (*CWS* 104). The problem, as Turner's critics saw it, was that Styron's liberalism, preoccupied as it was with the "slavery" experienced by whites working for the likes of IBM and "the big corporations complex," offered an impoverished and ultimately self-serving account of that "mutual humanity." Indeed, it seemed the novelist didn't require anything more than Turner's skin; he insisted that he was able to find within himself the essence of what it meant to be a black slave. He wanted to live within Turner's skin but articulate his own experiences.[44] "If I did do anything original in Nat Turner," he declared, "it was to, for the first time so far as I know, plunge a white consciousness into a black incarnation" (*CWS* 105). Killens was entirely right that the novel "reveals more about the psyche of the 'southern liberal' Styron, direct descendent of ol' Massa, than it even begins to reveal about the heart and soul and mind of black revolutionary Nat Turner" (*TBW* 36). Equally right was Lerone Bennett Jr., who claimed that "the voice in this confession is the voice of William Styron" and that Styron's Turner is therefore an "intellectual in blackface" (*TBW* 4, 19).

Styron wanted to hollow out the historical figure. He dubbed the actual Nat Turner "a person of conspicuous ghastliness," a "psychopathic monster" (441–442), and an "almost insanely motivated religious fanatic" (*CWS* 193). As self-satisfied as he was arrogant, he decided to endow his literary creation with capacities that he presumed Turner himself could not have had: "As a writer I think I gave this man a dimension of rational intelligence which he most likely did not really possess, and as a result smoothed down that stark fanaticism" (*CWS* 193). Styron thought slaves generally bereft of rational intelligence. Elaborating on the work of Stanley Elkins—who thought the plantation akin to the concentration camp in its totalitarian reduction of captive bodies to infantile states—Styron argued that slaves didn't have much of an interior life:[45]

> The Negro slave of antebellum years in the South, who was without any contact with white people, was so far down a psychological scale that he could hardly hate in this calm, intelligent way Nat describes. For one thing, I do not think the intelligence of the average Negro who lived in a shack at the edge of a big tobacco plantation had come to full flower. He had been reduced to the level of an animal, quite consciously so. (*CWS* 91)

Appalling in itself—the slave is mentally deficient because he's not in sufficient contact with whites—this formulation also accounts for another aspect of the novel that proved objectionable to critics. Styron represented Turner in the first person. Godlike, he spoke through and for his protagonist. Turner thinks himself an empty vessel for God's will and voice. But when he cites biblical passages, he seems an empty vessel for his literary creator: "*I will lay sinews upon you, and will bring up flesh upon you, and cover you with skin, and put breath in you, and ye shall live, and ye shall know that I am the Lord*" (319). Styron inspires Turner: he breathes life into what before was only animal.

At one point, Styron allegorizes and questions his decision to bring literary language to a person he thinks would otherwise be without it. Turner speaks in a vernacular black idiom only when the situation demands servility. His internal dialogue (which constitutes the bulk of the narrative) evinces a more self-consciously literary style. Entranced by motes of dust glistening in the evening light, Turner waxes profound:

> Perhaps, I thought, these grains of dust were the autumn leaves of flies, no more bothersome than an episode of leaves is to a man when he is walking through October woods, and a sudden gust of wind shakes down around him from a poplar or a sycamore a whole harmless, dazzling, pelting flurry of brown and golden flakes. For a long moment I pondered the condition of a fly, only half listening to the uproar outside the jail, which rose and fell like summer thunder, hovering near yet remote. In many ways, I thought, a fly must be the most fortunate of God's creatures. Brainless born, brainlessly seeking its sustenance from anything wet and warm, it found its brainless mate, reproduced, and died brainless, unacquainted with misery or grief. But then I asked myself: How could I be sure? Who could say that flies were not instead God's supreme outcasts, buzzing eternally between heaven and oblivion in a pure agony of mindless twitching, forced by instinct to dine off sweat and slime and offal, their very brainlessness an everlasting torment? So that even if someone, well-meaning but mistaken, wished himself out of human misery and into a fly's estate, he would only find himself in a more monstrous hell than he had even imagined—an existence in which there was no act of will, no choice, but a blind and automatic obedience to instinct which caused him to feast endlessly and gluttonously and revoltingly upon the guts of a rotting fox or a bucket of prisoner's slops. (26)

Representative of the novel as a whole in its highly wrought, figurative style, the first part of the passage embraces literary language: grains of dust are like "the autumn leaves of flies" (metaphor); falling leaves constitute "an episode of leaves" (ellipses); the falling leaves of an "October wood" (metonymy) are a "pelting flurry" (analogy) of "golden flakes" (metaphor). This is Styron speaking through Turner with relaxed aplomb. But in the second part of the passage, anxiety over inhabiting a "brainless" body condemned to the "pure agony of mindless twitching" goes hand in hand with anxiety over the viability of the vocal reincarnation that is the novel's central metaphor. The anxiety is Styron's, and born from what suddenly seems a too intimate identification with Turner. For a moment, Styron worries that there might be too much semantic impertinence in his effort to conjoin his white consciousness and Turner's black body. In the first part of the passage, "grains of dust" are like "autumn leaves of flies." But the fly rapidly changes from being the object of a fanciful literary comparison, to the most blessed of God's creatures, to the most cursed, and finally, to a figure for slaves. Contemplating the fate of the fly, Turner contemplates "my black shit-eating people [who] were surely like flies" (27). From this vantage, the above passage finds Styron contemplating his decision to enter into a black body—which he dichotomizes in familiarly racist fashion. Like flies, Styron's slaves shuttle "between heaven and oblivion," between a blissful freedom from misery and grief and a compulsive obedience to instinct. Already lodged within Turner's body, Styron worries about the fate of someone "well-meaning," but potentially "mistaken," who wishes himself into "a fly's estate." More specifically, he worries that the metaphoric conceit responsible for this haunting will lose its structure of difference, in which case he will, having lost the mediating function of figurative language, cease to be "like" a slave and become one literally.

The larger point here is not that the historical Nat Turner could not have thought as Styron has his character thinking. On his first abolitionist lecture tour, Frederick Douglass struggled against white sponsors, like William Lloyd Garrison, who wanted to replace his conspicuously literary rhetoric with a more seemingly primitive slave dialect.[46] The point is rather that Styron himself insists that the historical Turner could not have thought like his character. The slave, recall, "had been reduced to the level of an animal." Styron would reach down from on high and make one such animal not simply human but exceedingly literary. Toward the beginning of the novel, we find Thomas Gray, Turner's court-appointed lawyer, speaking to his client about the need to record his narrative: "This ain't supposed to represent your exact words as you said them to me. Naturally, in a court confession there's got to be a kind of, uh, dignity of style, so this here's more or less a reconstitution and *recomposition* . . . the quiddities of detail are the same—or at least I hope they are the same" (30). Of course it's not at all clear that Gray hopes "the quiddities of detail" are the same. He works for both the defense and the prosecution and his transcription of Turner's confessions is the principal evidence used in the case against Turner. Gray has only one end in mind; he wishes to quiet public alarm by proving—because the revolt was local, because slaves tended to defend their masters, and because Turner himself proved unable to fully participate in the bloodshed—that slaves "ain't a race made for revolution" (397). Gray's attempt to prove the race harmless closely resembles what is for Killens Styron's efforts to do the same.

Styron turned to the Turner rebellion because the historical record was as nearly mute about Turner as Styron imagined slaves to be in general. He said that "one of the benefits for me in Nat Turner's story was not an abundance of material but, if anything, its scantiness" (439). Given this dearth, Styron might make his subject whatever he needed him to be. But what other "benefits" did Nat Turner's story offer? Most obviously, it allowed Styron to be both master and slave: he imagines himself a slave even as he insists in and through this identification that he remains free in ways that the slave did not. In fact, he confesses that, like Gray, he is in some sense Turner's jailer, if not his owner. Giving life and voice to a body that remains in chains, Styron animates and retains possession of a literary property. From this vantage, he wanted inside Turner's skin to inhabit, manipulate, and render subject to exchange "a black man's skin." His novel was an exercise in how to detach, as it were, the souls of black folk from those folk, the better to bring their skins to market.

When at one point Turner looks into the eyes of a former master and dimly perceives there a "far-off abstract being who possessed my body" (388), we must imagine that he perceives Styron, who here and elsewhere makes himself Turner's master as much as his God. "For me," Styron declares, "starting a novel is like starting a plantation." These words mean to reference the deliberate cultivation of land: "Before the earliest signs are out," Styron continues, "there is a lot of planting and hoeing and traveling around to the seed salesmen. It evolves very slowly and sometimes very haltingly" (*CWS* 266). But Styron just as plausibly comments on the financial boon that Nat Turner—his property—represents. Nineteenth-century American slave narratives often proved windfalls for their white publishers. As William Andrews has it, bringing these narratives to market involved "a division of labor" not unlike slavery itself, "in which the Negro supplies the raw materials, the 'brute facts' of life, and the white man manufactures and packages them for public consumption."[47] This packaging paid large dividends: Frederick Douglass's 1845 narrative went through seven printings in four years; William Wells Brown's 1847 volume went through four in its first year alone. Thomas Gray, the author of the original *Confessions of Nat Turner*, anticipated such business: he printed 50,000 initial copies at his own expense.[48] Gray went broke, but Styron did not: his blackface paid handsomely. His novel garnered publishing guarantees of more than $1,000,000, an astonishing sum at the time.

In 1959, Mailer deplored Styron's practice of "the art of literary advancement." He accused the author of having spent "years oiling every literary lever and power which could help him on his way" and believed, prophetically enough, that there were "medals waiting for him in the mass media" (*A* 464).[49] In *Nat Turner*, Styron confesses as much. At one point Turner begins "to wonder if ownership of me did not presage a diminution of fortune" (44). The line is ironic; Styron knew before he finished writing just how much he stood to gain from impersonating Turner, and elliptically acknowledged his profiteering. Scrutinized by a roomful of whites, Turner feels "stripped down to the bare black flesh" (164). The same fate awaits him in literal form after his execution. The last page of the novel quotes from a historical source: "The bodies of those executed, with one exception, were buried in a decent and becoming fashion. That of Nat Turner was delivered to the doctors, who skinned it and made grease of the flesh." That gruesome fact becomes strikingly relevant in light of the next sentence: "Mr. R. S. Barham's father owned a money purse made of his hide" (429). As Styron later explained, "change purses were carved from [Turner's] skin" (*CWS* 81). If Barham's father owned one such purse, then surely Styron owned another, his literary subject an empty container of cured skin, to be filled not simply with his creator's voice, but with the money Turner made for him.

White Head, Liberal Seed

What does it mean, in Styron's words, to "plunge a white consciousness into a black incarnation"? Should we think of the result as vocal, taking shape through hypothetically black lungs, larynx, tongue, palate, cheeks, lips? Or is the result an immaterial affair, a disembodied because ultimately imaginary transcription of white consciousness? Turner tends to speak in a crude vernacular idiom and think in the broadly literary language that characterizes most of the novel. But this isn't universally the case, and Styron didn't consistently describe his novel's first-person voice as issuing from a white consciousness lodged within a black body. For example, he claimed that in writing the novel he "wanted to risk leaping into a black man's consciousness" (*CWS* 103). The "risk" here seems to inhere in the fact that Styron aimed to submerge his own consciousness within Turner's. Similarly, he recalled, "I realized that inevitably one of the most difficult things I would have to set up for myself would be the telling of this story from the point of view of Nat himself—a first-person narrative which would somehow allow you to enter the consciousness of a Negro of the early decades of the 19th century" (*CWS* 70). But what is the relation between leaping into a black mind, a "consciousness," on the one hand, and a black body, an "incarnation," on the other?

What's clear is that even as he waxes arrogant concerning his gift of language to his otherwise inarticulate protagonist, Styron imagines that in placing his consciousness in Turner's body, he both changes that consciousness and discovers the extent to which that change is no change at all, white consciousness being, finally, no different from black consciousness. Thus he will confirm the "mutual humanity" that he shares with his subject. It's no longer possible, in this regard, to know the difference between white author and black character: the former takes on a black body and the latter takes on a white consciousness, even as these acquisitions change the terms through which we understand white and black, consciousness and body, author and subject.

In fact, Styron's novel places its author and subject in a hall of mirrors. Soon after Gray explains to Turner the need to reconstitute and recompose his language, Turner sits "motionless, sweating, aware of the pounding in my heart. His words (mine? ours?) came back in my brain like a somber and doleful verse from Scripture itself" (37). Unable to source the language that he hears, Turner fails to distinguish between himself and Gray, which suggests at another level the difficulty of distinguishing between Styron and Turner. This confusion results, at least according to Styron, in a voyage of self-discovery. He noted, "If you start finding out about Nat, discovering things about Nat, well, of course, every passage, every chapter, every section is kind of a revelation both for yourself and for Nat. To this degree the book is also, I think, a psychological novel" (*CWS* 70). Understanding Nat means understanding your own psychology, and vice versa. Styron makes this even more clear when he quotes James Baldwin in his afterword: "Each of us, helplessly and forever, contains the other—male in female, female in male, white in black, and black in white. We are part of the other" (455).[50]

Styron's white skin covers Turner's black consciousness even as, *Nat Turner* suggests, Turner's black skin covers Styron's white consciousness: the novel offsets its oblique confessions to blackface with recurring visions of white exteriors and black interiors. Turner recalls playing with other slave children, covering their bodies in clay and then, after that clay had dried into a calcimine coating, screaming "in mad delight at our resemblance to white boys" (140). Later, Turner becomes white again—"white as clabber cheese, white, stark white, white as a marble Episcopalian"—when he sits in an empty plantation and surveys it. "Solitary and sovereign as I gazed down upon this wrecked backwater of time, I suddenly felt myself its possessor" (232). But if this is an assertion of the economic and political benefits of freedom, it's not immediately obvious who claims these benefits, since it's tempting to understand this moment as one in which Turner becomes an author, by virtue of taking possession of the historical record—now a "wrecked backwater of time." This incipient historical novelist is both Turner and Styron. As he takes imaginary possession of the deserted plantation, Turner thinks of "dainty and tiptoeing feet" and imagines "ladies in crinoline and taffeta." The language closely repeats Styron's account, published two years before the novel, of his own visit to the deserted Whitehead plantation, which housed the one person, a young southern woman, whom Nat Turner killed with his own hand. This is Styron listening for echoes of the past: "For an instant, in the silence, I could hear the mad rustle of taffeta, and rushing feet." Styron's time and Turner's time collapse: "Then that day and this day seemed to meet, melting together, becoming almost one, and for a long moment indistinguishable" (*QD* 30). Sharing language, Turner and Styron become for a moment indistinguishable. But they become even more so when Turner begins physically to take possession of plantations. His revolt begun, Turner plans to march his followers to Richmond, gathering slaves from plantations across the countryside as they go. But they are waylaid by slaves loyal to their masters, and deviate from their route. Styron depicts their path visually, by representing it on the page in the form of an outsized "S." The striking suggestion is that Turner marks the countryside with the initial of the author who creates him: even or especially in his moments of self-assertion, the liberated slave is one and the same with his would-be master.

Styron's ostensible contempt for Norman Mailer's sexual politics notwithstanding, he asserts this union most forcefully in his depictions of Turner's sexuality. Alone on an abandoned plantation, Turner imagines himself sovereign of all he surveys. He exercises his sovereignty and his newfound "privilege of ownership by unlacing [his] fly and pissing loudly on the same worn stone where dainty tiptoeing feet had gained the veranda steps a short three years earlier." Moments later he becomes "white—white as clabber cheese." Turner takes possession of the buildings, and becomes white, by marking them with urine. But Styron hints at another substance. Turner unlaces his fly while thinking of "dainty and tiptoeing feet"; he imagines "ladies in crinoline and taffeta [who] had laughingly dismounted upon carpeted footboards, their petticoats spilling on the air like snow as I steadied their arms." As he conjures these images— borrowed from Styron's account of his visit to the Whitehead estate—he experiences first "a sharp and growing excitement" and then a "strange, demented ecstasy!" (232). Exercising his sovereignty involves more than urination: the "clabber cheese" suggests semen, the product of Turner's imagined possession of white women. This semen, which issues forth the white inside, returns later in only slightly different form. Alone in his cell awaiting execution, Turner holds a Bible. He also holds his penis. He fantasizes about the white girl, Margaret Whitehead, whom he killed during the rebellion. They were friends, of a sort, before he took her life. He recalls her religious admonitions with erotic fervor: *"Love is of God; and everyone that loveth is born of God, and knoweth God."* He begins to masturbate. *"Then behold I come quickly"* (426), the paragraph begins, confusing sexual and religious release: "Come!" (428) a voice of unknown origin will boom to him as he leaves his cell for the last time. Then, in a moment of discharge that prefigures his impending death: "I pour out my love within her; pulsing flood; she arches against me, cries out, and the twain—black and white—are one" (426). This moment of congress takes place between Turner and Whitehead but also signals the unification of Turner and Styron. In a culminating confluence, Turner imagines filling Whitehead's body in just the same way that Styron has all along imagined his own "white head" filling Turner's body.

Similar moments in the fiction of the time begin to suggest the political dimensions of Styron's project. In Hal Bennett's *Lord of Dark Places* (1970), a black adolescent named Joe Market travels the South with his father, Titus, converting followers to the Church of the Naked Child, founded on the worship of Joe's penis. Titus parades Joe onstage and then reveals his "holy object." When confronted with members of his flock, Market thinks he ought "to drag out his tail and baptize all of them with come." Market dies as Turner dies: as he sits on the electric chair convicted of murder, "a terrible, flaming spirit entered his being, almost stifling his breath with the onslaught of his coming." When he dies, he ejaculates, and thinks, *"I am the Holy Ghost, I have come to redeem the world."*[51] The context is explicitly political. Though Joe is disaffected from politics, one of the first things he realizes about the woman he will marry is that "she looked like Jackie Kennedy" (84); "Joe really liked John Kennedy" (88). But he's aghast at "America in the Age of Johnson," which "was so jumbled and disarranged that the current Presidential contest lay between a happy little bumpkin like Hubert Horatio Humphrey and a less-humorous travesty in the person of Richard Milhous Nixon" (244). He's disgusted in general by the political process, which raises "big business to the level of government," and in which "black and white Americans alike sell their souls to the most attractive devil." He thinks people "are riotous and discontent" and "asking for their souls back" (245). He imagines himself capable of returning those souls, which is why he would "baptize all . . . with come." But the irony is bleak. While Joe's grandfather's name "was Roosevelt, after the one who carried the big stick" (1), Joe's surname is "Market," and his fantasy of wielding his own "big stick" against "big business" (and with Jackie Kennedy) is, finally, a fantasy in which he acquiesces to the depredations of a cultural and political marketplace that transforms him into a fetish: a walking penis.

John Updike's *Rabbit Redux* replicates those depredations, on behalf of the Democratic Party that Joe rejects. A social conservative and hawk during the Vietnam War, Harry "Rabbit" Angstrom takes in a black fugitive named Skeeter (Styron's African Americans are flies, Updike's are mosquitoes). Their relationship is fraught with a sexual tension that Skeeter casts in religious terms. "I am *the* black Jesus," says Skeeter to Angstrom. "Kiss my balls—they are the sun and the moon, and my pecker's a comet whose head is the white-hot heart of the glory that never does fail!" (183). Updike is self-referential in a manner that recalls Styron, who merges white author and black character in Margaret Whitehead. In *Rabbit Redux*, white author and black character merge in the body of Jill, a white teenager living with Rabbit and Skeeter. Watching Skeeter and Jill have sexual relations is, for Rabbit, like watching a drama between "ink and paper" (331). Sitting in a dark room with their entangled bodies, Rabbit turns on the light. "What he sees reminds him, in the first flash, of the printing process, an inked plate contiguous at some few points to white paper" (259). The fact that the flash reveals Skeeter's penis engulfed by Jill's mouth makes the metaphorical gambit clear: Jill is the white background upon which Skeeter writes, and her mouth draws from Skeeter's penis an ejaculate that Updike likens to ink. To see Skeeter's penis as an instrument of writing, however, is to immediately see it as an expression of an agency other than Skeeter's own: just as when Turner releases himself into Whitehead, we register the black penis as a vehicle for a white authorial presence.[52]

Updike's is a textbook instance of triangulated male desire, and illustrative of the nervous homosociality that often organized contemporary novels about hip. From the start of the novel, Rabbit thinks himself "de-balled" (224). He lives in "a world where inches matter" (16), and feels he's come up short. He understands this incapacity as a function of his whiteness: he feels like "a ghost, white, soft"

(49), "a large white man a knife would slice like lard" (30). Skeeter offers a way beyond this castration anxiety. As Sally Robinson aptly puts it, Skeeter enables Rabbit to get "re-balled."[53] Skeeter elicits from Jill what he calls "a demon-stray-shun of o-bee-deeyance" (258) and Rabbit watches transfixed, his desire for Skeeter laundered through Jill's body. "Never did figure your angle," Skeeter tells Rabbit, by way of saying good-bye. Yet his final gesture, and Rabbit's response to it, makes the angle clear: Skeeter takes Rabbit's hand and "tips it so the meaty pink creases are skyward." He then gently spits into the hand, his saliva "warm as skin," and appearing to Rabbit as "moisture full of bubbles like tiny suns." All at once, Rabbit notices of Skeeter, "when he laughs there is that complexity about his upper lip white men don't have, a welt in the center, a genial seam reminding Rabbit of the stitch of flesh that holds the head of your cock to the shaft" (292). Skeeter is to Rabbit a walking penis, and as such, a symbol of Updike's phallic literary authority.

The phallic fixations and sexual triangulations in *Rabbit Redux* participate in the novel's larger effort, which I detail in Chapter 3, to convert Rabbit from his pro-war commitments to Eugene McCarthy's "coalition of conscience," which reconciled the professional-managerial class to the counterculture. Updike effects this conversion in a manner that echoes Styron's transformative engagement with Turner. Rabbit understands Skeeter's anger; it matches his own as a disenfranchised white man, abandoned by his wife and soon to be unemployed because of technological changes in his workplace. Skeeter and Rabbit share this anger in a textually mediated experience of slavery. Participating in a "teach in" with Skeeter, Rabbit reads from *The Life and Times of Frederick Douglass*. He learns to "groove" while reading those passages that describe Douglass violently combating his owner, Covey. Reading Douglass, Rabbit discovers and embraces the revolutionary slave within—just moments before we witness Rabbit being created, metaphorically, in the "drama of ink on paper" that is Skeeter's black penis being engulfed by a white mouth. This, Updike suggests, is the seed of "lib-er-alism."

William Styron's Dreamboat

Styron adumbrates an analogous racial politics in a striking use of white on black that recalls Turner's transformation into something "stark white, white as a marble Episcopalian." Waking from sleep, half attuned to his external surroundings and half still in dreams, Turner envisions a "marble" building, perched on an ocean promontory, that is "stark white" on the outside and dark inside (422). The first two pages of the novel describe the vision, of which this is a part:

> Just as this building possesses neither doors nor windows, it seems to have no purpose, resembling, as I say, a temple—yet a temple in which no one worships, or a sarcophagus in which no one lies buried, or a monument to something mysterious, ineffable, and without name. But as is my custom whenever I have this dream or vision, I don't dwell upon the meaning of the strange building . . . for it seems by its very purposelessness to be endowed with a profound mystery which to explore would yield only a profusion of darker and perhaps more troubling mysteries, as in a maze. (4)

This sealed edifice—an "inscrutable paradigm of a mystery beyond utterance or even wonder" (422)—allows no ingress. It turns Turner toward his own interior: he can only "explore" its mysteries in his own mind. But when he contemplates the "darker" inside of the building, he stops short before its inscrutability. Turner refuses to interpret the glimpses of the building that he catches when he wakes from sleep into consciousness. He recognizes that the building is full of troubling mysteries and convinces himself that they should stay inviolate—evocative as they are of what he calls the "oceanic" (5). Seen this way, the inside of the temple is like nothing so much as an unconscious, rich with proscribed information. It expresses what remains hidden from the half-awake mind that conjures it. In this, it might seem to resemble the historical Turner, of whom Styron wrote, "What has helped make the man such a fascinating subject for speculation is his very inaccessibility" (452).

But if the building is an unconscious, it belongs equally to Styron and Turner. Styron waxed profound on the psychic significance of blacks to white southerners: they "impinge upon their collective subconscious to such a degree that it may be rightly said they become the focus of an incessant preoccupation, somewhat like a monstrous, recurring dream" (*QD* 10). Turner looking at the temple thus resembles Styron looking at the monstrous dream of Turner lodged within his own "subconscious." Wandering about the site of Turner's rebellion in 1965, Styron recalls feeling "that this Negro, who had so long occupied my thoughts, who indeed had so obsessed my imagination that he acquired larger spirit and flesh than most of the living people I encountered day in and day out, had been merely a crazy figment of my mind, a phantom no more real than some half-recollected image from a fairy tale" (*QD* 26). Styron wonders while contemplating Turner if he is dream or reality, confusing in the process his character's "spirit and flesh" with those of "living" people. Analogously, Turner wonders while contemplating the white building if he is having a dream or a waking vision. Appropriate, then, that Turner turns white as marble while adopting as his own the language Styron uses while visiting the deserted "Whitehead" plantation. The white building on the ocean promontory collapses author and character a second time, insofar as it depicts Styron's mind as a "white head" that is haunted by "a phantom" as "dark as the darkest tomb" (422).

This confusion is implicitly political. The white building sitting high on a promontory consciously invokes John Winthrop's "City Upon a Hill," a long-standing icon of the promise of American civic life (as does the original cover of *Ten Black Writers Respond*, which shows Winthrop's city with a lynching pole occupying the highest point of the hill). Equally, it evokes neoclassical government buildings, like those in Washington, into which Styron was often invited. He dined and smoked cigars with John Kennedy in the White House; he also sailed with Kennedy on "the good ship *Patrick J*" (*HC* 13), where he was asked about his work on *Nat Turner*. Responding, he "told Kennedy things about slavery he had obviously never heard before" (*HC* 15). Perhaps grateful for these insights, Kennedy later asked Styron for his help in reaching out to black men of letters: "Did I know any Negro writers? Could I suggest some Negro names for a meeting at the White House?" (*HC* 17). Kennedy wanted to bring black Americans into the marble corridors of Washington, and thought Styron might help. So did Lyndon Johnson, who asked Styron to contribute a phrase to his 1964 civil rights speech. Styron did ("our unending search for justice") and received a thank-you letter from the president in return.

Styron was a party man. But toward the end of the sixties, he soured on establishment Democrats and supported the party only "despairingly" (*HC* 81). He decided to inhabit the body of an angry black man, and write *Nat Turner*, during the period of his most intense disaffection from the Democrats, as he grew embittered over Johnson's war in Southeast Asia. At the start of 1966, as he was nearing completion of his novel, U.S. infantry moved into the Mekong Delta of South Vietnam. By the end of the year, when Styron finished writing, U.S. forces in and just outside Vietnam numbered 445,000. More than 6,000 Americans had been killed over the course of the year; 30,000 had been wounded. An estimated 61,000 Vietcong had been killed. In 1967 Styron hung

Johnson's letter by his toilet. In 1968, he pledged his allegiance to Eugene Mc-Carthy. With Robert Lowell, he accompanied McCarthy to the Democratic Convention of that year, where he served the candidate as a delegate challenger.[54] Outraged by Mayor Daley's brutal police tactics and by the eventual selection of Hubert Humphrey, Styron lambasted the party to which he had committed himself. He derided the "rigidity and blindness" and the "feebleness of thought, that have possessed the party at every level" (*QD* 234). He denounced the "petrification of a party that allowed such apathy and lack of adventurousness and moral inanition to set in . . . [and shape] its frozen logic." The convention culminated trends long in the making, within the party and within Styron. He saw now that the party was "a colossal dreamboat" (*QD* 235). And now, he wrote, "my detestation of politics attained an almost religious passion" (*QD* 236).

The language is suggestive, since "religious passion" captures what was to Styron the historical Nat Turner's most salient attribute. From this vantage, Styron inhabits Turner's body the better to channel—and in punishing that body, contain—his own potentially radical loathing of liberal politics. In his account of the 1968 convention, he recalls a journalist who likens the protestors' "violent confrontations" to "the show of muscle among the black militants" (*QD* 235). Two years earlier, when writing *Nat Turner*, Styron believed such confrontations unnecessary. But he did understand Turner's muscle, and its relation to the Democratic Party of 1831, in light of problems then facing the party in 1966. As Styron pointed out, Turner's revolt takes place during "the presidency of Andrew Jackson," which was, to Styron, "the very dawn of our modern history" (*QD* 15). Jackson's presidency represented the dawn of the modern Democratic Party, just as, to Styron and many others, the year 1966 suggested the sunset of that party. Jackson and Johnson mark the beginning and possible end of the party to which Styron was then ambivalently committed, which is perhaps why the first page of *Nat Turner* contains two interlocked symbols, a Greek A and Ω, for Alpha and Omega. The eschatological register reflects Turner's messianic mind-set, but it also might describe the waning of Styron's hope that liberalism, the best of "modern history," might right its own wrongs.

Defending his decision to write about Turner in the first person, Styron said, "A Negro should be able to come along and write a fantastic novel about Andrew Jackson" (*CWS* 103). The chiasmus—Styron assuming black skin and writing about Turner and a black writer assuming white skin and writing about Jackson—is suggestive. Historians of minstrelsy locate its origins in Jackson-era America—in 1831, to be precise, the very year of Turner's revolt. Eric Lott stresses the virtual coincidence of the rise of abolitionism and minstrelsy, and the intimacy of "these two instances of racial discourse, one middle class and one working class," which were "dialectical partners" in their "shared ambivalences." As Lott sees it, William Lloyd Garrison's "paternalist condescension" mirrored the "ridicule and wonder" at work, for example, in T. D. Rice's original performances.[55] At the same time, as Alexander Saxton notes, "overt partisanship" linked minstrelsy "to the Democratic party." Saxton elaborates on "the exclusiveness of [minstrelsy's] Jacksonian orientation": after noting that many of the most famous blackface troupes had "intimate contact with Democratic party leaders," Saxton reasons that "whiggish politics were precluded because the mass urban culture from which minstrelsy derived was itself an attack on the moral and economic premises of whiggery; and because, through its stylized form, it propagandized metaphorically the alliance of urban working people with the planter interest in the South." Saxton explains: "The price of unity" within the party, "as set by southern Democrats, was defense of the institution of slavery by the national party." Risking a "statement of the obvious," he notes that the "political stance" of blackface minstrelsy was, at bottom, "a defense of slavery."[56]

Styron's blackface performance of Turner aims to right this wrong, and thereby to save the Democratic Party from the legacy of its defense of slavery. Styron thought Turner a fulcrum of U.S. history, and in interviews and essays, he constructed an elaborate alternate history around the slave revolt. He claimed that Virginia in the early 1830s "had been edging closer to emancipation." It stopped short, he believed, because Turner's revolt generated a profound fear of emancipation in an otherwise liberalizing white population. This meant that had Turner not revolted, the Civil War might never have taken place. The implications of this were, to Styron, "awesome to contemplate" (*QD* 21). A staggering loss of life might have been avoided. Having freed its slaves without northern meddling, the South might have sidestepped its extreme backlash against the freedmen. The long-term consequences for the Democratic Party alone would have been profound. With no need for Abraham Lincoln, a Republican, to intervene on behalf of the North, the most unregenerate and race-baiting southerners would not have decamped to the Democratic Party. What would the New Deal have looked like if Franklin Roosevelt had not needed to appease conservative southern congressmen in his own party? What would Kennedy have done on behalf of civil rights, if he had not been beholden to these same interests? Styron was eager to point out that "a tradition of liberalism has of course existed honorably in the South and is as much a part of its history as its right-wing fanaticism. The South in the nineteenth-century had produced liberals of staunch moral fiber" (*QD* 32). Without the Turner uprising, those liberals might have gained control of the Democratic Party.

Instead, as C. Vann Woodward put it, the result of the North's military intervention in the South was that "the Democrats ceased to be a party *in* the South and became instead the party *of* the South. Politics was a continuation of Civil War history by other means."[57] One of Styron's closest friends, James Baldwin, glossed the consequences of this fact for black voters. In the South,

> the Republican Party was the *nigra's* friend, and, in the North, it was the Democrats who lovingly dried our tears. But, however liberal Northern Democrats might seem to be, nothing was allowed to menace the party unity—certainly not niggers—with the result that the presumed or potential power of the black vote in the North was canceled out by the smirk on the faces of the candidates in the South. The party had won—was in—and we were out. (BE 801)

The coalition that Baldwin describes held sway long after blacks in the South began voting with the Democratic Party, in large part because national Democrats, mindful of the continuing clout of southern conservatives within the party, urged caution when it came to civil rights. Constitutively cautious, Adlai Stevenson asserted, "We must proceed gradually, not upsetting habits or traditions that are older than the Republic." Though Kennedy made his support for civil rights clear, he avoided confrontation in federal versus states' rights issues in the South.[58]

All of this seemed to change with the landslide of 1964, which handed Lyndon Johnson the largest margin of victory won by any president since Franklin Roosevelt in 1936. "These are the most hopeful times since Christ was born in Bethlehem," Johnson declared while lighting the White House Christmas tree later that year.[59] A flurry of liberal legislation, beginning with the Economic Opportunity Act of 1964 and culminating in the Voting Rights Act of 1965, seemed to confirm this general sentiment. And yet just five nights after the passage of the Voting Rights Act, in a cruel turn of events that must surely have echoed Turner's fateful rebellion for Styron, the conflagration in Watts began.

Urban uprisings had erupted in major American cities the previous summer, but in scale and public visibility, Watts topped them all. As flames consumed Los Angeles, large portions of the nation's TV audience tuned in, and began to roil with the aggrieved outrage that would characterize the "silent majority" and decisively alter the face of both the Republican and the Democratic parties. Rick Perlstein sums up the subsequent Republican message for the 1966 congressional elections: "Vote Republican to preserve home and hearth, vote Democratic to surrender them." The Democratic Party suffered a devastating defeat, losing its majority by a margin of two to one—in large part because many of Johnson's staunchest supporters saw him moving too quickly on civil rights.[60]

The Democrats' share of the popular vote would drop 19 percentage points, from 61 percent in 1964 to 42 percent in 1968; 50 percent of those who voted for Nixon in 1968 had cast ballots for Johnson in 1964; 97 percent of all eligible blacks voted for the Democratic ticket in 1968, while only 35 percent of the white electorate did so.[61] Henceforth, the party would depend more heavily than it ever had on African American votes, which constituted roughly 20 percent of the total cast for the party in national elections in 1968 and 1972.[62] Styron suggested that all of this might have been different had Turner not rebelled—and, analogously, had African Americans not rioted in Watts. Tacitly, *Nat Turner* asks its readers to wonder what might have been, had these rioters embraced the democratic process, however torturously slow it was, instead of taking to the streets and setting their cities aflame. This was the question that preoccupied Styron as he wrote in 1966, when the effects of the riots had already taken their toll on the midterm elections and when the history of American liberalism seemed once more to be pivoting in dire fashion. His growing distaste for Johnson made him impatient and led him to believe that working within the system was almost impossible. But he couldn't support Turner any more than the rioters in Watts, however dismal their plight. Invariably, he advocated patience and deliberate action.

And so he leaves us with Nat Turner gazing in wonder at a white marble building that he cannot understand. Mesmerized, Turner is freed from his anger, and from what Styron would later term, in describing his intense disaffection from the Democrats, "religious passion." Calm and momentarily liberated from his antinomian mania, Turner floats beneath the mysterious building in a boat—or in what we might call a "dreamboat," which is what Styron, in his moment of pique, would call the party in 1968. This is a fantasy of leisure:

at rest, our protagonist neither organizes his revolt nor works for the profit of another. But this is also a fantasy of the revolutionary freed from his revolution, and momentarily pacified by the prospect of a resonantly institutional union of white and black, one in which creator and subject, master and slave, white and black, lose their distinctions and celebrate their "mutual humanity" within what looks like a government building. We can almost hear Styron sigh: would that Turner had trusted the State of Virginia to free him, as Styron was sure it eventually would have. What if, instead of knocking down the front door, he had come quietly 'round back?

6 Countercultural Capital, from Alaska to Disneyland

Each an expression of what we might call pornographic minstrelsy, William Styron's *The Confessions of Nat Turner* and John Updike's *Rabbit Redux* figure the mastery of the white liberal in the orgasms of black men. In graphically self-referential fashion, each novelist understands the (white) ejaculate issuing forth from a black penis as an instance of the ventriloquism with which he controls and speaks on behalf of his black characters. Norman Mailer's *Why Are We in Vietnam?* (1967) and E. L. Doctorow's *The Book of Daniel* (1971) dramatize a disembodied but no less disturbing version of this gambit. In both, narrators appropriate black voices by detaching them from what Mailer calls their "material physical site or locus" (26). Mailer and Doctorow's youthful and rebellious narrators acquire their hip voices by violently repudiating the black bodies from which they take them. Staging this expropriation, Mailer and Doctorow confess to the origins of their own literary voices, even as they capture the conflict inherent in contemporary efforts to deracinate, exchange, and at the same time preserve racial difference.

This conflict takes shape alongside each novel's preoccupation with rock and roll—which, by the sixties, had replaced jazz as the standard-bearer of liberalism's hip coalition culture. Over and beyond its purely musical appeal, rock assumed this prominence, at least in part, because of its ability simultaneously to gesture to and erase black bodies. By the time of Mailer's novel, the music was inextricably linked with the counterculture's larger commitment to integration and civil rights, even as it had transformed the ostensibly black sounds once associated with rhythm and blues into the stuff of a more homogenized mass culture. "There's two kinds," declared Miles Davis of rock, in 1969, "white and black, and those bourgeois spades are trying to sing white and whites are trying to sound colored. It's embarrassing to me."[1] But in fact, it was impossible to make these distinctions: by the early sixties, the convergences that were animating rock had confounded what it meant to sound either black or white. "I got it from them," declared Elvis Presley. "The colored folks been singing and playing it [rock and roll] just like I'm doing now, man, for more years than I know." All the same, this was no simple theft, as rock defied easy racial distinctions. "Don't give me any sophisticated crap," quipped John Lennon, "give me Chuck Berry." This preference was common enough, but Berry understood his sound in very sophisticated terms: "I stressed my diction so that it was harder and whiter," he said. "It was my intention to hold both the black and white clientele by voicing the different songs in their customary tongues."[2] As natural as they might have sounded, such unions were uneasy. Berry's remark recalls V. N. Volosinov, who claims that "the form of irony in general is conditioned by a social conflict: it is the encounter in one voice of two incarnate value judgments and their interference with one another."[3] We hear a version of this interference in the self-consciously hip voices examined below; even as they bind together disparate clienteles, Mailer and Doctorow express a conflict between styles and value judgments that, ultimately, reveals a conflict within imperial and capitalist social relations.

Put in Mailer's preferred terms, the two novelists considered below understand their voices as expressions of an abstract and necessarily disembodied black phallus. Each endows that phallus with a talismanic efficacy relevant to Vietnam-era politics. At the same time, each confesses the symbolic violence upon which his ambiguously raced voices depend, and acknowledges his larger complicity in the brutal power struggles of the era. "The novelist fashions a totem as much as an aesthetic," Mailer declares in his preface to *Why Are We in Vietnam?* "The book before you is a totem."[4] Mailer understood this totem as both a parody and an extension of "black magic" (2), and thought this magic crucial to the Democratic Party. In fact, he thought his black magic totem an expression of the party's contested authority. Eager to appear "before you," Mailer's novel offers a variant of what Jacques Derrida, also writing in 1967, called "phallogocentrism": narrative authority and a phallic sense of presence meet in a voice that the narrator asks us to understand as spoken and not written. This voice doesn't speak on behalf of patriarchy as such so much as it bespeaks the primal thirst for blood that drives the novel's maniacal, music-loving teenage narrator, D. J. Jethro, toward carnage in Vietnam. "Go out and kill," the aggressively hip D.J. imagines some dark divinity whispering in his ear, "fulfill my will, go and kill" (203). Uncomfortably like Lyndon Johnson,

Mailer's divinity would have D.J. violently appropriate black vocal styles the better to arm him for violence against the North Vietnamese. Mailer was appalled by the war in Vietnam; he thought it an egregious abuse of military and political power. And yet, at the same time, he sees D.J. as an extreme elaboration of his own hip commitments, and understands his protagonist's voice as an instance of his own.

Doctorow dramatizes the radical left's appropriation of black vocal styles. In *The Book of Daniel*, Daniel Isaacson is one of two children born to Paul and Rochelle Isaacson, American Communists, modeled on Julius and Ethel Rosenberg, who were tried and executed for supplying national secrets to the Soviet Union. Daniel's story—his book—explores how their prosecution and execution defined his life and the possibilities of American radicalism. Daniel feels abandoned by his parents, who might have prevented their execution by pleading guilty to the charges against them. He thinks them pseudo-sophisticates, lower-middle-class snobs whose high-minded radicalism amounted to self-absorption. His mother "had a profound distaste for the common man. Her life was a matter of taking pains to distinguish herself from her neighbors."[5] Daniel embraces a more populist, and self-consciously black, ethos. As "deliberately cool" (4) as D.J., he organizes his revolutionary sensibility around an insurrectionary black phallus. "It is aroused, man," he says, "the whole world is sticking up like a hard-on" (283). Doctorow manifests that global tumescence vocally, in an authoritative but disembodied black voice that encourages Daniel to be more hip than he is, and more potentially violent. Here, too, however, the novelist confesses his sins: Doctorow's black voice functions, finally, not on behalf of a militant left, but on behalf of the aspirant writer, Daniel, who would appropriate that voice for his own personal and artistic development.

"Nothing that's not tested, not voice tested"

The postwar period's regnant prophet of countercultural orgasm, Mailer celebrated the divine mystery and world-shaping power of phallic writing. Richard Poirier notes Mailer's easy movement "between sexual careers and the career of the novelist, between sexual creativity and the creative effort to shape history."[6] Second Wave feminists quickly keyed into Mailer's conflations. In 1968, Mary Ellmann described the tendency of male writers to view texts as extensions of the male body; as Kate Millett added in her devastating assessment of Mailer two years later, writers like him installed the male phallus at the heart of "a theology."⁷ But Mailer's political theology required a phallus that the novelist did not himself possess, and had instead to acquire in often violent acts of appropriation. "Hip" stood at the center of that theology because, compensatory, it suggested the transferable nature of the black phallus. Responding to Mailer's "The White Negro," James Baldwin noted that Mailer imagined the black phallus as a metonym for those properties that hip whites wanted to claim from blacks. Baldwin lamented "that to be an American Negro male is also to be a kind of walking phallic symbol; which means that one pays, in one's own personality, for the sexual insecurity of others."⁸ And indeed, "The White Negro" views white efforts to be hip as efforts to achieve the kinds of orgasm ostensibly experienced by black men: Mailer describes jazz, for example, not simply as "the music of orgasm" (*A* 341), but as the music of those black orgasms that white Negroes wanted for themselves. Ten years later, Mailer was still exploring this logic, albeit in a more critical fashion: being "cool," thinks D.J., the protagonist of *Why Are We in Vietnam?*, is to "get back cock" (188)—this just after he tells us that "in fact," he has "a dick like a nigger, but for hue, Renfrew" (161). Cool redresses a lack signaled by a simile.

"The White Negro" celebrates hipsters as "urban adventurers who drifted out at night looking for action with a black man's code to fit their facts" (*A* 341). These adventurers explore the nation's last unexplored territory: Mailer casts the urban hipster as "a frontiersman in the Wild West of American nightlife" (*A* 339). Mailer's invocation of a "Wild West" was torn from the headlines of the Civil Rights Movement: he wrote "The White Negro" just months after a 1957 article in the *Nation* described civil rights workers in Montgomery, Alabama, as "new frontiersmen, black and white, [who] may lead us—and some of the colored and white millions of the world—into a new experience of democracy." Mailer wanted a new experience of democracy, but his frontiersmen did not, as did the *Nation*'s, use the "weapons" of "Thoreau and Gandhi rather than Crockett and Boone." Mailer's frontiersmen were sinners, not saints, interested in desire and violence more than beatitude; given a choice of weapons, they would use guns and knives.⁹ By 1967, Mailer had pushed this logic to appalling conclusions. D.J. travels to an actual Wild West—Alaska's Brooks Range— armed with new weapons and a code that "The White Negro" traces to African Americans: "live a life of constant humility or ever-threatening danger" (*A* 341). Risking it all against grizzly bears in sub-zero Alaska provides the occasion for innumerable plays on the word "cool": "Make it cool, D.J., make it cool" (9), D.J.

sings. "It's square to be frantic," he tells himself, "so bring in the cool, bring in the cool" (27). For D.J., being cool doesn't mean being placid. It means being capable of dispassionate brutality. "The White Negro" celebrates the psychopath who murders "out of the necessity to purge his violence" (*A* 347). By 1967, that violence had grown in intensity: D.J. must push himself to ever more extreme acts of aggression, the better to retain his equanimity.

Mailer was writing for a new generation. A decade after having penned "The White Negro," he remained the voice of liberal members of the PMC—if not as the writer of "The White Negro" then as an instantly recognizable celebrant of hip.[10] This was his brand, but the rising tide of his fortune throughout the sixties depended in no small part on the diligence with which he sold it to an increasingly youthful readership, made up of young activists as well as older liberals ready to embrace the spirit if not the revolutionary conclusions of the New Left. In *Vietnam*, we find Mailer tending to his brand. Donald L. Kaufman notes, "The old-time 'White Negro' still survives" in the novel. D.J.'s is a "jive consciousness," articulated in a "kind of salt and pepper lingo." According to Kaufman, "*Vietnam?* is a blast of now language, America, 1967. A slice of pop dynamics."[11] The novel begins, "Hip hole and hupmobile, Braunschweiger, you didn't invite Geiger and his counter for nothing" (7), and most of what follows is a similarly hip mash-up of technology, popular culture, proper names, and fantasies of blackness. Thus D.J. describes himself as the "only American alive who could outtalk Cassius Clay, that's lip, duck the blip, Orlando, it's right on your radar screen" (22).

The novel's pop dynamics gesture toward new heroes on the American scene: radio "DJs," who brought wordplay, impious rhyming games, and hip rapping to teenagers during the fifties and sixties.[12] Cited in *Vietnam*, Marshall McLuhan thought radio a "cool medium" because it was aural, low resolution, and dependent upon listener participation. Enjoined to involve herself in the medium, the listener hears "echoes of tribal horns and antique drums" and feels "the resonating Africa within."[13] But there's a more prosaic context in which to understand Mailer's investment in radio. As Susan Douglas puts it,

> Radio—more than films, television, advertising, or magazines in the 1950s—was the media outlet where cultural and industrial battles over how much influence black culture was going to have on white culture were staged and fought. Increasingly, teenagers' music was written or performed by African Americans, and many of the announcers they love, who were white, tried to sound black. . . . [The important

point was that] whites themselves—the DJs, the performers, and their fans—embraced a hybridity that confounded and defied the existing racial order. And it was precisely because of radio's invisibility that such hybridizations could flourish.[14]

Mailer's D.J. captures this hybridity, and the music around which it was taking shape. "Go on, Dr. Jek tell the folk," he says in one of his first simulated radio broadcasts, "we're here to rock" (9). By 1967, that meant reworking the inheritance of R & B and, at almost every turn, borrowing heavily from early blues masters—Robert Jordon above all. But rock's genealogy was complex. Many rockers thought themselves indebted to bebop as well as the blues and R & B. Formed two years after Mailer's novel, Led Zeppelin would be sued twice for copyright infringement, by bluesmen Willie Dixon and Muddy Waters. At the same time, lead guitarist Jimmy Page had risen to fame in a band named the Yardbirds (a gesture to Charlie Parker), and leader singer Robert Plant would later recall, "I wanted my voice to be a tenor sax, really." "I wanted to be Coleman Hawkins. I wanted to be Dexter Gordon."[15]

But were these sounds identifiably black? Or did it no longer make sense, given the advent of radio, to talk of sounds as having colors? These questions go to the heart of *Vietnam*. D.J. is "Disk Jockey to Amer-ica" (208) in large part because, the narrator reminds us, we cannot see his body. He declares that "we have no material physical site or locus" (26) for his voice. We must, as he puts it, "hip into a little aggregate of fact" (191), which is that we hear him but cannot know whether his body is black or white. What if I'm not "true-blood Wasp-ass Texas," D.J. asks, but "some genius brain up in Harlem . . . ?" (27). The question remains unanswered, even as the demographic ambiguity gestures toward Lyndon Johnson's presidential campaign, whose presumed ability to carry Texas as well as New York loomed large as the Democrats anticipated the election of 1968. Indeed, given the extreme deracination at work in *Vietnam*, the question cannot be answered, for hip is not, here, an effort to build coalitions between bodies with different-colored skins; it is, rather, an effort to transform color so completely that it matters, if it matters at all, only in relation to disembodied voices that compete for prominence within the mind.

The short stories in Mailer's *Advertisements for Myself* had already experimented with disembodied narrative voices of unknown origin. The reader never discovers who narrates "The Man Who Studied Yoga," though she knows that he inhabits the sleeping mind of the protagonist. The narrator of "Prologue to a Long Novel" mockingly notes that "the duller minds among you cannot support the luxury of listening to a voice without a face unless you are handed some first approximation to my state"—before coyly suggesting that he might be a ghost or "an embryo eight instants old" (*A* 513). The voice turns out to be the expiring consciousness of a murder victim. The incorporeal nature of these voices makes a different kind of sense in each story: the protagonist of "The Man Who Studied Yoga" is sexually repressed and alienated from his body; the protagonist of "Prologue" is dead, having already left his body. More paradoxically, in *Vietnam*, D.J. insists on the irrelevance to his readers of a body we know to be rapacious in its appetites. Like the white Negroes Mailer described in 1957, D.J. wants to be "nearer to that God which every hipster believes is located in the senses of his body" (*A* 351); D.J. feels himself, like the narrator of Ralph Ellison's *Invisible Man*, "a man of substance, of flesh and bone, fiber and liquids" (3). But to the reader he is, like Ellison's most famous narrator, "invisible and without substance, a disembodied voice" (581).

D.J.'s is a blackface routine without the black face, and it's impossible, at least in theory, to know whether he is a White Negro or a Negro White. Ultimately, we cannot but understand D.J. as white, but our confusion about this fact is important. D.J. asks,

> Bishop Berkeley goes the mad comptometer in old D.J.'s head, am I the ideational heat of a real crazy-ass broken-legged Harlem Spade, and just think myself D.J. white boy genius Texan in Alaska imagining my opposite number in Harlem land, when in fact, Good Lord, when in fact, I, D.J., am trapped in a Harlem head which has gone so crazy that I think I sitting at a banquet in the Dallas ass white-ass manse remembering Alaska am in fact a figment of a Spade gone ape in the mind from outrageous frustrates wasting him and so now living in an imaginary white brain? (57–58)

The ostensibly white D.J. is in a "Harlem head," a "figment of a Spade gone ape in the mind," even as that head and mind is "living in an imaginary white brain"—and even as both "opposite numbers" exist only in the reader's mind. Here, the white inhabitation of a black brain is always potentially the black inhabitation of a white brain, and Mailer records this vertiginous confusion of inside and outside syntactically, when he uses commas to produce parenthetical phrases at one moment and then refrains from doing so the next. D.J. says "I am" in different ways. At one moment "D.J." is sharply delimited in a parenthetical, between "I" and "am": "in fact, I, D. J., am trapped in a Harlem head." Moments later, his language loses its focus and D.J. can no longer claim to "be" distinct from his (verbal) environment: "I think I sitting at a banquet in the Dallas ass white-ass manse remembering Alaska am in fact a figment of a Spade gone ape in the mind."

Mailer's voyage to the far reaches of Alaska—not unlike Styron's voyage backward through time and into the body of a slave—is matched by a self-conscious voyage inward, into the epistemologically uncertain landscape of his protagonist's mind. D.J. asks the novel's most important question: "Whose consciousness you getting?" (133).[16] The question has far-reaching implications as D.J. and his companion, Tex, strike out alone and travel northward. Mailer's novel describes the North Pole as a plastic valve, or anus, through which the world's dream energies enter the planet. The North Pole is, therefore, a site at which it becomes difficult to distinguish between the awake and the asleep, the conscious and the unconscious. Primal desires swirl about the two boys, who seem figments of each other's imaginations. D.J. (Dr. Jekyll) contemplates sexually mastering Tex (last name "Hyde") and wonders whether he is equal to the task. For Mailer, this is less an expression of homosexuality than a reiteration of the contest already under way inside the reader's mind, between a Texan white man and a Harlem black man, whose metaphorical skin, or "Hyde," promises D.J. the verbal authority he wants.

Mailer's metaphorical hides, detached from visible bodies, limn complex capitalist relations. Toward the beginning of the novel, D.J. announces, "America, this is your own wandering troubadour, brought right up to date, here to sell America its new handbook on how to live, how to live in this Electrox Edison world, all programmed out" (8). Edison is for D.J. the source of opportunity—insofar as he provides both the problems and the solutions from which D.J. would profit. Edison's sound technology is both poison and cure. The inventor brings into being a soulless world, "all programmed out," but he also perfects the technology through which sound can be separated from bodies and transmitted around the planet. D.J. figures this split—between the imprisoning and freeing aspects of sound technology—as one between work and leisure. He tells us that Edison becomes inspired while trying to increase the speed of the Atlantic cable, puts aside his original task (square in its commitment to efficiency), and promptly invents the phonograph, almost by accident. D.J. explains, "That's how Miles Davis was born. Bangalore don't snore—here's the bulge: Edison was hip, baby, the way you make it is on the distractions" (8). The most valuable work gets done creatively, off task, on break from routinized labor. Taking a break and playing around, Edison gives birth to Davis, who once described himself and a fellow musician as "scientists of sound," and who was then experimenting with rock rhythms and paving the way for what would later be called jazz-rock fusion. Completing the circuit, this new science of leisure opens up new areas for production and profit: D.J. draws on figures like Davis when selling his hip "up to date" manual on "how to live."

This reciprocity between the programmed and the creative, the square and the hip, replicates a larger reciprocity between white-collar production and consumption regimes. As Alan Liu has it, "cool" was in the postwar period "the delinquency, but also the mimicry, of Taylorism." He argues that cool involved "the construction of a bodily or social pose that perfectly expressed the adjustment of technique to technology—but for unproductive purposes." But as we saw in the case of Edison, unproductive labor doesn't stay unproductive. Edison takes a break from his efficiency work and opens expansive leisure markets with a new invention. Liu thinks this mutually reinforcing relation between work and leisure a characteristic of white-collar information economies. Technically proficient office workers go home and tinker with their stereos or, later, customize their laptops and play video games. These activities enhance the skills of the workers in question and result in the increase of their workplace efficiency. "Cool" is for Liu the lubricant of this reciprocity, especially insofar as it facilitates the "single, dominant mode of knowledge associated with the information economy."[17]

Preoccupied with a range of technologies organized around the recording and storing of transferable data, Mailer's *Vietnam* announces its interest in the information economy. Poirier notes that characters in the novel "do not exist as characters at all but as expressive filaments of some computerized mind" (137). This provides one answer to D.J.'s question, "Whose consciousness you getting?" As Poirier has it, D.J. "represents the oversoul as Univac." If Mailer's novel takes place within D.J.'s mind, it's nonetheless possible that that mind isn't human. For Poirier, D.J.'s consciousness is "a kind of computer bank in which is stored the fragmented consciousness of everyone else in the book" (140). Just before announcing his racial indeterminacy, D.J. suggests that his narrative finds its proper place in "the transistorized electronic aisles and microfilm of the electronic Lord" (26). These aisles and microfilms deracinate and reduce to fungible data everything from consciousness to once-resonant artifacts of high culture. D.J. is "up tight with the concept of dread" (34); reminding us that the narrative is a flashback, he says, "RTPY—Remembrance Things Past, Yeah, you remember?" (186); "Herman Melville, go hump Moby and wash his Dick" (26), he commands.

These gestures demonstrate D.J.'s mastery over and ultimate refusal of high culture; they suggest his ability, as Poirier has it, to "rend and shred" (136) dominant literary discourses. In this way, they exemplify how, according to Philip Ford, the populist discourse of hip important to rock and the sixties counterculture rejected the high-cultural elitism important to the more self-consciously modernist hip organized during the forties and fifties around jazz.[18] But D.J. also reproduces the deracinating processes of the information economy itself, and reveals that those disembodying processes require the mediation of something seemingly beyond their confines. As Liu has it, the workplace of that economy "became in imagination just a 'scene' from which one distanced oneself through regular indulgences in outlaw scenes. *I work here* [amid all these machines, protocols, procedures, codes], *but I'm cool*" (103). *Vietnam* is an extended outlaw scene, a fantasy of the ultimate work vacation. It narrates time taken off by D.J.'s father, Rusty, from his plastics corporation, even as it describes how that time off will advance his career. That vacation is also a scene of consumption, in which an Alaskan tour company sells values and experiences beyond the pale of office work. As the trip guide tells them, you pay "de-luxe prices" and in return experience a "proper paganism" (71) while hunting grizzly bears.

This scene of consumption understands voice as something like an industrial product. When not at work, Rusty has "a chameleon pussy sphincter changeling of a voice," which means that he alternates between "down home" talk and "Cosmo high-fashion dinner talk" (74) in what D.J. takes to be a less than admirable fashion. But being a vocal changeling doesn't cut it at Rusty's plastics firm. "Perfection breeds perfection," D.J. announces—"the critical ear gets as sharp as a mad dragster maniac-type genius listening to two 427 cubic inchers put in tandem." Rusty can't fake voice work: "those Texas ears too sharp" (52). Management, D.J. explains, "know enough not to try to read each other's corporate fish features when they can read each other's corporate ass voices. Man, they pick up what you're trying to slip by them, they buy nothing that's not tested, not voice tested" (51). That voice testing accounts for the principal events of *Vietnam*. Rusty needs to kill a grizzly bear to advance up the corporate ladder, lest he fall from it. He cannot advance without demonstrating that he's a ruthless alpha male, which to his superiors means successfully having hunted grizzlies. He cannot fake having done so by producing the "Hyde" of a bear. He needs actually to have killed a bear, because management will hear any lie in his voice and the voices of his underlings.[19] The bear promises a second skin, as we will see, but that skin must reside in Rusty's voice.

Purple Mountain Majesty

Rusty is as reactionary as his firm, and he and his employers see killing the bear as an outlet for social resentments, among which:

(1) The women are free. They fuck too many to believe one man can do the job. (2) The Niggers are free, and the dues they got to be paid is no Texas virgin's delight. (3) The Niggers and the women are fucking each other. (4) The Yellow races are breaking loose. (5) Africa is breaking loose. . . . (11) The white men are no longer champions in boxing. (12) The great white athlete is being superseded by the great black athlete. (13) The Jews run the Eastern wing of the Democratic party. (110)

The list continues. But the essential point remains, to Rusty and his ilk, that "he, Rusty, is fucked unless he gets that bear, for if he don't, white men are fucked more and they can take no more" (111). It makes sense, from this warped perspective, that D.J. conceives the entire hunting trip as a form of violence against African Americans. On separate occasions, he likens a caribou, a mountain goat, a ram, and an eagle to blacks. These animals tend to evoke caricatured elements of an older, quiescent black culture. As the caribou climbs, "each step" seems "a pure phase of the blues—take me away, Mr. Dixieland" (97); the goat strikes D.J. as an "old Negro heel-and-toe tap man" (99), the ram "an old Negro witch smelling gypsy money on a mark" (104). But where these lesser species evoke fading images of slavery and Jim Crow, the grizzly seems a pure product of post-bop jazz. To Mailer's hunters, the animal reigns supreme in its psychopathic capacities, and evokes dangerously empowered African Americans. One of these repellently racist hunters thinks of the grizzly as "a Nigger washerwoman gone ape with a butcher knife" (88) and D.J. and Rusty think "of grizzer as a big black man, about as frightening as a stone-black seven-foot 300-pound nigger" (135).

Seen this way, the animals are to D.J. phallic inversions of the handicapped man in Harlem with whom he vies for control of the narrative. We're told that the bears have "gone ape" (114) in ways that link them in D.J.'s mind not simply to black Americans but to the novel's most significant black man. D.J. asks us to think of his alter ego in Harlem as "the ideational heat" of "a Spade gone ape" (57, 58). The grizzly completes the circuit between ape and African American; it points back to the "something black-ass and terrible" (57) lurking in the heart of the Harlem narrator. The narrative offers no account of why this man is "broken legged." But we know that its events take place two years after the hunt, and it's from within this later time frame that D.J. refers to the Harlem man's condition. We might therefore venture that, in killing the grizzly, D.J. cripples the man in Harlem.

When Thomas "Daddy" Rice performed his first Jim Crow routines, he imitated a slave whose legs had been broken: symbolically manipulating the body of the other required symbolically breaking that body. Similarly, in *Vietnam*, by destroying the bear, D.J. destroys the body of an imagined rival narrator, the better to appropriate his voice. He thus refigures the logic that sends Rusty on the hunt: his father needs to kill a bear because he needs to be able truthfully to say that he has done so. The model is industrial: Rusty's voice is likened to an automobile engine, and he must show that he can make good engines. But D.J. needs to kill a bear so that his voice cannot be falsified or said to depend for verification on the body that speaks it. We might say, in only slightly different terms, that D.J. learns in killing the bear to produce voice as Rusty's firm produces plastic—as a wholly fabricated product that makes no claims to authenticity. Thus Mailer stages the birth of rock and roll—and its mass circulation over the radio—as the symbolic crippling of more identifiably black forms of music.

Whatever else characterizes it, the plastic voice that D.J. draws from the bear is recognizably cool. On the trail of his first grizzly, D.J. is "listening to the *mood, man*" (128) of the nature around them. "There's a fine cool in now," he offers, "they're off the fever of hunting and into the heart of it, the cool" (135). When finally D.J. and his father mortally wound a grizzly, something transpires between bear and teenager. D.J. sees his own alienation in the animal's eyes. He looks into its dying face and sees "wise old gorilla eyes." These eyes "locked into his, a message, fellow, an intelligence of something very fine and very far away, just about as intelligent and wicked and merry as any sharp light D.J. had ever seen in any Texan's eyes any time (or overseas around the world) those eyes were telling him something, singeing him, branding some part of D.J.'s future" (146). This act of branding transfers the bear's "soul"—understood as the spirit animating a range of black musical forms—into D.J. Writing as the man in Harlem at the start of the narrative, D.J. notes that "every Spade is the Shade of the White Man, and when we die we enter their mind, we are part of the Shade" (26). Dying, the bear enters D.J.'s mind. Mesmerized by this transfer, D.J. hears the bear speak to him in hip argot: "Baby, you haven't begun." Suddenly, he feels the forest emanating "the unspoken cool on tap in the veins of every tree" (147). The bear connects D.J. to the cool spirit of the wilderness, and by extension to soulful black musical styles. But it also leaves him with "psychic transistors in his ear (one more gift of the dying griz)" (151). These are the devices that allow him to imagine his narrative as a radio broadcast, coming from an internal terrain that is akin to either Harlem or Dallas, we know not which. And these transistors explain how it is that Mailer's text can be, at one and the same time, *pace* Derrida, a phallus and an instrument of the human voice, a primitive totem and an up-to-the-minute piece of broadcast technology.

Mailer's musical stories are political stories as well. He analogizes killing the grizzly to killing not simply black Americans but John F. Kennedy. The hunters are "Dallasassians" (99) and, at one point, lay an ambush for the animals on a "knoll" in "the middle of one emerald alpine meadow" (117)—which is to say a "grassy knoll." This novel advances, in other words, a version of the theory later championed by Oliver Stone: the Texas native Lyndon Johnson kills Kennedy, in order to safeguard the U.S. military's involvement in Vietnam. Written during the height of Johnson's power, *Vietnam* takes as its protagonist a Texan Dallasassian who violently appropriates and contains African American expressivity, as preparation for a tour of duty in Vietnam. It's tempting to read D.J.'s voice not simply as a figure for Johnson's interracial coalition but, more damningly, as a figure for the dangerous confusion that Johnson's commitment to Vietnam generated between violence against unruly blacks and violence against Vietnamese. Thus Richard Godden points out that the grizzly is likened both to King Kong and to the Vietcong.

This confusion notwithstanding, D.J. is not the same kind of hunter as his father. As he communes with his wounded grizzly, absorbing his soul, Rusty dispatches the animal, thereby precipitating the "final end of love of one son for one father" (147). Godden reads this generational schism in economic terms. For him, Mailer's novel traces "the perverse tactics of late capital, under which financier and state liaise to counter and disguise the tendency of the rate of profit to fall." Falling profits spur the overdevelopment of productive capacity and the creation of new markets, which eventuates in the speculative excess and inflation that characterized the end of the sixties. According to Godden, the entrepreneurial D.J. attempts to forestall this cycle when he breaks from the hunting group and treks farther into the Arctic Circle: he searches for new markets that might absorb the economy's productive surplus. D.J.'s Oedipal desire to kill Rusty is part of that search: the son wants to break an "incest taboo" that "impedes the flow of capital . . . in the name of the father." It is worth adding, however, that racial taboos impeded the flow of capital in more obvious ways than did incest taboos. As we saw in Chapter 3, corporate America was reaping the rewards of integration by learning to sell across racial barriers. Mailer's novel insists that we understand the generational divide between D.J. and Rusty in terms of these barriers: the son will engage in exploitative commerce with African Americans in ways that the father will not.[20] While no less racist than his father, the entrepreneurial and incipiently postindustrial D.J. depends upon the racial mixing that Rusty would avoid.

Hostile to the integration that his son has achieved in vocal registers, Rusty worries that he will be forced to watch whites like his son having sex with black women. "The time is soon coming," he thinks, "when fornication will be professional athletics, and everybody will watch the national eliminations on TV. Will boys like D.J. . . . be in the finals with a couple of playboy bunnies or black ass honeys?" (109). Rusty's terror of this scenario comes freighted with political overtones. He objects to the notion that blacks should have any place in national iconography; he almost writes a letter to Congress protesting the fact that the bald eagle is the national bird, because he sees a bald eagle attacking a wounded deer and thinks it "like a Nigger strutting his ass feathers" (132). This objection is more pointed when, in speaking of the "national eliminations," he worries, "What if Spades run away with the jewels? . . . Think of that in Color TV—all the purple majesty" (109–110). We hear in this last figure a reference to a popular national ballad, as we do in *Miami and the Siege of Chicago* (1968), when Mailer describes Americans like Rusty, for whom "the sweetest object of contemplation" is "nothing less than America the Beautiful herself." These hypothetical Americans recoil when their reverie is interrupted by "the face of an accusing rioting Black right in the middle of the dream."[21]

"America the Beautiful" was turning black, just as surely as "The Star-Spangled Banner" would, two years later, at the hands of Jimi Hendrix. But the more disturbing threat in *Vietnam* is that black men were providing the republic with its crown jewels and scepter all in one. In Rusty's nightmare, the "purple majesty" of a victorious black penis dominates and defines America the Beautiful, which D.J. thinks a once-glorious "land of purple forests," now overrun by "all those fucking English, Irish, Scotch, and European weeds" (205). One year earlier, Mailer wrote that "democracy flowers with style; without it, there is a rot of weeds." *Vietnam* suggests that democracy flowers best when fertilized with a hip purple majesty. As Mailer saw it, an increasingly sterile WASP establishment deployed that purple majesty in Vietnam, as even they feared the power it lent a new generation of young wanting to cross racial lines, appropriate new voices, and sing a new kind of national anthem.[22]

Antebellum minstrelsy had articulated a related set of concerns. As Ralph Ellison put it, "The mask was the thing (the 'thing' in more ways than one)." Eric Lott explains: "Bold swagger, irrepressible desire, sheer bodily display: in a real sense the minstrel man *was* the penis, that organ returning in a variety of contexts, at times ludicrous, at others rather less so." Lott argues that "white men's investment in the black penis appears to have defined the minstrel show," which provided white men an opportunity to negotiate the "homosexual attraction, male identification, and male rivalry" they experienced for and with black men. At the same time, minstrel shows raised the uncomfortable possibility that the voices that issued from the blackened lips of white performers blackened the national soul. "The Jim Crows, the Zip Coons, and the Dandy Jims, who have electrified the world," announced J. K. Kennard in 1845, "from them proceed our ONLY TRULY NATIONAL POETS." Kennard advances by way of Shelley: "The popular song-maker sways the souls of men; the legislator rules only their bodies. The song-maker reigns through love and spiritual affinity; the legislator by brute force. Apply this principle to the American people. Who are our true rulers? The Negro poets, to be sure! Do they not set the fashion, and give laws to the public taste?"[23] Kennard deplores this development, and his distinction between ruling souls and ruling bodies belies a deeper unease with the prominence that black expressivity enjoyed upon the stage of national culture.

Saul Bellow's *Mr. Sammler's Planet* (1970) further specifies the nature of the phallic authority bound up with fantasies of black expressivity at the end of the sixties. Toward the start of the novel, protagonist Arthur Sammler lectures at Columbia University. The lecture does not go well. He'd anticipated talking to a small group of enthusiasts about his association with H. G. Wells and the Bloomsbury circle; instead, the half-blind Sammler is led into a large and crowded auditorium. Off balance, he begins to speak about the idealism of the 1930s. Those were days, he tells the hall, when artists "set upon the building of a planned, orderly, and beautiful world society . . . based on a rational scientific attitude toward life."[24] But before getting much further, he is interrupted by a student radical who accuses him of defending counterrevolutionaries. "Why do you listen to this effete old shit?" the Levi's-wearing, bearded antagonist asks those around him in the audience. "What has he got to tell you? His balls are dry. He's dead. He can't come" (46). Shamed, Sammler quits the lecture hall and heads for the bus, marveling at this new generation's "will to offend" (47). But no sooner has he stepped on the bus than he sees a figure he has witnessed in action before: a tall and elegantly dressed black pickpocket. The figure looms over an old and unsuspecting victim. Sammler observes the thief reach in, open the victim's wallet, take what little cash there is, riffle through some cards and then discover and steal a Social Security check. The pickpocket sees Sammler witness the theft, so Sammler quits the bus and tries to disappear into the city's crowds. But the pickpocket finds Sammler as he heads home and forces the old man into his building's lobby. Here begins one of twentieth-century American literature's most notorious scenes. With an expression less menacing than "oddly, serenely masterful," the pickpocket drops his pants and exposes his penis with what Bellow calls a "mystifying certitude. Lordliness" (54). This, then, is the stunning culmination of the ambush Sammler received at Columbia University. If Sammler's antagonist at the lecture deemed him irrelevant because of his inability to come, then we find here, cradled confidently in the pickpocket's hand, the final and most ostensibly devastating form of that rebuke. You, Sammler, are impotent, most especially so when confronted by the pickpocket's "great oval testicles [and] large tan-and-purple uncircumcised thing—a tube, a snake" (53).

The message is clear: the counterculture derives its strength from sexually potent African Americans. Sammler describes the pickpocket's self-exposure to the professor who invited him to Columbia; he thinks Sammler cannot understand the meaning of the gesture. He responds that Sammler is "wise, but not hip" (123).[25] But though clearly not hip, Sammler understands well enough. Thinking back on the incident with the pickpocket, he describes the penis as "an object intended to communicate authority." The penis, he thinks to himself, "was a symbol of superlegitimacy or sovereignty" (59). In one respect, this is a national symbol that reaches back to the republic's founding documents. Likening the pickpocket's penis to an embodied natural right, Sammler thinks, "We hold these truths, man, to be self-evident" (59). Derisive of truths you can hold in your hand, Sammler prefers more abstract pleasures. But Bellow's "sov-

ereignty" more specifically indicates a Democratic Party sovereignty. He immediately follows the pickpocket's exposure with this: "Sammler now even vaguely
recalled hearing that a President of the United States was supposed to have
shown himself in a similar way to the representatives of the press (asking ladies
to leave), and demanding to know whether a man so well hung could not be
trusted to lead his country" (70). That well-endowed and extroverted president
is of course Lyndon Baines Johnson, famous for showing himself to reporters
and inviting aides into the bathroom while he did his business there. Bellow
figures the pickpocket's penis as the authority behind Great Society liberalism.

With Johnson now in hand, we can return to what Sammler sees on the
uptown bus. Having just waxed nostalgic about the utopian 1930s, and having been stopped in his tracks by a radical student, Sammler witnesses the
theft of the New Deal's most cherished legacy: Social Security. Johnson seems
in league with this theft. Reinventing the welfare state alongside his efforts
to secure comprehensive civil rights legislation, Johnson made it possible for
social reactionaries, like Sammler, to view that state as a distinctly African
American enterprise. The pickpocket's theft of the check takes place at the
back of a public bus. The smartly dressed man doesn't need to ride the bus;
he's wealthy enough to take a cab. In Bellow's universe, he rides only to steal
what isn't rightfully his; he does so, tellingly enough, by preying upon those
elderly whites who, following a trajectory of downward mobility, ride where
African Americans once rode. Thus the theft of the Social Security check feels
like a redistributive act taking place within mainstream liberalism: resources
pilfered from the nation's social insurance program and shunted into the gra-
tuitous pursuit of civil rights.

Skinning the White Liberal

In *St. George and the Godfather* (1972), Mailer described a party reshaping its
priorities and redistributing authority among its constituencies. He believed
that "every sense of power in the Democratic Party had shifted" (69–70)—
for the worse. Like Bellow, he cast the crucial divide facing liberalism as one
between youth and age. But unlike Bellow, who deplored what he took to be the
party's undue reliance on the young and African Americans, Mailer reflected
on the now baleful prominence of the PMC within the party. That constituency
was, alas, no longer hip. It was important to the Democrats' electoral success
in 1960, and had become progressively more important since then, but had

become the party's center of gravity only in the early seventies, by which time the mantle of hip it had once worn had passed to its children.

In *Miami and the Siege of Chicago*, Mailer described the Democrats' coalition as lacking any true center. Reporting from Chicago in 1968, he viewed it as a pastiche of "cosmopolitans, one-worlders, trade-unionists, Black militants, New Leftists, acid-heads, tribunes of the gay, families of Mafia, political machinists, fixers, swingers, Democratic lobbyists, members of the Grange, and government workers, not to include the *Weltanschauung* of every partisan in every minority group" (*MSC* 33). He liked this eclectic mix, and the incessant jockeying for position to which it gave rise. Four years later, however, a largely affluent constituency had gained the upper hand within the party and was endeavoring to hold these coalitions together. The old machines, as well as the working classes and the trade unions, no longer enjoyed their pride of place. Instead, George McGovern led what was once Eugene McCarthy's wing of the party, his core constituency "the newly prosperous liberals of the suburb [who] welcomed the idea that all principles of the Establishment—God, nation, family, marriage, patriotism, and the distinction of the sexes—were wrong or non-existent." Mailer thought that this group embraced "every idea which was anathema to the Establishment: women's liberation, welfare rights, minority rights, tax reform . . . they were also devoted to every right and liberty which would make humans more equal in soul and body" (*SG* 69). But their opposition was no longer vital; it was, instead, self-sacrificing.

In 1968, he viewed the Democratic Party as a concatenation of countervailing interests, made up of multiple groups fighting over their respective political properties. In 1972, on the other hand, the party seemed the ward of a benevolent professional-managerial class eager to represent the interests of every group except its own. He declares, "It was their pride, their delight, and their levitation from guilt that McGovern's tax reform would hit them hardest" (*SG* 68). Mailer denounces such self-sacrifice and warms to McGovern's followers only when, learning from their children, they realize that "the sanction to act came from within the body" and, enlightened, act as "swingers" (*SG* 68). The young matter as much as they do, Mailer thinks, because they represent the PMC's last contact with the invigorating black hip that was still, to him, the lifeblood of the party.

As he sees it, that hip instantiates the needs of the body as the ultimate arbiter of political action and short-circuits the white liberal's proclivity to legislate from guilt. Mailer thinks the Democratic Party desperately in need of this lesson. In 1966, he wrote that conservatives were "Cannibals" because they relished the brutal struggle at the heart of politics; liberals were "Christians," not because they believed in Christ—they generally didn't, he thought—but because they were bound by high moral principle. Speaking as a Christian, he explained, "We believe man is good if given a chance, we believe man is open to discussion, we believe science is the salvation of ill, we believe death is the end of discussion; ergo, we believe nothing is so worthwhile as human life" (*CC* 20–21). Yet Mailer would never rest easy with these beliefs; they denied the bestial needs that animated D.J. and old guard Democrats like Richard M. Daley. This bestiality was disappearing from the Democratic Party, but alive and well in the GOP. At the Republican convention of 1972, he therefore reports, "There is not a jive Black in sight, no smocks, no sarongs, or flaring Afros. No prime evil. Nothing carnal. The mood, if boring, is absolutely safe" (*SG* 164). These smiling corn-fed mannequins don't seem to follow their bodies. All the same, Mailer feels that beneath their implacably bland veneer, these WASPs— a "Faustian, barbaric, draconian, progress-oriented, and root-destroying people"—understand the nature of force, violence, and evil.[26] The professional and managerial classes at the center of McGovern's coalition, on the other hand, betray their bodies. The protesting students at the Chicago convention were belligerent about their desire for peace; they would have understood D.J. Jethro. But McGovern's core had inherited an angry countercultural ethos from these youths and transformed it into a smugly white-collar lifestyle. McGovern's is "a clerical revolution, an uprising of the suburban, the well-educated, the modest, the reasonable, and all the unacknowledged genetic engineers of the future" (26–27). This is Shelley without the romantic agon.

Democrats therefore needed "jive Blacks" in ways that Republicans did not. Liberals found in black Americans the "carnal" and "prime evil" qualities that they lacked, and that the Republicans, all appearances to the contrary, richly possessed. In the language of Chapter 5, blacks knew how not to be slaves; they knew how to rise up in anger and strike fear into their oppressors. Mailer had been arguing for more than a decade that the Democrats needed more anger, more violence, and more manly vigor. Celebrating Kennedy in "Superman Comes to the Supermarket" (1960), he derided Beats who were "weak before the strong" (*PP* 18). Similarly, Adlai Stevenson would be weak before the rapacious Kennedy, "the hipster as presidential candidate" (*PP* 21). Mailer imagines Kennedy's aides muttering that the Illinois governor "had nothing going for him but a bunch of Goddamn Beatniks" (*PP* 29). Attending the Democratic convention in Chicago in 1968, Mailer wants to know "if there was not real outrage in the Democratic Party" (*MSC* 95). He hopes there is, and fantasizes about top-level Democrats having "contacts" with members of the South Side "Blackstone Rangers, the largest gang of juvenile delinquents on earth, 2,000 by some count—one could be certain the gang had leaders as large in potential as Hannibal or Attila the Hun" (*MSC* 110, 87).

An alliance between party officials and black gangs was appealing to a mind like Mailer's. At the same time, it raised questions about the ultimate control of the Democrats, and these questions led back to Mailer's own exploitative relation to black culture. One year earlier, *Vietnam* had described D.J. as a potential Hannibal or Attila the Hun. But D.J. doesn't ally himself with violent blacks; rather, he expropriates them in the name of imperialism in Vietnam and a musical form (rock and roll) from which he means to profit. Doing so leaves in its wake the "broken-legged" body of the nameless African American in Harlem. Terry Southern would echo this conceit, and suggest its political implication, in his account of the 1968 Democratic convention. Having just arrived in Chicago, he witnesses "four boys each about ten years old and armed with small sticks" who "were flailing wildly at a huge crippled black man who reeled and staggered drunkenly among piles of debris in a deserted lot." Southern stops to help, but the man does not want help. Instead of offering a "verbal reply, his response was to seize a large, empty and battered ashcan [and] to raise it over his head." Southern writes, "A curious tableau—did it augur well, or mal, conventionwise?"[27] He doesn't return to the question, which ramifies uncomfortably.

Mailer is not sure that anyone at the Chicago convention views African Americans as more than negotiable pieces of political property. He admits to having grown impatient with the demands of blacks, and wonders how many white politicians felt otherwise. He likes the Blackstone Rangers, but doesn't like black politicians, this despite his readiness to acknowledge "all legitimate claims, all burning claims, all searing claims . . . that America's wealth, whiteness, and hygiene had been refined out of the most powerful molecules stolen from the sweat of the Black man" (*MSC* 52). Awash in racial resentments, he wonders if he has "become in some secret part of his flesh a closet Republican" (*MSC* 53). That's an open question, and it resonates with the racial deracination implicit in *Vietnam*, in which the commitment to refining white voice from black bodies requires destroying those bodies, lest they decide to speak for themselves.

At the Republican convention of 1972, Mailer thrills to a joke made by comedian Johnny Grant, in which Spiro Agnew, relentless in his Democrat bashing, is said to really "give 'em oral karate" (*SG* 197). Mailer pounces: "Swimming just out of reach we see the head of a liberal politician stuck onto some sort of pus-filled penile shaft (black presumably) and wham! go Agnew's teeth. What a karate chop! The head of the liberal has just been clipped off its black backing" (*SG* 198). A complexly grotesque image: Agnew as Ahab? Bruce Lee? Linda Lovelace? Certainly the image echoes Eldridge Cleaver's claim that white men had assumed for themselves the power of the brain, and ceded to black men the power of the body, while insisting on control of the black penis. This made black men what he called "Supermasculine Menials." Cleaver speaks as a white man in order to explain: "By subjecting your manhood to the control of my will, I shall control you. The stem of the Body, the penis, must submit to the will of the Brain."[28] Seen in more specifically political terms, Agnew's cutting of a white head from its black "backing" suggests cutting white liberals from the black constituencies in whose name and with whose voices they wished to speak, and from whom, at least according to Mailer, they would borrow their outrage and muscle.

But speaking in the name of those constituencies was not the same as allowing them to speak, as Mailer's self-conscious racial resentments suggest. And in 1972, the Democratic Party had yet to provide substantial opportunities for black leadership. The convention of that year gave the Black Caucus, which had been formed in 1969, its first chance to participate in the selection of a national ticket. Reforms adopted by the McGovern-Fraser Commission allowed for a significant increase of black delegates: 483 out of 3,203 attending were black.[29] Moreover, the convention saw the nomination of Shirley Chisholm as the first African American woman for president. But Richard Rubin notes that the convention was most significant for its largely symbolic use of blackness. As he puts it, "It was not the lack of a sizeable convention delegation or the lack of participation in the manifest business of the convention that was most notable, but rather the presence of symbolic representation *without* Blacks playing a direct and vital role in the primary function of the convention." The nomination of Chisholm was one such "symbolic representation." More generally, Rubin notes, "the public view of the convention activities (i.e., the number of speakers on the floor, in committee, and on the dais) suggested a far greater political input from Blacks than was actually made in power terms."

This suggests to Rubin that "the personal qualities so beneficial to non-party political leadership—charismatic, symbolic, and rhetorical—had [yet] to be welded to those other needed organizational, manipulative, and strategic talents required in party politics."[30]

And, indeed, contemporary accounts of the 1972 convention treat black style as little more than decor. Mailer turns to Willie Brown, who stages the first demonstration of the convention when he pushes aside a challenge to McGovern's California delegates. Mailer describes Brown as "lithe as a super-cat, and young, and super-cool as a dream of Black supremacy in his creamy stay-cool-forever clothes" (*SG* 45). Mailer relishes Chisholm telling the Black Caucus, "I'm the only one among you who has the balls to run for President." In his eyes, this leaves her "as related to politics as the air is to the wind" (*SG* 63). But figures like Brown and Chisholm seem valuable to Mailer largely for what they can teach their white audiences. As Hunter Thompson has it, Chisholm's candidacy mobilized black dispossession for the edification of a white constituency. He records Ron Dellums, a black congressman from Berkeley, introducing her on behalf of "the Nigger vote." Thompson notes that he "wasn't talking about skin pigment." By "America's Niggers," Dellums means "the Young, the Black, the Brown, the Women, the Poor—all the people who feel left out of the political process."[31] This was another version of the phenomenon reported by Joe McGinniss four years earlier when, speaking for those feeling dispossessed by the Nixon campaign of 1968, he quotes Gloria Steinem: "We're all niggers now."[32]

These and other visions of inclusiveness often functioned to consolidate the power of white politicians. For example, Mailer records the vocal transference of blackness, the way in which white candidates were learning to sound black. It was already commonplace in 1968 for politicians to mimic the rhetorical styles of African Americans; doing so offered a cost-free means of reaching out to black constituencies while promising them little. Thus Mailer observes as unlikely a politician as Nixon borrowing the rhythms of the recently assassinated King, "without shame and certainly without fear" (*MSC* 80–81). In 1972, Humphrey perfected this art, adopting a self-consciously black "rhythm when he spoke. He laid down every favor he had ever done for Blacks, did it in cadence, you could hear the repetitive roll of the soul drummer hearkening to a Black *duende* at these rhythmic calls on history" (*SG* 16). Thompson tells a similar story when he describes Humphrey ingratiating himself with black voters by "greeting all comers with the Revolutionary Drug Brothers handshake. It was like Nixon flashing the peace sign, or Agnew chanting 'Right On!' at a minstrel show" (*FL* 167).

Vietnam functions, similarly, at a second remove: no less than when Agnew disarticulates a white head from a black phallus, the novel dismembers the black body to control it and speak in its voice. This process was not reversible. We cannot know for sure whether D.J. is white or black. But Mailer does suggest the limits of this uncertainty when he notes, "It's easier for D. J. to imitate a high I.Q. Harlem Nigger time to time, since D. J. knows New York . . . than for a Harlem Nigger ever to know all this secret Texas shit" (133–134). It's safe to say, in other words, that few in Harlem would have access to the corporate boardrooms and mansions of Dallas. White kids could hear black musicians on the radio; they never had to enter black neighborhoods. Should they want to, however, they could enter those neighborhoods far more easily than black musicians (or novelists) could enter wealthy white enclaves, and in this context, D.J.'s voyage to the far reaches of Alaska indicates the ease with which he might also travel—gun or political platform in hand, it might not matter which— even to Harlem. In *American Dream*, former Democratic congressman Stephen Rojack enters Harlem and physically humiliates a black musician. Not unlike the Democratic Party of his moment, D.J. trumpets his capacity to do the same; more openly violent and, Mailer suggests, honest than that party, D.J. acknowledges that blacks cannot speak for him.

"To be free and creative"

E. L. Doctorow's *The Book of Daniel* extends concerns central to William Styron's *The Confessions of Nat Turner*, but does so in ways that echo Norman Mailer's *Why Are We in Vietnam?* Daniel, the novel's narrator, would understand himself as a black slave. He faults his working-class parents for having failed to perceive the class position they shared with blacks; in their minds, they "were not conditioned to accept slavery. Their minds were free." But Daniel disagrees, and lampoons them in an act of blackface: "Oh yes, Lawd. Oh yes, complacent lawd" (95). The momentary eruption of dialect suggests a return of what the Isaacsons repress. But Doctorow is more critical of his reliance on blackface than was Styron, and insists on his own predatory relation to the black bodies whose voices he would borrow. In *Daniel*, speaking in dialect requires disposing of black bodies, the better to use their voices as internal goads to personal development.

In an obvious sense, the Isaacsons are confirmed as slaves by the government that executes them. Daniel invokes Karl Marx, who uses the term "slavery" to describe the working classes' subjection to both the economic conditions of capitalism and the coercive authority of the state:

> As societies endure in history they symbolize complex systems of corporal punishment in economic terms. That is why Marx used the word "slavery" to define the role of the working class under capitalism. In times of challenge, however, the ruling classes restore their literal, un-symbolized right of corporal punishment upon the lower classes. (129–130)

Working class, Daniel's parents experience the slavery of wage labor. But they are also subject to the "symbolized" economic authority of the capitalist interests that pay their wages. The state articulates these interests and, feeling under threat, takes their lives. Daniel faults his parents for failing to grasp this eventuality: though deluded by their idealism into thinking otherwise, they are not special, and by the terms of their own Marxist analysis they possess little agency over the coercive authority to which they are subject.

Daniel's distaste for his parents' misguided sense of agency takes shape in relation to an African American named Williams who lives in the cellar of the Isaacsons' Bronx home when Daniel is a child. The Isaacsons think Williams "a man destroyed by American society because of his skin" (35). They see not a person but a social problem—little more than a symbol of oppression. Doctorow nods to Ralph Ellison: Williams is invisible to the Isaacsons, a glowering black man living in the cellar, ranting against the Communist Party. From Daniel's vantage, the Isaacsons view Williams in the same way that the government does. After their incarceration, they agree that "the black man can't take care of [the children]" (144–145). But Daniel wonders, and asks us to imagine Williams taking care of him and his sister, Susan, and thus saving the Isaacsons' home. In the state shelter, Daniel muses that "leaders are the only ones who ever feel at home," just before describing black kids whose athletic gifts make them just such leaders—and "unbelievable stars" (170) to boot. Moments later, he plans his escape. He has "this idea that if we went home to Williams, somehow that would have the effect of getting our mother and father home too" (172). Home as an angry black man: this is a mammy fantasy, gender-bent and updated for the sixties. Daniel's fantasy that Williams might have saved his home is part and parcel of his fantasy that Williams might have saved his parents' leftism from itself. It's as if Daniel imagines the Isaacsons having missed an opportunity to guide themselves out of bondage—both ideological and physical—by the light of this "unbelievable star."

Throughout, Daniel suggests that the Old Left failed to understand American race relations. Thus he recounts an incident that takes place when the Isaacsons travel upstate by bus to hear Paul Robeson, whom Daniel's father describes as "a proud black Communist" (47). No one considers inviting Williams. The oversight haunts the expedition. After the concert, in a fictional reenactment of the Peekskill Riots, racists assault the bus. Outraged that a policeman stands idly by, Paul Isaacson tries to leave the bus and complain. The mob breaks his arm, and the irony is heavy. These earnest but insular whites, going to hear their proud black Communist: not a colored face on the bus, they come off as ersatz Freedom Riders, architects of their own victimization. To Daniel, this is the Old Left at its most obtuse.

Loosely modeled on Abbie Hoffman, Artie Sternlicht offers a different approach. The novel's New Left mouthpiece, he tells Daniel that African Americans must lead the revolutionary struggle, because, he declares, "the only people in the U.S. who know they're slaves are the black people. I mean they are born with absolutely no tolerance for shit, they are born willing to die." This invocation of slavery accords black Americans a singular status; learning from black people, "the white dropout children [and] the derelict kids" learn that they too are part of "a runaway slave movement" (138). Sternlicht echoes the Free Speech Movement when he goes on to equate "all the spades murdered in their beds, and in every jail in the world" with all "the millions of kids murdered in their schools" (152). The movement's "We Want a University" (1964) held that "in a twentieth-century industrial state, ignorance will be the definition of slavery. If centers of education fail, they will be the producers of the twentieth century slave."[33] In a 1965 essay on the movement and its aftermath at Berkeley, Paul Goodman described higher education as a form of "exploitation" that imposes on children "the discipline of slaves." He suggested that calling students "kids" is "something like calling a Negro 'boy.' In many a Town-Gown fracas, the analogy of student and Negro is pretty obvious."[34]

The analogy was not simply obvious. It was the operating assumption of the mass activism of the sixties. Maurice Isserman and Michael Kazin remind us of the influence of the Civil Rights Movement on the New Left. "Without the civil rights movement," they say, "it is difficult to imagine the emergence of any of the new radical movements of the 1960s." In 1966, Irving Howe went further: "In the United States the civil rights movement has had a substantial liberating effect, not merely in gaining victories for the Negroes and providing the idealistic young with opportunities for activities and sacrifice, but also in opening up the country to fresh moods and sentiments." Along these lines, Todd Gitlin recalls, "In the sphere of music as in the sphere of justice, white America was drawing its juice from blacks." Paul Buhle stresses the far-reaching implication of the widespread affinity that white teens felt for blacks. "Everything," he wrote,

> started with the Blacks, and at least until the crest of the anti-war movement on the campuses, would remain so. Behind that strategic reality, a web of political understanding and personal growth entwined the white New Left's self-identity with the non-white world. . . . To affirm solidarity with Blacks in any political sense was a minority act; but the sympathy towards Black culture reached further among millions of teenagers than any previously Left-oriented effort could have envisioned.[35]

That sympathy was profound. Because of it, the sixties witnessed an unprecedented political awakening, as countless Americans fought for racial justice both within and beyond the United States.

But Buhle is most apposite to *The Book of Daniel* in describing "the web of political understanding" that connected acts of white sympathy to what he calls "personal growth." Activists used African Americans to model the repression and freedom at stake in a range of institutions, and in doing so tended to assume that whites were least free, and most like slaves, when they lost their capacity for creativity and self-expression and, conversely, were most possessed of black power when they found this capacity within themselves. When Mario Savio declared that "the same rights are at stake" in both Mississippi's Freedom Summer and Berkeley's Free Speech Movement of 1964, he added that these movements were "a struggle against the same enemy": "In our free-speech fight at the University of California, we have come up against what may emerge as the greatest problem of our nation—depersonalized, unresponsive bureaucracy. We have encountered the organized status quo in Mississippi, but it is the same in Berkeley."[36] Following this logic, Carl Davidson argued in "The New Radicalism and the Multiversity" (1968) that the cornerstone of twentieth-century "slavery" was "the regimentation and bureaucratization of existence." But the salient feature of this slavery was its suppression of creativity. Davidson derided Dow Chemical, for example, because it squelched the worker's desire "to be free and creative." And Savio suggested that whites might attain personal liberation by understanding themselves as blacks, because they would otherwise "suppress the most creative impulses that they have; this is a prior condition for being part of the system."[37]

This antithesis between an individual's (black) inner creative voice and a (white) "system" took on heightened significance after 1966, when organizations like SNCC expelled white liberals and radicals. Exiled from the movement, whites discovered within themselves new avenues for achieving integration and so advancing a struggle in which they could no longer directly participate. SDS national secretary Greg Calvert thought "white radicals" owed "SNCC a debt of gratitude for having slapped us brutally in the face." He heard in the emergence of Black Power a message: "go home and organize in white America which is *your* reality." He chastised liberals for failing to understand that this reality didn't refer to white neighborhoods so much as it referred to the white mind. "Radical consciousness," he claimed, turns inward, and focuses on closing "the gap between 'what one could be' and the existing conditions for self-realization." Such consciousness, he added, requires "the perception of oneself as unfree, as oppressed." It requires "the discovery of oneself as one of the oppressed." As he had it, "Only when white America comes to terms with its own unfreedom can it participate in the creation of a revolutionary movement." Calvert claimed that whites could help blacks only after they discovered that they too were slaves and began their own insurrectionary journeys toward "self-realization."[38]

This theory of liberation aligned political and literary aims. For much of the New Left, political action either required or eventuated in discovering and freeing the black slave within. But this discovery was also imagined to unearth the power of creative expression. Herbert Marcuse offered the most sophisticated version of this claim when he equated black liberation with the emancipatory potential of the aesthetic. For Marcuse, increasingly organized political and economic systems required progressively greater degrees of guilt, sexual repression, and ever more extreme sublimations of human sexuality into relations of production and work. Each reinvention of capitalism required an even more severe repression of instinct, and Marcuse held that a pre-genital, polymorphous sexuality not geared exclusively toward reproduction (coupled with a narcissistic autoeroticism) might reverse this tendency.

Marcuse's "An Essay on Liberation" (1969) dramatizes these terms in light of American race relations. The essay is symptomatic of New Left thinking in its rejection of "that whole network of parties, committees, and pressure groups on all levels" and its sense that "nothing that any of these politicians, representatives or candidates declares is of any relevance to the rebels."[39] It's equally symptomatic in its sense that African American bodies provide an alternative to this world of traditional politics. He thinks that the young want "to see, hear, [and] feel new things in a new way." He grants the "distorted" nature of this inescapably "private" desire for "a revolution in perception" and points to the fascination with the psychedelic as a debased version of this privatizing desire. At the same time, he regards the drive for "a new sensorium" as crucial to the vanguard of "social liberation" (37) and, like Norman Mailer before him, thinks African Americans hold the key to that liberation. Preoccupied by what it would mean to live "life not as masters and not as slaves, but as men and women" (52), Marcuse views African Americans as exemplars of a "new sensibility" that will replace traditional politics and the corporate capitalism that sustains it. Whereas the "needs and satisfactions" of capitalism "reproduce a life in servitude, liberation presupposes changes in [the] biological dimension, that is to say, different instinctual needs, different reactions of the body as well as the mind" (17). Marcuse thinks blacks express these changes and a corresponding "ascent of the life instincts over aggressiveness and guilt" (23).

Marcuse also shares with Mailer the conviction that because blacks embody the intimacy between biological and mental liberation, their cultural expressions exemplify the power of art generally to change reality. Marcuse imagines a dispensation in which "technique would . . . tend to become art, and art would tend to form reality." The resultant "aesthetic ethos" (24) "would mean the *Aufhebung* of art: end of the segregation of the aesthetic from the real, but also end of the commercial unification of business and beauty, exploitation and pleasure" (32). Crucially, this ethos derives force from the end of racial segregation: blacks break "real" physical boundaries even as their cultural expressions exemplify how art can "tend to form reality." Black liberation, he everywhere suggests, is more than the liberation of people—it is the liberation of sublimated energies that promise a fundamental reorganization of Western society. He thinks that "at present in the United States, the black population appears as the 'most natural' force of rebellion" (58)—"natural," in particular, because it represents a musical voice denied by corporate and state capitalism.

"Black music is originally music of the oppressed," Marcuse notes, and "the affinity between black music (and its avant-garde white development) and the political rebellion against the 'affluent society' bears witness to the increasing desublimation of culture" (47). He grants that this desublimation is a negation "easily absorbed and shaped by the market" (47), but says that it "'anticipate[s]' a stage where society's capacity to produce may be akin to the creative capacity of art, and the reconstruction of the world of art akin to the reconstruction of the real world." Not yet grounded in a material reorganization of society, the desublimation of culture manifest in black music nevertheless "constitutes an essential element of radical politics" (48). But Marcuse is most interested in the "linguistic rebellion" accomplished by

> blacks [who] "take over" some of the most sublime and sublimated concepts of Western civilization, desublimate them, and redefine them. For example, the "soul" (in its essence lily-white ever since Plato), the traditional seat of everything that is truly human in man, tender, deep, immortal—the word, which has become embarrassing, corny, false in the established universe of discourse, has been desublimated and in this transubstantiation, migrated to the Negro culture: they are soul brothers; the soul is black, violent, orgiastic; it is no longer in Beethoven, Schubert, but in the blues, in jazz, in rock 'n' roll, in "soul food." (36)

Desublimated black language rewrites Western metaphysics, as African Americans appropriate through mimicry the otherwise lily white. For Marcuse, this constitutes an "ingression of the aesthetic into the political" (36).

This ingression both signals and solves a problem. Though powerful in its ability to facilitate "the reconstruction of the world," language can only follow on the heels of inarticulate bodily states. As a consequence, aesthetic experience points toward what we cannot yet say. Marcuse speaks of the "abstract, academic, [and] unreal character" of any effort "to evaluate and even discuss the prospects for radical change in the domain of corporate capitalism" (79). "If we could form a concrete concept of the alternative today," he writes, "it would not be that of an alternative; the possibilities of the new society are sufficiently 'abstract,' i.e. removed from and incongruous with the established universe to defy any attempt to identify them in terms of this universe" (86). Again, African Americans play a densely emblematic role: they are aesthetic harbingers of the alternative that Marcuse cannot yet know. He thinks that "blues and jazz" are "not merely new modes of perception reorienting and intensifying the old ones; they rather dissolve the very structure of perception in order to make room—for what?" (38). He cannot know, but looks toward African Americans for answers. He concludes: "What are the people in a free society going to do? The answer which, I believe, strikes at the heart of the matter was given by a young black girl. She said: for the first time in our life, we shall be free to think about what we are going to do" (91).

"Oh baby, you know it now"

C. Wright Mills lamented the managerial demiurge because it robbed professionals of their capacity for "self-cultivation."[40] Speaking in 1966 of "the new generation of student activists [that] graduates into the professions," Tom Hayden, who had written his master's thesis on Mills, described a movement led by children from "professional homes" who grew up "independent of mind" but found themselves harnessed by "social institutions that denied them their independence."[41] Hayden, a founder of SDS, reasoned that African Americans taught these children how to release themselves from bondage. In emancipating themselves, blacks were "restoring the individual personality to a creative and self-cultivating role in human affairs."[42] Whites needed to learn how to do the same, not simply because they were themselves slaves, but because feeling and acting black promised, in addition to a liberated consciousness, an incipiently literary authenticity, whose authority depended on eliding stylistically the implicitly ideological question of what "people in a free society [were] going to do."

The Book of Daniel assumes this compatibility between the political and literary use of blackness. Daniel wants us to wonder about Williams and what he is doing in this novel. "Some colored man in the basement," he writes, "what is that all about? What has that got to do with anything?" (43). We might surmise that Williams is in this novel because Doctorow felt that the story of the Rosenbergs needed the story of Invisible Man—that the reader needed reminding of all that the Isaacsons' ideological fervor tended to repress. The Invisible Man, recall, leaves an organization very much like the Communist Party, and it's tempting to view Williams as a riposte to any who would forget Ellison's search for a more personal and experiential form of politics. Of course we might imagine that Williams is in the novel because Doctorow believed that failing to include a black face in the story of American radicalism was the narrative equivalent of failing to invite Williams to the Robeson concert. But Williams is not just a black face; he's an opportunity for literary blackface, for authorial emulation and imitation. As a young boy, Daniel "was fascinated by everything [Williams] did," in part because "everything he did was monumental" (90). Williams seemed to Daniel gripped by "constant anger" (90) and "incredibly gigantic" (91). The young boy imagines even his father "subject . . . to Williams' wrath" (37). Daniel envies that wrath, just as he longs for the monumental proportions of the man in the basement. More pointedly, Daniel wants the vocal power from which these proportions are indistinguishable. He describes Robeson's "as one of the greatest voices of our time" (45) before telling us that Robeson's voice reminds him of Williams's (48). The janitor had a voice, Daniel recalls, "of murder and menace, so deep it sounded like singing" (90). He remembers seeing Williams (almost exactly as Terry Southern had seen his angry black man in Chicago), with "his red eyes of menace," hoisting an ashcan over his head, and "riding his great flat feet with an eagle's grace, floating his body through the air like a song" (145). Daniel wants to sing that furious if wordless song, and we're meant to understand that the novel we read is the result of his efforts to do so.

This is emulation as self-discovery. Having broken out of the state shelter with Susan, Daniel finds his way home, now empty of his incarcerated parents. He's looking for Williams, who he hopes will raise him and his sister. But he finds only himself: "I hoisted myself up to look through the window of the cellar door. In the darkness I saw the light of my own eyes" (178). Writing his novel years later, Daniel looks for Williams again, but finds something different. Williams was broken by bondage; he is to Daniel a stock character, a black man forced to swallow his wrath and menace. Daniel needs a different muse, and invents one in a second and more mysterious black voice—one crucial to the radical aspirations of his narrative. We encounter this insurrectionary voice, unattached to any character, and so unattached to any body other than Daniel's, some twenty pages into the novel. Like some crafty Nat Turner, whose story Paul Isaacson tells his son (35), this black man within exhorts Daniel to free himself from bondage:

> Oh, baby, you know it now. We done played enough games for you, ain't we. You a smart lil fucker. You know where it's at now, don' you big daddy. You got the picture. This the story of a fucking, right? You pullin' out you lit-er-ary map, mutha? You know where we goin', right muthafuck? (23)

Sly and insinuating, self-consciously black, the voice renders knowledge erotic, an agent of tumescence. The "smart lil fucker" becomes a "big daddy" as he comes to know "it," which seems to be the fact that "this is the story of a fucking." Knowing as much means being able to mete out, rather than receive, the fucking in question—just as it means being able to take direction of the story. The voice thus challenges Daniel to grow up, sexually, and become a self-mastering author. It tells him how to place *himself* upon a literary map, which we find him "pullin' out" as he might his penis. This egregious shtick keeps the lesson simple: show that you can talk and write like this and you will have arrived in possession of your literary powers—having become a "baby" (hip, like this voice), rather than a "baby" (undeveloped, like an infant).

The Book of Daniel understands "fucking," and stories about it, as a form of political mastery. Daniel thinks that the American legal system immobilized his parents and "drove it in deeper" (161). The problem is that the men in Daniel's family cannot do the same. Daniel recalls being told at school "that General MacArthur flew all the way from Japan to cut off my father's prick with a scissors" (125). The boy grows up feeling castrated, his "little balls . . . encased in ice" (115). Susan confirms these feelings. Dismayed that Daniel's radicalism doesn't match her own, she tells Sternlicht that her brother is "politically undeveloped. She made it sound like undescended testicles" (150).

For Doctorow, as for Mailer and Updike, the symbolic acquisition of a black phallus redresses this disempowerment even as it safeguards an authoritative literary voice. Daniel first develops sexually under Williams's auspices. On one occasion he and Susan play hooky from a rally and hide in the basement, where Williams lives. Susan reads *The Enchanted Garden*; Daniel contemplates his groin. "I was growing hair around my penis," he recalls, "and I showed Susan" (295). Williams helps Daniel's garden grow. Analogously, Williams's voice solves for Daniel a problem in authorship occasioned by his sister. The principal events recalled by the narrative take place between Susan's attempted suicide and her death in an asylum. Susan haunts Daniel. "All I can say about your voice," he says of her, "is that it is so familiar to me that I cannot perceive the world except with your voice framing the edges of my vision. It is on the horizon and under my feet" (209). Williams offers something beyond Susan's dangerously encompassing vocal frame, because while Daniel here refers to Susan, his words remind us that it is Williams who lives in the Isaacsons' basement. His voice is, literally, under Daniel's feet. Emulating this buried voice, Daniel begins to move beyond the perceptual constraint occasioned by his incipiently incestuous attachment to his sister.

The unknown voice above completes this project by framing Susan even more explicitly. When it declares, "You got the picture. This the story of a fucking," it reformulates Susan's last words to Daniel: "'They're still fucking us,' she said. 'Goodbye, Daniel. You get the picture'" (9). Susan's claim that "they're still fucking us" echoes her father's claim, made to Daniel, "It's still going on. . . . it's still going on" (35). Paul Isaacson means this to refer to American society's continuing destruction of Williams. Figuratively, Susan and Daniel are raped in the same way that Williams is. But the agents of this rape are less immediately clear. Susan dies believing the whole world conspired to fuck her family; Daniel notes that when she says "they" are fucking us, she refers to "everyone else and now the left" (153). Returning to this totality later in the novel, Daniel describes it as a giant penis. Proclaiming that "the revolution" has gone "back to the people," he cries, "Look at the world today. It is aroused to its own education. It is aroused, man, the whole world is sticking up like a hard-on" (283).

This hard-on is the symbolic property of the unattributed voice that echoes and reframes Susan's language, a voice that seems to express a global left inspired by black nationalism (the events in the novel begin when "everyone was defining Black Power" [78]). In fact, the passage immediately preceding the appearance of this voice is the novel's only description of a revolutionary gathering. Taken to a rally in support of their jailed parents, Daniel and Susan are overwhelmed by a "roar" that "though directed at them, was not meant for them; it was meant for others who dwelled in a realm so mysteriously symbolic that it defied his understanding." He and Susan stand "transfixed by the placards, the oversized pictures of their mother and father everywhere above the crowd, going up and down in rhythm as the crowd roared Free them, free them, free them" (22). The placards' suggestive rhythm echoes Daniel's vision of the left as a global hard-on, and the crowd's demands for freedom find an answer in Daniel's "mysteriously symbolic" black voice, which represents a more ostensibly masculine left now "sticking up" for itself.

The unknown voice urges Daniel to adopt an engorging as opposed to a castrating radicalism—to wield the phallus of the left, instead of allowing himself to be fucked by the right—even as it urges him toward a more literary liberation. Daniel's struggle for that liberation is the tacit subject of this novel. Attending the 1967 March on the Pentagon, he catches a glimpse of Norman Mailer leaning purposively forward, "his left forearm on his left knee, his right fist on his right knee" (257). Mailer physically embodies the phallic literary authority at stake in Daniel's just-concluded experience. Referring to himself, Daniel writes,

> And suddenly he is there, locked arm in arm with the real people of now, sitting in close passive rank with linked arms as the boots approach, highly polished, and the clubs, highly polished, and the brass highly polished wading through our linkage, this many-helmeted beast of our own nation, coming through our flesh with boot and club and gun butt, through our sick stubbornness, through our blood it comes. My country. And it swats and kicks, and kicks and clubs—you raise the club high and bring it down, you follow through, you keep your head down, you remember to snap the wrist. Complete the swing, raise high bring down, think of a groove in the air, groove into the groove, keep your eye on the ball, eye on balls, eye on cunts, eye on point of skull, up and down, put your whole body into it, bring everything you've got into your swing, up from your toes, up down, turn around, up high down hard, hard as you can, hard as you can, harder harder: FOLLOW THROUGH. (256)

Initially, Daniel objectifies himself in the third person: "he is there." But as his perspective moves into the collective of which he is a part, his voice shifts, so that he speaks possessively of "our flesh" and "our blood." Daniel describes from within the violation of this organic union by the extravagantly polished appurtenances of approaching soldiers. This is the story of a fucking: linked "arm in arm" to those around him, he's part of a virginal body that is raped by "boot and club and gun butt." These phallic metonyms represent a "many-helmeted beast" of war that "comes" "through our blood" and "through our flesh." Brutal as it is, however, this rape results in what is to Daniel a new kind of belonging. No sooner is he the victim of the rape than he becomes its perpetrator: a simple if ironical phrase—"My country"—shifts the passage's voice to the second person: "You raise the club high and follow through, you keep your head down, you remember to snap your wrist." At one now with the agent of his persecution, Daniel addresses himself as a drill-sergeant-cum-batting-instructor. War having been turned into sport, it hardly matters which team Daniel plays for. It makes sense from this perspective that Daniel understands the many-helmeted beast of which he is now a part in terms of the decade's discourse of bondage and liberation. Already a drill sergeant and a private, a coach and a player, Daniel is, all at once, a master and a slave: his "up down, turn around" makes reference to the slave work song "Pick a Bale of Cotton," whose refrain is "Jump down, turn around, pick a bale of cotton / Jump down, turn around, pick a bale of hay."

Here as elsewhere, the figure of slavery holds together otherwise contradictory positions. While Daniel writes his dissertation in the Columbia University library, demonstrations erupt across the campus. A student sees him working and asks, "What's the matter with you, don't you know you're liberated?" (302). But it's not clear, by novel's end, whether Daniel is or is not liberated, and this ambiguity inheres in the deracinated black voice discussed above. Just as we can't know the ultimate origin of this voice, we can't know the nature of the liberation it offers. Indeed, we might ask what this voice tells Daniel. The outburst begins, "Oh, baby, you know it now." But in an important sense, the reader cannot know the referent of this "it." We recognize the hip stylings of the voice, but we cannot know in any definitive way what its words mean. Like Marcuse, Doctorow places significant store in the desublimating powers of black style, even as he refuses to articulate the nature of the liberation at stake in that style.

Put simply, *The Book of Daniel* dramatizes the equivocal liberation promised by an "aesthetic ethos" like hip or cool. On the novel's second page, Daniel writes of himself, "Let's face it, he looked cool, deliberately cool. In fact nothing about his appearance was accidental." All too self-conscious, "he was dressed in a blue prison jacket and dungarees" (4)—already by the sixties the garb of radical hip. This said, it's unclear what kind of ideology follows from Daniel's cool. Daniel writes of his mother, "Her life was a matter of taking pains to distinguish herself from her neighbors." Updating her mother's commitment to class distinction, Susan adopts an air of "ivy-league cool" (68). Along these lines, Daniel writes of the "total dissatisfaction" we feel from those "not smart enough, good-looking enough [or] cool enough" (62). At the same time, cool remains attached in some vague way to enlightened politics. During the march on the Pentagon, Daniel complains of having "to get through many levels of not particularly civilized let alone cool behavior" (255–256). Doctorow suggests we read this ambiguity as expressing something more than Daniel's ambivalence.

William Gibson's *Spook Country* (2007) equates cool with the withholding of information: "Secrets," declares one character, "are the very root of cool."[43] Similarly, state secrets are the very root of Doctorow's *The Book of Daniel*. The Isaacsons are accused of "giving secrets" (123). But their crime remains vague.

"The Isaacsons," Daniel writes, "are convicted of conspiracy to give to the Soviet Union the secret of the atom bomb. No—the secret of the hydrogen bomb. Or is it the cobalt bomb? Or the neutron bomb. Or napalm. Something like that" (205). It's as if, in some basic sense, he does not know the content of the crime of which they are accused—just as, more strikingly, he cannot determine whether there has been a crime at all. Doctorow has a secret off-limits to his narrator: "Perhaps," Daniel muses, they "are neither guilty nor innocent" (130). The novel is an enigma machine that cannot explain. Thus the very last paragraph, a messianic injunction from Doctorow to Daniel, taken from the biblical narrative that shares its name with this novel: "*Oh Daniel, shut up the words and seal the book*" (303). Recalling that Doctorow studied with John Crowe Ransom while at Kenyon, we might read this exhortation as fundamentally New Critical; his characters neither guilty nor innocent, his novel refuses translation.[44]

Going to Disneyland

Just as we cannot know the referent of "it," when the mysterious voice says, "Oh, baby, you know it now," so too we cannot know which "picture" that voice refers to when it asks us to "get the picture." Daniel litters his narratives with possible candidates, which include placards with Paul and Rochelle Isaacson's image held aloft at a rally held on their behalf (22); Daniel's vision of his sister's suicide attempt (28); the image in Daniel's head of his parents fucking (30–31); an image from a medical textbook that diagrams the anatomy of three generations of Isaacson women (71); a glimpse Daniel catches of his sister's genitals (208); a poster of Daniel looking militant that he mounts on Susan's hospital wall (211); a news photo of Daniel and Susan looking through the bars of the White House (253); the hand-drawn bomb schematics, never revealed, that Paul Isaacson is accused of relaying to the Soviet Union.

Among these many pictures, one does stand out. Before she dies, Susan means to deliver to Artie Sternlicht an old poster of Paul and Rochelle Isaacson. Sternlicht's partner is assembling a vast mural of American life,

> a collage of pictures, movie stills, posters, and real objects. Babe Shirley Temple in her dancing shoes, FDR, a bikini sprayed with gold paint, Marilyn Monroe on her calendar, Mickey Mouse, Gilbert Stuart's Washington with a mustache penciled on, a real American Legion cap, Fred Allen in front of a microphone, pinch-mouthed Susan B. Anthony, Paul Robeson, Sammy Baugh throwing a jump pass, Calvin Coolidge in Indian feathers, a World War One dogfight, a chain gang working on

the road, jackets of *Gone with the Wind* and *One World* by Wendell Willkie, a diaphragm sprayed with silver paint, a cluster of cigarette butts, a *Death of a Salesman* poster, a young Elvis, a black man hanging from a tree, a white man selling apples for 5 cents— (135)

The last sequence is resonant, as it encapsulates the vocal deracination that I describe in the previous section: the young Elvis seems to require a lynched African American; his voice, detached from a disposable black body, facilitates exchange, captured here in a white man selling what was once forbidden fruit. In a loosely analogous fashion, Sternlicht tells Daniel that Susan "would have been done with it" if she "had managed to get the picture here" (152). But with what exactly would Susan have been done after passing to Sternlicht an image of her parents' bodies? The question lingers because getting the image to the wall is in some sense indistinguishable from getting the meaning of the collage on the wall, which, we are meant to presume, is something like the meaning of America itself.

Daniel wonders whether any radical analysis can encompass such a meaning. The radical, he reasons, makes analytical "connections," until, "finally, he connects everything" (140). But he's not sure how to connect so many pictures. "I worry about images," he says.

> Take the word image. It connotes soft, sheer flesh shimmering on the air like the rainbowed slick of a bubble. Image connotes images, the multiplicity being an image. Images break with a small ping, their destruction is as wonderful as their being, they are essentially instruments of torture exploding through the individual's calloused capacity to feel powerful undifferentiated emotions full of longing and dissatisfaction and monumentality. (71)

Doctorow reproduces W. F. Haug's claims, examined in previous chapters, concerning the promissory nature of the commodity, which offers consumers enticing images, and the promise that those images can become, at the moment of purchase, something like a "second skin." Daniel implies the same: the image "connotes soft, sheer flesh shimmering on the air like the rainbowed slick of a bubble." It is a promise, extended to those absorbed in "longing and dissatisfaction" and otherwise bereft of the capacity to experience differentiated emotions.

Convinced that this promise offers only false consciousness, Daniel concludes that images "serve no social purpose." Sternlicht disagrees. "In less than a minute," he says, "a TV commercial can carry you through a lifetime." And everything you've ever dreamed of: "Giants, and midgets, and girls coming in convertibles, and knights and ladies, and love on the beach, and jets fucking the sky, and delicious food steaming on the table, and living voices of cool telling you how cool you are, how cool you can be" (139). Sternlicht sees revolutionary promise in images. And his enthusiasm for the "living voices of cool" that they provide helps to specify the metaphorical color of the "sheer" and "shimmering" flesh that Daniel associates with the image. Daniel's images are rainbow-colored bubbles, and in this respect extend the possibility of interracial solidarity. But we hear the word "pink" in "ping," and recall the novel's sublimation of the visibly black body into a deracinated black voice—one able to issue from skin like Daniel's. Thus, for example, when reminded that Daniel thrills to "the music of the Stones" (6), and of his claim that the "image" appeals to those gripped by "dissatisfaction," we hear in Sternlicht's "voices of cool telling you how cool you are, how cool you can be" an echo of Mick Jagger singing "(I Can't Get No) Satisfaction": "When I'm watchin' my T.V. / And that man comes on to tell me / How white my shirts can be." But Sternlicht's political fantasy doesn't sell a white shirt, or a white collar: it sells the deracinated blackness famously embodied in Jagger's voice, a blackness that Sternlicht thinks necessary to the revolutionaries of his time.

What does it mean to say that we hear blackness in Jagger's voice? Can we hear images, or see sounds? The voice that asks Daniel to "get the picture" sounds black, but it issues from a pointedly invisible source: blind, we have no picture of the body that speaks this voice. We think we hear the color in it, but the voice is, as in Mailer's *Vietnam*, detached from a material site or locus— which reminds us of the futility of any effort fully to know "it" or to "get the picture." As Haug describes it, the commodity promises a totality of experience: it would have consumers believe in a perceptual synesthesia in which sights can be sounds and sounds can be sights. But this is only a lure, which Daniel suggests when he describes "images" breaking "with a small ping." The image combines sight and sound in what Daniel would insist is an unsustainable moment. Daniel's narrative consistently countermands this fantasy of synesthesia. "I remember your voice," he writes of his sister, "but how can I expect them to remember your voice. You can't write out voices" (208). Daniel remembers voices, but struggles to reproduce them, presumably, because writing them "out" means rendering them visual, an image.

Doctorow dreamed of working in radio as a child and remained fascinated by it as an adult:

> Radio is oral culture and related to storytelling. I think that's unquestionable, because whether you hear it over the airwaves as it's dramatized with different voices or it's one person sitting and telling you this story and doing all the voices, you still have it in your mind, the depthless mind. . . . It's like a dream where things change radically from one thing to another and you don't mind—it seems logical and natural that they do.[45]

The unknown voice that prompts Daniel to know "it" and to "get the picture" issues from this dreamscape. The problem, however, is that like the promissory lures of advertising, the private, vanishing images that issue from this dreamscape cannot be falsified. Daniel traces what he calls "the vulnerability of my radical affectations" (285) to his ability to invent stories from whole cloth. Thus he will commit to what he calls "the theory of the other couple," the better to dramatize and explain why Selig Mindish betrayed his parents and why they accepted their execution without pleading down the charges against them. According to the lore of the left, he tells us, there was a second couple, not the Isaacsons, who did steal important secrets for the Soviet Union. Soon after Daniel's father was arrested, it is said, that couple disappeared. This theory in hand, Daniel dramatizes a courtroom scene to Linda Mindish. His mother sits glowering at Selig, only to discover in one fateful glance, when he looks at her as "one comrade to another," that Selig believes in the existence of the other couple. As does her husband: "Complicitors in self-sacrifice" (281), the two men wish to put the FBI off the other couple's scent and take the fall for the greater glory of their cause.

Armed with this story, Daniel travels to Orange County to confront Mindish. But first he must convince Selig's daughter Linda, with whom he played as a child, to grant him access to her father. The two argue, and he chastises her for her conservative lifestyle; "You're not the little hipster I used to know," he adds. Far from it: she's betrothed to a lawyer with "Disney-animal eyelashes, square clothes [and a] skinhead haircut." He strikes Daniel as "a dangerous, wide-hipped whitey" (272). Linda's chosen profession is similarly square. She has become a dentist; she disinfects and guards against what Daniel's adoptive mother calls the "foulmouth" (27). While Daniel wants a black voice, Linda keeps teeth white and mouths clean. And yet Doctorow will suggest that Daniel's ostensible hip is not so different after all from Linda's Disney lifestyle. Once Linda hears the story of the other couple, she agrees to grant Daniel access to her father. Significantly, Daniel will later relate that story to Selig within the confines of Disneyland. That story, it would seem, is just another version of the rides contained within the amusement park—and the commercials that absorb Sternlicht.

Doctorow's novel describes the role Disneyland played in transitioning the United States from a war economy to a leisure economy and consequently suggests, as Richard Godden has it, that the amusement park—with all its ancillary entertainments—effectively redirects the electrical current that killed the Isaacsons.[46] Disneyland's sanitized vision is as totalitarian as it is capitalist. With its disturbingly efficient mechanisms for controlling the bodies and minds of large crowds, the park sits "somewhere between Buchenwald and Belsen" (285). In Disneyland, entertainment scrubs the consumer clean, erasing his past and his capacity to experience anything more than momentary pleasure. Thus transformed, the consumer might occupy any subject position. In 1994, William Styron reacted in dismay to Disney's plans to build in northern Virginia a theme park with exhibits devoted to American slavery. Styron quotes Imagineering head Robert Weiss: "We want to make you feel what it was like to be a slave, and what it was like to escape through the Underground Railroad." Weiss adds that the exhibits would "not take a Pollyanna view," but would be "painful, disturbing and agonizing" (*HC* 127). Styron decries the exhibit because however painful it should prove, it would inevitably place slavery safely in the past. "But the drama has never ended" (*HC* 131), he insists. Styron is also concerned that the exhibits will simplify the troubling complexity of American slavery, the way in which it produced "almost unlimited permutations of human emotions and relationships" between master and slave. He worries, how could Disney "show that there were white people who suffered torment over the catastrophe?" (*HC* 129). Though less preoccupied with the master's pathos, Doctorow makes a related point: Disney's goal is to reduce all complexity to incipiently commercial "images." Daniel points out that, in Disneyland, novels like *Alice in Wonderland* and *Huckleberry Finn* change into rides, becoming "sentimental compression[s] of something that is itself already a lie" (288). These compressions militate on behalf of consumption: "The ideal Disneyland patron may be said to be one who responds to a process of symbolic manipulation that offers him his culminating and quintessential sentiment at the moment of a purchase" (289).

These claims resonate uncomfortably with Daniel's theory of the other couple and, ultimately, with his carefully cultivated cool. Daniel wants to run his theory by Mindish, and is allowed to do so in Disneyland. The theory thus seems just another sentimental compression. Daniel begins by writing a dissertation at Columbia, on the prosecution and execution of his parents, and ends by telling stories in Disneyland. With this trajectory, Doctorow confesses to his own compressions. Confronted with the Rosenbergs, he too writes a novel, and would have us know that this act does not escape radical analysis. He has profited from the death of the Rosenbergs, and for this he would atone. "After the radical is dead," Daniel observes, thinking of his parents, "his early music haunts his persecutors." But, he continues, "Liberals [later] use this [music] to achieve power" (140). Doctorow's metaphor aligns the liberal's parasitical relation to radicalism with the white's parasitical relation to black culture, and in so doing confuses radical analysis not simply with black music but with the black voices that capture for Daniel the insurrectionary power of that music. The Isaacsons disapprove of jazz because it shows "the cultural degeneracy of the bourgeois with their rhythms stolen from the southern Negro, cheapening a people's music" (194). These remarks haunt Daniel's novel, whose reliance on an angry black muse partakes of the degeneracy of Disneyland. Park rides, Daniel says, invite customers "to participate in mythic rituals of the culture" (286). At Disneyland, these rituals are pitched to the "wide-hipped whiteys" that populate Orange County. But in dropping into a sly black voice while urging himself toward liberation, Daniel invokes a ritual of American culture no less mythic—and capitalist—for being practiced by the hip.[47]

Conclusion
Joan Didion and the Death of the Hip Figure

Set during the final days of the Vietnam War, Joan Didion's *Democracy* (1984) recounts the dissolving marriage of Inez and Harry Victor. Harry is a Democratic senator who once ran for president. Born in Hawaii, Inez comes from a family of wealthy colonialists—the pointedly named Christians. The collapse of the Victors' marriage dramatizes the waning of U.S. global power and, as John McClure suggests, Inez's subsequent decision to move to Kuala Lumpur captures the opportunities for high romance that present themselves on the peripheries of a crumbling empire.[1] The failing marriage also expresses fateful tensions within the Democratic Party between the party's liberal wing and what Harry's manager calls "the American business class."[2] Didion relates these tensions to the waning of U.S. empire, and demonstrates how the racial narratives that surrounded the Vietnam War coded more properly domestic dramas between black and white. But she also prefigures a break that would transform the Democratic Party ten years after the events in her novel are set. In 1985, one year after the publication of *Democracy*, prominent Democrats from the South and the Sunbelt formed the Democratic Leadership Council (DLC) to counteract the party's by then long-standing commitment to civil rights and the new social movements of the sixties. Empowered by Walter Mondale's humbling defeat by Ronald Reagan, the DLC embraced neoliberal tenets and rejected the state activism inaugurated by Roosevelt's New Deal and reaffirmed by Lyndon Johnson's Great Society. Didion's *Democracy* anticipates that retrenchment by radically revising the form and function of what I have been calling the hip figure.

For many of the novelists in this study, John F. Kennedy served as the quintessential hip figure, a touchstone for demonstrating how expressive bodily styles derived but safely distant from the period's musical subcultures might, when part of a literary project, reconcile white suburbanites and working-class African Americans beneath a metaphorically elastic second skin. Didion repudiates that project, we will see, by attacking its fundamental assumptions about the nature and political efficacy of metaphor, as well as by providing an alternate history of Kennedy and his famous family. Harry Victor is, as McClure has it, "a left-leaning liberal transparently modeled after the Kennedys"— "less a character than an *ad hominem* attack on sixties liberalism."[3] Inez is a thinly veiled Jackie Kennedy. "Surely you remember Inez Victor campaigning," Didion teases, "Inez Victor speaking her famous Spanish at a street festival in East Harlem" (106). The reader might remember Jackie Kennedy doing the same, but doesn't know, Didion insinuates, that Jackie thought "politics was for assholes" (176). Didion adds that liberalism is for assholes—most powerfully when its interracial coalitions threaten the economic interests of families like the Christians.

Disgusted with Harry's liberalism, Inez runs away with an entrepreneurial intelligence officer, Jack Lovett, whose date of death matches almost exactly that of Aristotle Onassis. The fantasy at the heart of this surprisingly sentimental novel is that Jackie and Aristotle were in love all their lives, and that Kennedy was a cuckold as well as a cheat. Lovett is as unapologetic as Harry is committed to the politics of white guilt. Where Victor expresses "uneasiness" (48) with economic and racial privilege, Lovett relishes the Vietnam War "as a specifically commercial enterprise" (159). Among his many shady international dealings, Lovett is rumored to be, like Onassis, "in the aircraft business" (97), and has been in and out of Vietnam since 1955, "setting up lines of access" in what he then called "the insurgency problem" and would later call "the assistance effort" (90). In 1975, when the principal events of the novel take place, Lovett feverishly extracts capital from the crumbling Republic of Vietnam—on one occasion, gold bullion, on another, "the officers and cash reserves of the Saigon branches of the Bank of America, the First National City Bank, and the Chase Manhattan" (195). Like Onassis—who once illegally acquired and then fronted his ownership in surplus U.S. military tankers—Lovett moves in "a fluid world," manipulating for his own ends "the interests of state and non-state actors" (218), on behalf of capital flows that recognize no national borders.[4]

The end of the Vietnam War precipitated a momentary disarticulation of the interests of certain state and non-state actors. Families like the Christians had invested heavily in the U.S. occupation, and needed agents like Lovett to recover those investments as the occupation drew to an end. But their capital would find an alternate conduit into American political life. "During the 1970s," writes Thomas Edsall, "the political wing of the nation's corporate sector staged one of the most remarkable campaigns in the pursuit of power in recent history." By the start of the eighties, "Washington's corporate lobbying community in particular had gained a level of influence and leverage approaching that of the boom days of the 1920s." Edsall reasons that during the seventies, "business refined its ability to act as a class, submerging competitive instincts in favor of joint, cooperative action in the legislative arena."[5] Crucial in this respect was the Supreme Court's 1976 decision that a corporation had a right to make unlimited monetary contributions to political parties. As a result of this ruling, the number of political action committees in the United States went from 89 in 1974 to 1,476 in 1982.[6] For Edsall, this rise in corporate class consciousness made the Republican Party more coherent than it had been in years—it would now appeal directly to concentrated financial interests. The same development left the Democrats in a state of civil war. Elites in the party wanted to appeal to big business in order to remain competitive with the GOP in fund-raising, while liberals struggled to sustain the party's "ties to various groups in society"—like "women, blacks, labor, the elderly, Hispanics, urban political organizations"— none of which stood "clearly larger than the others."[7] But the writing was on the wall: invariably, the corporations from which the party would raise money were hostile to the visions of social justice embraced by the party's liberal wing.

To those who identified their interests with the business class ascendant within the Democrats, Jesse Jackson epitomized the party's problems, just as Bill Clinton would later epitomize the solution to those problems. Published during Jackson's 1984 presidential bid, Didion's novel looks back on the seventies from the vantage point of Jackson's emergent Rainbow Coalition, a political formation that expressed the utopian social aspirations of postwar liberalism. Her heroine rejects the interracial vision that Jackson would come to express and "Joan Didion," the novel's narrator, who moves easily in the Christians' world, seems herself eager to turn back the clock on the Democrats' liberalism, by tacitly endorsing the roiling white resentments that facilitated the eventual rise of the business class within the party. The narrator wants the Christian fortune and the interests of the party tended by Lovett and not the likes of Harry Victor. Inez concatenates those fortunes and interests, and the novel goes so far as to suggest that her marriage to Harry constitutes a kind of miscegenation. *Democracy* would punish Harry for this relationship and, by extension, discipline the political ambitions of those African Americans for whom he speaks.

But the novel is nothing if not equivocal; it embraces the very racism from which, at another level, it would save the Democratic Party. A Democrat when she wrote *Democracy*, Didion offers a version of the Janus-faced racial code that she would attribute to Bill Clinton many years later. "There was often just this chance," she wrote, "when Governor Clinton spoke about race, to hear what he very clearly said and yet to understand it quite another way." When he condemned "race-baiting" and "the politics of division," she heard an address to two audiences. He appealed to those wanting to condemn racial intolerance. But he seemed also to recognize that "it had been within memory the contention of large numbers of white Americans that civil rights legislation itself represented the politics of division."[8] Analogously, *Democracy* asks to be understood in two ways, as both an appeal to and a condemnation of white resentment. The novel achieves this mixed message by forgetting at one moment what it seems eager to recall at another—by reproducing the selective memory that Didion consistently attributed to the Democrats. By 1992, the Democrats seemed to her "a party determined to present itself as devoid of all history save that one sunny day in the Rose Garden, preserved on film and repeatedly shown, when President John F. Kennedy shook the hand of the Boy's Nation delegate Bill Clinton, who could be seen on the film elbowing aside less motivated peers to receive the grail: the candidate's first useful photo opportunity" (129). Didion's distaste for Clinton notwithstanding, *Democracy* recalls and forgets Kennedy in a similarly uneven fashion, and for similar ends. It would kill the hip figure, the better to reinstall it in neoliberal form.

Back to the Stone Age

Toward the end of *Democracy*, Paul Christian, Inez's father, renounces his family and fortune, begins to speak on behalf of Cambodian orphans, and threatens to deliver "the goods on the Christians, let the chips fall where they may" (131). Cryptically, he adds, "lest we forget" (135). Nobody admits to understanding the nature of these "goods," in part because Paul has just shot his other daughter, Janet, and is apparently insane, but also because while the Christians openly acknowledge the nature of their financial stake in Hawaii and Vietnam, they're less eager to grant the tribalism that animates their business dealings in these locales. Paul shoots his daughter while shooting a Nisei congressman who opposes the Vietnam War, and with whom his daughter has been cheating on her husband. We know the Japanese American politician represents a threat to some of the Christians' financial interests; we're left to presume that he represents, also, a racial threat to the endogamous kinship group in whose name Paul pursues those interests.

In *Slouching Towards Bethlehem* (1968), Didion records the "conversationally delicate" status of integration on Hawaii. She quotes a wealthy white islander: "The Orientals are—well, discreet's not really the word, but they aren't like the Negroes and the Jews, they don't push in where they're not wanted" (201–202). This attitude helps explain Paul's outraged reaction to an "Oriental" who does in fact "push in"—into the sacred heart of the family's "goods." When Adam Stanton shoots Willie Stark on the steps of the state capitol in Robert Penn Warren's *All the King's Men*, we see Henry Sutpen from William Faulkner's *Absalom, Absalom!* (1936) shooting Charles Bon at the gates of Sutpen's Hundred. In each novel, the incestuous passion of a landed gentleman for his sister dovetails with horror over the miscegenation that ostensibly threatens that sister. Similarly, Paul's rage over his daughter's sexual transgression suggests rage over his daughter's choice of lover. But just as understanding Warren's relation to Faulkner requires reading Stark figuratively, as simultaneously white and "Negro," so too understanding Didion's relation to Warren and Faulkner, and above all to Norman Mailer and the politics of hip, requires understanding the manner in which she confuses African Americans, Asian Americans, and Asians.

After he shoots his daughter, Paul speaks to Inez of an early romance he enjoyed with a native Hawaiian. "Leilani and I were like brother and sister," he tells her. "Parties night and day. Leilani singing scat. I was meant to marry her. Not your mother" (139). Presumably, the fact that he and his lover were "like brother and sister" qualifies the fact that she was Hawaiian and he was white: they were not categorically different because they were akin to kin. This revelation might be understood as strategic: it seems to clear Paul of any racist motive for his assassination of the congressman and, just as importantly, of an incestuous jealousy regarding his daughter. Not meant to marry her mother, he is in a sense not really her father. Revealingly, however, Paul launders his lover's racial alterity through a particular vision of blackness. Leilani sang scat, and after communicating this information, Paul himself hums a few bars of "The Darktown Strutters' Ball." A fox-trot written in 1917 by Sheldon Brooks, an African American, the piece was recorded first, and most famously, by the Original Dixieland Jazz Band, a white group that enjoyed fame and fortune by selling itself to white audiences as the inventors of jazz. Humming this tune, Paul asserts his ability to remain fluid in his racial identifications and sympathies, and to return to his whiteness when necessary. He speaks for Cambodian orphans in one moment, shoots a Japanese American opposed to the Vietnam War in the next, and then recalls his love for a native Hawaiian, even as he invokes and recapitulates in deracinated form her vocal blackening.

Paul's suggestion that he and Leilani were both kin and destined lovers allows him simultaneously to be the same as and to desire a racial other. His gesture to jazz achieves this characteristically hip admixture: he and Leilani are rendered identical, and erotically distinct, through their performances of black culture. Leilani's scat in particular facilitates this contradictory amalgam. Writing against the notion that scat is "nonsense," a "fall" from language, Brent Edwards argues that scat stages a tension between semantic and linguistic meaning when it offers "contradictory indices that seem to be saying all too much at once."[9] But ultimately, Edwards reasons, because scat phonetics are indexical, and work within a regular musical syntax, scat results in "an augmentation of expressive potential rather than an evacuation or reduction of signification" (649). This coded dynamic is particularly rich, he points out, when one considers that, from its beginnings in the early twentieth century, scat "was concerned with the representation of the foreign: alterity projected on the level of linguistic impenetrability and absurdity" (627). Scat staged the foreign as inassimilable even as it rendered that foreignness coherent and familiar through the framework of the music. Edwards reminds us that performances of faux Chinese played a particularly prominent role in early scat, from Gene Green's 1917 imitation of Chinese in "From Here to Shanghai" to Cab Calloway's "Chinese Rhythm" and Slim and Slam's "Chinatown, My Chinatown" in the thirties. But as was not the case for black musicians, for whom "Oriental" linguistic alterity mediated and reconciled perceived differences between white and black, Leilani becomes less of a native Hawaiian, and therefore more like a sister to Paul, by mouthing a contingent blackness. That triangulation is fragile, and ultimately insufficient. Presumably, Paul forswore Leilani because of pressure from his family. Humiliating, then, that his white wife, to whom he is unhappily married, precipitates a "local scandal" (22) by stepping out with a man from Hong Kong, and doubly humiliating that his daughter Janet does the same with a man of Japanese descent. Punishing his daughter, and his wife, for their indulgence in what he refused himself, he destroys the figurative mediation of seeming opposites facilitated, originally, by the jazz culture he shared with Leilani.

Didion figures Paul's murderous rage, and his insanity generally, as a manifestation of the conservative's fear, experienced by the Christians and their class, that "Orientals" in Hawaii as well as Southeast Asia were starting to "push in," and were as a consequence becoming more like the mainland African Americans then militating for greater access to all levels of U.S. society—be they sexual or institutional. In fact, Paul's racial ventriloquism reaches its pitch during the final moments of the U.S. evacuation of Vietnam: racial others enter his mouth, as he hums "the Darktown Strutters' Ball," at the moment that the North Vietnamese push into Saigon. Slipping into a whitewashed jazz standard, Paul tenuously contains that threat.

Jack Lovett performs a similar if more extreme act of containment when, as a television behind him plays images of U.S. helicopters lifting off from Saigon rooftops, he waxes rhapsodic about the grandeur of the atomic explosions he witnessed in the fifties. His tacit message is offered on behalf of the Christians and their class: brown peoples of the world, keep your place, or suffer annihilation. To Mailer, the use of atom bombs in Japan suggested new avenues of interracial identification. As Andrew Ross suggestively puts it in *No Respect*, Mailer's white Negroes exemplify "'radical hip,' Bomb style" (88). It's easy to see why. Mailer argues that, along with the Holocaust, the Cold War precipitated by the destruction of Hiroshima and Nagasaki made whites and Negroes in effect the same: all now labor under the threat of sudden death as a result of actions not their own. But if for Mailer murdered Asians mediate a correspondence between white and black, for Didion they serve as proxies for blacks. Toward the end of *Democracy*, Inez sits in Vientiane, listening to a shortwave radio, waiting for Bing Crosby's "I'm Dreaming of a White Christmas"—the secret signal that will announce the final stage of the U.S. evacuation from Saigon. This is the last white Christmas for the very white Christians, and the song captures the novel's longing for days when such families held uncontested sway over American politics. "Not privileged," explains Janet Christian of her life on Hawaii; "I'd just call it a marvelous simple life that you might describe as gone with the wind" (67). Gone with the wind indeed: in this bleached novel—devoid of speaking Vietnamese or African Americans—the loss of Vietnam feels like the loss of the Old South, and the murder of a Japanese American congressman evokes Hiroshima and Nagasaki even as it feels of a piece with reactionary efforts to restore "law and order" on American city streets.

Harry Victor stands between this novel's considerable appetite for violence and the racial others upon whom it would release that violence. He concatenates all that Didion reviles in early seventies liberalism. Lamenting her memory loss, Inez tells a news crew that political life amounts to "something like shock treatment" (51). Her husband ran for president in 1972, and Inez's comment gestures to the primary of that year, during which the press revealed that Thomas Eagleton, George McGovern's running mate, was on Thorazine and had undergone shock treatment for severe depression. Although most obviously a figure for Kennedy, Harry is also a caricature of McGovern and the liberalism that he defined. Harry trades in class guilt: "the demographics" of his "phantom constituency were based on comfort and its concomitant uneasiness" (48). He thinks this constituency—smaller than he imagines it to be—is committed to the counterculture. He therefore takes part in "the sit-ins at Harvard and at the Pentagon and at Dow Chemical plants in Michigan and Pennsylvania and West Virginia" (47). During the 1968 Chicago convention, he contrives to get "photographed for *Life* getting tear-gassed in Grant Park" (49). He delivers lectures on civil disobedience in Ann Arbor, crusades against the Vietnam War, and founds the Alliance for Democratic Institutions (110), the kind of think tank overseen in the early seventies by "New Liberals" eager to reconcile student radicals with the Democratic Party. But above all, Harry's liberal legitimacy derives from the minority populations to whom, Didion insists, he panders. He's photographed crossing a police line with Coretta King and participates in marches in Mississippi and the San Joaquin Valley. He founds the "Neighborhood Legal Coalition" in East Harlem and publishes "*The View from the Street: Root Causes, Radical Solutions and a Modest Proposal*" (47). A gesture to Jonathan Swift and to the Donner Party with whom Didion's forebears briefly traveled: Harry claims to speak for African Americans as well as Mexican and Puerto Rican Americans, but devours them all for his own ends. Inez suggests as much when she spits, "Harry Victor's Burden" (180). Rudyard Kipling's "White Man's Burden" justified U.S. imperialism in the Philippines on the grounds that its native population was childlike and in need of guidance. Harry Victor's burden is to treat the young as if they were symbolically colored, and in need of his noblesse oblige.

Didion had already identified an analogous stance within the counterculture, which she depicted as preying upon the disenfranchisement of African Americans, often over the strident objections of black individuals. In *Slouching Towards Bethlehem*, she observes the San Francisco Mime Troupe, composed entirely of whites in blackface, in the Haight-Ashbury in the summer of 1967. One performer from the agitprop group wears a sign on his back that asks, "Who Stole Chuck Berry's Music?" An African American in the crowd responds, "Nobody stole Chuck Berry's music, man." He thinks the music "belongs to *every*-body" (125–126). An inconvenient obstacle to the politics of white guilt, the black man is shouted down. Here, as elsewhere, Didion wants us to know that she likes people who happen to have black skin; what she doesn't like, she insists, is any form of symbolic blackness. And yet the hostility she directs toward the Mime Troupers is indistinguishable from her hostility for those who would militate on behalf of civil rights, or any identifiably black interests.

That hostility is acute. She's more than just disdainful of Harry's liberalism. She would obliterate it. Preparing to begin her novel, the narrator visits Berkeley in 1975. "It so happened," she writes, "that I had been an undergraduate at Berkeley, which meant that twenty years before in the same room or one like it . . . I had considered the same questions [about the relation between style and democracy] or ones like them" (72). With this, the narrator points to an essay in *The White Album* (1979), "On the Morning After the Sixties" (1970), in which Didion contrasts the Berkeley she attended to the school convulsed by the countercultural liberalism of the late sixties. She confronts the legacy of her fifties-era education: "the historical irrelevancy of growing up convinced that the heart of darkness lay not in some error of social organization but in man's own blood. If man was bound to err, then any social organization was bound to be in error" (206). Convinced of original sin and human fallibility, she cannot believe in the counterculture, and echoes Miles Coverdale at the end of Hawthorne's *The Blithedale Romance*: "If I could believe that going to a barricade would affect man's fate in the slightest I would go to that barricade, and quite often wish that I could, but it would be less than honest to say that I expect to happen on such a happy ending" (208). Her morning after the sixties is thus a mourning of her own distance from the sixties; she wishes she could have taken part. But it is also a self-mutilating reflex against this wish: she would destroy her own sentimental longing for political commitment.

Didion's belief in the inevitability of sin offered compensations, however; she recalls the moment when, as an undergraduate reading on a fraternity couch, she found "real joy" at discovering "that the central line of *Heart of Darkness* was a postscript" (207). This elliptical reference—to the concluding line of Kurtz's report on "The Suppression of Savage Customs": "Exterminate all the brutes!"—haunts Didion's writing, which is violently ambivalent toward those who climb barricades. Conrad's line is her own. "One senses Conrad in Miss Didion's *Democracy*," writes Mary McCarthy in her review of the novel. "He has passed through this territory, making trail blazes. The novel seems closer to *Heart of Darkness* than the literal-minded movie *Apocalypse Now* did, which was also trying to talk about the end of Vietnam and unspeakable 'horrors,' located upriver in the film."[10] McCarthy doesn't explain her insight, but we might do so by way of Lovett, Didion's Mr. Kurtz. Didion provides a series of examples of how Lovett sees meaning where others do not: "A Laotian village indicated on one map and omitted on another suggested not a reconnaissance oversight but a population annihilated, x number of men, women, and children lined up one morning between the maps and bulldozed into a common ditch" (36–37). Lovett knows that missing information indicates unspeakable horrors. Does the reader know as much? Does she understand, as Lovett does, what it means that "the heart of Africa was an enrichment facility" (37)?

With this line, we are all at once in Conrad's heart of darkness, and it's hard not to think of the related forms of economic and sexual "enrichment" that the white Negro Kurtz derives from the natives with whom he lives. But it's doubly hard not to grasp Didion's violent reaction to one version of that enrichment. Sympathetic to commerce, she repudiates the ostensibly altruistic embrace of things African by embracing that continent's most potentially explosive export: "weapons-grade uranium" (37). Ore from the heart of Africa sits at the core of the atomic explosions that leave Lovett thinking he has seen the mind of God, and throughout the novel we hear echoes of the line to which Didion alludes in "The Morning After the Sixties": "exterminate all the brutes!" Ultimately, Lovett codes a desire to wipe away the bureaucratic tedium and doublespeak of career politicians, but Didion seems perfectly willing to accept as necessary collateral damage the elimination of the subaltern constituencies for whom liberals like Harry claim to speak. Impatient with those who work within the beltway, Lovett would be done as well with the world's postcolonial residuum: those to whom Democrats claimed to be committed, and who provided yet another occasion for the bad faith and hypocrisy of an entrenched liberal elite. Lovett's peripatetic commitment to the commerce of war thus merges with Kurtz's desire to wipe out hordes of Africans; Lovett shares Kurtz's desire to use and then in an act of self-cleansing exterminate the natives (all the while idealizing a Christian, an "Intended," waiting for him back home).

Though Lovett never goes native, as does Kurtz, he is in many ways a white Negro. He marvels that Inez's family tolerated his lifelong flirtation with her, begun in the fifties when she was a teenager. "I'm surprised," he thinks back, "the whole goddamned Christian Company wasn't turned out for the lynching" (14). Here, Lovett likens himself to an unruly slave eyeing the plantation owner's daughter. But the Christian Company does tolerate Lovett; more than this, it depends on him. He is less a slave than an overseer: his role in Vietnam is to make the country safe for American capital. And if Lovett is a hipster by figuratively bridging black and white, he attains this status only by insisting that, finally, his hip cannot be understood in conventional terms. As if to assert his freedom from restrictive identifications, Didion places him beyond color. "The hair on the back of Jack Lovett's wrist was translucent," she writes, "almost transparent, no color at all" (103). She adds, "What Jack Lovett did was never black or white" (219). With this metaphor, Didion would have us believe that the palpably embodied and thrill-seeking Lovett is, like Mailer's hipster, beyond conventional moral coordinates. His actions "devoid of ethical content altogether" (219), he gravitates to Vietnam, "because it was kind of the place to be" (170). At the same time, Didion seems to suggest that Lovett is something of a hipster by virtue of being neither simply black nor white—by being beyond race altogether, if not beyond category of any kind.

A spy, Lovett is indefinable. Harry Victor seems to "spring out, defined"; Lovett resists Didion's narrative. Though his hair is almost transparent, he is himself "wary to the point of opacity, and finally elusive" (84). So opaque is Lovett that he will condemn politicians for their reliance on the written word. "You people really interest me," he says to Victor and his fact-finding retinue in Southeast Asia. "You don't actually see what's happening in front of you. You don't see it unless you read it" (100). Recalling readers to their bodies, Lovett chastens those who would substitute any form of representation for lived life. He wants only the immediacy of physical experience. At a public reception, Victor, who sees himself as an "incorporeal extension[] of policy" (83), declares breezily "that Americans were learning major lessons in Southeast Asia." Lovett, who understands war "not abstractly, but viscerally" (159), counters that he "could think of only one lesson Americans were learning," that "a tripped Claymore mine explodes straight up" (99–100).

In *Political Fictions* (2002), Didion explains the importance of this kind of lesson to her ideas about democracy. She describes "the last true conflict of cultures in America, that between the empirical and the theoretical" (24). Empirical or inductive thinking begins with an embodied relation to observable detail. Conversely, theoretical, abstract, or deductive thinking begins, she will reason, with what we think we already know, or with what we want to know, and requires rendering commensurable the otherwise disparate. Her own empiricism, she suggests, derives from a populist commitment to realism—to the fact that there are particular things "out there" (like people's bodies and pain) in need of accurate transcription. Didion traces her populism to her rapport with persons somehow more palpably actual than those assembled for focus groups. While watching the national conventions of 1988, she proclaimed "that it had not been by accident that the people with whom I had preferred to spend time in high school had, on the whole, hung out in gas stations . . . they had knocked up girls" (19). These gritty, everyday folk remain unknown to "a self-created and self-referring class, a new kind of managerial elite" made up of reporters, candidates, and political consultants who prefer "the theoretical to the observable" and "dismiss that which might be learned empirically as 'anecdotal'" (20). For her, "the defining characteristic" of this permanent political class is "its readiness to abandon those not inside the process" (9) and to overlook "the contradictions inherent in reporting that which occurs only in order to be reported" (30). Democracy is most problematic, Didion will insist, when it remains autonomous and distinct, a delimited preserve worked by a class of experts.

That said, *Democracy* has little interest in replacing that class with the likes of Lovett. Part of the managerial elite that Didion disdains, Victor can't understand the Vietnam War. But Lovett's "lesson" is no lesson at all: the trajectory of an exploding mine suggests to him the impossibility of drawing usable conclusions from the war. His empiricism tends toward disarticulation and decomposition, and it's in this respect appropriate that he dies within the novel, just after he and Inez finally unite. Swimming in a hotel pool in Jakarta, he suddenly expires from an obscure circulatory condition. As if to emphasize the fact that he is now nothing more than a body, mere matter, Didion describes in detail Inez's arduous transportation of Lovett's lifeless corpse back to the United States. As she moves his inert form, Inez imagines "papers shredded all over the pacific" (228). Though this is a reference to the paper trail of his illicit dealings, we can also understand these papers as pages torn from the novels of Didion's predecessors, those who would mobilize their readers on behalf of liberalism; Lovett's death is the death of metaphor, if not of representation itself.

More specifically, it's the death of the fantasy that Mailer anchored in John F. Kennedy. "We admire the Adlai Stevenson character," Didion writes in *Slouching Towards Bethlehem*, "the rational man, the enlightened man, the man not dependent upon the potentially psychopathic mode of action." But he is not someone we "secretly desire" (72). Mailer thought Kennedy both things at once: an enlightened psychopath. But Didion's aesthetic requires fission and disarticulation, not fusion and synthesis: it dismantles Kennedy's coalition, and even divides Kennedy himself. Resigned to the impossibility of our ever desiring a member of the permanent political class, *Democracy* splits Kennedy into the high-minded if mealy-mouthed Victor, given to opportunistic alliances with African Americans, and the charismatic Lovett, ardent connoisseur of atomic blasts. Victor is the Kennedy who might have taken the United States out of Vietnam; as much as "Jack" Lovett resembles Onassis, he is also a version of a Kennedy we never had, one who, never assassinated, might have used the bomb to end the conflict there. Didion loves the swashbuckling Lovett but, resigned, knows Victor will ultimately be victorious, even if not as president: Lovett dies within the novel, but Harry survives to fight another day.

Impenetrable Polish

According to Fredric Jameson, writing the same year that Didion published her novel, Vietnam was "the first terrible postmodernist war." Its story "cannot be told in any of the traditional paradigms of the war novel or the movie."[11] Didion adds that its story can barely be told at all. On a Pacific atoll in the fifties, Lovett witnesses an atomic explosion. "The light at dawn during those Pacific tests was something to see," the novel begins:

> Something to behold.
> Something that could almost make you think you saw God, he said.
>   He said to her. Jack Lovett said to Inez Victor.
>   Inez Victor who was born Inez Christian.
>   He said: the sky was this pink no painter could approximate, one of the detonation theorists used to try, a pretty fair Sunday painter, he never got it. Just never captured it, never came close. (11)

This is narrative laboring against inertial forces that would defeat it. Lovett's lines struggle to clarify their relation to each other, struggle to bring order in the face of an overwhelming event that tolerates neither translation nor literary practice. It's not clear that Didion wants to win this struggle. Rather, Lovett's explosion is the palm, held up in interdiction, at the end of this novel's mind; a mystified expression of the Christians' interests in Vietnam and the racial resentments that animate their business dealings in Hawaii, it's what you see when you look too closely at those interests and resentments. Beyond representation, it ends discussion. Put in different terms, Lovett's explosion captures the way in which Didion's prose sublimates its otherwise unspeakable social resentments, and generative family traumas, into style.

Versions of that sublimation permeate her nonfiction. Didion begins *The White Album*, for example, by claiming that "flash pictures"—"images with no 'meaning' beyond their temporary arrangement" (13)—organize her memory of the sixties and seventies. She liked the Doors, she tells us, because these "Norman Mailers of the Top 40" (21) were amenable to such "flash" recordings; they embraced "anything about revolt, disorder, chaos, about activity that appears to have no meaning" (22). At the same time, she's preoccupied, in her suggestively titled collection, with cryptograms of racial hatred and genocidal fantasy. *The White Album* dwells on Charles Manson, who thought he heard in the Beatles' *The White Album* coded instructions for how to precipitate an apocalyptic war between whites and blacks. Littered with overheard fragments of commercial song, *Democracy* understands its own style as both a flash image that disables discriminating apprehension and, at the same time, a coded expression, uncomfortably similar to Manson's, of aggression directed at African Americans. A fetishistic style organized around empiricism and technology, Didion's is a techno-cool like the one described by Alan Liu; it constitutes what he calls "*information designed to resist information.*" Additionally, Didion embraces the Anglo-American cool that Joel Dinerstein associates with figures like John Wayne and Clint Eastwood (both referred to in *Democracy*) and that he contrasts with the West African cool at work in musicians like Lester Young. The "information" that Didion's Anglo-American cool would only partially "resist" asserts white racial dominance; her style codes the barely restrained capacity for violence that Dinerstein associates with Anglo-American cool, and directs it toward the black musical and cultural traditions that her cool would displace.[12]

In Didion's hands, those cultural traditions often look sentimental and self-indulgent. In *The Year of Magical Thinking* (2010), for example, she recalls the strange comfort that she took as a child from the prospect of atomic annihilation. The fact that these devices could "destroy the works of man might be a personal regret but remained, in the larger picture I had come to recognize, a matter of abiding indifference. No eye was on the sparrow. No one was watching me."[13] She refers to the popular spiritual "His Eye Is on the Sparrow," made famous by Ethel Waters, who titled her autobiography *His Eye Is on the Sparrow*. The song asserts, in effect, that Jesus is watching one and all. Didion's rejection of this prospect as a ten-year-old child is pointed, and offers a glimpse of the fitfully obscured resentment that subtends *Democracy*: no god that I knew of was watching me; nobody felt or cared about my pain; I didn't sing the blues, offer self-indulgent cries of grief, or ask for sympathy from fellow citizens. "People in grief think a great deal about self-pity," Didion writes. But most of all, she adds, "We worry it, dread it, scourge our thinking for signs of it" (192). The Didion of this memoir is neither the Didion of *Democracy* nor Didion the child: she now longs to be known and wants the eyes of the world upon her. But the scourge that she recalls from her youth finds an echo in the memoir's contemporary frame. So seemingly dispassionate is she over the loss of her husband that a social worker terms her "a pretty cool customer" (15). Following this agent of the welfare state, Didion will call her composed demeanor "the pretty cool customer effect" (46). That cool effect rejects agents of the state and, we might hazard, the racially marked populations to whom those agents minister.

Inez, too, is a pretty cool customer and, at least initially, the narrator views her "capacity for passive detachment as an affectation of boredom, the frivolous habit of an essentially idle mind." But Didion comes to see that detachment as "the essential mechanism for living a life in which the major cost was memory" (70). In some general sense, that "life" is "political life"; but equally, Inez's memory loss is itself an essential mechanism for living with unresolved family trauma. A hardened survivor, she loses her mother at an early age but cannot confront her absence. Instead, she internalizes images (often in the form of photographs) of the glamour that she associates with her mother. Nicholas Abraham and Maria Torok describe something like this as "incorporation"—a process of failed or refused mourning in which a melancholic chooses "photographic images" over language itself.[14] Typical mourning involves a substitution of language for the void occasioned first by the removal of the mother's once nourishing breast and, later, by the loss of the mother herself. Incorporation is anti-figurative to the extent that the melancholic, unable to fill the emptiness of her mouth with words, instead ingests the whole of the lost object, as image. Resistant to the substitutive logic of language, the incorporated object acquires what Abraham and Torok call "a genuinely magical power," and becomes an "encrypted" presence within the melancholic.[15] For Abraham and Torok, this requires "*demetaphorization* (taking literally what is meant figuratively) and *objectification* (pretending that the suffering is not an injury to the subject but instead a loss sustained by the love object)."[16]

The concept of encryption speaks powerfully to *Magical Thinking*, which is an elaborate study of incorporation. But Didion's other memoir, *Where I Was From* (2003),[17] is more apposite to *Democracy*, because it suggests the extent to which Didion's stylistic commitment to "demetaphorization" emerged from ultimately inextricable personal and political losses. On its final page, the memoir describes a scene between Didion and her dying mother, who hands her a parting gift: a soup ladle. The odd insufficiency of this object captures the encrypted void produced throughout Didion's life by her mother's chronic depression. The mother's stoicism inculcated in Didion an abiding loneliness, and a reflexive suspicion of the very possibility of human community and collective action, as well as an implacable confidence that the "old stock" Didions were somehow superior to those other, often racially marked, Californians. Didion's mother was lost to her, as a source of warmth and consolation, long before her actual death, but she is abidingly present as the source of resentments and antisocial impulses. With her death, however, Didion gains perspective on her own long-standing reflexes—especially those pertaining to government and class analysis. *Where I Was From* represents maternal loss as an impetus to a wholesale reevaluation of received political wisdom. Didion sees after the death of her mother that the prosperity enjoyed in California during most of her lifetime depended from the start on federal largesse. More broadly, the memoir acknowledges that "the greater game of capital formation"(986) in California depended on the fact that members of Didion's class shared with her a "fairly tenacious wish not to examine whatever it was I needed to believe" (1075). In sum, Didion suggests that in overcoming what she calls "my own barricade" (1091), she overcomes her resistance, described earlier, to climbing barricades.

Some twenty years earlier, however, those barricades were still in place, even if they showed signs of falling. Didion's tenacious wish not to see, and its attendant commitment to "demetaphorization," consumes the narrator of *De-*

mocracy, who resists the implications of her enterprise. She "would skim stories on policy" while researching her characters, she confesses, "and fix instead on details" (73). Fixing obsessively on details, she recognizes, amounts to practicing "magic" (108). In *The Year of Magical Thinking*, a text explicitly preoccupied with how magic functions as a defense mechanism, Didion confesses her "sense that meaning itself was resident in the rhythms of words and sentences and paragraphs," and that the "impenetrable polish" of "technique" facilitated "withholding whatever it was I thought or believed" (7).

"Joan Didion" the narrator is herself a barricade. She is an authorial stand-in from which the historical Joan Didion achieves safe distance, a fictionalized character forgiven in advance for her uncomfortable proximity to the Christians and "the greater game of capital formation" in which they participate. In general, Didion's fictional narrators embrace markedly more conservative political and cultural sensibilities than her nonfictional narrators do—they function, one speculates, to concretize the atavistic impulses from which the historical Didion struggles to escape. This helps to explain why *Democracy* describes the feelings of ambivalence that dog its own composition, and the generation of its style. Unsure of herself or her story, the narrator goes to Berkeley, where she teaches a seminar that considers "the idea of democracy in the work of certain post-industrial writers." The class studies "similarities" between the "style" of a given author and his "ideas about democracy" (71). She uses as an example Norman Mailer, with whom she shares much, but whose style and ideas about democracy she tacitly repudiates.

Where Mailer's Rabelaisian excess conglomerates the seemingly different, Didion's minimalism sets itself against the assimilative properties of metaphor and, in the process, disarticulates the liberal coalitions in whose name Mailer wrote. In *Political Fictions*, Didion describes liberalism's commitment to the "'Black,'" insofar as that commitment militated on behalf of "a reasonable constituency composed exclusively of blacks and supportive liberal whites" (53). She will suggest, instead, in her fiction, that words like "black" be understood to indicate nothing more or less than the absence of color or light, and that constituencies be broken down into their constituent parts—there being nothing but bad faith binding those parts together. Hostile to metaphor, and to any representation that combines what should be inviolate (or "discrete," to recall her account of Hawaiian "Orientals"), she is also hostile to novelists and politicians who represent black voices and interests. The deadpan, laconic style of her protagonist and narrator embodies this hostility to the synthetic powers of representation. Confronted with Lovett's demise, Inez renounces her U.S. citizenship, moves to Kuala Lumpur, and reluctantly lets Didion interview her about her time with him. After the interview, Didion asks,

> What did I think about this.
>
> Finally I shrugged.
>
> Inez watched me a moment longer, and then shrugged herself. (229)

This exchange, in which Inez's speech, unadorned with quotation marks, collapses into the narrator's, captures both at the height of their cool. Faced with loss, they shrug.

Didion shrugs as well. Politics is for assholes, and she's not interested in producing blueprints for how to change the world. She's interested, rather, in weapons that can destroy it. Didion makes an arms dealer the hero of *A Book of Common Prayer* (1977). She fondly recalls atomic blasts in *Magical Thinking*. In *Slouching Towards Bethlehem*, she longs for atomic apocalypse, alongside one of Mailer's fictional hipsters: she imagines going "out onto the desert with Marion Faye, out to where he stood in *The Deer Park* looking east to Los Alamos and praying, as if for rain, that it would happen: ' . . . *let it come and clear the rot and the stench and the stink, let it come from all of everywhere, just so it comes and the world stands clear in the white dead dawn*'" (161). In *Democracy*, the bomb promises to clear the rot and the stench of Washington, DC, if not all collectivizing forms of representation. It is for Lovett and Didion alike a bracingly "actual" antidote to the hermetic world of professional politics, and to the ersatz ethical sway those politics would exert upon more properly visceral enterprises.

But the bomb promises to change the novel as well. Lovett loves atomic blasts because their efferent trajectories promise to shatter the myopic self-enclosure of the professional civil servants whom he despises: "pencil pushers" (196), he calls them. In opposing the bomb to pencil pushers, *Democracy* nods to Mary McCarthy, whose 1960 essay "The Fact in Fiction" describes the bomb as antithetical to the "enclosed space" of "institutions," "closed corporations," and ultimately the novel itself.[18] McCarthy asserts that, along with the blinkered professional, the novelist "has become specialized, like the worker on an assembly line whose task is to perform a single action several hundred times a day or the doctor whose task is to service a single organ of the human body" (456). When confronted by the bomb, the writer is "embarrassed by the insignificance . . . of his finite world" (455) and ceases to invent such worlds. As a consequence, the novel dissolves "into its component parts: the essay, the travel book, reporting, on the one hand, and the 'pure' fiction of the tale on the other" (458). For McCarthy, the bomb breaks apart the novel. Acknowledging that she is herself a "pencil pusher," the narrator of *Democracy* extends this conceit, and explodes her novel.

As Mailer put it, form is "the record of a war"—the lineament of what survives, it "proclaims the value of what is kept." Form, he adds, is also "the physical equivalent of memory," especially insofar as it attests to a selective reshaping of what has come before (*CC* 369–373). Didion's *Democracy* is the record of a war, in two senses: a testimonial to the impact of the Vietnam War on its characters, it is also, at the same time, a record of the breaking and reassembling of an earlier and abandoned effort to narrate the life of Inez. Lovett describes an atomic blast on the first page of the novel, and likens it to evidence of God. But *Democracy* begins in an act of genesis that serves as testimonial to an act of destruction: we read the remains, "or shards" (29), of what was once a realist novel written in the spirit of Anthony Trollope. That earlier effort was a "study in provincial manners, in the acute tyrannies of class and privilege by which people assert themselves against the tropics" (22). But Didion explodes this novel, as if unwilling to hear what it might tell her, and surrounds us with stylized fragments.

The Goldwater Girl

"Politics," Didion writes in *Political Fictions*, "is push and pull, give and take, the art of the possible, an essentially pragmatic process by which the differing needs and rights of the nation's citizens get balanced and to some degree met" (335). And yet she represents herself as having actively resisted writing about domestic politics. She was reluctant to begin covering campaigns, she confesses, because to her, "there remained about domestic politics something resistant, recondite, some occult irreconcilability that kept all news of it just below my attention level" (4). A few pages later: "There was to writing about politics a certain Sisyphean aspect. Broad patterns could be defined, specific inconsistencies documented, but no amount of definition or documentation seemed sufficient to stop the stone that was our apprehension of politics from hurtling back downhill" (8). Her own meaning is resistant, recondite; what is it about her "apprehension of politics" that chases her down the hill and causes her to look away?

It is surprising, given her demonstrable reluctance to answer this question, that she doesn't understand why she is "asked with somewhat puzzling frequency" about her politics. People seem to think, she complains, that they "were eccentric, opaque, somehow unreadable." They are not, she insists; they are the

> logical product of a childhood spent among conservative California Republicans (this was before the meaning of "conservative" changed) in a postwar boom economy. The people with whom I grew up were interested in low taxes, a balanced budget, and a limited government. They believed above all that a limited government had no business tinkering with the private or cultural life of its citizens. In 1964, in accord with these interests and beliefs, I voted, ardently, for Barry Goldwater. Had Goldwater remained the same age and continued running, I would have voted for him in every election thereafter. (7)

This is an innocuous account of the Arizona governor, who championed white backlash. He was notoriously hostile to civil rights activism and declared on one occasion that he was "not impressed by the claim that the Supreme Court's decision on school integration is the law of the land."[19] Moreover, Goldwater's libertarianism was more absolutist than Didion's description suggests. "Throughout history," he wrote, "government has proved to be the chief instrument for thwarting men's liberty." He would end government: "My aim is not to pass laws," he declared, "but to repeal them. It is not to inaugurate new programs, but to cancel old ones."[20] Liberals were for the apparatus of politics; he was for wiping it away. From this perspective, "new programs" and "laws" are embarrassingly trivial in light of the grander struggle between those who want government and those who want none, and Didion's politics are safely beside the point.

Goldwater had no truck with the "essentially pragmatic process" of politics, and it makes a strange kind of sense, from this perspective, that Didion's loyalty to him should lead her to the enemy's camp: she tells us that she was "shocked and to a curious extent personally offended" when California Republicans once enamored of Goldwater shifted to embrace Ronald Reagan. As a consequence, she registered with the Democrats. This was no small decision, given her family's long-standing loyalties. She claims to have been "the first member of my family (and perhaps in my generation still the only member)" (7) to register with the Democrats. But conveniently enough, the betrayal turned out to be no betrayal at all: that joining the party "did not involve taking a markedly different view on any issue was a novel discovery, and one that led me to view 'America's two-party system' with—and this was my real introduction to American politics—a somewhat doubtful eye" (7–8). This "novel" discovery resonates with *Democracy*, which finds its most salient political differences within the Democratic Party, as opposed to between the Democrats and the Republicans.

These differences take shape in Inez's two children. The son slavishly extends his father's vision; he wants to "bring [his] generation into the dialogue," and works at "finding a way to transfer anti-war sentiment into a multi-issue program" (173). The daughter steers her own course; an embarrassment to her father, she succumbs to and then masters a heroin addiction and, on a whim, hops a military transport to Vietnam, where she gets a job serving French fries at the American Legion Club in Saigon. The significance of the difference between the siblings emerges in light of their names. The son, "Adlai," embraces the meretriciously empty language and countercultural commitments of his father and, by implication, two-time loser Adlai Stevenson. In *The White Album*, Didion describes an event held on behalf of Eugene McCarthy that had "a certain *déjà vu* aspect to it, a glow of 1952 humanism" that was pleasing to those who had "voted for Adlai Stevenson" (87). If McCarthy was the son of Stevenson, in *Democracy*, Adlai is the son of a candidate a lot like McCarthy, and Didion wants us to know that Harry's outmoded liberal guilt guarantees future defeat: he will lead the party to years of failure, as did Stevenson and McCarthy. Conversely, the Victors' daughter, "Jessie," is the "crazy eight" (164) in *Democracy*, the principle of unpredictability that dogs her father's steps and scorns his establishment ambitions. Didion chose this name in 1984, at the moment that Jesse Jackson's first run for the presidency was challenging the complacency of the Democratic Party.

"I have the dream," Didion writes toward the start of *Democracy*, "in which my entire field of vision fills with rainbow" (16–17). A reference to Jackson's Rainbow Coalition, by way of Martin Luther King Jr.'s famous dream? Perhaps; but it matters that, moments later, Didion watches "the spectrum separate into pure color." Her coalitions inevitably disarticulate themselves into their constitutive parts—never more so than in relation to color. In fact, Jessie Victor is a metaphor for the novel's tendency to reduce all differences of color to a final difference between the presence and absence of light. Didion thinks Jessie possessed of an "incandescent inscrutability" and "luminous gravity" (172). What does it mean to describe a character by attributing light ("luminosity," or "incandescence") to a physical law ("gravity") whose ultimate expression (a black hole) results in the absence of light, and thus a kind of "inscrutability"? "In 1975," Didion writes, "time was no longer quickening but collapsing, falling in on itself, the way a disintegrating star contracts into a black hole" (72). The image of a black hole captures the novel's recursive nature. First circling about a wide range of seemingly disjointed events, and then falling in on itself, collapsing down with increasing speed on a smaller range of now interrelated events, Didion's narrative mimics what it calls "the black hole effect" (73). Not unlike the bomb, the black hole figures unreadable information. As she puts it in *Magical Thinking*, "information swallowed by a black hole could never be retrieved from it" (181). It makes sense, then, that while *Democracy* associates the atomic bomb's centrifugal release of blinding light with Lovett, it associates the black hole's centripetal absorption of light with what it takes to be the next generation's hip figure, Jessie. Each in his or her own way, Lovett and Jessie disable representation.

And yet, the figure with which Didion describes Jessie suggests the possibility of retrieving information. A black hole is literally black—it emits no light. Jessie's "luminous gravity," on the other hand, is contradictory. Her charismatic "blackness" gives off light, which is perhaps just to say that, like Lovett, she is never black or white, even as she is somehow both at once. Surprisingly enough, Didion likes Jesse Jackson, and associates Jessie Victor with him, because the politician strikes her as similarly contradictory: inextricably linked to blackness, he transcends that category and joins black and white in ways that previous liberal politicians never did.

In *Political Fictions*, Didion waxes exuberant describing Jackson's candidacy in 1988. She attends his campaign party just after he concedes defeat to Michael Dukakis. The event is centrifugal, and inclusive: "Jackson parties tended to spill out of ballrooms onto several levels of whatever hotel they were in, and to last until three or four in the morning: anyone who wanted to be at a Jackson party was welcome at a Jackson party" (57). At its core stands the hip figure: she spots Jackson across the room, "taking off his tie and throwing it to the crowd, like a rock star." Jackson's gravity is luminous: a collapsing political star, he's nevertheless enough of a rock star to give off an "energy level in defeat notably higher than that of other campaigns in victory" (56). Jackson's contradictory relation to light and energy suggests the contradictory relation to color embedded in the familiar narrative toward which Didion gestures. While she concedes that calling Jackson a "rock star" produces "a narrative of its own," and therefore reproduces idealist as opposed to empirical thinking, she considers the particular narrative "a relatively current one, and one that had, because it seemed at some point grounded in the recognizable, a powerful glamour for those estranged from the purposeful nostalgia of the traditional narrative" (57). Of course this "relatively current" narrative forgot what it did not want remembered: to Didion, the rock star transcends race; Chuck Berry belonged to and seemingly came from "everybody," and so too, it seems, did Jackson.

Didion insists that the "historic" aspect of Jackson's candidacy "derived from something other than the fact that he was black, a circumstance that had before been and could again be compartmentalized, segregated out" (52). Or left in for symbolic purposes: she mocks the Dukakis campaign, and American liberalism generally, for believing that "'black' . . . could be useful, and even a moral force, a way for white Americans to attain more perfect attitudes" (53). No, she insists, something other than "'black,' by itself and in the right context" was at work in Jackson's candidacies. The electoral process couldn't accommodate him because he eschewed the familiar clichés, and because he rejected "the notion that the winning and maintaining of public office warranted the invention of a public narrative based at no point on observable reality" (54). No surprise that "they were not idealists, these white Jackson voters, but empiricists" (55). Removing the isolating scare quotes from "black," Jackson threatened to break political frames in a fashion that recalls *Democracy.* Jackson was a crazy eight, a force so disruptive that his fellow Democrats saw him, in her words, as "a bomb that had to be defused" (54). Didion wanted that bomb to go off. She gleefully recalls the "sense of panic" that "swept the party" as the Jackson campaign gained momentum. This was a candidate who "could take the entire Democratic Party down with him" (52).

Bill Clinton's Neoliberal Hip

Jessie Victor is hip, but not in any way we might associate with the counterculture: "she never considered her use of heroin an act of rebellion, or a way of life, or even a bad habit of particular remark." Rather, her hip expresses a version of the capitalist spirit that animates Lovett. Jessie considered her heroin use "a consumer decision. Jessie Victor used heroin simply because she preferred heroin to coffee, aspirin, and cigarettes, as well as to movies, records, cosmetics, clothes, and lunch" (172). Didion divests Jessie's lifestyle of political meaning, and celebrates it for its commitment to commerce. In a related fashion, Didion likes Jackson not because he extended the Democratic Party's commitment to countercultural blackness, but because he ended it, not because he committed to social justice, but because he was, at bottom, outside the political process and in some basic sense an opportunist. She likes the fact that Jackson bypassed official channels, and appreciates the candidate, one feels, precisely because he struck even his supporters as "a con man" (54). Didion would happily endorse, one imagines, Adolph Reed's description of Jessie Jackson as an aggrandizing opportunist who, drawing from a church-based protest tradition on its way to obsolescence, leapfrogged over and effectively damaged a burgeoning network of elected black leaders. She embraced Jackson precisely because, as Reed has it, he undermined the efficacy of black participation within the Democratic Party at the moment that he seemed to announce its triumph, and thus abetted, or at least failed adequately to retard, "the proliferation of much of what is known as 'neoliberalism' within Democratic ranks."[21]

As David Harvey sees it, the decisive year in the advent of neoliberalism was 1979, when the United Kingdom elected Margaret Thatcher as its prime minister, and when she began to replace her government's Keynesianism with monetarist "supply side solutions" to the problem of stagflation. Thatcher also set about

> confronting trade union power, attacking all forms of social solidarity that hindered competitive flexibility (such as those expressed through municipal governance, and including the power of many professionals and their associations), dismantling or rolling back the commitments of the welfare state, the privatization of public en-terprises (including social housing), reducing taxes, encouraging entrepreneurial initiative, and creating a favorable business climate to induce a strong inflow of foreign investment.[22]

That same year, Paul Volcker, Jimmy Carter's Federal Reserve chairman, effected a fundamental shift in U.S. monetary policy. Where before the Fed had focused its energies on sustaining maximum employment, it would now primarily seek to combat inflation. Elected one year later, Reagan followed this initiative with deregulation, tax cuts, budget cuts, and assaults on trade union and professional power. He used the Treasury Department and the International Monetary Fund to force similar reforms on credit-hungry nations around the globe. As Harvey has it, "All of this connected to the strong burst in activity and power within the world of finance. Increasingly freed from the regulatory constraints and barriers that had hitherto confined its field of action, financial activity could flourish as never before, eventually everywhere." The effects of this reorganization were profound. By 1996, the net worth of the 358 richest people was equivalent to the combined income of the poorest 45 percent of the world's population—some 2.3 billion people. Between 1994 and 1998, the world's 200 richest people more than doubled their net worth, to more than $1 trillion.[23]

Reagan's significance aside, however, it would be wrong to attribute the rise of neoliberalism solely to the Republican Party, and this not simply because Paul Volcker, a Democrat, inaugurated what would prove to be a decisive shift in monetary policy. For Sheldon Wolin, "neoliberalism emerged as the New Deal's residuary legatee and found its icon in JFK." Kennedy liberals wanted a "strong state" to oppose Soviet communism, but were unwilling "to intervene to control the 'excess' of capital and to respond, at least minimally, to the new challenge of broadening political along with social democracy." And, indeed, although Kennedy was the first Democratic president to offer support to the Civil Rights Movement, he did so in the context of a newfound commitment to concentrated economic power. "I do not believe in big government," he declared in 1960, well on his way to winning over significant numbers of those socially liberal Republicans who controlled Wall Street. "I do not know whether to regard with alarm or indignation the common assumption of an inevitable conflict between the business community and the Democratic Party. That is one of the great political myths of our time, carefully fostered." By and large, Lyndon Johnson believed in that myth, and as a consequence constructed strong bulwarks against injustice. All the same, he began to distance the Democrats from the Keynesian fiscal policy of the thirties and embrace an early version of neoliberal monetary policies. Even as the party's 1964 platform advocated the pursuit of civil rights and hinted at the legislation that would facilitate the emergence of a "Great Society," it declared support for a "continuation of flexible and innovative fiscal, monetary, and debt management policies, recognizing the importance of low interest rates." John Gerring points to this quote when he argues that by the sixties, the scientific maximization of economic output had replaced earlier, New Deal emphases on regulation and redistributive justice. Steve Fraser and Gary Gerstle echo Gerring when they argue that despite Johnson's intentions to the contrary, the Great Society "ruled out a politics of more vigorous intervention in the marketplace." Paul Frymer describes, in a different vein, how Johnson, faced with pressure from southern Democrats, ultimately weakened organized labor by developing "a bifurcated system of power that assigned race and class problems to different spheres of government."[24]

This study has pursued a different intimacy between the Democrats and the emergence of neoliberalism. In accounting for the phenomenon's origins, Harvey emphasizes the revolutionary unrest of the sixties. Specifically, he identifies an incompatibility between the "values of individual freedom and [those of] social justice" at the heart of the period's radicalism. This was an incompatibility open to exploitation, as we just saw with respect to Jessie Victor, who embraces heroin as a consumer even as she rejects her brother's political commitment to the counterculture. "Neoliberal rhetoric," Harvey avers, "with its foundational emphasis upon individual freedoms, has the power to split off libertarianism, identity politics, multiculturalism, and eventually narcissistic consumerism from the social forces ranged in pursuit of social justice through the conquest of state power." In the United States, radical social movements often bundled their attacks on an interventionist state and corporate power, which at that moment seemed synonymous with each other. Neoliberal rhetoric took advantage of this confusion by offering a "market-based populist culture of differentiated consumerism and individual libertarianism." Such rhetoric allowed business interests to capture large segments of the voting public because it "emphasized the liberty of consumer choice, not only with respect to particular products but also with respect to lifestyles, modes of expression, and a wide range of cultural practices."[25]

White fantasies of black hip had been crucial to the liberal coalitions of the sixties. And if, as Harvey points out, the radicalism of that moment was characterized by its uneasy amalgam of the desire for individual liberty on the one hand and social justice on the other, then hip facilitated this amalgam and elided its constitutive contradictions. Just as the plight of black Americans was central to the liberalism of the sixties—and to bringing liberalism and radicalism closer to each other than they had been since the thirties—so too the imagined hip lifestyles, modes of expression and cultural practices of those same Americans sustained that liberalism by reconciling its most basic tensions, by confusing consumer need with utopian politics.[26] But ultimately, consumer need is no more intrinsically related to social justice than, to recall E. L. Doctorow, the radical's music is to his social analysis. Hip provided a sustaining fiction, a promissory image that amalgamated otherwise incompatible positions.

Bill Clinton exploited that fiction such that it might serve his neoliberal program. Active early on in the DLC, he helped move the organization and its beliefs into the party's mainstream. He did so by reassuring whites that the Democratic Party did not belong to African Americans. Starting in 1966, white working-class voters in the North and white voters from across the economic spectrum in the South and the West had begun to leave the party because, most historians have tended to assume, they were alienated by the depth of its commitment to civil rights and the aspirations of blacks generally.[27] In the early nineties, a spate of books, such as Peter Brown's *Minority Party*, pointed to this ongoing trend and argued that the Democrats would never win so long as they were closely associated with blacks and, by extension, the welfare state. Clinton's solution to this state of affairs was simple. He updated the African American patina that the party had always possessed, but did so in an act of crucial distancing that disarticulated the twined imperatives of hip, its emphasis on individual liberty on the one hand and social justice on the other. Baiting Jesse Jackson and denouncing "angry" rap musicians like Sister Souljah, he promised to downsize the welfare state. At the same time, he surrounded himself with black faces and, famously, blew his sax for Arsenio Hall's late-night audience.

The musical performance scandalized the press. "Am I such an old fogey that I thought it was undignified?" Barbara Walters asked on *This Week with David Brinkley*. "The association with jazz music and dark shades and *The Arsenio Hall Show*, I don't think that's an asset in running for the presidency," added Tom Wicker in the *New York Times*.[28] Of course these reactions were beside the point, for they only confirmed the myopia with which establishment journalism then treated political life. Walters was indeed an old fogey, because her dignity left her insensitive to the demotic style that the candidate aimed to embrace. But this didn't indicate anything so simple as a cleavage between popular and high culture. As we have seen, serious novelists had long elaborated upon what it meant for politicians to aspire to hip.

And they would do so again: six years into Clinton's presidency, Toni Morrison wrote in the *New Yorker*, "White skin notwithstanding, this is our first black President. Blacker than any actual black person who could ever be elected in our children's lifetime," Morrison's Clinton "displays almost every trope of blackness." Suggesting that Clinton could conceivably be "blacker" than a man with black skin, Morrison insisted on the primacy of his metaphoric as opposed to his "actual" body. This allowed her, in turn, to assert the importance of her own craft to Clinton's power. Expressing disgust with corporate media, Morrison declared that the real story behind his impeachment, for example, lacked "a coherent sphere of enunciation. There seem to be no appropriate language in which or platform of discourse from which to pursue it."[29] But she supplied that language and discourse when she argued that the president's impeachment stemmed from and further confirmed his blackness. She claimed to understand the struggle for power enacted over his body because, as a novelist, she was expert with "tropes," able in her use of language to transform our experience of the "actual." Her essay was a literary coronation, and culminated the tradition begun when Norman Mailer declared John F. Kennedy "the Hipster as Presidential Candidate": Morrison didn't simply observe that Clinton was the first black president; she insisted that only one adept in figurative language might place the crown upon his head.

Writing during Obama's campaign, from a broadly liberal point of view, journalist Jeff Yang sang Obama's praises by favorably contrasting his ethnic and cultural hybridity with Bill Clinton's. Yang revisited the way in which "Toni Morrison granted our 42nd president, William Jefferson Clinton, a kind of cadet membership in the grand cultural narrative of black America." Obama's inauguration seemed to represent the fulfillment of that narrative; his was no cadet membership: he seemed authentically hip in ways Clinton could never be, and thus not in need of literary shepherding. A model of effortless grace, Obama stayed within himself, and the media's declarations of his hipness simply confirmed the triumph of his ease, the comfortable manner with which he laid claim to his identity and the grand cultural narrative associated with it. But Yang wasn't interested in that particular narrative. He thought "that the tropes that surround and define Obama can just as easily be read as those of another community entirely. Which raises the question: Could it be that our true first black president might also be our first Asian American president?"[30] Yang made his case: Obama was raised in Hawaii, he spent formative years in Jakarta, and some of his closest friends and congressional aides were or are Asian; above all, he displayed the concatenation of aspiration, pragmatism, and hard work that Yang takes to be central to the Asian American experience.

The ultimate goal of these identifications, at least for Yang, is not a commitment to social justice but the licensing of new kinds of unfettered global commerce. Morrison's article ends with retreat from the corporate media into the seemingly archaic pleasures of reading—and political protest. "Early this week, a neighbor called to ask if I would march. Where? To Washington, she said. Absolutely, I answered, without even asking what for. 'We have to prevent the collapse of our Constitution,' she said." Morrison concludes, "We meet tonight." Yang's article ends differently: it tells us that the author "forecasts global consumer trends for the market-research company Iconoculture." A trip to the company's Web site, advertised in the article, explains the service it provides: "Get closer to your consumer with insights and data derived from an in-depth global consumer study measuring values, category indicators, lifestyle choices and demographics across 17 countries, including emerging markets—Brazil, Russia, India and China." No surprise, then, that Yang published an article in Salon.com titled "Brand-aid" just before extolling Obama's Asian bona fides. "Global marketing execs agree," the article crows, "America's image is in the toilet. The cure? One presidential candidate has what it takes, they say, to save Brand USA."[31] That candidate was Obama, and Yang's endorsements might be said to express one endpoint of the trajectory that *Hip Figures* describes, in which the once literary making of the Democratic Party winds up in the hands of marketing execs and brand managers.

It's worth noting that Barack Obama is the legatee of Clinton's neoliberalism—most obviously in his adherence to Chicago School economics and in his decision to extend the policies of Clinton's secretary of the treasury, Robert Rubin. In this context, Obama's hip represents something other than the achievements of the Civil Rights Movement and Johnson's Great Society. Cultural conservatives tend to hate Obama for the very reasons that economic conservatives love him. Before Obama came to office, reactionary ideologues perfected the art of railing against what Rush Limbaugh called "the medical elites, the sociology elites, the education elites, the legal elites, the science elites . . . and the ideas this bunch of people promote through the media."[32] Obama represents the still-further removal of these allegedly arrogant professional cadres from "the people"; to the white supremacists who constitute a significant part of the Tea Party movement, for example, he is a member of an elite that comes from everywhere and nowhere, and that therefore remains alien to American values and traditions. Claims like these resonate with celebrations of the president's transnational origins. As the conservative columnist David Brooks puts it, Obama "has a mentality formed by globalization, not the S.D.S. With his multiethnic family and his globe-spanning childhood, there is a little piece of everything in Obama. He is perpetually engaged in an internal discussion between different pieces of his hybrid self—Kenya with Harvard, Kansas with the South Side of Chicago—and he takes that conversation outward into the world."[33] The fact that one wing of the Republican Party hates Obama for the very deracination that elicits love in another wing suggests, in turn, that it's by no means clear that a hybridity formed by globalization is liberal rather than conservative.

What is apparent, however, is how effortlessly the logic of hip mobilizes ethnic and racial hybridity in the service of selling commodities the globe over. This became clear during Clinton's tenure in the White House. According to Naomi Klein, hip assumed its most explicitly corporate form in the early nineties, when black hip provided "the make-or-break quality in 1990s branding." According to Klein, marketers turned to "cool consultancies" such as Sputnik, *The L. Report*, and Bureau de Style. These consultancies studied "young black men in American inner cities"—who became "the market most aggressively mined by the brandmasters as a source of borrowed 'meaning' and identity"— and concluded that hip-hop was "the perfect identity for product-driven companies looking to become transcendent image-based brands."[34] "Transcendent" is right, and this not simply because hip did for globalizing brands what it did for liberalism during the sixties: provide an image designed to pass over and go beyond difference. As Klein puts it, "The 'got to be cool' rhetoric of the global brands is, more often than not, an indirect way of saying 'got to be black.' Just as the history of cool in America is really (as many have argued) a history of African American culture—from jazz and blues to rock and roll to rap—for many superbrands, cool hunting simply means black-culture hunting." Nike was one such global superbrand: "So focused is Nike on borrowing style, attitude and imagery from black urban youth that the company has its own word for the practice: *bro-ing*. That's when Nike marketers and designers bring their prototypes to inner-city neighborhoods . . . and say, 'Hey, bro, check out the shoes,' to gauge the reaction to new styles and to build up a buzz."[35]

A small leap from here to branding the nation: as Klein reports, "Since his election in 1997, England's young prime minister, Tony Blair, has been committed to changing Britain's somewhat dowdy image to 'Cool Britannia.'"[36] More than any president before him, Clinton set out to make the United States cool. But to Clinton, hip wasn't angry, any more than it has been for Obama, and his cool did not necessarily mean "got to be black." As Morrison had it, Clinton was the first black president. But Joe Eszterhas was perhaps more accurate when he called Clinton the first "rock and roll president." To be sure, Eszterhas relished the president's facility with black culture. "Bill Clinton could get down," he declared, while describing the president's affinity for African Americans. He "had *flow, ease, soul.*"[37] But Clinton's blackness was deracinated many times over, his ease safely detached from any untoward associations with angry African Americans. As Didion would point out, he was the master of mixed signals. He didn't play John Coltrane on *The Arsenio Hall Show*, or anything like hip-hop; he played Elvis Presley. Different groups would find in that performance different musical genealogies, from the blues to bluegrass, and different visions of how and why culture mattered to political life.

Notes

Introduction

1. Reported on March 2, NPR.org.

2. *American Prospect*, February 4, 2008. Michelle Cottle, "The Cool Presidency," *New Republic*, March 4, 2009, in *Best American Political Writing, 2009*, ed. Royce Flippin (New York: PublicAffairs Books, 2009). Sam Fulwood III, "For Obama, Hipness Is What It Is," *Politico*, April 24, 2009.

3. Quoted in *New York Times*, March 18, 2008. Cottle, "The Cool Presidency," 162, 165, 164.

4. David Riesman, with Nathan Glazer and Reuel Denney, *The Lonely Crowd: A Study of the Changing American Character*, rev. ed. (New Haven, CT: Yale University Press, 2001), 164–165.

5. Mailer, "Superman Comes to the Supermarket," reprinted in Mailer, *The Presidential Papers* (New York: Berkeley Medallion Books, 1963), 44; hereafter cited in text as *PP*.

6. William Styron, *This Quiet Dust* (New York: Random House, 1982), 32; hereafter cited in text as QD.

7. Tate, *Everything but the Burden: What White People Are Taking from Black Culture* (New York: Harvest Moon, 2003).

8. Karl Marx and Friedrich Engels, *Capital: The Process of Capitalist Production*, trans. Samuel Moore and Edward Aveling, ed. Friedrich Engels (Chicago: Charles H. Kerr, 1912), 83.

9. Susan Willis, "I Shop Therefore I Am: Is There a Place for Afro-American Culture in Commodity Culture?" in *Changing Our Own Words*, ed. Cheryl Wall (New Brunswick, NJ: Rutgers University Press, 1989), 189, 183.

10. Haug, *Critique of Commodity Aesthetics* (Cambridge, UK: Polity, 1986), 50; Mark McCrindle, *Seriously Cool: Marketing and Communication with Diverse Generations* (New South Wales, Australia: McCrindle Research, 2007), 30.

11. Doctorow, *Essays and Conversations*, ed. Richard Trenner (Princeton, NJ: Ontario Review Press, 1983), 27.

12. Quoted in Doug McAdam, *Political Process and the Development of Black Insurgency, 1930–1970* (Chicago: University of Chicago Press, 1999), 80. Political scientists

debate the relationship between the party as an intuitional formation and the liberalism that ostensibly subtended it. William Schneider argues that in the early 1960s voters began to identify themselves as "liberal" or "conservative," in place of and often at the expense of their party affiliations. See Schneider, "Democrats and Republicans, Liberals and Conservatives," in *Emerging Coalitions in American Politics*, ed. Seymour Lipset (New Brunswick, NJ: Transaction Publishers, 1978). E. J. Dionne examines the same phenomenon in light of the "New Politics" reform movement of the late sixties and early seventies. See Dionne, *Why Americans Hate Politics* (New York: Simon and Schuster, 2004), 47. Gerald Pomper thinks that the presidential election of 1964 evidenced the rise of issue voting and the decline of party identification. Warren Miller claims that after the presidential election of 1972, "the predictive power" of party identification fell to an all-time low. Pomper and Miller, cited in Theodore Rosenof, *Realignment: The Theory That Changed the Way We Think About American Politics* (Lanham, MD: Rowman and Littlefield, 2003), 128, 127. Andrew Gelman contends that Democratic Party partisanship has become more intense since Southern Democrats went Republican. Gelman, *Red State, Blue State, Rich State, Poor State* (Princeton, NJ: Princeton University Press, 2009). Similarly, the "Michigan School's" *The American Voter* (1960) stresses the importance of party identification over particular issues, and the essential continuity of the Democrats' appeal over time.

13. See, for example, Edward G. Carmines and James A. Stimson, *Issue Evolution: Race and the Transformation of American Politics* (Princeton, NJ: Princeton University Press, 1989); Paul Frymer, *Black and Blue: African Americans, the Labor Movement, and the Decline of the Democratic Party* (Princeton, NJ: Princeton University Press, 2007); Ralph Gomes and Linda Williams, eds., *From Exclusion to Inclusion: The Long Struggle for African American Political Power* (Westport, CT: Greenwood, 1991); Peter Brown, *Minority Party: Why Democrats Face Defeat in 1992 and Beyond* (Washington, DC: Regency, 1991).

14. As John Gerring puts it, the party changed forever with "the reemergence of the race question on the national political agenda. The symbolic power of this issue within a party historically devoted to the cause of white supremacy can hardly be overestimated." Gerring, *Party Ideologies in America: 1828–1996* (New York: Cambridge University Press, 2001), 253. For the impact of the Civil Rights Movement on Lyndon Johnson's Great Society, see Sidney Milkis and Jerome Mileur, eds., *The Great Society and the High Tide of Liberalism* (Amherst: University of Massachusetts Press, 2005), 3–5.

15. Michael Rogin, *Blackface, White Noise: Jewish Immigrants in the Hollywood Melting Pot* (Berkeley: University of California Press, 1996), 14.

16. Ralph Ellison, *The Collected Essays of Ralph Ellison*, ed. John Callahan, preface Saul Bellow (New York: Modern Library, 2003), 85, 557; hereafter cited in text as *CE*.

17. Dick Hebdige, *Subculture: The Meaning of Style* (New York: Routledge, 2002) 3, 179.

18. Quoted in Richard King, *Race, Culture, and the Intellectuals, 1944–1970* (New York: Woodrow Wilson Press, 2004), 291.

19. On "interest group liberalism," see Reynolds, *Democracy Unbound: Progressive Challenges to the Two Party System* (Boston: South End Press, 1997), 69. John Gerring argues that during the fifties, the Democrats rejected "the class appeal of Populism"

important to Roosevelt and instead embraced an "agenda that kept spreading outward . . . incorporating the demands of an ever wider set of ethnic, racial, sexual, and issue-based groups." For him, "the organizing theme of Democratic ideology changed from an attack against special privilege" to "an appeal for inclusion"; *Party Ideologies*, 244, 232. As Daniel Bell saw it, the New Deal laid the groundwork for this change by organizing its theory of politics and justice around the proliferation of "interest blocs." Bell, "America's Un-Marxist Revolution: Mr. Truman Embarks on a Politically Managed Economy," *Commentary*, March 1949, 207–209.

20. Kennedy, cited in Arthur Schlesinger, *A Thousand Days: John F. Kennedy in the White House* (New York: Mariner, 2002), 1015; Vidal, *United States: Essays 1952–1992* (New York: Random House, 1995), 44.

21. John Leland, *Hip: The History* (New York: Ecco, 2004), 288. The etymology of the word "hip" is disputed: some trace it to nineteenth-century opium dens, in which frequent users developed a bruise on the hip while they consumed the drug on their sides. More dubiously, others trace the word to the Wolof verb *hepi*, "to see," or *hipi*, "to open one's eyes"; see ibid., 5.

22. Eric Lott, *Love and Theft: Blackface Minstrelsy and the American Working Class* (New York: Oxford University Press, 1993), 3, 50, 6, 5, 53. For a more celebratory account of minstrelsy, see W. T. Lhamon Jr., *Raising Cain: Blackface Performance from Jim Crow to Hip Hop* (Cambridge, MA: Harvard University Press, 1998).

23. Andrew Ross, *No Respect* (New York: Routledge, 1989), 78.

24. Cornel West, *Prophetic Fragments: Illuminations in the Crisis in American Religion and Culture* (Grand Rapids, MI: Eerdmans Publishing, 1993), 176–177.

25. Ross, *No Respect*, 96.

26. Updike, *Rabbit, Run* (New York: Fawcett, 1996), 150.

27. On Black, see Nat Hentoff, *American Music Is* (Cambridge, MA: Da Capo, 2004), 122; LeRoi Jones, *Blues People: Negro Music in America* (New York: William Morrow, 1999), 148, 149; hereafter cited in text as BP.

28. *Down Beat*, cited in Penny M. Von Eschen, *Satchmo Blows Up the World: Jazz Ambassadors Play the Cold War* (Cambridge, MA: Harvard University Press, 2004), 97.

29. James Baldwin, *The Fire Next Time*, in James Baldwin, *Collected Essays* (New York: Library of America, 1998), 315; hereafter cited in text as BE.

30. Billy Lee Brammer, *The Gay Place* (Austin: University of Texas Press, 1994), 56; Saul Bellow, *Mr. Sammler's Planet* (New York: Viking Press, 1970), 59; John Updike, *Rabbit Redux* (New York: Fawcett, 1971), 229, 241.

31. See Eric Sundquist, *To Wake the Nations: Race in the Making of American Literature* (Cambridge, MA: Harvard University Press, 1993), introduction.

32. John Williams, *The Man Who Cried I Am* (New York: Thunder's Mouth Press, 1994), 209, 18; Ishmael Reed, *The Free-Lance Pallbearers* (New York: Dalkey, 1999), 109, 74, 110, 108.

33. See Scott Knowles DeVeaux, *The Birth of Bebop: A Musical and Social History* (Los Angeles: University of California Press, 1999).

34. Mailer, *Advertisements for Myself* (1959; Cambridge, MA: Harvard University Press, 1992), 197; hereafter cited in text as *A*.

35. Lukács, *History and Class Consciousness: Studies in Marxist Dialectics* (Cambridge, MA: MIT Press, 1972), 41.

36. For the classic account of political parties as organizational structures, see Robert Michels, *Political Parties: A Sociological Study of the Oligarchical Tendencies of Modern Democracy* (New Brunswick, NJ: Transaction, 2002).

37. For an account of Burns and his relation to the politics of the sixties, see Garry Wills, *Nixon Agonistes: The Crisis of the Self-Made Man* (1970; reprint, New York: Houghton Mifflin, 2002). For an illuminating account of the figure of the president in American literature, see Sean McCann, *A Pinnacle of Feeling: American Literature and Presidential Government* (Princeton, NJ: Princeton University Press, 2008).

38. David Lewis Cohn, *The Fabulous Democrats: A History of the Democratic Party in Text and Pictures* (New York: Putnam, 1956), 183, 184.

39. On Lakoff and the Democrats, see Matt Bai, "The Framing Wars," *New York Times Magazine*, July 17, 2005. Himelstein, quoted in James MacGregor and Georgia J. Sorenson, *Dead Center: Clinton-Gore Leadership and the Perils of Moderation* (New York: Simon and Schuster), 245. Edsall, quoted in Theodore Rueter, *The Politics of Race* (New York: M. E. Sharpe, 1995), 95.

40. Saxton, *The Rise and Fall of the White Republic: Class Politics and Mass Culture in Nineteenth-Century America* (New York: Verso, 1990), 165.

41. Morris Dickstein, *The Cambridge History of American Literature*, vol. 7, *Prose Writing, 1940–1990*, ed. Sacvan Bercovitch (New York: Cambridge University Press, 1999), 228.

42. Ricoeur, "Metaphor and the Central Problem of Hermeneutics," in *Hermeneutics and the Human Sciences*, ed. and trans. John B. Thompson (New York: Cambridge University Press, 1981), 170, 174, 180.

43. Ricoeur, "The Metaphorical Process as Cognition, Imagination, and Feeling," *Critical Inquiry* 5 (Autumn 1978): 148, 153.

44. J. L. Austin, *How to Do Things with Words* (Cambridge, MA: Harvard University Press, 1975), 12, 26. Pierre Bourdieu, *Language as Symbolic Power* (Cambridge, MA: Harvard University Press, 1999), 111, 126, 54.

45. White, *The Making of the President, 1960* (New York: Buccaneer, 1961), 234.

46. Warren, *So Black and Blue: Ralph Ellison and the Occasion of Criticism* (Chicago: University of Chicago Press, 2003), 67.

47. See Eric Santner, *The Psychotheology of Everyday Life* (Chicago: University of Chicago Press, 2001), Chapter 3.

48. For Wolfe's quotes and on his relation to Fanon, see Gayle Wald, "Mezz Mezzrow and the Voluntary Negro Blues," in *Race and the Subject of Masculinities*, ed. Harry Stecopoulos and Michael Uebel (Durham, NC: Duke University Press, 1997), 134; for Wolfe's relation to bebop, see Scott Saul, *Freedom Is, Freedom Ain't* (Cambridge, MA: Harvard University Press, 2003), 51.

49. Ford, "Somewhere/Nowhere: Hipness as an Aesthetic," *Musical Quarterly* 86, no. 1 (Spring 2002): 55, 56, and "Hip Sensibility in an Age of Mass Counterculture," *Jazz Perspectives* 2, no. 2 (November 2008): 137, 138.

50. Richard Godden, "Labor, Language, and Finance Capital," *PMLA* 126, no. 2 (March 2011):417–418.

51. Gouldner, cited in Charles Derber, William A. Schwartz, and Yale R. Magrass, *Power in the Highest Degree: Professionals and the Rise of a New Mandarin Order* (New York: Oxford University Press, 1990), 178.

52. Leland, *Hip*, 133; Saul, *Freedom Is, Freedom Ain't*, 34; Mezzrow, quoted in Brent Hayes Edwards, "Louis Armstrong and the Syntax of Scat," *Critical Inquiry* 28, no. 3 (Spring 2002); Alan Liu, *The Laws of Cool: Knowledge Work and the Culture of Information* (Chicago: University of Chicago Press, 2004).

53. DeVeaux, *The Birth of Bebop*, 28; on Shago Martin and Miles Davis, see Mary V. Dearborn, *Mailer: A Biography* (New York: Mariner, 2001), 117; Davis, in Miles Davis and Quincy Troupe, *Miles: The Autobiography* (New York: Simon and Schuster, 1990), 63. Gerald Early describes bebop musicians as "uncompromising professionals" who were "no more in tune with the black masses" than the often vilified Louis Armstrong and his generation, "and, in some sense, were probably less so" (quoted in DeVeaux, *The Birth of Bebop*, 26). Eric Hobsbawm argues that "the [black] hipster aspired to the white man's status as a professional"; Hobsbawm, *The Jazz Scene* (Cambridge, MA: Da Capo, 1975), 219.

54. Rogin, *Blackface, White Noise*, 38, 5. For two accounts of blackface opposed to Rogin's, see Michael Alexander, *Jazz Age Jews* (Princeton, NJ: Princeton University Press, 2001), and Andrea Most, *Making Americans: Jews and the Broadway Musical* (Cambridge, MA: Harvard University Press, 2004).

55. For a comprehensive account of how Jewish and black writers understood themselves in relation to each other in postwar America, see Eric Sundquist, *Strangers in the Land: Blacks, Jews, Post-Holocaust America* (Cambridge, MA: Harvard University Press, 2005).

56. Norman Mailer, *Armies of the Night: History as a Novel, the Novel as History* (New York: Plume, 1994), 94, 28.

57. Norman Mailer, *The Prisoner of Sex* (Boston: Little, Brown, 1971), 183, 184.

58. Ehrenreich and Fraiman, in Fraiman, *Cool Men and the Second Sex* (New York: Columbia University Press, 2003), xv, xiii.

59. Robin Morgan, "Goodbye to All That," in *Dear Sisters: Dispatches from the Women's Liberation Movement*, ed. Rosalyn Baxandall and Linda Gordon (New York: Basic Books, 2000), 53–57.

60. Lisa Young, *Feminists and Party Politics* (Vancouver: UBC Press, 2000), 91–92.

61. See G. Calvin Mackenzie, *The Irony of Reform: Roots of American Political Disenchantment* (Boulder, CO: Westview Press, 1996), 46; Joyce Gelb, *Feminism and Politics: A Comparative Perspective* (Berkeley: University of California Press, 1990), 64; Ronald Walters, *Black Presidential Politics in America: A Strategic Approach* (Albany, NY: State University of New York Press, 1998), 73.

62. Mailer, *St. George and the Godfather* (New York: Arbor House, 1972), 56; hereafter cited in text as *SG*.

63. Frank, *The Conquest of Cool: Business Culture, Counterculture, and the Rise of Hip Consumerism* (Chicago: University of Chicago Press, 1997), 233.

64. Brown, *Life Against Death* (Middletown, CT: Wesleyan University Press, 1985), xvii.

65. Baldwin, *Another Country* (1962; New York: Vintage, 1992), 212; on Thompson, see Marc Weingarten, *The Gang That Wouldn't Write Straight: Wolfe, Thompson, Didion, and the New Journalism Revolution* (New York: Crown, 2005), 126; Didion, *Slouching Towards Bethlehem* (New York: FSG, 1990), 4.

66. Plath, *The Bell Jar* (New York: Harper Perennial, 2005), 82.

67. Millett, *Sexual Politics* (Urbana: University of Illinois Press, 2000), 23, 24.

68. Macdonald, *The Root Is Man* (Brooklyn, NY: Automedia, 1995), 39.

69. Mills, *The Sociological Imagination* (New York: Oxford University Press, 2000), 16, 17; Lukács, "Realism in the Balance" (1938), in *Aesthetics and Politics: Theodor Adorno, Walter Benjamin, Ernst Bloch, Bertolt Brecht, George Lukács*, afterword by Fredric Jameson, trans. and ed. Ronald Taylor (New York: Verso, 1988), 47–48.

70. Lukács, "Realism," 38, 48.

71. On vocal blackening in literary modernism, see Michael North, *The Dialect of Modernism: Race, Language, and Twentieth-Century Literature* (New York: Oxford University Press, 1994), 77, 78.

72. Greenberg, "Avant-Garde and Kitsch," in Greenberg, *Perceptions and Judgments: 1939–1944*, ed. John O'Brien (Chicago: University of Chicago Press, 1988), 10.

73. Scott DeVeaux, "Constructing the Jazz Tradition," in *The Jazz Cadence of American Culture*, ed. Robert G. O'Meally (New York: Columbia University Press, 1998), 498. See also Bernard Gendron, *Between Montmartre and the Mudd Club: Popular Music and the Avant-Garde* (Chicago: University of Chicago Press, 2002), Chapter 7.

74. Howe, *Politics and the Novel* (Chicago: Ivan R. Dee, 2002), 161, 17; hereafter cited in text as *PN*.

75. Howe, *Steady Work: Essays in the Politics of Democratic Radicalism* (New York: Mariner, 1967), 43.

76. Howe, *A Margin of Hope* (New York: Mariner, 1984), 321.

77. Howe, *The Critical Point: On Literature and Culture* (New York: Dell, 1975), 204.

78. Howe, *Steady Work*, 39, 38.

79. Kushner, *Angels in America: A Gay Fantasia on National Themes* (New York: Theater Communications Group, 2003), 74.

80. Lou Ann Bulik, *Mass Culture Criticism and "Dissent": An American Socialist Magazine* (Berne, Germany: Peter Lang, 1993), 69, 60, 61, 64.

81. Howe wants an escape from the scientism of systematic thinking; Blotner wants to study the political novel like a political scientist. His study seeks to merge "his technical competence in one branch of learning with his informed and enthusiastic interest in another," and thereby "build[] bridges between the social sciences and the humanities"; Blotner, *The Political Novel* (New York: Doubleday, 1955), v.

82. Howe, *A World Elsewhere* (New York: Horizon Press, 1963), 87.

83. Zola, *Thérèse Raquin*, trans. Leonard Tancock (New York: Penguin, 1962), 22; Symons, quoted in Hugh Kenner, *The Pound Era* (Berkeley: University of California Press, 1971), 134; T. S. Eliot, "Philip Massinger," in *Selected Prose of T. S. Eliot* (New York: Houghton Mifflin Harcourt, 1975), 160; Zola, *The Fortune of the Rougons*, trans. Ernest Vizetelley (New York: Mondial, 2004), 6; *Robert Penn Warren Talking: Interviews, 1950–1978*, ed. Floyd Watkins and John T. Hiers (New York: Random House, 1980), 35, 36.

Chapter 1

1. Ransom, "Reconstructed but Unregenerate," in *I'll Take My Stand: The South and the Agrarian Tradition* (Baton Rouge: Louisiana State University Press, 1977), 26–27.

2. Allan J. Lichtman, *Prejudice and the Old Politics: The Presidential Election of 1928* (Lanham, MD: Lexington Books, 2000), 153.

3. On the Dixiecrats and their relation to Nixon's Southern Strategy, see Kari Frederickson, *The Dixiecrat Revolt and the End of the Solid South, 1932–1968* (Chapel Hill: University of North Carolina Press, 2001).

4. V. O. Key, *Southern Politics in State and Nation* (New York: Knopf, 1949), 44, 5. For an excellent review of Key, see Richard Hofstadter, "Key, V. O., Jr. *Southern Politics* (Book Review)," *Commentary* 9 (1950).

5. Adam Fairclough, *Race and Democracy: The Civil Rights Struggle in Louisiana, 1915–1972* (Atlanta: University of Georgia Press, 2008), 22; W. J. Cash, *The Mind of the South* (1941; reprint, Garden City: Doubleday, 1954), 291; Roy Wilkins, "The Irrelevance of Race," in *Huey Long*, ed. Hugh Davis Graham, Great Lives Observed series (Englewood Cliffs, NJ: Prentice-Hall, 1970), 78.

6. See Nick Kotz, *Judgment Days: Lyndon Baines Johnson, Martin Luther King, Jr., and the Laws That Changed America* (New York: Houghton Mifflin Harcourt, 2005), 25–26.

7. Mailer, *Armies of the Night*, 49, 51.

8. *The Public Papers of Lyndon B. Johnson* (Washington, DC: Government Printing Office, 1963–1969), 1965:840–842.

9. Joe Klein, *Primary Colors* (New York: Random House, 2006), 300. Eric Lott thinks Klein embraces this servitude at the expense of the antinomian characteristics that Burton associates with his father. To Lott, Klein's novel "is told in literary blackface by a Jewish writer": Klein raises his stock among the media elite by castigating the militant stance of black leaders committed to identity politics. See *The Disappearing Liberal Intellectual* (New York: Basic Books, 2006), 140, 145. Lott suggests that Klein's most significant antecedent is Gunnar Myrdal's *An American Dilemma* (144). But in fact, Klein borrows from Warren's novel everything from proper names (Stanton, Burton for Burden) to its basic narrative structure.

10. See Gary Boulard, *Huey Long Invades New Orleans: The Siege of a City, 1934–36* (Gretna, LA: Pelican, 1998), 262.

11. Joe Eszterhas, *American Rhapsody* (New York: Knopf, 2000), 275.

12. Cleanth Brooks, *The Hidden God: Studies in Hemingway, Faulkner, Yeats, Eliot, and Warren* (New Haven, CT: Yale University Press, 1963), 117, 118, 4.

13. Warren, introduction to *All the King's Men* (New York: Random House, 1953), v–vi.

14. Joseph Blotner, *Robert Penn Warren: A Biography* (New York: Random House, 1997), 229; hereafter cited in text as *RPW*. John Whalen-Bridge claims, "Politics for Warren is that which sharply limits the possibilities of interpretation, and this limitation of interpretative possibilities is what makes literature, unlike politics or journalism, the realm of 'deeper concerns.'" See *Political Fiction and the American Self* (Urbana: University of Illinois Press, 1998), 174.

15. Warren, *The Legacy of the Civil War* (New York: Random House, 1961), 45; hereafter cited in text as *LCW*.

16. Martin Horwitz, *Transformations in American Law, 1870–1960: The Crisis of Legal Orthodoxy* (New York: Oxford University Press, 1992), 254–255.

17. Norman O. Brown, *Love's Body* (Berkeley: University of California Press, 1966), 16, 126. In 1961, Philip Rieff would declare Freud's "primal crime" the "crime to end all crimes." "Society *begins* with a crime," Rieff explains. "Man *begins* as a killer." He adds, "not merely a killer, but a *remorseful* killer"; Rieff, *Freud: The Mind of a Moralist* (New York: Doubleday, 1961), 218. Ernest Gellner thinks Freud's fiction of the primal horde "probably the most important single text for understanding the moral climate of the twentieth century" (93) because it offers a vision of the social contract based not on ideas but on "a pattern of feeling" that transforms psychic ambivalence into a morally binding guilt; Gellner, *Anthropology and Politics: Revolution in the Sacred Grove* (Cambridge, MA: Oxford University Press, 1995), 66, 75.

18. Robert Penn Warren, Floyd Watkins, John Hiers, and Mary Weaks, *Talking with Robert Penn Warren* (Athens: University of Georgia Press, 1990), 46.

19. Sterling Brown suggests a similarity between Mailer and Warren, whom he wryly concludes is, in 1966, "currently the authority on the Civil War and Segregation and, in some quarters, of the Civil Rights Revolution." See Brown, "A Century of Negro Portraiture," *Massachusetts Review* 7, no. 1 (1966): 96.

20. Warren, *Band of Angels* (Baton Rouge: Louisiana State University Press, 1994), 285.

21. Robert Penn Warren, *Conversations with Robert Penn Warren*, ed. Gloria L. Cronin and Ben Siegel (Jackson: University Press of Mississippi, 2005), 55.

22. Warren, *Who Speaks for the Negro?* (New York: Alfred A. Knopf, 1965), 96, 97; hereafter cited in text as *WS*.

23. Forrest G. Robinson, "A Combat with the Past: Robert Penn Warren on Race and Slavery," *American Literature* 67, no. 3 (1995): 524, 515, 517, 525.

24. Mark Tushnet, *The American Law of Slavery, 1800–1860* (Princeton, NJ: Princeton University Press, 1981); Jay Mandel, *Not Slave, Not Free: The African American Economic Experience Since the Civil War* (Durham, NC: Duke University Press, 1992).

25. Godden, *Fictions of Labor: William Faulkner and the South's Long Revolution* (Cambridge: Cambridge University Press, 1997), 115.

26. *Who Owns America?* (Freeport, NY: Books for Libraries Press, 1970), 220.

27. Godden, *Fictions of Labor*, 2, 117.

28. Richard Godden, *An Economy of Complex Words* (Princeton, NJ: Princeton University Press, 2007), 3. As Godden has it, the nature of this whiteface was changing rapidly during the 1930s, when Warren sets his novel. The New Deal was intervening decisively in southern agriculture, with the result that African Americans were beginning to leave southern fields in unprecedented numbers. Burden's melancholia, akin to the kind Godden finds in texts like *Go Down, Moses* and *The Hamlet*, springs from the loss of this constitutive but disavowed labor—from anxiety initiated by the departure of the subaltern population upon whose backs Burden's class first comes into self-consciousness.

29. Frederick Breithut, "Common Wonders," *Railroad Telegrapher* 21, pt. 2 (1904): 1156.

30. Lott, *Love and Theft*, 59, 62, 39.

31. Relevant here is Fredric Jameson's account of Andy Warhol's *Diamond Dust Shoes*. As Jameson has it, Warhol's work "turns centrally around commodification." *Diamond Dust Shoes* does so in part because its color "has been stripped away to reveal the deathly black-and-white substratum of the photographic negative"; Fredric Jameson, *Postmodernism, or, The Cultural Logic of Late Capitalism* (Durham, NC: Duke University Press, 1991), 8–10.

32. Samuel Charters, *A Trumpet Around the Corner: The Story of New Orleans Jazz* (Jackson: University Press of Mississippi, 2008), 31.

33. Jones, *Blues People*, Chapters 6 and 10. On the racial politics of New Orleans jazz, see Charles Hersch, *Subversive Sounds: Race and the Birth of Jazz in New Orleans* (Chicago: University of Chicago Press, 2008). On jazz history and its relation to New Orleans, see Bruce Raeburn, *New Orleans Style and the Writing of American Jazz History* (Ann Arbor: University of Michigan Press, 2009), and Burton Beretti, *The Creation of Jazz: Music, Race, and Culture in Urban America* (Urbana: University of Illinois Press, 1994). On the employment of jazz musicians on riverboats and in New Orleans clubs, see Charters, *A Trumpet Around the Corner*, Chapter 18.

34. Warren, introduction to *All the King's Men*, 1953, v.

35. Kenner, *The Pound Era*, 123.

36. Hemingway, *Death in the Afternoon* (1932; New York: Charles Scribner's, 1999), 154.

37. John Guillory, *Cultural Capital: The Problem of Literary Canon Formation* (Chicago: University of Chicago Press, 1993), 159, 136.

38. Mark Jancovich, *The Cultural Politics of the New Criticism* (Cambridge: Cambridge University Press, 1993), 22.

39. Quoted in Jeffrey Moran, "Reading Race into the Scopes Trial: African-American Elites, Science, and Fundamentalism," *Journal of American History* 90, no. 3 (December 2003): 901.

40. Richard Gray, *Writing the South: Ideas of an American Region* (Baton Rouge: Louisiana State University Press, 1998), 143–145.

41. Jameson, "Reflections in Conclusion," in *Aesthetics and Politics* (London: New Left Books, 1977), 202.

42. Brooks on *I'll Take My Stand*, quoted in Vincent Leitch, ed., *The Norton Anthology of Theory and Criticism* (New York: Norton, 2001); Brooks to Warren in Mark Winchell, *Cleanth Brooks and the Rise of Modern Criticism* (Charlottesville: University of Virginia Press, 1996), 119, 388.

43. Paul Bové, *Mastering Discourse: The Politics of Intellectual Culture* (Durham, NC: Duke University Press, 1992), 126. Thomas Wolfe, *The Web and the Rock* (New York: HarperCollins, 1973), 230. On childhood friend, see Blotner, *Robert Penn Warren*, 25.

44. Jancovich, *The Cultural Politics*, 14. Graff, *Professing Literature* (Chicago: University of Chicago Press, 1987), 146. On the New Critics' embarrassment, see Karen O'Kane, "Before the New Criticism: Modernism and the Nashville Group," *Mississippi Quarterly* 51, no. 4 (Fall 1998): 683–697.

45. Liu, "Understanding Knowledge Work," *Criticism* 47, no. 2 (2006): 255.

46. Ibid., 256.

47. Liu, *The Laws of Cool*, 179; emphasis in original.

48. Kermit Lansner, "Burke, Burke, the Lurk," *Kenyon Review* 13 (1951): 324; Brooks, *The Hidden God*, 4, 7, 117–118.

49. Robert Penn Warren, *New and Selected Essays* (New York: Random House, 1989), 56–58.

50. Invoking a well-worn New Critical tenet, *Democracy and Poetry* attributes this animating capacity to the non-instrumental and self-referring nature of the well-wrought text; it claims that literary "means and ends interpenetrate in a process and in an object which finally embodies its own meaning, *is* its own meaning"; *Democracy and Poetry* (Cambridge, MA: Harvard University Press, 1975), 82; hereafter cited in text as *DP*. Warren describes Stark years earlier as autotelic in an identical way; unlike most individuals, he is "essential" and therefore without "accidental parts." Possessed of an intrinsic design, he stands above fate. Life for individuals like Stark is a process of "discovering what they really are, and not, as for you and me, sons of luck, a process of becoming what luck makes us" (63).

51. Having just visited with representatives of the United States Information Agency in Washington, Trilling wrote a letter to Brooks, dated November 22, 1965 (two months after the NEA received congressional funding), in which he offered to write the *New York Times* urging Johnson to grant the cultural attachés more funds and "the rank of Minister"; Lionel Trilling Papers, Columbia University 10267 (1979)/Brooks, Cleanth V.p. 1965–1969.

52. *Papers of Lyndon B. Johnson*, 1965:732.

53. Cited in Deak Nabers, "Past Using: James Baldwin and Civil Rights Law in the 1960s," *Countercultural Capital: Essays of the Sixties from Some Who Weren't There*, ed. Sean McCann and Michael Szalay, special issue, *Yale Journal of Criticism* 18, no. 2 (Fall 2005): 221–242, 229.

54. For an elaboration of this claim with respect to James Baldwin, see ibid.

55. *Segregation: The Inner Conflict in the South*, in *Reporting Civil Rights, Part One, American Journalism, 1941–1963* (New York: Library of America, 2003), 284, 330, 320, 321.

56. http://www.neh.gov/whoweare/jefflect.html.

57. Lionel Trilling, *The Liberal Imagination* (New York: NYRB Classics, 2008), 94.

58. Marcus Klein, *Foreigners: The Making of American Literature, 1900–1940* (Chicago: University of Chicago Press, 1981), 101.

59. William Blake, *The Marriage of Heaven and Hell*, intro. Geoffrey Keynes (Oxford: Oxford University Press, 1975), 56.

60. Lionel Trilling, *The Moral Obligation to Be Intelligent: Selected Essays*, ed. Leon Wieseltier (Chicago: Northwestern University Press, 2009), 491–493.

Chapter 2

1. Mailer, *Presidential Papers*, 40.

2. Brossard, *Who Walk in Darkness* (New York: Herodias, 2000), 115.

3. Wolfe, *Memoirs of a Not Altogether Shy Pornographer* (New York: Doubleday, 1972), 148.

4. Riesman, Glazer, and Denney, *The Lonely Crowd*, xxxiv, 208–209, 250, 164.

5. Pells, *The Liberal Mind in a Conservative Age: American Intellectuals in the 1940s* (Middletown, CT: Wesleyan University Press, 1989), 248, 243.

6. Hofstadter, "The Pseudo-Conservative Revolt," in *The Radical Right*, ed. Daniel Bell (New Brunswick, NJ: Transaction Publishers, 2001), 84.

7. Saul, *Freedom Is, Freedom Ain't*, 45.

8. *Dictionary of Literary Biography*, vol. 16, *The Beats: Literary Bohemians in Postwar America* (Detroit: Gale Group, 1983), 43–45.

9. See Kenneth C. Davis, *Two-Bit Culture: The Paperbacking of America* (Boston: Houghton Mifflin, 1984).

10. Anatole Broyard, *When Kafka Was the Rage: A Greenwich Village Memoir* (New York: Vintage, 1993), 28.

11. Ondaatje, *Coming Through Slaughter* (New York: Vintage, 1996), 8.

12. "Dizzy Gillespie's Style, Its Meaning Analyzed," *Down Beat* 13 (February 11, 1946): 14.

13. Ross, *No Respect*, 69–70.

14. For an excellent account of Broyard, see Philip Ford, "Somewhere/Nowhere: Hipness as an Aesthetic," *Musical Quarterly* 86, no. 1 (Spring 2002): 49–81.

15. Hemingway, *The Sun Also Rises* (New York: Scribner, 2006), 153.

16. Broyard, "A Portrait of the Hipster," reprinted in *The Scene Before You: A New Approach to American Culture*, ed. Chandler Brossard (New York: Rinehart, 1955), 116, 113. Reisner's essay collected in Andrew Clark, ed., *Riffs and Choruses: A New Jazz Anthology* (New York: Continuum, 2001), 335.

17. Mezzrow and Bernard Wolfe, *Really the Blues* (New York: Citadel, 1946), 53; Herbert Gold, *The Age of Happy Problems* (Piscataway, NJ: Transaction, 2002), 83; Broyard, "A Portrait," 113–114; Clark, *Riffs and Choruses*, 335.

18. Theodor Adorno, Walter Benjamin, *The Complete Correspondence, 1928–1940*,

ed. Henri Lonitz, trans. Nicholas Walker (Cambridge, MA: Harvard University Press, 2001), 321.

19. Broyard, *When Kafka Was the Rage*, 29–30.

20. Brossard was close enough to Broyard to know his secret: he had been the best man at his wedding. See Henry Louis Gates, "The Passing of Anatole Broyard," in *Thirteen Ways of Looking at a Black Man* (New York: Random House, 1997), 180–214.

21. See Gerald M. Boyd, *My Times in Black and White: Race and Power at the "New York Times"* (New York: Lawrence Hill, 2010).

22. Irving Howe, *A World More Attractive* (New York: Horizon Press, 1963), 67, 65, 68.

23. On this claim, see Walter Michaels, *Our America* (Durham, NC: Duke University Press, 1997).

24. For a fuller version of this claim, see my "Modernism's History of the Dead," in *Blackwell Concise Companion to American Writing, 1900–1950*, ed. Peter Stoneley and Cindy Weinstein (Oxford: Blackwell, 2008), 158–185.

25. On Hemingway and taxidermy, see Richard Godden, *Fictions of Capital: The American Novel from James to Mailer* (New York: Cambridge University Press, 1990).

26. Steinbeck, *The Grapes of Wrath* (New York: Penguin, 2006), 214; Steinbeck, *The Harvest Gypsies: On the Road to the Grapes of Wrath*, intro. Charles Wollenberg (Berkeley, CA: Heyday Books, 2002), xi.

27. Ross, *No Respect*, 85.

28. Cited in Milton Klein, *The Empire State: A History of New York* (Ithaca, NY: Cornell University Press, 2005), 667.

29. Reich, *The Greening of America* (New York: Random House, 1970), 325; *Time*, quoted in Orrin Klapp, *Inflation of Symbols: Loss of Values in American Culture* (New Brunswick, NJ: Transaction Publishers, 1991), 30.

30. Anderson, *Deep River* (Durham, NC: Duke University Press, 2001), 131. *New Republic*, quoted in Geoffrey C. Ward and Ken Burns, *Jazz: A History of America's Music* (New York: Knopf, 2005), 240; Brown, cited in Arthur Knight, *Disintegrating the Musical: Black Performance and American Musical Film* (Durham, NC: Duke University Press, 2002), 200.

31. Penny Marie Von Eschen, *Satchmo Blows Up the World* (Cambridge, MA: Harvard University Press, 2004), 34; Saul, *Freedom Is, Freedom Ain't*, 15, emphasis in original; Willis Conover, "Who Is Conover? Only We Ask," *New York Times Magazine*, September 13, 1959; Lisa Davenport, *Jazz Diplomacy: Promoting America in the Cold War Era* (Jackson: University Press of Mississippi, 2009), 147.

32. Gillespie, quoted in Ingrid Monson, "The Problem with White Hipness: Race, Gender, and Cultural Conceptions in Jazz Historical Discourse," *Journal of the American Musicological Society* 48, no. 3 (Fall 1995): 409. As Coleridge Goode recalled, "It was the bebop tradition to freeze out strangers" (cited in Leland, *Hip*, 135). Ford, "Somewhere/ Nowhere," 73.

33. Panetta, *Viva Madison Avenue!* (New York: Harcourt Brace, 1957), 3.

34. Hemingway, *Death in the Afternoon*, 266.

35. Kennedy, *Profiles in Courage* (New York: Harper Perennial, 2004), 1.

36. Cited in Gerring, *Party Ideologies*, 287.

37. Cohn, *The Fabulous Democrats*, 8.

38. Norman Mailer, *Miami and the Siege of Chicago* (New York: NYRB Classics, 2008), 20; hereafter cited in text as *MSC*.

39. Austin, *How to Do Things with Words*, 99–100.

40. Charles, quoted in Glenn Altschuler, *All Shook Up: How Rock 'n' Roll Changed America* (New York: Oxford University Press, 2003), 51.

41. See Larry Bartels, *Unequal Democracy: The Political Economy of the New Gilded Age* (Princeton, NJ: Princeton University Press, 2010), 77.

42. Goodwin, quoted in Jon Bradshaw, "Richard Goodwin: The Good, the Bad, and the Ugly," *New York Magazine*, August 18, 1975, 41.

Chapter 3

1. Riesman, Glazer, and Denney, *The Lonely Crowd*, 189.

2. See Kathleen Hall Jamieson, *Packaging the Presidency: A History and Criticism of Presidential Campaign Advertising* (New York: Oxford University Press, 1996).

3. See Judith Trent and Robert Friedenberg, *Political Campaign Communication: Principles and Practices* (New York: Rowman and Littlefield, 2007), 384.

4. Schneider, *The Golden Kazoo* (New York: Rinehart, 1956), 71.

5. See Macdonald, "Masscult and Midcult," in *The New York Intellectuals Reader*, ed. Neil Jumonville (New York: Routledge, 2007).

6. Andrew Hacker, *American Political Science Review* 51 (1957): 1015. Baltzell liked the fact that Hacker thought structures of deference important to liberalism. He thinks Hacker's liberalism is "gentlemanly" and not, as is typical, a form of "human engineering." Baltzell and Howard Schneiderman, *Judgment and Sensibility: Religion and Stratification* (New Brunswick, NJ: Transaction Publishers, 1994), 172.

7. Bell, *The Cultural Contradictions of Capitalism* (New York: McGraw-Hill, 1976), 71–72. Susman, *Culture as History: The Transformation of American Society in the Twentieth Century* (New York: Pantheon, 1984), xxiv, xxviii.

8. Mailer, *Of a Fire on the Moon* (New York: Little, Brown, 1971), 10.

9. Broyard, "A Portrait of the Hipster," 116; Broyard, "Keep Cool, Man," *Commentary* 11 (1951): 361.

10. Stephen Fox, *The Mirror Makers: A History of American Advertising and Its Creators* (Urbana: University of Illinois Press, 1997), 273.

11. See Frank, *The Conquest of Cool*, 69, 68. For a response to Frank that is sympathetic to the advertising industry, see Joseph Heath, "The Structure of Hip Consumerism," *Philosophy and Social Criticism* 27, no. 6 (2001): 1–17.

12. Frank, The *Conquest of Cool*, 31.

13. Elizabeth Cohen, *A Consumer's Republic: The Politics of Mass Consumption in Postwar America* (New York: Knopf, 2003), 295.

14. Ibid., 301.

15. Cited in William Leiss, Stephen Kline, Sut Jhally, and Jacqueline Botterill, eds., *Social Communication in Advertising: Consumption in the Mediated Marketplace*, 3rd ed. (New York: Routledge, 2005), 319.

16. Jones, *Blues People*, 100, 101, 129.

17. Fox, *The Mirror Makers*, 278

18. Cohen, *A Consumer's Republic*, 299, 324, 325, 327.

19. Jason Chambers, *Madison Avenue and the Color Line: African Americans in the Advertising Industry* (Philadelphia: University of Pennsylvania Press, 2008), 120; Ellison, *Three Days Before the Shooting . . .* (New York: Random House, 2010), 46–47.

20. Klonsky, *A Discourse on Hip: The Selected Writings of Milton Klonsky* (Detroit: Wayne State University Press, 1991), 137.

21. See Todd Pittinsky and Laura Maruskin, "Allophilia, Beyond Tolerance," in *Positive Psychology: Exploring the Best in People*, vol. 1, *Developing Human Strengths*, ed. Shane Lopez (Westport, CT: Praeger, 2008).

22. Cited in Jeffrey Meikle, *Twentieth Century Limited: Industrial Design in America, 1925–1939* (Philadelphia: Temple University Press, 2001), 10.

23. Altschuler, *All Shook Up*, 50.

24. Rothenberg, *Where the Suckers Moon: The Life and Death of an Advertising Campaign* (New York: Vintage, 1995), 66.

25. Ross, *No Respect*, 96, 71.

26. See, for example, Susan Gubar, *Racechanges: White Skin, Black Face in American Culture* (New York: Oxford University Press, 1997), 45.

27. Nathan Hare, *The Black Anglo-Saxons* (New York: Marzani and Munsell, 1965), 15, 16.

28. For a relevant analysis of the phrase "African American," see Toni Morrison, *Playing in the Dark: Whiteness and the Literary Imagination* (New York: Vintage, 1993).

29. What it meant to be "black" or "Negro" would change. Hare issued his study one year before Stokely Carmichael proposed the term "Black Power." Carmichael aimed to consolidate a nationalist movement that would reject the epithet "Negro." Part of that movement, John Oliver Killens thought "the American Negro" was "an Anglo-Saxon invention, a role the Anglo-Saxon gentleman created for the black man." Preferable were designations like "black" and "African American." These new monikers were different from Hare's. Carmichael's "Black" is both an adjective and an exclusive identity category; the same is the case with "African" in "African American": it makes as little sense, given these terms, to speak of becoming black as it does to speak of becoming of African descent. Killens, quoted in Alexs D. Pate, foreword to John Oliver Killens, *The Cotillion: or One Good Bull Is Half the Herd* (New York: Coffee House Press, 2002), xi.

30. Richard Condon, *The Manchurian Candidate* (New York: Jove, 1988), 51.

31. Greil Marcus, *The Manchurian Candidate* (London: British Film Institute, 2002), 15.

32. For an account of the film's distribution history, see J. Hoberman, *Dream Life: Movies, Media, and the Mythology of the Sixties* (New York: New Press, 2003).

33. Richard Hofstadter, *The Paranoid Style in American Politics* (New York: Knopf, 1965).

34. Richard Condon, *And Then We Moved to Rossenarra; or, The Art of Emigrating* (New York: Dial, 1973), 267, 8, 201.

35. Packard, cited in *Cultural Studies* 5, no. 2 (1991), ed. Lawrence Grossberg and Janice Radway. Elaborating on Condon's response to Packard, Matthew Jacobson and Gaspar González describe Shaw as "the automaton as hero," in *What Have They Built You to Do? The Manchurian Candidate and Cold War America* (Minneapolis: University of Minnesota Press, 2006), 48.

36. Jack Kerouac, *Dharma Bums* (New York: Penguin, 1971), 29.

37. Gold, *The Age of Happy Problems*, 87. As Norman Mailer puts it in 1957, hip language resembles abstract painting; it "is a pictorial language, but pictorial like non-objective art." It represents "immediate experiences . . . abstractly" as a "vector in a network of forces." Rather than being simply "static," "hip is a language of energy, how it is found, how it is lost" (*A* 348–349). Mailer would have known that these claims echoed Ezra Pound on the Chinese written character. As Pound had put it in 1913, "The thing that matters in art is . . . energy." The Chinese written character was to Pound "pictorial like non-objective art." Hugh Kenner (*The Pound Era*) notes that the Chinese written character struck Pound as "a picture of an active thing" (159) and therefore crystallized his belief that "energy creates pattern" and that "emotion is an organizer of form" (146). Working in "composition à la mode *chinoise*," Pound advanced what Kenner calls the "*Ars Poetica* of our time" (230).

38. Updike, *Rabbit, Run*, 45, 63.

39. See Jacobson and González, *What Have They Built You to Do?*, 19, 10.

40. Christopher Matthews, *Kennedy and Nixon* (New York: Free Press, 1997), 152.

41. See Philip J. Deloria, *Playing Indian* (New Haven, CT: Yale University Press, 1999).

42. Marcus, *Candidate*, 28.

43. On the fellaheen, see Stephen Prothero, "On the Holy Road: The Beat Movement as Spiritual Protest," *Harvard Theological Review* 84 (1991); Cassady, quoted in Neal Cassady, *Collected Letters, 1944–1967*, ed. Dave Moore (New York: Penguin, 2005), 206.

44. Kevin Phillips, interview with James Boyd, *New York Times Magazine*, May 17, 1970.

45. Hoffman, "The New Niggers," in Hoffman, *Revolution for the Hell of It* (New York: Thunder's Mouth Press, 2005), 71, 74, 76.

46. On McLendon, see Gina Caponi-Tabery, *Jump for Joy: Basketball and Black Culture in 1930s America* (Amherst: University of Massachusetts Press, 2008), 85; Podhoretz, *Doings and Undoings: The Fifties and After in American Writing* (New York: FSG, 1964), 367.

47. On Kerouac, see Updike, *Conversations with John Updike*, ed. James Plath (Jackson: University Press of Mississippi, 1994), 17; hereafter cited in text as *CU*. On the title of *Rabbit, Run*, see Updike, *Rabbit Angstrom: The Four Novels* (New York: Knopf, 1995), x.

48. Altschuler, *All Shook Up*, 176.

49. Charlie Gillett, *The Sound of the City: The Rise of Rock and Roll* (Cambridge, MA: Da Capo Press, 1996), 207.

50. Updike, *The Early Stories: 1953–1975* (New York: Random House, 2004), 151.

51. Rabbit lives in a fictionalized suburb of Reading, Pennsylvania (Brewer), and such suburbs were crucial to Kennedy's victory. See Earle and Merle Black, *Divided America: The Ferocious Power Struggle in American Politics* (New York: Simon and Schuster, 2008), 100. For a breakdown of how Pennsylvania counties voted in 1960, see http://www.uselectionatlas.org/RESULTS/datagraph.php?year=1960&fips=42&f=0&off=0&elect=0; on the origins of Diamond County and Brewer, see Jack De Bellis, *The Up-dike Encyclopedia* (Westport, CT: Greenwood, 2000), 138, 374; on the role of religion in the 1960 Pennsylvania election, see Albert J. Menendez, *The Religious Factor in the 1960 Election: An Analysis of the Kennedy Victory over Anti-Catholic Prejudice* (Jefferson, NC: McFarland, 2011), Chapter 6.

Chapter 4

Portions of this chapter appeared as "Ralph Ellison's Unfinished Second Skin," *American Literary History* 23, no. 4 (Fall 2011).

1. Box I:164, Folder 16, Ellison Papers, Manuscript Division, Library of Congress, Washington, DC.

2. Ellison to Albert Murray, in *Trading Twelves: The Selected Letters of Ralph Ellison and Albert Murray*, ed. John F. Callahan (New York: Modern Library, 2000), 197–198.

3. Ellison, *Three Days Before the Shooting . . .* (New York: Random House, 2010), 1099.

4. Ellison, *Collected Essays of Ralph Ellison*, 118.

5. Saul, *Freedom Is, Freedom Ain't*, 69.

6. Mailer, "Superman Comes to the Supermarket," 44, 31.

7. Kenneth Warren, *So Black and Blue: Ralph Ellison and the Occasion of Criticism* (Chicago: University of Chicago Press, 2003), 21.

8. Ellison, *Invisible Man* (New York: Vintage, 1995), 33.

9. On *Invisible Man* in light of the period's preoccupation with office work, see Andrew Hoberek, *Twilight of the Middle Class: Post–World War II American Fiction and White-Collar Work* (Princeton, NJ: Princeton University Press, 2005).

10. Cited in Ralph Ellison, *Living with Music*, ed. Robert O'Meally (New York: Modern Library, 2001), xxviii, 244, 245, 247; hereafter cited in text as *LM*.

11. As Ken Warren might put it, Ellison valued the blues and swing because, unlike bebop, they expressed a specifically "Negro" sensibility. See Warren, *So Black and Blue*.

12. Warren, "Chaos Not Quite Controlled: Ellison's Uncompleted Transit to *June-teenth*," in *The Cambridge Companion to Ralph Ellison*, ed. Ross Posnock (Cambridge: Cambridge University Press, 2005), 199.

13. Mezzrow, quoted in Gayle Wald, *Crossing the Line: Racial Passing in 20th Century U.S. Literature and Culture* (Durham, NC: Duke University Press, 2000), 57. John Howard Griffin, *Black Like Me* (New York: Signet, 1962), 15–16.

14. James Baldwin, *The Fire Next Time* (New York: Vintage, 1993), 104; Norman Podhoretz, *The Norman Podhoretz Reader: A Selection of His Writings from the 1950s*, ed. Thomas Jeffers (New York: Free Press, 2003), 64.

15. Ross, *No Respect*, 82–83.

16. Cited in Larry Neal, "Ellison's Zoot Suit," in *Ralph Ellison's Invisible Man: A Casebook*, ed. John Callahan (New York: Oxford University Press, 2004), 92.

17. See Arnold Rampersad, *Ralph Ellison: A Biography* (New York: Knopf, 2007), 39.

18. Lott, *Love and Theft*, 98.

19. Box I:126, Folder 8, Ellison Papers.

20. Box II:53, Folder 8, Ellison Papers.

21. Theodor Adorno and Walter Benjamin, *The Complete Correspondence, 1928–1940*, ed. Henri Lonitz, trans. Nicholas Walker (Cambridge, MA: Harvard University Press, 2001), 321.

22. Timothy Bewes, *Reification, or The Anxiety of Late Capitalism* (New York: Verso, 2002), 211.

23. See Saul, *Freedom Is, Freedom Ain't*, 155, 168, 152, 151; O'Meally suggests that Mingus might be a model for Minifees in *Living with Music*, 214.

24. Box I:116, Folder 1, Ellison Papers.

25. For Kennedy's relation to Jews, see Herbert Druks, *John F. Kennedy and Israel* (New York: Praeger, 2005). For Kennedy's relation to regional interests, see Sean Savage, *JFK, LBJ, and the Democratic Party* (Albany: State University of New York Press, 2004), 19, 44.

26. David Pietrusza, *1960: LBJ vs. JFK vs. Nixon* (New York: Union Square, 2008), 292–293; http://www.livingroomcandidate.org/commercials/1960.

27. *Negro Digest* 11, no. 1 (November 1961): 46.

28. Jameson, *Valences of the Dialectic* (New York: Verso, 2009), 56, 50, 17.

29. Ibid., 17, 20.

30. Cited in Savage, *JFK, LBJ*, 36.

31. Lawrence Jackson, *Ralph Ellison: The Emergence of Genius* (New York: Wiley and Sons, 2002), 217; Rampersad, *Ralph Ellison*, 332.

32. Perlstein, *Before the Storm* (New York: Hill and Wang, 2001), 47, 135.

33. See William Duiker, *The Communist Road to Power in Vietnam* (Boulder, CO: Westview Press, 1996), 36.

Chapter 5

1. *Lay My Burden Down: A Folk History of Slavery*, ed. B. A. Botkin (Chicago: University of Chicago Press, 1945), ix.

2. Ibid., ix, xiii; Jerre Mangione, *Dream and the Deal* (New York: Little, Brown, 1972), 270.

3. See Joanne Gabbin, *Sterling Brown: Building the Black Aesthetic Tradition* (Charlottesville: University of Virginia Press, 1994), 73.

4. Considerable bias and abuse existed on the projects. John A. Lomax was the first director of the Folklore Division. He claimed to have "discovered" Huddie Ledbetter, a.k.a. Lead Belly. When Lomax met him, the folksinger was incarcerated and about to be released. Lomax deceived Ledbetter into believing that he had secured his parole and

then hired him to be his driver and help negotiate the "seamy side of Negro life" in the cities they visited together. See Nolan Porterfield, *Last Cavalier: The Life and Times of John A. Lomax* (Urbana: University of Illinois Press, 1996), 170, 301, 330–331.

5. WPA Records, Record Group 69/8. National Archives.

6. On the relation between the Folklore Project and African American votes for Roosevelt, see Guido van Rijn, *Roosevelt's Blues: African American Music and Gospel Songs on FDR* (Jackson: University Press of Mississippi, 1997), xvii.

7. Jack Balch, *Lamps at High Noon*, ed. Michael Szalay (Urbana: University of Illinois Press, 2000), 35.

8. Michael Sandel, "The Procedural Republic and the Unencumbered Self," in *Twentieth-Century Political Theory*, ed. Stephen Eric Bonner (New York: Routledge, 1997), 81.

9. See Lauren Sklaroff, *Black Culture and the New Deal: The Quest for Civil Rights in the Roosevelt Era* (Chapel Hill: University of North Carolina Press, 2009), Chapter 1.

10. See, for example, A. A. M. van der Linden, *A Revolt Against Liberalism: American Radical Historians, 1959–1976* (Atlanta: Editions Rodopi, B.V., 1996), 194.

11. See Sklaroff, *Black Culture*, 15, 143. See also van Rijn, *Roosevelt's Blues*.

12. For a useful summary of that debate, see Brendon O'Connor, *A Political History of the American Welfare System: When Ideas Have Consequences* (New York: Rowman and Littlefield, 2003), Chapter 9.

13. Two novels exemplify that shift. In 1966, Margaret Walker published *Jubilee*, about a black woman living in Georgia just before and after the American Civil War. Walker had worked for the Illinois Works Progress Administration and her novel captured the spirit that animated the WPA's collection of slave narratives. Based on oral histories and preoccupied with folkways, it was, like the narratives, history from the bottom up; as the book jacket declared, *Jubilee* was "steeped in knowledge of and feeling for . . . the people." At the same time, Walker drew on years of archival research while writing a novel committed "to showing the interrelationships of class as well as race and . . . how these interrelationships shape the political, economic, and social structure in the entire panorama of the novel." A work of social realism, *Jubilee* situates individuals with respect to impersonal structural forces over which they have no control. The novel was heavily indebted to Georg Lukács, whom Walker admired; according to Hazel Carby, Lukács inspired Walker "to fuse popular memory with her extensive historical research in order to represent the transformations of history as the transformations of popular life" (quoted in Hazel Carby, *Cultures in Babylon: Black Britain and African America* [London: Verso, 1999], 149, 154, 152). As Carby has it, *Jubilee* failed to resonate with readers in part because of its debt to the thirties. Committed to the analysis of economic forces, it "entered the cultural conditions of 1966" with what by the standards of the moment seemed "a severely limited historical, psychological and aesthetic vision of the possibilities of a free black community." In this, Carby agrees with Hortense Spillers (154).

A colleague of Walker's on the Illinois WPA, Arna Bontemps published a novel about slavery that was also based on oral traditions and slave narratives. But though published in 1936, and thus thirty years removed from Walker's, this novel was closer to the heart of sixties-era cultural nationalism, in style, subject matter, and gender orientation. In fragmented interior monologues and from multiple points of view, Bontemps's *Black Thunder* describes an 1800 slave revolt in Virginia. Writing a preface for a new edition in 1968, Bontemps acknowledged his novel's currency. He tells us that he wrote his tale in Watts, California, and speculates that had Watts erupted in violence when *Black Thunder* was first issued, as opposed to in 1965, "more readers might then have been in a mood to hear a tale of volcanic rumblings among angry blacks—and the end of patience." According to Bontemps, "the theme of self-assertion by black men whose endurance was strained to the breaking point was not one that readers were prepared [then] to contemplate," as they very much were in 1968. (Bontemps, *Black Thunder: Gabriel's Revolt: Virginia, 1800* [Boston: Beacon Press, 1992], xxiii).

14. Leland, *Hip*, 116.

15. Quoted in DeVeaux, *The Birth of Bebop*, 24.

16. Steven Brint argues that professionals move leftward during periods of intense social change. But they also tend to move back to the center during periods of prosperity and, in fact, did vote with managers and businessmen during the fifties; Brint, *In an Age of Experts: The Changing Role of Professionals in Politics and Public Life* (Princeton, NJ: Princeton University Press), 104.

17. Schlesinger, "The Future of the Democratic Party," *New York Magazine*, November 4, 1968, 23.

18. C. Wright Mills, *White Collar: The American Middle Class* (New York: Oxford University Press, 1951), 114, 113.

19. White, *The Making of the President, 1960*, 222.

20. For Talcott Parsons on professionals, see Howard Brick, *Transcending Capitalism: Visions of a New Society in Modern American Thought* (Ithaca, NY: Cornell University Press, 2006), 132–135; Brint, *Age of Experts*, 42–43; Louis Menand, *Discovering Modernism: T. S. Eliot and His Context* (Oxford: Oxford University Press, 1987), 114. On the role of professionalism in postwar literature, see Stephen Schryer, *Fantasies of the New Class: Ideologies of Professionalism in Post-War American Fiction* (New York: Columbia University Press, 2011).

21. Bernard Wolfe, "Ecstatic in Blackface: The Negro as Song-and-Dance Man," in Brossard, *The Scene Before You*, 51, 53.

22. Jameson, "The Vanishing Mediator," in *The Ideologies of Theory: Essays 1971–1986*, vol. 2, *Syntax of History* (Minneapolis: University of Minnesota Press, 1988), 34.

23. Cited in Schryer, *Fantasies of the New Class*, 26.

24. Meier, *A White Scholar in the Black Community, 1945–1965: Essays and Reflections* (Amherst: University of Massachusetts Press, 1992), 207.

25. Broyard, "A Portrait," 119.

26. Tom Wolfe, *Radical Chic and Mau-Mauing the Flak Catchers* (New York: Bantam, 1971), 109, 147, 161.

27. The Mario Savio quote is from Larry Spence, "Berkeley: What It Demonstrates," in *Revolution at Berkeley*, ed. Michael Miller and Susan Gilmore (New York: Dell, 1965), 220; Herbert Marcuse, *One-Dimensional Man: Studies in the Ideology of Advanced Industrial Society*, 2nd ed. (Boston: Beacon Press, 1991), 1. On the pathos surrounding downward middle-class mobility during the same period, see Hoberek, *Twilight of the Middle Class*; and Catherine Jurca, *White Diaspora: The Suburb and the Twentieth-Century American Novel* (Princeton, NJ: Princeton University Press, 2001).

28. *Conversations with William Styron*, ed. James L. W. West (Jackson: University Press of Mississippi, 1985), 46; hereafter cited in text as *CWS*.

29. Karl Marx, *Economic and Philosophical Manuscripts of 1844*, trans. M. Milligan, ed. Dirk Struik (New York: International Publishers, 1964), 128.

30. Liu, *The Laws of Cool*, 82, 81, 84–85, 43.

31. Barbara Ehrenreich and John Ehrenreich, "The Professional-Managerial Class," in *Between Labor and Capital*, ed. Pat Walker (Boston: South End Press, 1999), 12; Barbara Ehrenreich, *Fear of Falling* (New York: Pantheon, 1989), 153.

32. Martin Luther King Jr., *The Papers of Martin Luther King, Jr.*, vol. 6, *Advocate of the Social Gospel, September 1948–March 1964* (Berkeley: University of California Press, 2007), 168.

33. Richard Poirier, *A World Elsewhere: The Place of Style in American Literature* (Madison: University of Wisconsin Press, 1985), 4.

34. Ferenczi, cited in Eli Zaretsky, *Secrets of the Soul: A Social and Cultural History of Psychoanalysis* (New York: Vintage, 2004), 89.

35. John Berryman, "The Imaginary Jew," *Kenyon Review* 8, no. 4 (1945): 539. As Andrew Gross puts it, "It was widely assumed in mid-century psychological theories that prejudice turns its object into an inverted mirror, simultaneously reflecting and alienating those aspects of personality the bigot is incapable of facing in himself." Gross, "Imaginary Jews and True Confessions," *Journal of Transnational American Studies* 1, no. 1 (2009).

36. Styron, *The Confessions of Nat Turner* (New York: Vintage, 1992), 435.

37. George Steiner described *Nat Turner* as "less an anatomy of the Negro mind than a fiction . . . of the relationship between a present day white man of deep Southern roots and the Negro in today's whirlwind"; "The Fire Last Time," in *The Critical Response to William Styron*, ed. Daniel W. Ross (Westport, CT: Greenwood, 1995), 123.

38. John Lewis, cited in Van Gosse, *The Movements of the New Left, 1950–1975* (New York: Palgrave Macmillan, 2005), 77.

39. Malcolm X and Alex Haley, *The Autobiography of Malcolm X* (New York: Ballantine, 1999), 191; Addison Gayle, "Nat Turner vs. Black Nationalists," *Liberator* 8 (February 1968): 44; Larry Neal, "The Black Arts Movement," in *Visions of a Liberated Future: Black Arts Movement Writings*, ed. Michael Schwartz (New York: Thunder's Mouth Press, 1989), 72; Eldridge Cleaver, *Soul on Ice* (New York: McGraw-Hill, 1968), 110. On Turner's relation to the literary imagination of the civil rights era, see Eric Sundquist, "1855 / 1955: From Antislavery to Civil Rights," in *Frederick Douglass and*

Herman Melville: Essays in Relation, ed. Robert Levine and Samuel Otter (Chapel Hill: University of North Carolina Press, 2008). Also see Albert E. Stone, *The Return of Nat Turner: History, Literature, and Cultural Politics in Sixties America* (Athens: University of Georgia Press, 1992).

40. Harper Lee, *To Kill a Mockingbird* (New York: HarperCollins, 2006), 42.

41. William Styron, *Havanas in Camelot* (New York: Random House, 2008), 122; hereafter cited in text as *HC*.

42. *William Styron's Nat Turner: Ten Black Writers Respond,* ed. John Henrik Clarke (Boston: Beacon Press, 1968), 43–44; hereafter cited in text as *TBW*.

43. Styron, *Set This House on Fire* (New York: Vintage, 1993), 116.

44. Anthony Stewart makes a similar point. See his "William TurnerGrayStyron, Novelist(s): Reactivating State Power in *The Confessions of Nat Turner,*" *Studies in the Novel* 27, no. 2 (Summer 1995): 169–185.

45. On Turner's relation to Elkins, see Tim Ryan, *Calls and Responses: The American Novel of Slavery Since Gone with the Wind* (Baton Rouge: Louisiana State University Press, 2008).

46. See William Andrews, *To Tell a Free Story* (Urbana: University of Illinois Press, 1986), 107.

47. Ibid.

48. See Mica Hilson, "Slave Subjectivity and Narrative Voice," *Literary Griot* 14, nos. 1–2 (Spring/Fall 2003): 110.

49. Ralph Tutt sees Styron responding to Mailer's accusations throughout his career. See his "Stingo's Complaint: Styron and the Politics of Self-Parody," *Modern Fiction Studies* 34, no. 4 (Winter 1988): 584.

50. Styron's biographer suggests that the author modeled Turner on Baldwin: the novel "was an attempt to represent the common history of black and white people, but on another and more private level, it was 'our' history, the history of two individual men—Baldwin's and Styron's together." See James L. W. West III, *William Styron: A Life* (New York: Random House, 1998), 336–337.

51. Hal Bennett, *Lord of Dark Places* (New York: Turtle Point Press, 1997), 21, 36, 284.

52. Reading the sequence of events leading to Jill's fellatio, Sean McCann sees Rabbit as a "Presidential" figure able to absorb the violent tensions of the nation. A latter-day Abraham Lincoln, McCann's Rabbit absorbs and allays the suffering of others. See McCann's impressive study, *A Pinnacle of Feeling: American Literature and Presidential Government* (Princeton, NJ: Princeton University Press, 2008), 161.

53. See Sally Robinson, *Marked Men: White Masculinity in Crisis* (New York: Columbia University Press, 2000), 38.

54. On Styron and Johnson, see Raymond Sokolov, "Into the Mind of Nat Turner," *Newsweek,* October 16, 1967, 65–69. On Styron and McCarthy, see West, *A Life,* 382–383.

55. Lott, *Love and Theft,* 111.

56. Alexander Saxton, *The Rise and Fall of the White Republic: Class Politics and Mass Culture in Nineteenth-Century America* (New York: Verso, 1990), 165, 175, 176.

57. C. Vann Woodward, "The Chaotic Politics of the South," *New York Review*, December 17, 1972, 37.

58. Stevenson, cited in Richard Rubin, *Party Dynamics: The Democratic Coalition and the Politics of Change* (New York: Oxford University Press, 1976), 124.

59. See Rick Perlstein, *Nixonland: The Rise of a President and the Fracturing of America* (New York: Scribner, 2008), 6.

60. Ibid., 151. By September 1966, more than half of those in the North thought the president was pushing integration too quickly. See Richard M. Scammon and Ben J. Wattenberg, *The Real Majority* (New York: Coward-McCann, 1970), 116.

61. Doug McAdam, *Political Process and the Development of Black Insurgency, 1930–1970* (Chicago: University of Chicago Press, 1982), 195.

62. See Benjamin Ginsberg and Alan Stone, *Do Elections Matter?* (New York: M. E. Sharpe, 1996), 9–11. On voter demographics before 1968, see Alan Ware, *The Democratic Party Heads North, 1877–1962* (Cambridge: Cambridge University Press, 2006).

Chapter 6

1. Charles Shaar Murray, *Crosstown Traffic: Jimi Hendrix and the Post-war Rock 'n' Roll Revolution* (New York: St. Martin's Griffin, 1991), 78.

2. Presley, Lennon, and Berry, quoted in Altschuler, *All Shook Up*, 30, 167, 63.

3. V. N. Volosinov, *Freudianism: A Marxist Critique*, trans. I. R. Titunk (New York: Academic Press, 1976), 113.

4. Norman Mailer, *Why Are We in Vietnam?* (New York: Picador, 2000), 4–5.

5. Doctorow, *The Book of Daniel* (New York: Random House, 2007), 94.

6. Richard Poirier, *Norman Mailer* (New York: Viking, 1972), 86. Poirier's is perhaps the best study of Mailer yet written.

7. Millett, *Sexual Politics*, 334. Germaine Greer offered an apt evaluation of Mailer's tendency to see "his spirit as a triumvirate of phallus, ego and talent." Dismissing his archaic celebrations of motherhood and femininity, she wrote, "To an abused woman it is a bitter blasphemy to explain, as Mailer would, that her humiliation is enacted simply to prove the 'power and glory of the grandeur of the female in the universe' for she feels only the female in her debased self. What does it mean to the woman raped and bashed to learn that her assailant did it to show that the power of the feminine 'can survive any context or abuse'? Not that it's even unusual—many a rapist says 'I love you'"; Germaine Greer, "My Mailer Problem" (1971), reprinted in *The Madwoman's Underclothes: Essays and Occasional Writings* (New York: Atlantic Monthly Press, 1990), 82, 83.

8. James Baldwin, "The Black Boy Looks at the White Boy," *Nobody Knows My Name*, in *Collected Essays*, 269–270.

9. *Nation*, January 1957, 361.

10. My analysis accords with Thomas Schaub's claim that the "antisocial behavior" of Mailer's hipster "has liberal, socially responsible effects surprisingly in harmony with the assumptions and biases of consensus discourse." See Schaub, *American Fiction in the Cold War* (Madison: University of Wisconsin Press, 1991), 160.

11. Kaufman, "Catch-23: The Mystery of Fact (Norman Mailer's Final Novel?)," *Twentieth-Century Literature* 17, no. 4 (October 1971): 249; final quote, 254.

12. See Saul, *Freedom Is, Freedom Ain't*, 39–40.

13. Marshall McLuhan, *Understanding Media: The Extensions of Man* (New York: McGraw-Hill, 1965), 299, 301.

14. Susan J. Douglas, *Listening In: Radio and the American Imagination* (Minneapolis: University of Minnesota Press, 2004), 222.

15. http://www.npr.org/templates/story/story.php?storyId=129993435.

16. Tony Tanner believes that D.J.'s "voice aims at exploiting all the available speech levels of America, from the obscenities of Harlem slang to the pedantries of the academe. We cannot possibly 'fix' the identity of this narrator"; Tanner, "On the Parapet: A Study of the Novels of Norman Mailer," *Critical Quarterly* 12 (June 1970): 174. Fredric Jameson notes in passing what he calls "the Free Speech Movement quality of the narrator's language" but says nothing about D.J.'s ultimate identity; Jameson, "The Great American Hunter, or, Ideological Content in the Novel," *College English* 34, no. 2 (November 1972): 186.

17. Liu, *The Laws of Cool*, 102, 101, 7.

18. See Ford, "Hip Sensibility in an Age of Mass Counterculture," *Jazz Perspectives* 2, no. 2 (November 2008): 121–163.

19. Mailer's grizzly is a descendant of William Faulkner's famous bear. See Joanna Durczak, "Norman Mailer's *Why Are We in Vietnam?* as an Epilogue to William Faulkner's Hunting Sequel of Big Bottom Woods," *Studia Anglica Posnaniensia* 11 (1979): 183–202. The grizzly is also a descendant of Melville's Moby Dick, as Poirier notes in *Norman Mailer* (130–136).

20. Godden, *Fictions of Labor*, 147, 189, 196. Godden reads Rusty and D.J. as representative of a Republican right that wants to digest black bodies. But there are different ways of eating flesh, and not all accord it a magical power. For Emile Durkheim, writing on the Arunta tribe of central Australia, the totem was a manifestation of the mysterious force, or "mana," that watched over and gave power to a given clan. According to Durkheim, a totem animal needed to be protected, representing as it did the health of the tribe. Nevertheless, the tribe often ate the animal's flesh to absorb its power (more practical, Malinowski thought totem animals were sacred in the first place because they were "good to eat"). Unlike his father, D.J. wishes to eat the grizzly-as-black-American because he understands it as the totem of his tribe: the Democrats. On Durkheim and Malinowski, see Jeffrey Alexander and Philip Smith, *The Cambridge Companion to Durkheim* (Cambridge: Cambridge University Press, 2005), 249; and Thomas Barfield, *The Dictionary of Anthropology* (Malden, MA: Wiley-Blackwell, 1998), 468.

21. Mailer, *Miami and the Siege of Chicago*, 51.

22. Norman Mailer, *Cannibals and Christians* (New York: Pinnacle Books, 1966), 84; hereafter cited in text as *CC*.

23. Eric Lott, *Love and Theft*, 25–26, 121–122; Kennard, quoted in ibid., 99.

24. Bellow, *Mr. Sammler's Planet*, 45.

25. Sammler's friend sets out to take pictures of the pickpocket in action on the uptown bus, so that he can discuss Sammler's experience on NBC. Sammler understands his efforts otherwise: "You're thinking of . . . how close you could bring together the TV and that person's genitalia" (126). Earlier, when exposed to the pickpocket's "transmission" (54), Sammler experiences "a temporary blankness of spirit. Like the television screen in the lobby, white and gray, buzzing without image" (54). TV preoccupies the novel: one character, a German Jew who spent World War II in Buchenwald, has a sexual fetish for the brown arms of Latina women; Bellow names the man Walter Bruch, after the German engineer who spent the war operating a closed-circuit television system that allowed the German military to monitor the launch of V-2 rockets safely. Bruch later invented color television.

26. Mailer, *Of a Fire on the Moon,* 10.

27. Terry Southern, "Grooving in Chi," in *Now Dig This: The Unspeakable Writings of Terry Southern, 1950–1995* (New York: Grove Press, 2002), 118–119.

28. Cleaver, *Soul on Ice,* 194.

29. For an account of how the reform affected the party in 1972, see Caroline Arden, *Getting the Donkey out of the Ditch: The Democratic Party in Search of Itself* (Westport, CT: Greenwood, 1988).

30. Rubin, *Party Dynamics,* 133, 134, 135.

31. Hunter S. Thompson, *Fear and Loathing: On the Campaign Trail '72* (New York: Warner, 1983), 46, 125; hereafter cited in text as *FL.*

32. Joe McGinniss, *The Selling of the President* (New York: Penguin, 1988), 127.

33. George R. Vickers, *The Formation of the New Left: The Early Years* (Lexington, MA; D. C. Heath, 1975), 104.

34. Paul Goodman, quoted in Irving Howe, *The Radical Imagination: An Anthology from Dissent Magazine* (New York: New American Library, 1967), 206, 211.

35. Isserman and Kazin, *America Divided: The Civil War of the 1960s* (New York: Oxford University Press, 1999), 142; Howe, *Steady Work,* 10; Gitlin, *The Sixties: Years of Hope, Days of Rage* (New York: Bantam Books, 1993), 38; Buhle, *Marxism in the United States* (New York: Verso, 1991), 224.

36. Savio, "An End to History," in Massimo Teodori, ed., *The New Left: A Documentary History* (Indianapolis: Bobbs-Merrill, 1969), 159.

37. Davidson, quoted in Teodori, *New Left,* 328, 324; Savio, quoted in Teodori, *New Left,* 161.

38. Calvert, quoted in Teodori, *New Left,* 414–415.

39. Herbert Marcuse, *An Essay on Liberation* (Boston: Beacon, 1969), 63; hereafter cited in text.

40. Mills, *White Collar,* 112.

41. Hayden, "The Politics of 'The Movement,'" in *The Radical Papers,* ed. Irving Howe (Garden City, NY: Doubleday, 1966), 364, 362. For an account of the relation between white-collar downward mobility and race, see Hoberek, *Twilight of the Middle Class.*

42. Mitchell Cohen and Dennis Hale, *The New Student Left: An Anthology*, rev. ed. (Boston: Beacon Press, 1967), 288.

43. William Gibson, *Spook Country* (New York: Viking, 2007), 106.

44. "I tend not to accept any modification of the word novelist," Doctorow declared in New Critical fashion. "So if you ask am I a historical novelist, I say no. Am I a political novelist? No. Am I an ethnic novelist? No. I am a novelist." Novels might resist the state, but only by discovering that literature offered a modality categorically different from the state's. Just after *Daniel*, Doctorow likened "nonfictive" uses of language to expressions of "*the power of the regime*" and "fictive" uses of language to expressions of "*the power of freedom*." He thought "the language of politicians, historians, journalists and social scientists always presumes a world of fact to be discovered." Speaking on behalf of novelists who would oppose that language, he said, "We have it in us to compose false documents more valid, more real, more truthful than the 'true' documents of the politicians or the journalists or the psychologists." Doctorow, *Essays and Conversations*, ed. Richard Trenner (Princeton, NJ: Ontario Review Press, 1983), 95, 16–17, 21, 26.

45. Interview with Doctorow by Michael Wutz, Winter 1994. http://weberstudies .weber.edu/archive/archive%20B%20Vol.%2011–16.1/Vol.%2011.1/11.1Wutz.htm.

46. Godden, *Fictions of Capital*, Chapter 9.

47. Back in the Bronx at the end of the novel, Daniel seems to step out of Disneyland; he contemplates "a ruined city," strewn with "great plastic bags of garbage." He sees two black children playing on the stoop of his old home. This is a less romantic image than the one he conjured years earlier, when he imagined Williams raising him and his sister. He "gets the picture," but he's no longer in it. He considers asking to be let inside, but turns away. "It's not his house now" (299).

Conclusion

1. See John McClure, *Late Imperial Romance* (New York: Verso, 1994), Chapter 3.

2. Didion, *Democracy* (New York: Vintage, 1995), 128. Alan Nadal reads the novel as an expression of a Cold War preoccupation with containment in "Failed Cultural Narratives: America in the Postwar Era and the Story of Democracy," *boundary 2* 19, no. 1 (1992): 95–102. Others read it as an ironic comment on the limits of democratic representation. See, for example, Richard Levesque, "Telling Postmodern Tales: Absent Authorities in Didion's *Democracy* and in DeLillo's *Mao II*," *Arizona Quarterly* 54, no. 3 (Autumn 1998): 69–87; and Paul Jude Beauvais, "Postmodernism and the Ideology of Form: The Narrative Logic of Joan Didion's *Democracy*," *Journal of Narrative Technique* 23, no. 1 (Winter 1993): 16–30. Michael Tager reads the novel as a critique of the Vietnam War in "The Political Vision of Joan Didion's *Democracy*," *Critique* 31, no. 3 (Spring 1990): 173–184. On Didion's interest in the relation between the domestic sphere and politics, see Janis Stout, "Moving into the Political: Joan Didion and the Imagination of Engagement," in *Through the Window, Out the Door* (Tuscaloosa: University of Alabama Press, 1998), 188–225.

3. McClure, *Late Imperial Romance*, 83.

4. On Onassis and military tankers, see Peter Evans, *Nemesis: Aristotle Onassis, Jackie O, and the Love Triangle That Brought Down the Kennedys* (New York: Harper, 2004), 3.

5. Thomas Edsall, *The New Politics of Inequality* (New York: Norton, 1985), 107, 128.

6. Harvey, *A Brief History of Neoliberalism* (New York: Oxford University Press, 2005), 49.

7. Edsall, *New Politics of Inequality*, 235.

8. Didion, *Political Fictions* (New York: Vintage, 2001), 137.

9. Brent Edwards, "Louis Armstrong and the Syntax of Scat," *Critical Inquiry* 28, no. 3 (Spring 2002): 647.

10. *New York Times*, April 22, 1984. See also McClure, *Late Imperial Romance*, 77–78.

11. Quoted in Beauvais, "Postmodernism and the Ideology of Form," 84.

12. Joel Dinerstein, "Lester Young and the Birth of the Cool," in *Signifyin(g), Sanctifyin', & Slam Dunking: A Reader in African American Expressive Culture*, ed. Gena Dagel Caponi (Amherst: University of Massachusetts Press, 1999), 253–254.

13. Didion, *The Year of Magical Thinking* (New York: Knopf, 2005), 190; hereafter cited in text.

14. Abraham and Torok, *The Shell and the Kernel*, vol. 1, ed., trans., and intro. Nicholas Rand (Chicago: University of Chicago Press, 1994), 127.

15. Abraham and Torok, *The Wolf Man's Magic Word: A Cryptonymy*, trans. Nicholas Rand (Minneapolis: University of Minnesota Press, 1986), 19.

16. Abraham and Torok, *The Shell and the Kernel*, 126–127.

17. In Joan Didion, *We Tell Ourselves Stories in Order to Live: Collected Nonfiction*, intro. John Leonard (2003; New York: Everyman's Library, 2006).

18. McCarthy, "The Fact in Fiction," *Partisan Review* 27, no. 3 (Summer 1960): 454.

19. Rick Perlstein, *Before the Storm: Barry Goldwater and the Conservative Revolution* (New York: Hill and Wang, 2001), 65.

20. Barry Goldwater, *The Conscience of a Conservative* (Washington, DC: Regnery Gateway, 1990), 17.

21. See Reed, *The Jesse Jackson Phenomenon* (New Haven, CT: Yale University Press, 1986), 133. In 1988, the *Nation* saw it differently, and cast Jackson as a direct challenge to a then ascendant neoliberalism. See "For Jesse Jackson and His Campaign," *Nation*, April 16, 1988.

22. Harvey, *Neoliberalism*, 23.

23. Ibid., 33, 34–35.

24. See Wolin, *Democracy Incorporated: Managed Democracy and the Specter of Inverted Totalitarianism* (Princeton, NJ: Princeton University Press, 2010), 221; Gerring, *Party Ideologies*, 236; Fraser and Gerstle, *The Rise and Fall of the New Deal Order, 1930–1980* (Princeton, NJ: Princeton University Press, 1989), 187; Frymer, *Black and Blue: African Americans, the Labor Movement, and the Decline of the Democratic Party* (Princeton, NJ: Princeton University Press, 2008), 2. For a sympathetic view of Johnson's commitment to economic redistribution, more representative of the scholarly consensus, see

Robert H. Haveman, *Poverty Policy and Poverty Research: The Great Society and the Social Sciences* (Madison: University of Wisconsin Press, 1997).

25. Harvey, *Neoliberalism*, 41–42.

26. To Numan Bartley, the Civil Rights Movement (and works like Gunnar Myrdal's *An American Dilemma*) led liberals to embrace personal and moral development at the expense of economic reform. See King, *Race, Culture, and the Intellectuals*, 2.

27. Rick Perlstein's *Nixonland* represents the consensus when it insists on the importance of white backlash to the Democrats' fall from power starting in the late sixties; Larry Bartels's *Unequal Democracy* questions that consensus, and the more general assumption that working-class whites have slowly left the party.

28. Quoted in Joseph Hayden, *Covering Clinton: The President and the Press in the 1990s* (Westport, CT: Greenwood, 2002), 19.

29. Quoted in Morrison, *What Moves at the Margin: Selected Nonfiction* (Jackson: University Press of Mississippi, 2008), 149–153.

30. Yang, "Could Obama be the first Asian American president?" SFGate.com, July 30, 2008.

31. Yang, "Brand-aid," Salon.com, March 3, 2008.

32. Limbaugh, quoted in Thomas Frank, *What's the Matter with Kansas?* (New York: Metropolitan Books, 2004).

33. David Brooks, *New York Times*, October 19, 2006.

34. Naomi Klein, *No Logo: Taking Aim at the Brand Bullies* (New York: Flamingo, 2000), 68–75.

35. Ibid.

36. Ibid., 70.

37. Eszterhas, *American Rhapsody*, 13, 272.

Index

abolitionism, 193, 204; Warren on, 45, 46–47, 50
Adams, Henry, 32, 136
Adams, John Quincy, 106
Adderley, Cannonball, 9, 139
Admiral Tones, the, 139
Adorno, Theodor, 168; on jazz, 160; on reification, 94, 159–60
advertising, 94, 117, 124–26, 127, 138–39, 141, 247; and Brossard's *Who Walk in Darkness*, 86–90, 96, 97–98, 109–10, 142; "Daisy" advertisement, 119–20; and Ellison's *Three Days Before the Shooting…*, 158–59, 161, 162–63; Galbraith on, 121; Haug on, 88, 154–55; Mailer on, 13, 106; and market segmentation, 120–23, 131; and Panetta's *Viva Madison avenue!*, 103–4, 115–16; Pepsi Generation, 121; in politics, 113–14, 119–20; Riesman on, 82–83; Volkswagen ad campaign, 118–19, 124
African Americans: as advertising copywriters, 125–26; as athletes, 137–38; black church, 148, 159, 166; the black phallus, 11, 198, 199, 200, 209, 222, 223, 224–25, 229, 231, 240, 241–42; and Bill Clinton, 41, 42, 254, 277–78, 280–81; as consumers, 121–23, 222; and Democratic interracial coalition, 3, 5–6, 13, 40–41, 82, 111, 123, 135–37, 142–44, 149, 167–68, 170, 171, 177–78, 206, 227–31, 251–52, 267, 277; Great Migration, 65, 135–36, 166, 167; vs. Jewish Americans, 25–26; labor of, 12–14, 42, 50, 51–52, 53–59, 61–62, 64–65, 68, 70, 78, 99–100, 139, 156, 291n28; language of, 65–66, 72–73, 150–51, 231; literary traditions of, 11; Marcuse on, 236–38; in middle class, 126; and PMC,

3–4, 180–82, 184, 185–86; and radio, 213–14; and rock and roll, 209–10. *See also* Civil Rights Movement; race; slavery
Agnew, Spiro, 229, 231
Allen, Henry J., 38
allophilia, 124
Alsberg, Henry, 176
Altschuler, Glenn, 139
American Bandstand, 139
American Prospect, 1
Anderson, Paul: on jazz, 101
Andrews, William, 194
Apocalypse Now, 260
Aristotle: on metaphor, 18
Armstrong, Louis, 9, 60, 61, 90, 99, 148, 287n53
Arnold, Matthew, 62
Arts and Humanities Act, 73
Arvey, Jake, 115
Austin, J. L.: on performative speech, 19, 20, 110–11
Avalon, Frankie, 139

Bacon, Francis, 69
Baldwin, James, 196, 303n50; *Another Country,* 189; on Democratic Party, 205; *The Fire Next Time,* 153–54; on Mailer, 146, 212; on security, 28; on white fantasies of black America, 10
Baltzell, E. Digby: *Judgment and Sensibility,* 295n6; *The Protestant Establishment,* 115
Baraka, Amiri (LeRoi Jones): on bebop, 178–79; on the blues, 160–61, 178–79, 181; *Blues People,* 178, 181; on jazz, 10, 59–60, 122; on the Negro as consumer, 122
Bartel, Larry: *Unequal Democracy,* 309n27
Bartley, Numan, 308n26